32.50

COPY 1

DATE DUE

D1801230

C 0037001
738.0979 COPY 1
Col

Cumberland Trail Library System
Flora, Illinois 62839

HANDBOOK OF NORTHERN ARIZONA POTTERY WARES

AMS PRESS
NEW YORK

Jar of Deadmans Fugitive Red from Medicine Cave, San Francisco Mountains. Date about 1000 A.D. Stage Pueblo II ($\frac{1}{6}\times$).

MUSEUM OF NORTHERN ARIZONA
Bulletin No. 11

HANDBOOK OF NORTHERN ARIZONA POTTERY WARES

BY

HAROLD SELLERS COLTON

AND

LYNDON LANE HARGRAVE

NORTHERN ARIZONA SOCIETY OF SCIENCE AND ART
FLAGSTAFF
August 1937

Library of Congress Cataloging in Publication Data

Colton, Harold Sellers, 1881–
   Handbook of northern Arizona pottery wares.

   Reprint of the 1937 ed. published by the Northern Arizona Society of Science and Art, Flagstaff, which was issued as Bulletin no. 11 of the Museum of Northern Arizona.
   Bibliography: p.
   Includes index.
   1. Indians of North America—Arizona—Pottery. 2. Pottery—Arizona.   I. Hargrave, Lyndon Lane, 1896–   joint author.   II. Title.   III. Series: Flagstaff, Ariz. Museum of Northern Arizona. Bulletin; no. 11
   E78.A7C74   1979   738.3   76-43677
   ISBN 0-404-15511-1

738.0979

0037001/5

First AMS edition published in 1979.

Reprinted from the edition of 1937, Northern Arizona. [Trim size of the original has been slightly altered in this edition. Original trim size: 13.2 × 21 cm. Text area of the original has been maintained.]

MANUFACTURED
IN THE UNITED STATES OF AMERICA

CONTENTS

CHAPTER		PAGE
	Introduction	xi
I.	Types, Series, and Wares	1
II.	Techniques of Pottery Making	6
III.	Methods of Studying Potsherds	9
IV.	Styles of Design	14
V.	Naming Pottery Types and Priority in Naming	19
VI.	Dating Pottery Types	23
VII.	Geographical Focus of Manufacture and Distribution by Trade	27
VIII.	Introduction to Pottery Descriptions	29
	A Word about Dates	35
IX.	Key to Northern Arizona Pottery Types	36
	How to Use the Key	37
	Key A: Primary Key	37
	Key B: Surface Altered	40
X.	Oxidizing Atmosphere	42

Key C: Surface not Altered; Exterior Surface Brown, Orange, Yellow, or Buff............42
A: Pottery Constructed by Coiling.....................44
Mogollon Brown Ware. **Key 1**............44
Alma Series. **Key a**.................46
    San Lorenzo Red-on-brown.................46
    Mogollon Red-on-brown.........................47
    San Francisco Red..............48
Winona Series. **Key b**.........................51
    Winona Red......................51
    Winona Smudged.........................52
    Winona Black-on-red.................53
    Winona Red-on-tan.........................54
    Winona Corrugated.........................55
    Walnut Corrugated.........................56
Woodruff Series. **Key c**...........................58
    Woodruff Brown.........................58
    Woodruff Red.........................58

CONTENTS

Woodruff Incised.................................59
Woodruff Smudged................................59
Linden Series. Key d.............................60
   Linden Corrugated............................60
   McDonald Corrugated..........................61
   Silver Creek Corrugated......................62
Flagstaff Series.................................63
   Elden Corrugated.............................63
Salado Series. Key e.............................64
   Salado Red...................................65
   Salado White-on-red..........................65
San Juan Red Ware. Key 2.........................67
Bluff Series.....................................68
   Bluff Black-on-red...........................69
Deadmans Series..................................70
   Deadmans Black-on-red........................71
   Medicine Black-on-red........................72
   Tusayan Black-on-red.........................74
   Citadel Polychrome...........................75
Alameda Red Ware. Key 3..........................77
Homolovi Series. Key f...........................78
   Showlow Black-on-red.........................78
   Arauca Plain.................................80
   Homolovi Black-on-red........................80
   Black Ax Polychrome..........................81
   Homolovi Polychrome..........................82
Chavez Pass Series. Key g........................84
   Chavez Pass Black-on-red.....................84
   Chavez Pass Polychrome.......................84
Roosevelt Red Ware. Key 4........................86
   Pinto Polychrome.............................87
   Gila Polychrome..............................88
   Tonto Polychrome.............................90
Tsegi Orange Ware. Key 5.........................92
   Tsegi Orange.................................93
   Tsegi Red-on-orange..........................94
   Tsegi Black-on-orange........................95
   Tsegi Polychrome.............................96
   Tusayan Polychrome...........................96
   Dogoszhi Polychrome..........................98
   Kayenta Polychrome...........................99
   Kiet Siel Polychrome........................100
White Mountain Red Ware. Key 6..................102
Fourmile Series. Key h..........................104
   St. Johns Polychrome........................104
   Pinedale Black-on-red.......................106
   Pinedale Polychrome.........................107
   Fourmile Polychrome.........................109
   Showlow Polychrome..........................111
Hawaikuh Series. Key i..........................113
   Pinnawa Black-on-red........................113
   Heshotauthla Polychrome.....................113
   Wallace Polychrome..........................114
   Pinnawa Polychrome..........................115
   Adamana Polychrome..........................117
Houck Series. Key j.............................118
   Wingate Black-on-red........................118
   Wingate Corrugated..........................119
   Puerco Black-on-red.........................120
   Houck Polychrome............................121
   Querino Polychrome..........................122

CONTENTS

Klageto Series. Key k............................123
   Klageto Black-on-yellow........................123
   Klageto Polychrome............................124
Kintiel Series. Key l.............................125
   Kintiel Black-on-orange........................125
   Kintiel Polychrome............................126
Zuni White Ware. Key 7..........................128
   Pinnawa Red-on-white.........................129
   Hawikuh Glaze-on-white.......................130
   Arauca Polychrome............................131
Homolovi Orange Ware. Key 8.....................132
   Homolovi Plain................................133
   Homolovi Corrugated..........................134
Winslow Orange Ware. Key 9......................135
Winslow Series...................................136
   Tuwiuca Orange...............................136
   Tuwiuca Black-on-orange......................137
   Tuwiuca Polychrome..........................138
   Winslow Polychrome..........................139
Kwaituki Series..................................140
   Jeddito Black-on-orange........................141
   Jeddito Polychrome...........................142
Awatobi Yellow Ware. Key 10.....................143
   Jeddito Corrugated............................144
   Jeddito Plain..................................144
   Jeddito Tooled................................145
Jeddito Yellow Ware. Key 11......................146
Kokop Series. Key m.............................148
   Kwaituki Polychrome..........................148
   Kokop Black-on-orange........................149
   Kokop Polychrome............................149
Jeddito Series. Key n.............................150
   Jeddito Black-on-yellow........................150
   Bidahochi Polychrome.........................151
   Sikyatki Polychrome...........................152
   Jeddito Stippled...............................153
   Jeddito Engraved..............................154
   Awatobi Polychrome..........................155
   Kawaioku Polychrome........................156
B: Pottery Constructed by Paddling..................157
Alameda Brown Ware. Key 12.....................158
Adamana Series. Key o...........................159
   Adamana Brown..............................159
   Adamana Fugitive Red.........................160
Rio de Flag Series. Key p..........................161
   Rio de Flag Brown.............................161
   Rio de Flag Smudged..........................162
   Winona Brown................................162
   Sunset Red....................................163
   Turkey Hill Red...............................165
Tonto Series.....................................166
   Tonto Red....................................166
Verde Series. Key q..............................167
   Verde Brown.................................167
   Verde Red-on-buff.............................168
   Tuzigoot Red..................................169
   Tuzigoot Black-on-red.........................170
   Tuzigoot White-on-red........................171
   Tuzigoot Red-on-black.........................171
   Tuzigoot Black-on-gray........................172
Gila Series. Key r................................173

CONTENTS

Gila Plain..174
Santan Red..175
Gila Red..176
Gila White-on-red...............................177
Coconino Buff Ware. Key 13................179
   Walnut Wiped..................................180
   Winona Red-on-buff.......................181
   Coconino Red-on-buff......................182
Prescott Gray Ware. Key 14.................184
   Verde Black-on-gray........................184
   Verde Polychrome............................186
   Prescott Black-on-brown..................186

XI. Reducing Atmosphere........................188

Key D: Surface not altered; Exterior Surface Gray or White..188
A: Constructed by Coiling.....................189
Tusayan Gray Ware. Key 15.................190
Tsegi Series..191
   Lino Gray.......................................191
   Lino Fugitive Red............................193
   Lino Black-on-gray..........................194
   Kana-a Gray...................................195
   Tusayan Corrugated........................196
   Moenkopi Corrugated......................197
   Kiet Siel Gray.................................198
   Medicine Gray................................199
   O'Leary Tooled...............................200
   Coconino Gray................................201
Honani Series.....................................202
   Honani Tooled................................202
Tusayan White Ware. Key 16................203
Kayenta Series. Key s..........................205
   Kana-a Black-on-White....................205
   Deadmans Black-on-white................208
   Dogoszhi Black-on-white..................209
   Sosi Black-on-white.........................211
   Tusayan Black-on-white...................213
   Betatakin Black-on-white.................215
   Kayenta Black-on-white...................217
Polacca Series.....................................218
   Kio-ko Black-on-white......................219
   Polacca Black-on-white....................220
   Hoyapi Black-on-white.....................222
Wupatki Series....................................225
   Flagstaff Black-on-white..................225
   Wupatki Black-on-white..................227
Mesa Verde White Ware. Key 17............229
   Mancos Black-on-white....................230
   Mesa Verde Black-on-white...............231
Little Colorado Gray Ware...................232
   Little Colorado Corrugated...............232
Little Colorado White Ware. Key 18.......234
Walnut Series.....................................235
   Dead River Black-on-white...............235
   Holbrook Black-on-white..................235
   Padre Black-on-white......................236
   Walnut Black-on-white....................237
Tularosa Series...................................240
   Tularosa Black-on-white..................240

CONTENTS vii

    Pinedale Black-on-white..........................241
    Klageto Black-on-white...........................242
  Bidahochi White Ware...............................245
    Bidahochi Black-on-white........................245
  Miscellaneous Types................................246
    Jeddito Black-on-white..........................247
    Kokop Black-on-white............................248
    Wide Ruin Black-on-white........................249
  B: Constructed by Paddling..........................251
  San Francisco Mountain Gray Ware. **Key 19**............251
    Deadmans Gray..................................252
    Deadmans Fugitive Red...........................252
    Deadmans Black-on-gray..........................253

Glossary... 255
Bibliography... 260
Index.. 265

KEYS

Key	A	Primary Key.................................	37
Key	B	Surface Altered..............................	40
Key	C	Surface not altered; exterior surface brown, red, orange, yellow, buff.....................	42
Key	D	Surface not altered; exterior surface gray or white.................................	188
Key	1	Mogollon Brown Ware........................	44
Key	2	San Juan Red Ware..........................	67
Key	3	Alameda Red Ware...........................	77
Key	4	Roosevelt Red Ware..........................	86
Key	5	Tsegi Orange Ware...........................	92
Key	6	White Mountain Red Ware...................	102
Key	7	Zuni White Ware.............................	128
Key	8	Homolovi Orange Ware.......................	132
Key	9	Winslow Orange Ware........................	135
Key	10	Awatobi Yellow Ware........................	143
Key	11	Jeddito Yellow Ware.........................	146
Key	12	Alameda Brown Ware........................	158
Key	13	Coconino Buff Ware..........................	179
Key	14	Prescott Gray Ware..........................	184
Key	15	Tusayan Gray Ware..........................	190
Key	16	Tusayan White Ware.........................	203
Key	17	Mesa Verde White Ware.....................	229
Key	18	Little Colorado White Ware..................	234
Key	19	San Francisco Mountain Gray Ware...........	251
Key	a	Alma Series..................................	46
Key	b	Winona Series...............................	51
Key	c	Woodruff Series..............................	58
Key	d	Linden Series................................	60
Key	e	Salado Series................................	64
Key	f	Homolovi Series..............................	78
Key	g	Chavez Pass Series...........................	84
Key	h	Fourmile Series..............................	104
Key	i	Hawikuh Series..............................	113
Key	j	Houck Series.................................	118
Key	k	Klageto Series................................	123
Key	l	Kintiel Series................................	125
Key	m	Kokop Series.................................	148
Key	n	Jeddito Series................................	150
Key	o	Adamana Series.............................	159
Key	p	Rio de Flag Series...........................	161
Key	q	Verde Series.................................	167
Key	r	Gila Series...................................	173
Key	s	Kayenta Series...............................	205

FOREWORD

This Bulletin is an outgrowth of a check list of Southwestern Pottery Types. The original plan called for a systematic classification of all Southwestern pottery types described in literature. To this it was planned to add the descriptions of all northern Arizona types which had been recognized since Bulletin I of this series had been published. It was soon found that it was impossible for the authors to venture outside the area in which they were personally familiar because pottery types frequently were indefinitely and incompletely described. Therefore the geographic area has been constantly reduced until only wares occurring in northern Arizona have been retained. Instead of printing references to published descriptions, all types treated herein have been redescribed following a definite, consistent plan. Much care, time, and thought has been given to this work and the authors hope that some of the ideas expressed will be useful to others who are trying to unravel the complicated facts that pottery studies present.

The material used in this study is a part of the Museum sherd collection. That part dealing with Tsegi Orange Ware, almost without exception, was, however, acquired as the result of a joint survey with the Rainbow Bridge—Monument Valley Expedition of 1933.

Although the authors have collaborated throughout, Chapters VIII, IX, X, and XI are almost entirely the work of Mr. Hargrave.

The authors particularly wish to thank Mr. Watson Smith for his valuable criticism of the text and for his aid in preparing the glossary, Mr. Kenneth B. Disher for his work on rim types, and Mr. John C. McGregor for reviewing Chapter VI; also, thanks are due Mr. Virgil Hubert for making the drawings.

The work proved more difficult than the authors anticipated and the long delay, more than three years, is due to constant revision of the manuscript. It is our hope that we have made a definite contribution to the general study of ceramics. Time alone can tell.

HAROLD S. COLTON, *Director*
Museum of Northern Arizona

This edition limited to 600 copies.

ERRATA

HANDBOOK OF NORTHERN ARIZONA POTTERY WARES

By H. S. Colton and Lyndon L. Hargrave

Museum of Northern Arizona, Bulletin 11, Flagstaff, Aug. 1937

Page 13, line 12: for "impacted," read *"compacted,"* and throughout the book.

Page 14, line 33: For "Tusayan Red Ware," read *"San Juan* Red Ware."

Page 39 and 40, under **EXAMPLE 2**: For "Key 10," read "Key *12.*"

Page 45, under **ALMA SERIES**: For "northwestern," read *"southwestern."*

Page 67, In Key 2: point 2, read "Not polychrome - - - - - - *3."*

Page 119, under **REMARKS**: for "Hawikuh," read *"Houck."*

Page 129, under **TIME**: read "Probably between *1250*-1400 A. D."

Page 136, under **RANGE**: read "Chavez Pass Pueblo on Clear Creek, *Coconino* County, Arizona."

Page 232, in 3rd paragraph, under **LITTLE COLORADO GRAY WARE**, for "Little Colorado White Ware," read "Little Colorado *Gray* Ware."

INTRODUCTION

In the present status of Southwestern Archaeology, Ceramics is the one cultural factor that can be studied at almost every site—even at sites that have not been excavated. Therefore, ceramics has an importance all out of proportion to its position in the complex of cultural traits. This being so, it is of immediate necessity to organize the study of Southwestern Ceramics so that the trends and influences can be recognized and studied and the details of Southwestern History can be compiled.

In any branch of science it is necessary first to analyze the material on which the science is based, to separate it into as many pigeon holes as possible. Bateson (1913, p. 249) once stated, "they will serve Science best by giving names freely and by describing every thing to which their successors may possibly want to refer, and generally by subdividing their material into as many species as they can induce any responsible journal to publish." But analysis is but one side of the picture. After analysis comes synthesis. By this we mean that the data collected should be assembled into a story, as complete as possible. In this paper we are considering Southwestern Ceramics in that light. We are attempting to analyze the pottery types that are found on the plateau of Arizona, north of the Mogollon Rim and south of the Utah border, and using these types as a basis, to build up a history of the region.

Pottery types will be described and named but the describing and naming of pottery types is not an end in itself but is the basis on which synthesis must be built. *Synthesis is only as accurate as the analyses which preceded it.* Many students think that Southwestern Archaeology is a finished study because works of synthesis have been published, but the analysis that preceded this synthesis is, in many cases, insufficient for the conclusions drawn.

The outline of such an analysis and the immediate fruits thereof may be indicated as follows: First, the identification of materials used, which, in a broad, although practical, manner determines certain groups of ceramic factors to be characteristic of certain regions (this is a stable character); second, recognition and knowledge of certain techniques of manufacture which make it possible to trace genetic relationships in time and space (another stable character since it is inherited); and third, characters acquired through personal contact as revealed in vessel form, style of design, and in other methods of ornamentation which reflect such factors as trade relations, and vogue. Through a proper correlation of this knowledge with knowledge from other sources, it then should be possible to determine pottery indigenous to a locality (based upon a study of materials used); to recognize the advent into a locality of new peoples (through changes in techniques that are inherited); or to trace the trend of the times as they swept across the country from one people to another (through a study of styles of design). Factors of these three kinds, over a long period of time, would combine to produce a variety of pottery types in a given region. Since we are trying to combine the stories of all of these types into one history, we cannot overlook the opportunity offered through recognition of each change in pottery. Because pottery is so durable and yet is so sensitive to change much is retained and preserved for all time in the firing of the vessel.

Most cultural factors, other than architecture and ceramics, give us relatively little material for study. At present, changes in cultural traits in the short time of pueblo evolution and geographic distribution in bone, stone and textiles have been determined in their broadest outlines only. This does not mean that textiles cannot tell as complete a story as does pottery, but it does mean that studies of textiles, to reach the same point as that of pottery, must be eminently costly. As an example, the Museum of Northern Arizona, in order to procure textiles from a dated site known to contain textiles, spent about $3,000.00 at Wupatki Pueblo and procured only a few fragments. In four years of study of 101 Pueblo II pithouses, the Museum found arrowpoints on pithouse floors in but two cases. The very sparseness of this material makes it difficult to build up a chronology based on textiles or stone points as has been done with pottery.

Textiles seem as sensitive to stylistic changes as does pottery but in very few cases have textiles been correlated with tree ring dates; moreover, much of the material is stored in eastern museums and must be studied in that area. We hope that some of the eastern institutions will turn their students to those important problems, for the material is available and crying for study.

Implements of bone and stone have been investigated but they are so insensible to individualistic expression that they have contributed very little to pueblo history. Architecture, being more sensitive than bone, has therefore contributed much but still is less sensitive to change than is pottery.

INTRODUCTION xiii

Having realized the value of pottery in recognizing time and cultural change, it is feasible to use pottery as a stage indicator. In assigning pottery types to designated chronological stages we use herein the terminology proposed at the First Pecos Conference in 1927 (Kidder, 1927) for the Basket Maker—Pueblo Culture; for the Hohokam, we use the terminology proposed at the Globe Conference in 1931 as modified by Gladwin (1934, p. 3). These stage designations are now firmly established in literature so until some radical change is made in the determination of cultural stages we believe this terminology should be continued in use.

Recognition of stages of cultural development came through the use of stratigraphy by Southwestern archaeologists. These stages were later dated by dendro-chronologists led by Dr. A. E. Douglass (Colton, 1935).

The approximate dates of the stages represented in northern Arizona differ from those in New Mexico. There seems to be about 100 years of cultural lag before 1200 A.D. Previous to that date, Arizona stages date later in time than do the same cultural levels in northern New Mexico. We cannot use dates from northern New Mexico in outlining Arizona history. Arizona has its own chronology, in part, as follows:

BASKET MAKER – PUEBLO STAGES IN NORTHERN ARIZONA

Pueblo V Stage; 1600–1900 A.D.; European influence
Pueblo IV Stage; 1300–1600 A.D.; Great pueblos
Pueblo III Stage; 1100–1300 A.D.; Pueblo evolution
Pueblo II Stage; 900–1100 A.D.; Emergence from pithouse to pueblo
Pueblo I Stage; 750–900 A.D.; Ceramic expansion; house type nearly static
Basket Maker III Stage; 500–750 A.D.; Introduction of pottery
Basket Maker II Stage; ?–500 A.D.; Pre-pottery

HOHOKAM STAGES IN SOUTHERN ARIZONA*

Modern	1700–1900 A.D.
Recent	1500–1700 A.D.
Classic	1200–1500 A.D.
Sedentary	900–1200 A.D.
Colonial	? – 900 A.D.
Pioneer	?

* Gladwin, 1934, fig. 10.

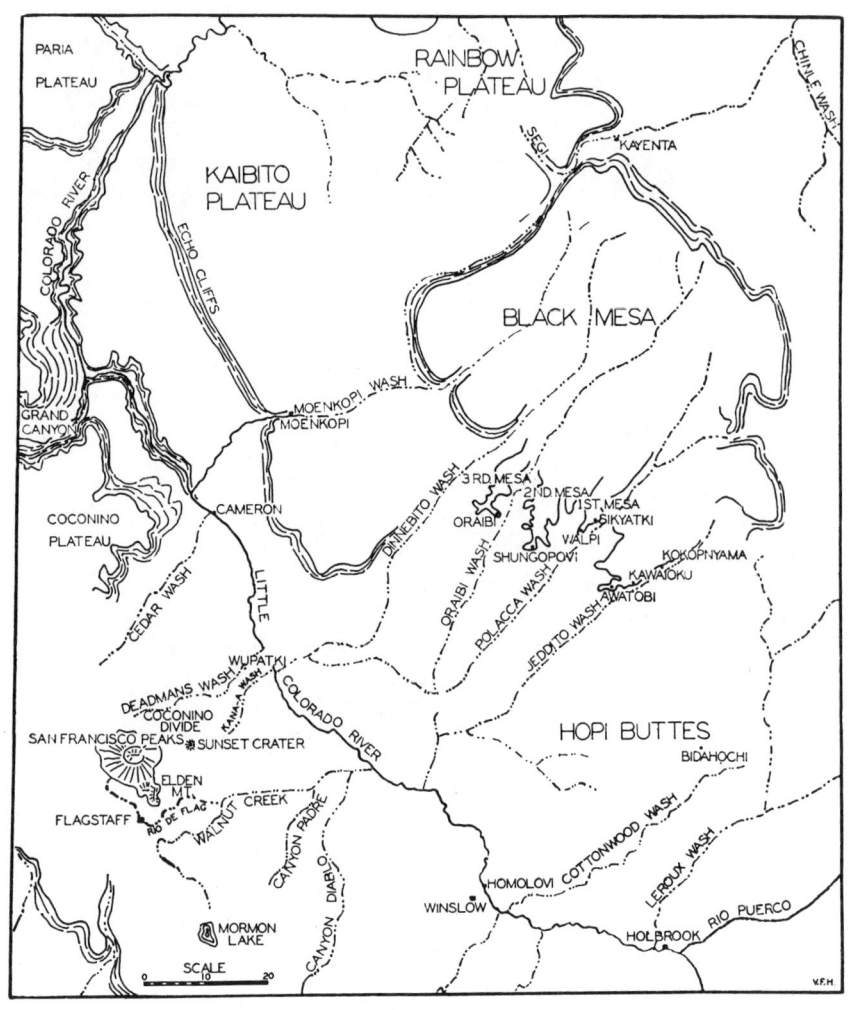

Map of the portion of Northern Arizona for which this handbook has been especially prepared.

CHAPTER I

TYPES, SERIES, AND WARES

THIS work is the result of an attempt to organize the study of Southwestern Ceramics as it appears in a small area, i.e., Northern Arizona. Until the pottery types of this area are arranged and classified it is impossible to interpret the information gathered in excavations. Because we do not know what to look for and what to record, information important in unravelling the history of the Southwest frequently is lost.

Few people outside of the active workers in Southwestern Archaeology realize the great variety of pottery that the prehistoric inhabitants of the Southwest manufactured nor do they realize how vitally pottery is contributing to an understanding of the history of the region. Not only do pottery types vary in time but they also vary from place to place at a given time. When two investigators have worked in a region, in many cases they have given different names to the same pottery type; in other cases when studies have been made in neighboring regions, investigators have failed to compare the pottery types from the two regions. In Arizona a sufficient number of pottery types have been described and named to make a system of classification possible (Hargrave, 1932). It may seem that any system is premature because so many types have been inadequately described and others have been described but not named, but the mere publication of the described types will focus attention on the weak spots and so will lead to their rapid obliteration.

Of the pottery types described from the Southwest, some are quite alike and some differ by many characters. When we have to deal with a large number of diverse objects it is necessary to arrange them in groups so that we may better grasp their characteristics. This is the reason for a system of classification.

Hargrave (1932) proposed a classification of pottery types based on fundamental structure of the material, such as paste, temper, and surface treatment. His classification is ideally perfect in that the material falls into definite pigeon holes. But because it does not always bring together in groups pottery types obviously related genetically, i.e., having a common derivation, it does not satisfy certain requirements of a logical classification system. For this reason a more realistic definition of *ware* becomes necessary. In practical use it has been found unnecessary to refer to Hargrave's "genus" and "order," but the subdivisions, whatever they may be called, are useful in building a key that may be used for aid in identification. In a classification of pottery the *ware* is the important group.

Stevenson (1883, p. 319) was the first worker in the Southwest to use the word *ware* as a basis of classification. He was followed by Holmes (1886) who spoke of *Whiteware, Redware,* etc., and Fewkes (1904) who spoke of *Coarse Gray Ware, Black-and-white Ware, Yellow Ware, Brown Ware,* etc. Thus there is plenty of respectable precedent for the use of the word *ware* as a group term in ceramic classification.

Before we can define a ware we must define the word "type," because the definition of a ware is dependent upon the types within the ware. *A pottery type is a group of pottery vessels which are alike in every important characteristic except* (possibly) *form.* In general these characteristics are as follows:
1. Surface color—white, buff, yellow, red, and gray.
2. Method of handling the clay—thinned by scraping ("coiled") or by pressure ("paddle-and-anvil").
3. Texture of the core—varying from almost no visible temper to coarse temper.
4. Chemical composition of the temper if the difference is obviously caused by a difference in technique. For example: sand gathered from a stream bed might show differences in mineral content from one place to another and so is not of much significance in determining a type; but the addition of ground sherds or crushed rock to a paste is a difference in technique and is important.
5. Chemical composition of the paint—such as carbon, iron-carbon, manganese, or lead.
6. Styles of design in decorated pottery.

The definition of a ware may then be stated thus: *A Ware is a group of pottery types which has a majority of* (the above) *characteristics in common but that differ in others.*

While studying certain types in the preparation of this Handbook, it became obvious that wares could and should be subdivided on the basis of genetic series of types that were observed in several wares. These types were readily recognized as belonging to a certain ware but consistently occurred within a given subdivision of the ware area. Since genetic relationships

TYPES, SERIES, AND WARES 3

within the ware clearly are revealed and since also a change in ecological factors is seen to have resulted in the development of new pottery types in minor geographic areas, recognition of these facts is indicated through the use of the term "series."

For many years series have unconsciously been spoken of in this manner when speaking of "Zuni glazes" or "Hopi Yellow." The unconscious recognition of the existence of series was indicated, although this fact has never been analyzed or systematized for general usage to the extent of definitely grouping specific types together according to a uniform system. Nothing new, therefore, is being proposed in the present method of classification.

In selecting a series name, the geographic portion of the name adopted was usually that of a late or culminating type in the series.

A Series, therefore, *is a group of pottery types within a single ware in which each type bears a genetic relation to each other, including all those types and only those types that occur:*

(a) *in the direct line of chronological genetic development from an original primitive or ancestral type to a late type: and*

(b) *as collateral developments or variations from any type in that line of development, but which are not themselves followed in chronological genetic sequence by derived types other than types derived through the main line of development from the type of which the collateral type is a development or variation*, as illustrated below. Fig. 1.

The earliest known type in a series is called the *ancestral type* of that series; several series may (and usually do) have a common ancestral type. Any type, however, may be spoken of as *ancestral* to all other types chronologically subsequent to it in the same series.

A type is called a *derived type* with reference to other types preceding it chronologically in the same series.

Two or more types in the same series which are derived immediately from the same ancestral type are said to be *collateral*.

Two or more types which are derived from a common *ancestral type*, no matter how remote, and two or more series which are derived from the same ancestral type, no matter how remote, are said to be *related* through that type.

The geographical occurrence of a series usually (although not necessarily) is limited to a definable subdivision of the ware area. An example may be graphed as follows:

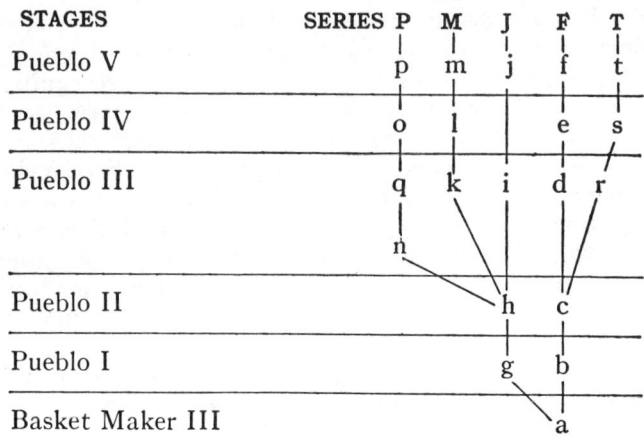

Fig. 1.
Example of Series within a ware.

Series F is composed of Types a, b, c, d, e, f.

In figure 1, type A is ancestral to all other types; type C is ancestral to types d, e, f, r, s, and t; type C is collateral to types d and r, derivative from type b, and ancestral to types f and t; all types are related to each other through type a; types i, j, k, l, and m, are related to each other through type h; types q and n are both ancestral to type o, but collateral to each other, and derivative from types h, g, and a.

The important thing in a classification is to have material, obviously related, placed in the same pigeon hole. So we must try to place pottery types obviously related in the same ware. It is impossible to make rules that will pigeon-hole the material automatically because in humanly manufactured articles so many variable influences have governed their manufacture and have affected their finished condition. Only personal judgment can care for some cases. A classification to be of value must aid our minds in grasping relationships. It cannot, however, be mathematically absolute.

Satisfactory and useful classification is impossible, however, without an orderly system of nomenclature wherewith to discuss the material classified. An object without an individual and significant name might be said not to exist in the mind of an observer. In general, most persons perhaps would admit this fact, but with some southwestern workers there is still a belief that names should not be given to various kinds of pottery, at least before the history of a type is known. But certain field and laboratory workers who have worked seriously and intensively in the field of ceramics, long ago recognized the need and value of names for various kinds of pottery in order that they might better understand each other. The action of the

1927 Pecos Conference (Kidder, 1927) in making a rule for naming pottery types is a general recognition of this need, which admittedly is most vital to those students active in purely technical investigation. The question may be asked: "Why are such purely technical studies necessary?" The answer is: "To understand and to command the full value of a thing or a condition, each factor that has influenced or that is responsible for a thing or a condition must be isolated and studied separately so that the whole may be understood and properly interpreted." Complete analysis followed by synthesis is the only means known by which to accomplish this result.

Let us consider the technical study of ceramics. The principal object in studying ceramics is to learn as much about pottery as it is possible to learn, so that the accumulated data may be correlated with data contributed from other sources. Specifically the technical study of pottery already has contributed much. As early as 1928, Hargrave had worked out the sequence of pottery types so that the relative ages of many ruins were known. With this knowledge Dr. A. E. Douglass was directed to desired sites which gave timbers or charcoal.

As definite evolutionary characters were recognized at definite horizons in different regions—which incidentally destroyed the old theory that color and design were characteristic of clans—divisions of pottery types became necessary; such broad terms as "black-on-white" or "black-on-red" pottery no longer would fulfill the needs of the student. Regional, or geographic, names became necessary.

With the recognition of types, series, and wares we are thus able to understand better the intricate archaeological history of local districts. We are able to recognize migrations and to evaluate the part played by the acculturation of certain arts of the people. Moreover, this analysis, as applied herein to pottery, must precede synthesis in reconstructing this history of the prehistoric inhabitants of the Southwest.

CHAPTER II

TECHNIQUES OF POTTERY MAKING

IN CONSIDERATION of the conspicuousness of pottery as a product of the Pueblo People and of its special use by students (Hargrave, 1932; Colton, M. R. F., 1931) there have been published astonishingly few papers which deal with materials and particularly with methods of construction. A paper by Holmes (1886) appeared early in the study of Southwestern archaeology but, in spite of a thoroughness rarely since equalled, it does not seem to be familiar to most students of the past and present generations. Holmes treated his subject in a practical manner and his attitude could well have been taken by many later students. Unfortunately, his successors failed to profit by the foundation laid for them.

As an introduction to techniques of pottery making one can do no better than to quote from Holmes. "The study of prehistoric art leads inevitably to inquiries into the origin of races. Solutions of these questions have generally been sought through migrations, and these have been traced in great measure by analogies in archaeological remains; but in such investigation one important factor has been overlooked, namely, the laws that govern migrations of races do not regulate the distribution of arts. The pathways do not correspond, but very often conflict. The arts migrate in ways of their own. They pass from place to place and from people to people by a process of acculturation, so that peoples of unlike origin practice like arts, while those of like origin are found practicing unlike arts. The threads of the story are thus so entangled that we find it impossible to trace them backward to their beginnings" (p. 266). Had the immediate successors of Holmes treated pottery objectively as did Holmes, instead of endeavoring to trace the migrations of peoples, much data on materials and methods would now be generally known and less confusion would exist.

A step of major importance in the study of pottery types has resulted from archaeological surveys. From such surveys pottery problems have been studied from potsherds rather than from whole vessels. Although methods of study have been developed for a better treatment of sherd material, yet these methods also may be applied in part to a study of whole vessels. The study of whole vessels must follow, of course, but since such material is found in widely scattered collections and thus

TECHNIQUES OF POTTERY MAKING

is less available, more time is required to examine the material. An analytical study of sherd material of a given type or ware should be followed by a similar study of whole vessels. The study of sherd material therefore presupposes the methods used and presented by Holmes but in many respects it is essentially the same.

Before methods of studying sherds are discussed it is essential that knowledge of techniques of manufacture be had. First comes the gathering of materials—clay, temper, and pigments. Usually the clay is from a convenient source and may be of varying mineral content which is sometimes shown by color (Guthe, 1925, pp. 19-20; Colton, M. R. F., 1931). The clay is refined and, generally, kneaded with temper. Temper is added so that the vessel will not break while drying. Various substances are used for temper. In prehistoric times sands were most generally selected for this purpose although in some regions or by some peoples, tempering material was purposely prepared. Rarely, and so far as known, organic matter was used only by the Basket Makers (Morris, 1927); inorganic matter (sand, rock, potsherds, etc.) was used in all other pottery whether Hohokam or Pueblo.

Pigment presumably was gathered as opportunity offered or was acquired by trade. Carbon, a common substance, was prepared by charring organic matter before or during the process of firing. Metals in mineral form occur approximately in the relative frequency as given in the following order: iron (usually as hematite), manganese (as pyrolucite), aluminum (as kaolin), lead (as galanite), and copper (in various forms).

Manufacture begins with the preparation of the basic materials. After the paste has been prepared by mixing the dry clay with water and temper, the vessel generally is started by moulding a base, either with the hands or in a base mold. When base molds or pot-rests are used they are made or shaped for the purpose. Baskets and pottery are known to have been used. With the foundation laid, a hunk of clay, rolled into a "rope" is pressed into the molded base. This rope is spiralled upward to the desired height. Small vessels frequently were entirely molded. Some aboriginal people have modified the coiling process in shaping vessels (Gifford, 1928; Rogers, 1936.) by using a paddle-and-anvil. Whereas, in vessels constructed by coiling, the vessel wall may be thinned by removing excess paste with a scraper, similar results may be attained by flattening the walls with a paddle. A pottery or clay anvil or a naturally shaped small cobble-stone of a convenient size was held inside the vessel to support the clay while pressure from the paddle was applied on the outside. After the vessel has been shaped, it is placed in the shade to dry.

Refinement of the surfaces were variously treated by different peoples. Techniques in refining the surface are here spoken of as surface treatment or finish. Variations occur, but the surface treatment of a smoothly finished vessel, which begins after the vessel has been dried, may be in the following order: (a) abrading the surface with a piece of sandstone, (b) moistening the surface with water and polishing with a fine grained polishing stone, and sometimes (c) coating the unabraded surface with a slip.

The decoration, if painted, is applied with a fiber brush. After the decoration has dried the surface is sometimes polished again over the freshly applied paint.

Little is known about methods of firing. We do know that in prehistoric times pottery was fired in an oxidizing or in a reducing atmosphere. The oxidizing atmosphere, in which an excess of oxygen is present was used generally throughout North, Central, and South America. Because of red oxides of iron, this resulted in pottery vessels having colors of varying shades of buff, brown, or red. The reducing atmosphere in which oxygen was prevented from reaching the vessel apparently was known only to some Southwestern Pueblo Indians. This atmosphere always produced a shade of gray or white. Nevertheless, when the clay is very low in iron some white surfaces are produced from firing in an oxidizing atmosphere. The color of a vessel then, generally, is more dependent upon the method of firing than upon the clays used since in most clays there is enough iron to color the surface of the vessel if an oxidizing atmosphere is used. If a reducing atmosphere is used, the vessel surface will be a gray or white, or, possibly sometimes purplish or black if much iron is present. Surface color then is a result of a specialized technique of firing a vessel, the *intensity* of the color being primarily dependent upon the amount of iron in the clay selected, if the oxidizing atmosphere is used.*

Knowledge of techniques of manufacture is essential in the study of the products of a primitive people. These techniques are basic, in that they are handed down from one generation to another so they are less susceptible to change. It is possible, therefore, to trace migrations of peoples, as well as cultural diffusion, by means of techniques of pottery making rather than by styles of design that are expressive of time or vogue.

* Numerous experiments have been performed in the laboratory of the Museum in which this theory has been satisfactorily tested.

CHAPTER III

METHODS OF STUDYING POTSHERDS

IN THE past few years many new methods have been used in the study of Southwestern Ceramics and in the use of these methods new fields of research have been opened. Although the use of these methods has not progressed far enough so that definite conclusions can be drawn in every case, yet, as a result of the application of these methods, certain trends of culture can now be observed so that bits of history that have been obscure now are reasonably clear. Methods of surface surveying have been developed by Mera, Gladwin, and Colton; Hawley has used simple chemical tests in determining paint pigments occurring on pottery; Shepard has studied the temper of pottery by petrographic methods; Fowler* has studied potsherds by means of the spectroscope; Shepard and Chapman have studied the firing temperature of modern Pueblo potters; Shepard, Fowler,* and Colton have studied the effect of oxidizing and reducing atmospheres upon various wares and clays; and Woodward has proposed a nomenclature for describing vessel forms. The importance of these new methods in the study of southwestern Ceramics cannot be too greatly stressed. A beginning has been made which will lead in time to definite conclusions.

A new method that has proven of practical value deals with the analysis of vessel rims. This method is herewith presented in print for the first time. Most readers have experienced difficulty in clearly understanding descriptive terms generally used when writers have referred to rim forms. That there is a great variety of rim forms is well known to students of Southwestern Archaeology, and, though attempts to describe these rims have been frequent, verbal or written descriptions have fallen short of accuracy and clarity. In some instances drawings have been made; these are better than word pictures. But neither of these means is adequate. Not only should the shape of the form be shown, as in a drawing, but there must be some way which, when referred to verbally, will bring to mind a picture of the rim form. A name will do that but before a name can be conveniently used there must be an adequate "description." Because of the instability of descriptive terms in certain branches

* Manuscript in files of Museum of Northern Arizona.

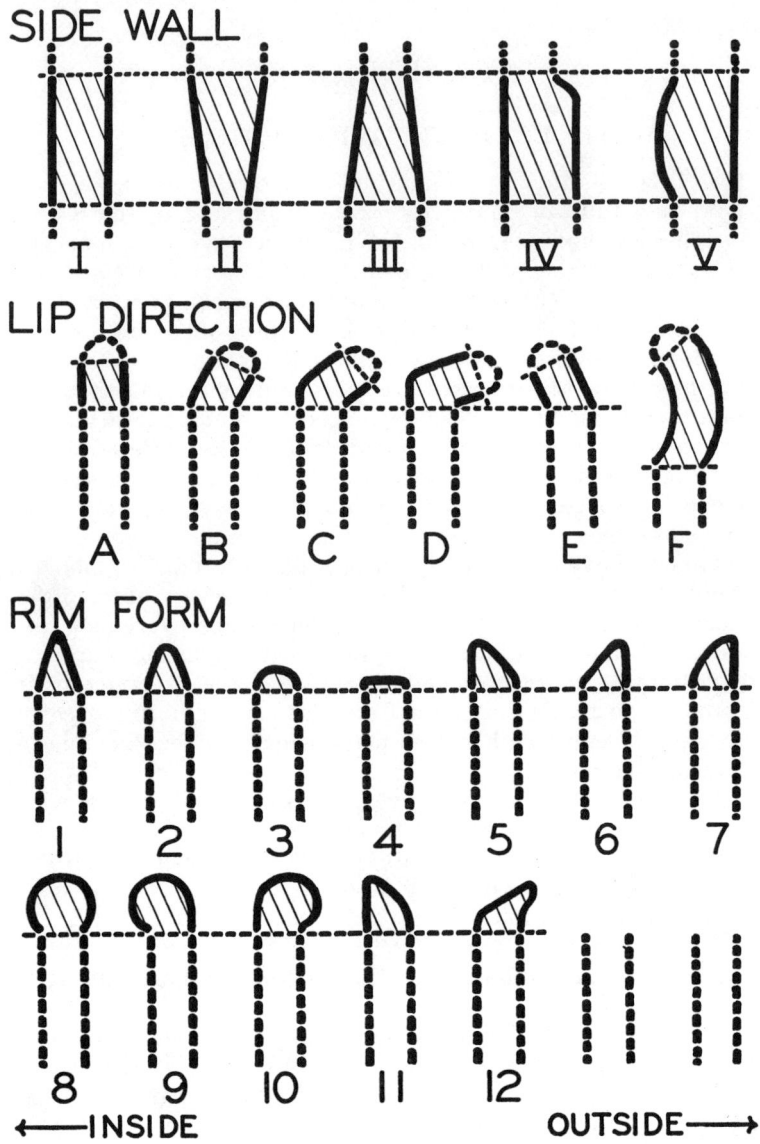

Fig. 2. Rim Types.

METHODS OF STUDYING POTSHERDS

of Southwestern Archaeology the Museum has devised a mechanical method of analyzing a rim form, a symbol being used in lieu of descriptive terms. An advantage of this method is that all rim forms can be analyzed, thus segregated from other forms, and, further, all examples of a given form can be properly placed as to form. By using symbols, in conjunction with a model chart, any form can be referred to in print and by always using the master chart, consistency in form determination is maintained. Familiarity with the rim forms designated by various symbols makes it possible to use these symbols in lieu of a name. Although technically these symbols, when spoken, are names, they are not meant to be interpreted as such.

To use the chart (Fig. 2) view a sherd in vertical cross-section and compare the shape of the vertical cross-section with that section of the chart indicated by the Roman numerals (i.e., vessel walls); next, determine the lip direction, indicated by capital letters; and, finally, compare the rim form, indicated by Arabic numerals. The symbol for the rim analyses would be the combination of the three divisional symbols, say "IA3."

This method is flexible and can be used on any forms of pottery vessels by adding to the chart any forms not previously recorded.

In the study of potsherds there are several preparatory steps. The material having been gathered, the study is begun by a dry examination for which the sherds are prepared by brushing off all loose earth, etc., so that sherds decorated with fugitive paint can be recognized. All sherds then should be washed and those sherds that are coated with lime should be placed in a crock containing a weak solution of hydrochloric acid until the lime has been removed. Sherds should be washed again to remove the acid. Concentrated acid may stain gray or white sherds.

After cleaning, major separations are made of the material, as black-on-white, black-on-red, corrugated, etc. The detailed study is started by breaking off a small piece of each sherd in a group. The core is examined (preferably with a 10× hand lens) for kinds, quantity, and mixture of temper. Temper will be recognized as grains of sand, as angular fragments of crushed rock or sherds, or may not be detected at all if the temper is very fine and of the same color as the core. Temper frequently is difficult to identify as to material, particularly when the temper is crushed rock. For instance, sands may be composed of particles or crystals of several minerals in which case a broad descriptive term must be used. The crushing of material for temper is a technique of manufacture. Although it is known that in some regions, at least, potsherds were crushed and used as temper (Haury, 1931, Pl. 10) still it is difficult definitely to identify temper as "sherd." Light-colored angular fragments is the designation used for sherd temper, and, in fact, for any temper having the appearance of ground-up potsherds.

Since the size of temper is an important criteria in recognizing types, some standard is necessary in describing size. Therefore, in the Handbook we will use a series of standards based on common pottery types. Examples of these are on file in the Museum of Northern Arizona. Very coarse temper—Jeddito plain, over .8 mm. Coarse temper—Tusayan corrugated, about .5 mm. Medium temper—Tusayan polychrome, about .2 mm. Fine temper—Deadmans Black-on-red, about .1 mm. Very fine—Jeddito Black-on-yellow, less than .1 mm and invisible to naked eye. (Hargrave and Smith, 1936.)

Other characters are noted at this time, as color of the core, presence of carbon streak, fracture, and general appearance of the core in cross-section. Color aids in determining the method of firing. *If the core has shades of color other than gray, white, or black, the specimen was fired in an oxidizing atmosphere.* The methods used in firing vessels slipped with iron-free clay can best be determined by the color of the core; in whole vessels this color may be seen in spots where the slip has worn away. Sherds of Zuni White Ware illustrate this case (p. 128).

Carbon streaks probably are a result of incomplete oxidation of organic matter within the paste. These streaks most frequently are seen in sherds fired in a reducing atmosphere, possibly because the lack of oxygen prevents the burning out of the carbon.* Moreover, core color of sherds fired in a reducing atmosphere often may be a gray on one or both surfaces, darkening, sometimes to black, as the center of the core is approached. Sherds fired in a reducing atmosphere have a greater strength, normally, than sherds fired in an oxidizing atmosphere and seem to have been fired at a higher temperature.

Methods of firing are most frequently determined by surface color, *the color of the exterior surface in nearly all instances being the criterion.*

Fracture, or the manner in which a sherd breaks under force, is determined by a combination of factors: materials, relative amounts of the mixed materials; and the degree of firing. Sherds containing large amounts of coarse temper, when fired in an

* Colton has mixed organic carbon with clay and fired it in oxidizing and reducing atmospheres.

oxidizing atmosphere, will crumble when broken; those containing small amounts of fine, or sometimes even a coarse temper, when fired in a reducing atmosphere, will have a clean break, sometimes flaking or shattering. The appearance of the cross-section is dependent primarily upon the size and quantity of temper plus firing temperature. This appearance is recorded as "shattering" or "crumbling."

Subdivision of the color groups may be conveniently made at this time by separating sherds with painted decoration from those without a painted decoration. Both groups should be subdivided further on the basis of surface finish, i.e., unpolished, polished, impacted, or slipped. Among sherds with painted decoration usually will be found more than one style of design. The smaller divisions should be types but in some cases type identification cannot be determined definitely until a comparison has been made with known material or until it has been checked with a good description.

If the Handbook is used for reference, comparison by use of the key should simplify ware and type identification, if the ware or type is listed. Should specimens not key to one of the wares, regroup the unidentified specimens on the basis of materials used and techniques of manufacture employed. This grouping is to determine WARE characters.

When dealing with undescribed material, separate into types and describe each following the order used herein.

The study of Southwestern Ceramics is a promising field of research and the above methods all are far from perfect. Much technical information is needed to round out descriptions of pottery types and wares; ranges must be determined and mapped; and, finally, a synopsis of each type giving all known characters and correlations should be made.

CHAPTER IV

STYLES OF DESIGN

WE MUST recognize the fact that in ceramics, as well as in other man-made objects, we have two influences at work on the finished product. The first influence comes through methods of technique that are passed on from mother to daughter by apprenticeship and which is similar to a biological "line." Wares, as already discussed, are a result of this influence. The second influence at work is one not encountered in biology and may be called *acculturation*. It is the acceptance of ideas by one group of people from people of a different line. There is nothing like this in the study of animals other than man, so is very important in studying man.

Among the factors of acculturation as applied to the pottery of the Southwest, is one that may be referred to as the diffusion of styles of design. When more is known of the dates of pottery types and of the centers of manufacture we will be able to picture in detail the waves of influence that passed over the Southwest from centers where potters showed creative ability. We can dimly perceive these influences now but as yet we cannot speak of them with much confidence.

To speak of Styles of Design or Styles of vessel forms, it is necessary to have a common terminology. In Styles of Design we must realize that design elements, such as lines, dots, or the simplest geometric figures (Fig. 3), when combined form motifs (Fig. 4), such as the "hourglass" motif which is the combination of triangle elements (Fig. 4, No. 27). When an element or motif is repeated in an orderly manner, the result is a pattern. The finished design will consist of a single element, a single motif, a pattern, or any combination thereof.

Elements and motifs* found in wares from northern Arizona are illustrated in Figures 3 and 4.

In Northern Arizona, the most common and best known wares are Tusayan White Ware, Tusayan Gray Ware, Little Colorado White Ware, Tusayan Red Ware, White Mountain Red Ware, Jeddito Yellow Ware, and Tsegi Orange Ware.

To become *Style of Design* a certain given element, motif, or pattern, must occur on two or more pottery types.

---

* The elements and motifs as illustrated herein are a part of a separate study and have not been applied to pottery descriptions in Chapters X and XI. In the future, descriptions can be made clearer by a consistent use of the names of elements and motifs and by the illustrations in Figures 3 and 4.

STYLES OF DESIGN

In Tusayan Gray Ware, Tusayan White Ware, and Little Colorado White Ware several *Styles of Design* are recognized. To refer to a *Style of Design* without inflicting the student with a new and greatly increased terminology, the authors have chosen the geographic designation of the name of a pottery

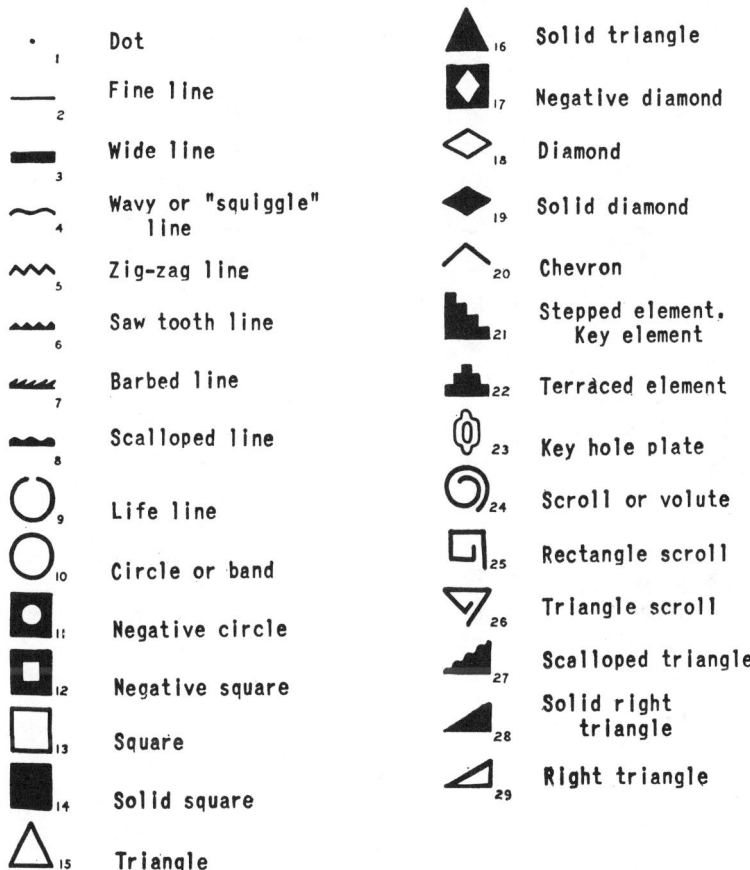

Fig. 3. Design Elements.

type characteristic of a *Style of Design* as the geographic name for the style of design. This does not mean that the style is confined to that type alone, since it may, and frequently does occur in another ware. More than one *Style of Design* may occur on a given type. Some of the prominent *Styles of Design* are illustrated in Figure 5. Briefly they are described as follows:

Lino Style is represented by crude lines and dots. It is found

NORTHERN ARIZONA POTTERY WARES

on Lino Black-on-gray and is characteristic of Basket Maker III.

Kana-a-Style is represented by triangles and fine parallel lines which frequently are not drawn carefully at angles. It is found on Kana-a Black-on-white and Dead River Black-on-white, and is characteristic of Pueblo I.

Deadmans Style is represented by broad lines, large triangles and often by pendant dots. It is found on Deadmans Black-on-

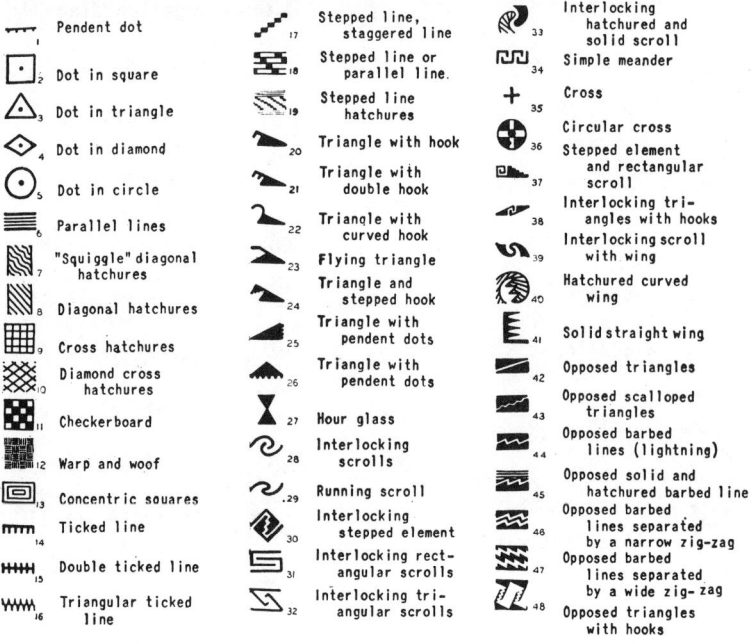

Fig. 4. Design Motifs.

white, and Holbrook Black-on-white and is characteristic of Pueblo II.

Flagstaff Style is represented by variations of the barbed line. It is found on Flagstaff Black-on-white, often on Walnut Black-on-white, and occurs in late Pueblo II and early Pueblo III.

Dogoszhi Style is represented by cross hatching in running panels. It is found on Dogoszhi Black-on-white, and on Tusayan Black-on-red. It occurs in late Pueblo II and early Pueblo III.

Kayenta Style is represented by dark masses on a white field, underlaid by a network of crossed lines like a mosquito bar. It appears on Kayenta Black-on-white, and Hoyapi Black-on-white. It occurs in late Pueblo III sites.

STYLES OF DESIGN

Walnut Style is characterized by interlocking stepped elements and flying triangles. It is found on Walnut Black-on-white and has been recognized on unidentified types from the southeastern part of the area.

These are only a few of the Styles of Design that may be met with. They are so common in the area treated that the authors feel they deserve specific names.

Styles are important time correlation criteria. They may be used in a manner similar to the use of index fossils in paleontology.

Fig. 5. Styles of Design.

It would be possible to classify pottery types by *Styles of Design*. In many ways that method of classification would be convenient, especially in teaching. Be that as it may, a consideration of *Styles of Design* leads to important conclusions relative to the diffusion of ideas.

A striking character of Pueblo pottery is the extreme conservatism rather than the expression of individual creative instinct of the craftsman. Not until it is realized that this conservatism permeated the whole cultural life of these craftsmen can this slavish following of style be understood. Occasionally a potter of the past, even as Nampeyo among the Hopi, would break from tradition, but it is a rare attribute. The artist did not give full reign to her creative ability, except in intervals so rare that they may be statistically ignored. Of course, someone must have first created the combination of elements into motifs and patterns, but when motifs and patterns were developed the only chance for creative expression seems to have been the combination of motifs into a complete design. These do vary to a considerable degree but the style of elements, motifs, and patterns seem, within a type, remarkably constant.

In studying the prehistoric pottery of northern Arizona before 1300 A.D. one is struck with the far-flung influences of *Styles of Design* over wide areas.

CHAPTER V

NAMING POTTERY TYPES AND PRIORITY IN NAMING*

THE reasons and necessity for systematically naming pottery types have been set forth in Chapter I. We will not, therefore, further expand the subject except to emphasize again that almost every author who has worked in the Southwest in the past has felt free to give names to pottery types as his whim pleased him without reference to what had been done previously. Those who have wished to follow a definite procedure have had no guide. The authors of this Handbook propose the following rules to determine the name that should be adopted. As these rules follow, in general, those that have been developed by biologists from the time of Linnaeus, nearly two hundred years ago, we see no reason why they cannot, in a modified form, be applied to pottery.

In this attempt at standardization certain arbitrary decisions have been made. It has not been the aim of the authors to be dogmatic in a personal way but each decision has been made after careful consideration of each problem. In the describing and naming of types, series, or wares the idea of personal credit is not admitted. It has been deemed necessary to record the name of the original describer, so that the *responsibility* of placing a description before students may be publicly assumed. The recording of the name of the person naming the type, and the source of reference, is, likewise, the placing of responsibility but, in addition, is recognition of an attempt at least to help straighten out the existing muddle.

RULES FOR NAMING A POTTERY TYPE, A POTTERY SERIES, OR A POTTERY WARE

RULE 1:

The description of a Type, a Series, or a Ware must be sufficiently clear so that it does not conflict wholly with the published description of another Type, Series, or Ware.

The distinguishing point, or points, should be made clear, and, if possible, a diagnostic character should be indicated. Distinctions, upon which type recognitions are based, are variable, type standing being determined by the presenter.

* See Colton and Hargrave, 1935a, Hargrave, 1935b, and Hargrave and Colton, 1935 for other discussions on this topic.

RULE 2:

The name of a Type, a Series, or a Ware must be a geographic name followed by a descriptive term (Kidder, 1927). Example: Deadmans Black-on-white; Mogollon Brown Ware.

It seems best to reserve as Ware names those geographic names that refer to large areas. Example: Little Colorado, Mogollon. Names of Series should be taken from areas intermediate in extent between those used in ware and type names, respectively. Type names may be borrowed from any geographic area, but preferably from a small one. Ideally, the pottery divisions should have approximately the same areal distribution as the geographic names applied to them.

The descriptive term of a type, if undecorated, refers either to the color of the vessel (example: Sunset Red), or to a condition of the surface finish (example: Jeddito Plain); if decorated the descriptive term either refers to a painted decoration (example: black-on-white); to changes in the vessel surface for ornamental purposes (example: corrugated, incised, tooled); or to a conspicuous difference in the color or in the technique of one surface as compared to the other (example: Deadmans Fugitive Red, Woodruff Smudged).

Gladwin (1930) states that the geographic name need not be the spot where the type was first found nor its area of greatest density but that the name would simply serve as a label for reference. This idea cannot be too greatly stressed. Many students feel that if a type is originally named for some place on the periphery of its area of distribution its name should be changed to that of a locality in the center of the area. This would only lead to endless confusion and a useless synonymy. The first name given, if properly constructed, and if the description is clear, should stand.

RULE 3:

Names should be as short as practicable (example: Chaco) *and may be abbreviated if the geographic original is long and unwieldy* (example: Kokopnyama, abbreviated to Kokop).

RULE 4:

Unnecessary adjectives should be omitted (example: North Creek Gray Corrugated should read North Creek Corrugated).

RULE 5:

The geographic name must not be combined with a prefix (example: Proto-Kayenta, Pre-Hawikuh), *or an adjective* (example: Upper Gila), *except where a prefix or an adjective has become an*

NAMING POTTERY TYPES

accepted part of a geographic name (example: Little Colorado, Dead River, Grand Canyon).

RULE 6:

A Type or Ware is designated "New Type" or "New Ware" when a description and name, formulated in accordance with Rules, appear in print together for the first time.

RULES OF PRIORITY

In any region where many papers dealing with one subject have appeared over a long period many differences in treatment and mention of subject matter are bound to occur if no standard has been set for presenting the information. The authors have been forced to recognize and to acknowledge priority. Although they hope that all matters of priority within the scope of this Handbook will be settled, still students interested in areas beyond its scope undoubtedly will encounter problems similar to those met here. To facilitate organization wherever these similar problems may be encountered, the writers are presenting a set of rules, upon which this Handbook is partly based.

RULE 1:

The name of a pottery type if printed without an adequate description is not acceptable.

RULE 2:

A name given prior to the 1927 Pecos Conference is acceptable if the geographic source can be inferred and a descriptive term of the type is given within the same work (hypothetical example: a printed reference to a specific black-on-white from Piedra, Colorado, may be called Piedra Black-on-white).

RULE 3:

In the event that a certain name has been erroneously applied in a publication to a pottery type which had previously been properly named, then the name thus erroneously applied becomes a synonym for the earlier name, and may not thereafter be used as the name of any other type.

RULE 4:

A name applied in a publication to a newly identified pottery type, without an accompanying description, becomes a synonym for the name applied to this type by the person who first publishes a description of it, and such name may not thereafter be used as the name for any other types.

Cumberland Trail Library System
Flora, Illinois 62839

RULE 5:

The date of acceptance for publication, when conforming to Rule 2, supersedes the date of publication in matters of priority. (This rule has not been applied to the Handbook prior to 1932.)

RULE 6:

When a name is adopted in accordance with Rule 2, the original description only is the responsibility of the describer while the inferred name is credited to the writer first formulating the name in accordance with Rules of Naming.

RULE 7:

The publication containing the description of the new type must be printed, litho-printed, or mimeographed, and not less than 50 copies must be distributed to libraries or field workers.

With the published description and name of a type should be stated the disposition of the type material. In studies conducted by the Museum certain sherds, illustrating type characters are set aside for future reference and comparison. These are designated as "type sherds." When possible whole vessels also should be designated as type vessels, i.e., type jar, type bowl, etc. Only material used in an original description is designated as "type," however. But if an original description is elaborated by the addition of published new information, part of the new material should also be filed and in print should be noted as "cotype." Any sherd of a given type, from the type site, i.e., from the site from which came the material used for the original description, or from a site designated a type site, is called a "topotype." Theoretically, topotype sherds are best for comparative purposes and when possible should be made available to interested parties. Experience has shown, however, that to properly identify, classify, catalogue, and prepare sherds for shipment requires much time. If sherds are sent to the Museum for identification, at least two of each supposed type should be sent; one sherd will be kept by the Museum and catalogued while the other, or others, will be returned identified to the one who wished the identification made.

CHAPTER VI

DATING POTTERY TYPES

THERE are three methods of dating pottery types, namely: relative dating by seriation as a result of archaeological surveys, seriation resulting from stratigraphy, and dating through direct correlation with dated wood specimens. To make seriation clear let us take a concrete example. In an archaeological survey let us suppose that we discover on certain sites both Flagstaff Black-on-white and Deadmans Black-on-white, and on other sites both Kana-a Black-on-white and Deadmans Black-on-white. Since Deadmans Black-on-white is common to both sites we can make a series. Kana-a Black-on-white, Deadmans Black-on-white and Flagstaff Black-on-white, but without data from another source we cannot state which type lies at the older end of the series. By cutting a trench through a trash heap, suppose we discover the same series but in addition we can now determine the oldest member of the series which, in simple cases will be on the bottom of the section. In this example, the oldest is Kana-a Black-on-white and the latest Flagstaff Black-on-white. By means of Dendrochronology or the dating of wood specimens by studying the annual rings, we can now actually date each member of the series in terms of our own era. Although this may occasionally be done with accuracy the method is cast about with difficulties.

To date pottery types by the tree ring method it is necessary to excavate a large number of small sites which were occupied but a short time. Besides these sites must be in a region where Yellow Pine, Douglas Fir or Piñon wood was used in the construction of the houses because these species, at the present time, are the only ones that furnish reliable rings for dating.

Large sites usually furnish poor material for dating pottery (1) because during a long occupation of a site the pottery fragments from many time periods may be recovered and (2) because beams from one portion of a site were sometimes robbed to roof new rooms. Besides we find that as the end of a long period of occupation approaches, while the pueblo was diminishing in population, no new trees were cut and the robbing of old rooms was the general practice. This occurs at the Hopi pueblos at the present time.

In reviewing situations under which ceramic specimens occur in correlation with datable timbers we find that there are occasions when the student would assign specific dates, or to make positive correlations of dates with sherds, where no such correlation is certain, because sherds occur in many situations and each situation should be carefully studied. Sherds from an excavation, for instance, consist of (1) surface sherds, (2) sherds within the earth fill of a room which may have come from the clay of the roof or from within the walls, (3) sherds resting upon the floor, (4) sherds that obviously belong to vessels crushed by falling walls or the roof, (5) sherds associated with charcoal in the fire pit and (6) sherds mixed with charcoal in trash or ash heaps

When a pit house or kiva is abandoned the roof collapses as well as a portion of the side walls, sherds on the surface of the ground, sherds that may have been imbedded in the clay of the roof as well as sherds in the fill behind the walls are found in the fill of the room. There is, therefore, no positive correlation between those sherds and the dates derived from the timbers. They may be much earlier. In a surface pueblo the fill in the rooms will contain sherds, (1) these may have been originally placed in the mortar found between the stones, (2) may have been supplied by sherds imbedded in the clay of the roof or (3) from trash deposited in the room after the room was abandoned. These sherds might cover a considerable time interval and may not be correlated with the timber found in the room. No positive correlation between sherds from within the earth fill of a room can be made with beams from this fill or with pottery specimens from within the structure proper, i.e., the dates from the two situations *cannot* be the same.

Sherds found upon or almost resting upon the floor are often considered contemporary with the structure. It must be mentioned that small miscellaneous sherds are not habitually seen knocking about floors of occupied pueblos. We cannot assume that this was true in prehistoric times. If datable timbers are recovered dates *cannot* be assigned to miscellaneous sherds found upon or near the floor since these sherds most probably came from the collapsed roof or wall, unless modifying conditions were encountered in the excavation. They must then be considered with the same doubt as "surface sherds." Moreover, it is not only possible but is probable that the dates from timbers may be of one stage while all sherds, surface and otherwise, may belong to an earlier stage. This condition was observed when a Pueblo II structure (based upon dated timbers) was built immediately upon an old Pueblo I site (based upon surface sherds). Not one single sherd of a type occurring later than Pueblo I was found in the room which was devoid of all artifacts suitable for time determination. Therefore, the structure was built, occupied, and abandoned, without leaving either whole or parts of vessels that would indicate the period of occupation.

Another case comes to mind, where every sherd found, indicated Pueblo I but a single pottery object, definitely Pueblo II, was found on the floor. Its position *directly upon the floor*, its size, and depth beneath the ground surface (about 7 feet), minimized all chances of the object having reached this position accidentally. Pueblo I sherds were found on the surface. Thus this site was Pueblo II in point of time, as the preceding example must also have been. It is to be recalled that in neither case was there found one sherd definitely referable to Pueblo II alone, yet in one site the occupation stage was determined by tree-ring dates, and in the other by ceramics. The time of abandonment of these two sites is thus stated as Pueblo II.

Sherds that belong to vessels crushed by falling walls or roofs or whole vessels in situ or in the floor, constitute a more definite criterion for accurately correlating pottery with dated house timbers. But even there, the elapsed period of time between the construction of the room and its abandonment would make an error of some years.

A more accurate determination of the *date of abandonment* might be made by studying charcoal and sherds from firepits, but branches which were used for fire wood are poor material for dating. The rings are unreliable, the record short and the outside rings are usually lost.

Hawley (1934) has used the sixth method—the dating of charcoal from fuel used in cooking, associated with sherds in a trash heap. It is assumed that when a firepit is cleaned out and the charcoal is carried to the heap, potsherds from recently broken vessels will become associated with it. Hence there will be a direct correlation. The method is sound but open to the same difficulties as is charcoal from firepits.

Even with the difficulties that have been outlined which are mostly concerned with a long or multiple occupation of a site, if many small sites of short occupation are studied, it is possible to date pottery types with reasonable accuracy. Although it is not possible to give a date more accurate than within twenty-five years, this is accurate enough for most purposes.

In Northern Arizona, the Museum has excavated more than one hundred small sites of short occupation from which a number of pottery types have been dated. These types bear what we like to call "index styles of design." When these types are associated with other types in a great number of small sites, these other types become dated also.

The approximate dating of pottery types has been one of the greatest advances in Southwestern Archaeology in the last ten years. By the recognition of index styles of design it has been possible to date with reasonable accuracy nearly every prehistoric site in Northern Arizona on which pottery fragments are found. For purposes of Archaeological synthesis, the importance of these results cannot be overstressed.

CHAPTER VII

GEOGRAPHICAL FOCUS OF MANUFACTURE AND DISTRIBUTION BY TRADE

A RESULT of the study of pottery types and sherds collected on archaeological surveys is the idea that there is a definite, often small, geographic area in which a pottery type is manufactured.

In every area it seems that at least two kinds of pottery may be expected to occur, a relatively thin "table type," often called "non-culinary," which generally is decorated; and an undecorated "utility type" that may have been used for cooking or for storing water or grain. Sometimes this latter kind is called "culinary." The "utility type" is usually found in the form of large vessels that would be difficult to transport and which usually are indigenous to the region. On the other hand, the "table type" often is a small piece that is easily transported. Small pieces are found over a wide area far from their place of manufacture. This statement is particularly true if the pieces are durable and of an attractive design.

The hypothesis that there existed foci for the distribution of certain pottery types, thus the recognition of trade pieces, is supported by the following axioms:

(1) *A trade piece should be small enough to be easily transported.* Example: Vessels of Jeddito Yellow Ware found in the Verde River Valley, Arizona, almost always are small bowls under 12 inches in diameter, or are parts thereof.

(2) *The companion utility type of a vessel after it has been traded to another region is a different utility type than the companion utility type of the vessel at its focus of distribution.** Example: Large vessels of Awatobi Yellow Ware, the companion ware to Jeddito Yellow Ware in the Hopi Country, are absent in the Verde River Valley where the utility types belong to Alameda Brown Ware and Prescott Gray Ware and are made of local materials.

---

* A vessel may have two kinds of companion types, i.e., those types normally associated with it "at home" or "domestic companion types," and those associated with it "away from home" or "foreign companion types."

(3) *The materials, of which a trade piece is made, are foreign to the locality where the suspected trade is found.* Example: To determine if a specimen is a trade piece, sometimes spectroscopic or petrographic tests of the paste might be necessary to determine the locality of origin. Spectroscopic tests made by Fowler† in the Laboratory of the United Verde Copper Company have shown that Jeddito Black-on-yellow, a table type from the Verde River Valley ruins, was made of clay not found in the Verde Valley, while Tuzigoot Red, one of the utility types abundant in the Verde Valley, has never been found in the Hopi Country.

The archaeological survey of the Museum of Northern Arizona indicated that the above hypothesis applies quite generally but until laboratory tests are made it will remain but an hypothesis. For each pottery type we must look for a focal area of manufacture, this area, in turn, surrounded by a trade area. We believe, as in the examples, cited above, that Jeddito Black-on-yellow was manufactured in the Hopi Country and that it was traded to peoples in the Verde River Valley. When more laboratory studies have been made we hope to be able to plot the focus of manufacture and the area of trade for every pottery type.

We can think of the small decorated bowls as a kind of currency. The people of the Verde Valley had salt, cotton, and malachite. The Hopis had little or none of these, but the Hopi made an attractive yellow pottery. The people of the Verde Valley made no well decorated pottery but apparently they liked it. Exchange was possible and so yellow Hopi pottery flooded into the Verde Valley.

Although it is possible to point out a few exceptions, yet there is a general rule that small objects which include small pieces of pottery were widely traded. On the other hand large objects such as large storage jars were infrequently carried long distances. These facts give us a means whereby to determine local foci of manufacture and make it possible to locate routes of trade.

† Notes on these tests are in the files of the Museum of Northern Arizona but have not been published in full.

CHAPTER VIII

INTRODUCTION TO POTTERY DESCRIPTIONS

ALTHOUGH no classification is proposed in this work, the order of presenting each ware, series, and type is dependent upon *convenience*.

An attempt has been made to describe each ware and type as fully and concisely as our knowledge and the purpose of this work permits, following a standard arrangement for presenting each character.

Old and new types are described. In dealing with old types a "revised" description is given. In this revision descriptive characters presented in the original, or supplementary, description have been condensed and rearranged. New information on old types has been included in the revised description. No attempt has been made to separate "old" from "new" information, the important point being the description and not the describer or describers. The large number of papers dealing with Southwestern Archaeology have prohibited thoroughness in presenting certain phases of this work. It is believed, however, that all papers specifically treating with pottery from Northern Arizona have been reviewed but some titles possibly have been overlooked. Although consistency and standardization in terminology have been constantly borne in mind, old synonyms commonly in use frequently have unconsciously appeared in the text and undoubtedly some will be seen in printed form. The list of synonyms is not complete but the more familiar colloquial names occurring in the publications have been listed. Besides these synonyms, some types are familiarly known by other so-called "lab" or "field" names. Type names must be made stable if type names are to be kept usable. The synonyms given for a type are believed to be sufficient to identify an unfamiliar name with a familiar type. The selection of a good name for a new type frequently has been a source of much concern. Since type names must begin with a geographic name and since in some extensive geographic regions, pottery types exceed in number the published place names, geographic features first have been given names, or an admittedly bad choice for a type name has been made. This is regrettable but is not serious since, in time, the name habitually calls to mind type characters, with a proportionate lessening of geographic or other significance. On first hearing a name, as "Deadmans Black-on-white" or

"Dead River Black-on-white," one would be inclined to smile. It is true that unfamiliar, meaningless names, as "Kana-a," "Lino," etc., not only are admirably adapted to use as type names but are readily accepted by the most critical persons. Unfortunately, such appropriate names were not always available.

Also, late in the preparation of this work, has come the realization that some terms consistently used do not convey the intended thought. Late consideration has also shown that for clarity many of these terms rightly are deserving of much discussion that cannot be given at this time. An example at hand is the general use of "constructed by coiling" and "constructed by paddling." The authors realize that "coiling" is an early stage in the application of both methods of building pottery vessels, but "coiling" versus "paddling" is even yet generally used to contrast the two methods so these terms have been retained, even though it is believed that the principles involve *thinning vessel walls by removing a part of the coils*, i.e., by scraping, and *thinning vessel walls by displacement*, through means of applied pressure. This thought should be borne in mind when using descriptions.

In many instances the method of constructing a vessel of a given type might be questioned. It is admitted that in all vessels, or parts thereof, this technique is not shown, much evidence frequently having been removed by later processes of construction. The statements in description that a given type was "constructed by coiling" or was "constructed by paddling" are based upon information not necessarily revealed in every sherd but that has been seen on an example of the type in question. Neatly finished and painted bowls "constructed by coiling," for instance, generally do not show evidence of coils if the surfaces of the bowl have been scraped and highly polished. Jar forms of the same type, but with restricted orifices, on the other hand, frequently have vestigial coils *within* the neck where a scraper could not be used effectively or because of the hidden position there was no need for fineness of finish. *Corrugated surfaces in decoration can be produced only by coiling; never by paddling.* Moreover, anvil marks generally show on the interiors of large jars, frequently on the interiors of bowls of some types, and not uncommonly paddle marks may be detected as flat planes or areas on the exterior surface of bowls and jars if "constructed by paddling."

It is admitted that all specimens of a type will not fit the description perfectly. The description is based upon a number

POTTERY DESCRIPTIONS

of "typical" sherds. By typical sherd, is meant a sherd that is not over-fired, under-fired, or re-fired. Control of heat could not be perfect, thus vessels frequently were defective. Defects of firing are a separate discussion to be presented sometime. However, experience in handling sherds will give one assurance in recognizing standard material. The following descriptions should fit the majority of sherds of a given type in any collection from the range of the known type.

Occasionally comparison of questionable material with examples of known types is advised. Because positive identification cannot be made by means of a published description does not in the least mean that a pottery type is not valid or that an adequate description should not be attempted. Pottery types differ one from another by some *visible* character as a result of influence from one or more factors. Even though a consistent difference can be *seen*, one cannot always *tell* exactly what is seen. That the describer is deficient does not lessen the truth of a material difference that has been extant for centuries. In identifying pottery types of recognized value in making certain correlations or deductions, direct comparison not only is often advisable, but frequently is necessary. Numerous precedents in various branches of scientific research support this statement.

In addition, there are sherds that are intermediate between types. Common in this class are areal and temporal intergrades. Usually, however, these intergrades may be readily recognized. Type determination would generally be made on the basis of dominant type characters. There are other examples of intergrades that would require a similar assignment. These result from partial adoption of a Style of Design from another region or type. Acknowledgment of these exceptions and familiarity with standard material lessens the chances for misidentification.

The recognition of types, with few exceptions, depends upon technical processes other than the method of construction and the method of firing. If the surface is scraped and lightly rubbed it would be one type; if a surface has been altered for decorative purposes by tooling, i.e., incising, punching, or by coiling, corrugating, etc., each variation of decorative technique would be a sound basis for type separation, since technique is learned through apprenticeship. Other types would be admissible with the addition of substances to the vessel surfaces, as slip, paint, or clay strips or knobs (applique); by variations in technique of application or manner of use of decorative material, as drawing a design with paint, by outlining a design with another color, by the local use of a slip, i.e., on a restricted part of a vessel, or by combinations thereof; by smudging, stippling, or engraving a painted surface. All are processes of decorative technique and are type determinants.

The first exception to the preceding paragraph is the recognition of a type on the basis of the *kind of temper*. Type recognition on this basis rarely would be made. An example is Sunset Red in the construction of which black volcanic sand was used. This temper is so conspicuous that trade pieces are readily recognized outside the area where vessels of this type were manufactured. In a detailed comparative study of the pottery types from two or more localities, petrographic analysis might show differences in temper or clay sufficiently great to warrant separation of other types. Other factors than minute differences in temper and paste, however, should determine the value of recognizing a new type. Material, or more specifically temper, used in the manufacture of pottery is of minor or local importance.

The second exception also deals with material. Hawley has clearly demonstrated that the kind of paint pigment used is an important cultural character. Prepared pigment is a result of technique. Pigment then certainly is an acceptable point for the recognition of a type, particularly if other characters, as surface finish and style of design, are the same on another type having a different pigment. But paint is of greater value since technique of preparation and the kinds of pigments used are restricted regionally and correlate with other regional cultural characters. Pigment then may be a ware determinant as well as a type determinant.

Vessel form is a possible exception to technical processes as a basis for type recognition. Proposing a type on this basis probably should be made only when all other ceramic characters are equal in kind and number to the characters of a previously described and named type. The need of a new type in cultural analysis and synthesis would warrant the recognition of a type on the basis of form (Fig. 6).

Some types are recognized by Styles of Design. Stress long has been placed upon this determinant. The Pueblo Stages are identified by style of design, and, in fact, Pueblo I and Pueblo II, in some regions can be identified definitely in many instances by this criterion only. Styles of design are widespread and thus are good stage criteria.

There may be some doubt as to the validity of types proposed on all points noted above, for instance, processes of incising, punching, smudging, stippling, engraving painted areas, etc.

POTTERY DESCRIPTIONS

Recognition of these decorative processes has value since the processes themselves, with the exception of engraving painted areas, are more widespread than are the space ranges of individual types based upon them. They are thus fundamental criteria in the recognition of cultural diffusion, or probably, even in tracing the movements of peoples; especially is this true if basic correlative cultural traits occur with them. Also, types recognized through use of these criteria serve excellently as time gauges. An example is Jeddito Engraved. This type has painted areas with engravings in the paint. Such engravings are not known to occur throughout the life of Jeddito Black-on-

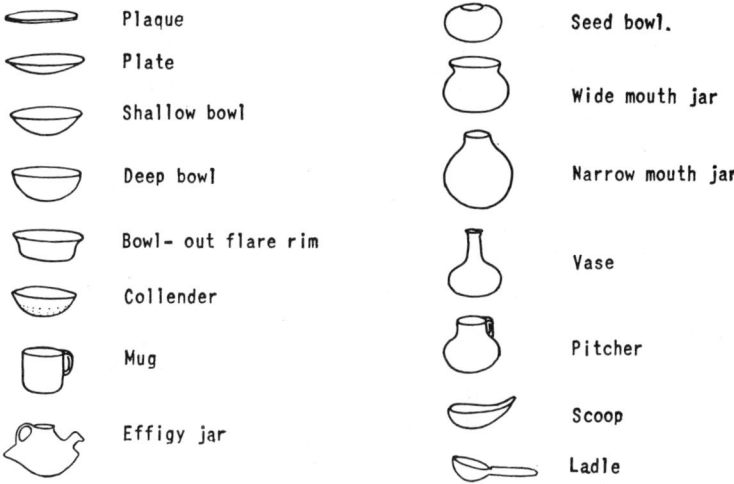

Fig. 6. Vessel Forms.

yellow, a companion type, so that the time range of Jeddito Black-on-yellow can be divided by recognizing Jeddito Engraved on the basis of the character "engraving," a decorative technique. Moreover, the recognition of the type Jeddito Engraved is necessary because Jeddito Black-on-yellow has too long a time range for accuracy in correlative dating. Jeddito Black-on-yellow and Sikyatki Polychrome (rarely) both occur at Misheptanga but Jeddito Engraved has not been reported from there. There is thus reason to believe that Jeddito Black-on-yellow is the earliest of the three types, and that Jeddito Engraved is the youngest. The time range of Jeddito Black-on-yellow would be broken into the following periods: the birth of Jeddito Black-on-yellow to the birth of Sikyatki Polychrome;

from the birth of Sikyatki Polychrome to the birth of Jeddito Engraved.

In considering type determinants we may summarize as follows: (1) materials, as temper and pigment when contrasted to temper and pigments of other kinds in other localities; (2) techniques of manufacture and processes thereof, as manner of finishing the vessel surfaces; (3) form; (4) decorative technique, as alteration of vessel surfaces, and minor processes or uses of decorative material; and, (5) styles of design in painted decoration.

After a type description has been published much difficulty has been experienced when attempting to identify ceramic material from printed words. And this difficulty increases proportionately with the appearance of each description of a new type. As early as 1932 an effort to lessen this difficulty was made at the Museum of Northern Arizona. In "Guide to Forty Pottery Types from the Hopi Country and the San Francisco Mountains, Arizona" (Hargrave, 1932) the pottery types were arranged in the table of contents with classification sub-heads which were then thought to be appropriate and understandable. It was intended that this table of contents would be viewed objectively and that it would be used as a "key" for the identification of types presented. Genetic relationships between these types were not meant to be considered. But since Hargrave did not explicitly state that the guide was to be used *objectively*, there resulted a misunderstanding of the use of the classification and of its purpose (Kidder & Shepard, 1936, p. xxviii). Since the publication of that work the senior author has suggested a more practical method of identifying Southwestern Pottery Types. The method is herewith presented for the first time as a "Key to Northern Arizona Pottery Types."

This key is not perfect. Conceivably it could be elaborated so that by its aid all described varieties of all types could be separated from a mass of sherds. But its bulk and intricate workings would be prohibitive to effective use in the field.

Much improvement can be made in its present form but this improvement must be a result of practicable application of the principle. Undoubtedly defects in descriptions will be recognized through the application of the key, but in time both the key and the manner of describing a pottery type should become standardized, at least to the extent that both will be of inestimable value in the identification of pottery types.

For convenience, the key has been broken into sections and

POTTERY DESCRIPTIONS

each section has been placed where it is believed identification will be made easier.

A WORD ABOUT DATES

A word about dates of pottery types. The dates as given are not meant to be exact and are intended to be used as an aid only. It was a desire to give dates as determined from dated wood and by other correlations but in most publications reviewed so little specific data was given that it seemed futile to strive for accuracy in dating pottery without a great deal of research. The range of years given for pottery types, is frequently reached from a number of, sometimes even diverse, correlations and sometimes are little more than "impressions" held by the authors.

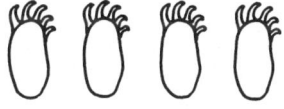

CHAPTER IX

KEY TO NORTHERN ARIZONA POTTERY TYPES

THE principal purpose of this key is to assist one to locate an unknown type *in the Handbook*. To one not familiar with type names the key, therefore, is essential to the proper use of the text.

The key is not built to identify or to isolate types not treated herein and if applied to pottery types from other regions might indicate the wrong type by name, a type that in some respects might differ greatly from the type keyed in the Handbook. If one is familiar with a given type name, its position in the Handbook can be learned from the table of contents, or from the index. There is no need to use the key in this case. But if one has at hand a sherd from northern Arizona and wishes to identify it, the key should indicate that section of this book that treats of it or of similar material. The authors do not hold that positive type identification can always be made by use of the key. If the material being keyed is an example of a type included in the Handbook, the chances are that it will key to a section of the text where detailed information will show if one is right or wrong. Certainly the specimen will key so that only a few pages of text need be read.

Many persons have been used in testing the key. Few had specific knowledge of the test material yet the results were highly satisfactory. On the other hand, the inadvisability of using relative terms in the key was emphasized. Unfortunately the use of such terms could not be avoided; but fortunately there are only three such cases—color, relative thickness, and anvil marks or no anvil marks.

Individual designation of color is so variable that type identification can sometimes be made only by repeated trials; also elimination by trial may often be necessary when considering thickness of slip and anvil marks. Realizing the indefiniteness of these relative terms an attempt to compensate has been made when possible. In keying some types the terms "thick slip" or "thin slip," or "anvil marks" or "no anvil marks" are not so important since they have been made to key either way. In other types, several attempts may be necessary before the type keyed checks with a detailed type description.

In using the key attention always should be paid to the exact

KEY TO POTTERY TYPES

wording of a statement and when checking a statement with type characters only that character being compared should be considered at that time. We may illustrate the working of the key by running several examples through.

HOW TO USE THE KEY
KEY A: PRIMARY KEY

1. Surface altered.................................Key B (p. 40)
   Surface not altered.. 2
2. Exterior surface Brown, Red, Orange, Yellow, or Buff....Key C (p. 42)
   Exterior surface Gray or White......................Key D (p. 188)

EXAMPLE 1:

Suppose we have a sherd in hand. We first turn to "Key A" where we see that the first character to check is whether or not a surface has been intentionally altered. By this is meant if the surface has been altered by cutting into the surface, as "incising," or "tooling"; if structural coils have been altered or merely left for decorative purposes; if the normal appearance of the surface has been altered by applying additional paste as "applique" in the form of knobs, etc. (See Fig. 7.) *A painted surface is not here considered as altered.*

We see that in our sherd the structural coils have been manipulated for decorative purposes. "Key A" then directs us to "Key B" (p. 40) where we find that "color" is the first consideration. Beginning at "1" we read each statement until the color of our sherd checks with the statement, which is "Exterior surface color gray or white." Our sherd is gray so we disregard the term "white." Reading after the statement of color we see the numeral "11." We are thus directed to turn to the eleventh point for our next consideration.

Here we have three alternatives. We know that our specimen is not "tooled" so we disregard this point. Next is "corrugated," a character that checks with our specimen so, as directed, we check with "13." Of the two characters queried we see that our example checks with the second, "body corrugated," so, in order, we move to "14" where inspection of the cross-section through our sherd shows us that in our specimen the temper is not "light-colored angular fragments." Then being directed to "15" we learn that, since on our sherd the corrugations are "not flattened and not partially obliterated," we must then check with the detailed description of "Tusayan Corrugated." This description fits our sherd so we can call our sherd "Tusayan Corrugated."

38 NORTHERN ARIZONA POTTERY WARES

Fig. 7 Altered Surface
(See opposite page for explanation)

KEY TO POTTERY TYPES

Had the description of "Tusayan Corrugated" not fit our sherd we should then run through the key again to see if we could have made an error. Satisfied that we were right we then conclude either that the type to which our sherd belongs is not in the Handbook or else our specimen is abnormal in some respect.

EXAMPLE 2:

But when checking with "Key A" if we had seen that our sherd was "surface not altered" we then would have checked with "2" where we would have learned that we were directed to "Key C" because our sherd was Brown, or Red, Orange, Yellow, or Buff (it doesn't matter which).

Turning to "Key C" we learn that color is of primary consideration. We will not try to split on shades of color but will make our decision on first impression, say "brown." Moving to "2" and checking as previously we see that our specimen does not have a painted design so on to "3." At "3" we might get into difficulty but again decide quickly, "no anvil marks" (anvil marks frequently have been completely removed but if they can be recognized at this point the specimen will key out sooner). Our next move is to "4" where we are directed to "5." We immediately admit that our specimen has a dull brown slip, so we turn to "Key b," this key being listed first has preference over "Key 10" and should be the correct key *if we have made the right choice*, in all previous comparisons. Turning to "Key b" we check through to two type descriptions and see that we could not possibly be correct in our key identification.

There are two alternatives. When keyed out of "Key C" we were given choice of two minor keys so we try the second, "Key 10." In "Key 10" we see that type identification is made on the basis of "temper." This does not mean that the type originally was recognized by this character solely but that "temper" later proved to be the most (or only) distinguishing character from another type in "Key 10." Checking through "Key 10" we are directed to "Key m" or to "Tonto Red."

Fig. 7. Altered Surface.

A. Corrugated (Medicine Gray)
B. Wiped (Walnut Wiped)
C. Tooled (Honani Tooled)
D. Tooled (Jeddito Tooled)
E. Punched (O'Leary Tooled)
F. Partially Obliterated Coils (Moenkopi Corrugated)
G. Flattened Coils (Kana-a Gray)
H. Corrugated (Winona Corrugated)

"Key m" does not identify the type but the description of "Tonto Red" fits the sherd. In the description of this type we learn that anvil marks generally are conspicuous on vessels of this type. We know then that we made the identification by a route made longer by our previous inability to distinguish anvil marks.

Let's go back to "Key C, no. 3" and agree on "anvil marks." Immediately we are directed to "Key 10" where we get the same results as by going the long way. The sherd is "Tonto Red."

EXAMPLE 3:

Trying another sherd "Key A" directs us to "Key D." Our sherd is very smooth, bright, and "lively"; we even see polishing marks, so we follow on to "3." Fracturing the sherd, with the naked eye we see temper in the core. Following through we note that the temper is not mica; at "5" we note further that the temper is "not light-colored angular fragments"; at "6" we agree that the surface is "whitish" but although the surface might be impacted there is the appearance of a slip so we move to "7." Here we have a choice of two styles of design. Referring to the illustration of styles of design, immediately we identify our type as "Jeddito Black-on-white." But we cannot be certain of the key name so we turn to the description of "Jeddito Black-on-white." Here we learn that we are wrong. Briefly reviewing "Key D" we stop again at "6" where we decided that our sherd was "slipped." Obviously there was a chance for error so we try "white, not slipped" and are directed to "Key 16: Tusayan White Ware," where we learn that our type is "Kayenta Black-on-white."

Identification of these examples may have seemed to require much time but actually a sherd can be run through the key in less time than it takes to explain it. Even so, when the number of types treated herein and the time required to check by reading are considered, the time required to run through the keys, even several times, is of little consequence.

KEY B: SURFACE ALTERED

1. Exterior surface color brown or red.................................... 2
   Exterior surface color orange, yellow, or buff..................... 9
   Exterior surface color gray or white............................... 11
2. Corrugated.. 3
   Incised...Woodruff Incised (p. 59)
   Wiped..Walnut Wiped (p. 180)

KEY TO POTTERY TYPES

3. Interior surface black painted design.......Wingate Corrugated (p. 119)
                                    Walnut Corrugated (p. 56)
   Interior surface not painted................................. 4
4. White painted decoration over corrugations................... 5
   No painted decorations over corrugations..................... 6
5. Corrugations always partially obliterated...Salado White-on-red (p. 65)
   Corrugations always clear and prominent........................
                                      McDonald Corrugated (p. 61)
6. Exterior surface purplish-red...................Salado Red (p. 65)
   Exterior surface not purplish-red.............................. 7
7. Corrugations appear as horizontal flutings or ribs (Fig. 00).........
                                Silver Creek Corrugated (p. 62)
   Corrugations do not appear as horizontal flutings or ribs........... 8
8. Black volcanic sand temper................Elden Corrugated (p. 63)
   Not black volcanic sand temper............Linden Corrugated (p. 60)
                                  Homolovi Corrugated (p. 134)
                                    Winona Corrugated (p. 55)
9. Corrugated... 10
   Tooled.....................................Jeddito Tooled (p. 145)
   Wiped.....................................Walnut Wiped (p. 180)
10. Exterior surface orange; core pinkish.....Homolovi Corrugated (p. 134)
    Exterior surface yellow; core not pinkish....Jeddito Corrugated (p. 144)
11. Tooled... 12
    Corrugated.. 13
    Neck coils; not tooled........................Kana-a Gray (p. 195)
12. Neck coils trimmed with tool..................Coconino Gray (p. 201)
    Tool marks as isolated punchings.............O'Leary Tooled (p. 200)
    Tool marks as series of lines................Honani Tooled (p. 202)
13. Neck corrugations only.....................Medicine Gray (p. 199)
    Body corrugations... 14
14. Temper (in part) conspicious light-colored angular fragments ......
                                 Little Colorado Corrugated (p. 232)
    Temper not light-colored angular fragments.................... 15
15. Corrugations flattened and partially obliterated..................
                                   Moenkopi Corrugated (p. 197)
    Corrugations not flattened and not partially obliterated...........
                                   Tusayan Corrugated (p. 196)

CHAPTER X

OXIDIZING ATMOSPHERE

THIS chapter deals only with wares fired in an oxidizing atmosphere while Chapter XI deals with wares fired in a reducing atmosphere. The order given may seem reversed since the reducing atmosphere was used in the greater part of northern Arizona before the oxidizing atmosphere appeared there. However, priority in order of presentation is given the oxidizing atmosphere because oxidized pottery seems to have appeared in southern Arizona before reduced pottery appeared anywhere in the state. Further, the oxidizing atmosphere is almost universally used to fire pottery by primitive peoples of prehistoric or historic times, while the reducing atmosphere, in America, is of comparatively recent "discovery" and occurred in a relatively small area.

KEY C: SURFACE NOT ALTERED
EXTERIOR SURFACE BROWN, RED, ORANGE, YELLOW, OR BUFF

1. Exterior surface brown or red................................. 2
   Exterior surface orange, yellow, or buff........................ 16
2. Painted design on vessel...................................... 6
   No painted design on vessel................................... 3
3. Anvil marks...Key 12 (p. 158)
                                         Deadmans Fugitive Red (p. 252)
   No anvil marks... 4
4. Pinkish surface generally thin and watery......... Arauca Plain (p. 80)
                                         Deadmans Fugitive Red (p. 252)
                                             Lino Fugitive Red (p. 193)
   Surface not pinkish; not thin and watery....................... 5
5. Slip bright red, highly polished, reflects light. San Francisco Red (p. 48)
                                                              Key b (p. 51)
                                                             Key 12 (p. 158)
   Slip dull, generally brown.............................Key c (p. 58)
                                                             Key 12 (p. 158)
6. Interior surface (bowl forms) white........................... 7
   Interior surface (jar forms) white............................ 8
   Interior surface (any form) not white......................... 8
7. Paint on interior surface, glaze....................... Key i (p. 113)
   Paint on interior surface, not glaze................... Key 4 (p. 86)
8. Glaze paint... Key 6 (p. 102)
   Not glaze paint.. 9
9. Red painted design; paint same as slip.........................
                                         San Lorenzo Red-on-brown (p. 46)
                                             Winona Red-on-tan (p. 54)
   Red painted design; paint not same as slip......................
                                             Mogollon Red-on-brown (p. 47)
                                             Tuzigoot Red-on-black (p. 171)
                                             Citadel Polychrome (p. 75)

OXIDIZING ATMOSPHERE

    No red painted design.................................... 10
10. Heavily slipped... 11
    Not heavily slipped.. 12
11. Temper conspicuous on red polished surface............Key 2 (p. 67)
                                                                       Key j (p. 118)
                                                                       Key 3 (p. 77)
    Temper conspicuous (?) on brown polished surface........Key 1 (p. 125)
    Temper (mica) conspicuous on brown or red surface......Key g (p. 84)
    Temper not conspicuous on red surface.................Key 6 (p. 102)
                                                  Tuzigoot Black-on-red (p. 170)
                                                         Kiet Siel Polychrome (p. 100)
                                                               Gila Polychrome (p. 88)
                                                                      Key m (p. 148)
12. Polychrome, red surface.............................Key 6 (p. 102)
                                                         Kiet Siel Polychrome (p. 100)
                                                         Citadel Polychrome (p. 75)
                                                              Gila Polychrome (p. 88)
                                                                        Key 3 (p. 77)
    Polychrome, brown surface...............Kintiel Polychrome (p. 126)
    Not polychrome.. 13
13. Brown surface.....................Kintiel Black-on-orange (p. 125)
                                                                      Key 14 (p. 184)
                                                          Verde Black-on-gray (p. 184)
    Red surface.. 14
14. Temper conspicuous on surface......................Key 2 (p. 67)
                                                                        Key j (p. 118)
    Temper not conspicious on surface............................ 15
15. Slip watery; base color shows through..................Key 3 (p. 77)
                                                                       Key m (p. 148)
    Slip not watery....................Deadmans Black-on-red (p. 71)
                                                            Bluff Black-on-red (p. 69)
16. Painted design on vessel..................................... 19
    No painted design on vessel................................. 17
17. Temper quartz sand; conspicuous on surface......Jeddito Plain (p. 144)
    Temper quartz-like sand; not conspicuous on finished surface........
                                                              Tuwiuca Orange (p. 136)
    Temper quartz-like sand and light-colored angular fragments....... 18
18. Sand predominantly reddish or brown..........Homolovi Plain (p. 133)
    Sand not predominantly reddish or brown........Tsegi Orange (p. 93)
19. Core yellow; no apparent temper....................Key 11 (p. 146)
    Core yellow; temper apparent...........Kwaituki Polychrome (p. 148)
                                                                    Key 6 (p. 102)
    Core not yellow.. 20
20. Polychrome.. 23
    Not polychrome.. 21
21. Red painted design only.................Tsegi Red-on-orange (p. 94)
                                                                     Key 13 (p. 179)
    Black painted design only.................................. 22
22. Design elements straight or curved lines only............Key k (p. 123)
                                                      Tsegi Black-on-orange (p. 95)
    Design elements lines and other elements................Key 9 (p. 135)
                                                                     Key 6 (p. 102)
                                                     Kintiel Black-on-orange (p. 125)
23. Exterior decoration white painted lines only......................
                                                              Jeddito Polychrome (p. 142)
                                                              St. Johns Polychrome (p. 104)

44 NORTHERN ARIZONA POTTERY WARES

Exterior decoration red painted lines only...............Key 5 (p. 92)
Key j (p. 118)
Black and white paint on red slip (any surface)........................
Kiet Siel Polychrome (p. 100)
Black Ax Polychrome (p. 81)
Black and red (paint or slip) on orange (any surface).....Key 5 (p. 92)
Citadel Polychrome (p. 75)
Black and white on orange (any surface)...............Key 9 (p. 135)
Key 6 (p. 102)
Homolovi Polychrome (p 82)

A: POTTERY CONSTRUCTED BY COILING

In considering the first division of oxidizing atmosphere, the technique of building the vessel by coiling is presented first, on the assumption that steps followed in this method are more primitive than those followed when the paddle-and-anvil is used (Gifford, 1928).

MOGOLLON BROWN WARE

The order in which wares are presented often is arbitrary. This ware, however, is placed first because Mogollon Brown Ware appears to be ancestral to, or else techniques first appearing in this ware exerted influences upon, later developed wares of the north. The majority of the described types in this ware occur indigenously beyond the southern boundary of the area treated herein. It was from peoples producing Mogollon Brown Ware at an early date that ceramic knowledge probably was transmitted to peoples living further north that the foundation for ceramic development and expansion in the northern part of the Pueblo Area was laid.

KEY 1: MOGOLLON BROWN WARE

1. Temper quartz-like sand....................................... 2
   Temper predominantly light-colored angular fragments...Key a (p. 46)
   Key b (p. 51)
   Temper black volcanic sand.................Elden Corrugated (p. 63)
   Temper copper-colored mica..........................Key e (p. 64)
2. Smooth surfaces......................................Key c (p. 58)
   Corrugated surface...................................Key d (p. 60)

OXIDIZING ATMOSPHERE

MOGOLLON BROWN WARE: new ware

STAGES: Basket Maker III–Pueblo IV.
TIME: Probably pre-700-ca 1150 A.D.
DESCRIPTION:
Constructed: by coiling. *Fired:* in oxidizing atmosphere. *Core:* gray or brown, sometimes almost black, occasionally pinkish, tan, or brick-red. *Temper:* coarse to fine quartz[1] sand (in Woodruff Series); light colored angular fragments, gray or white with lesser amounts quartz (in Alma Series); principally quartz sand (in Linden Series); black volcanic sand (in Flagstaff Series); flecks copper-colored mica (in Salado Series). *Texture core:* fine to coarse. *Walls:* weak to strong, *Fracture:* slightly crumbling. *Surface finish:* bowl interiors and jar exteriors, smoothed, in several types well polished, or corrugated; bowl interiors coated in three types—red on Woodruff Red, reddish-brown on San Francisco Red, light brown or pinkish-brown on Mogollon Red-on-brown; bowl exteriors coated with thin reddish-brown slip on San Lorenzo Red-on-brown; jar exteriors coated with thin slip on two types—reddish-brown on San Francisco Red, pinkish or light brown on Mogollon Red-on-brown; jar interiors scraped, not usually smoothed; bowl and jar exteriors, frequently manipulated coils on jar necks often unobliterated, sometimes flattened, sometimes indented. *Surface color:* brown, orange, buff, tan, pinkish, brick-red. *Forms:* bowls, jars, pitchers, seed-jars, figurines, eccentric. *Rims:* IA3, IA4, IA12, IIIA1, IIIA12, IB2, IB3, IB6, IB13, IIIB2, IC3, IIIC3, IE13.[2] *Paint:* reddish-brown; pigment, hematite; white paint, kaolin. *Painted Decoration:* only on bowl interiors of San Lorenzo Red-on-brown, bowl interiors and jar exteriors of Mogollon Red-on-brown; white line decoration on McDonald Corrugated, and Salado White-on-red.

RANGE:
Arizona south of the Little Colorado River to the north edge of the southern desert (lower Sonoran Zone), southcentral and southwestern portions of New Mexico, and the northern part of Chihuahua, Mexico.

ALMA SERIES

This group of related pottery types occurs in northwestern New Mexico and southeastern Arizona. These types, even at

---

[1] When used in Description "quartz" means having the appearance of Quartz.
[2] See Figure 2 for rim analysis.

this early date, are perfectly constructed. Earlier types, of Mogollon Brown Ware, that probably belong to this series, may be expected.

KEY a: ALMA SERIES

1. Painted decoration... 2
   No Painted decoration....................San Francisco Red (p. 48)
2. Lines in sets as framers for design units.........................
   Mogollon Red-on-brown (p. 47)
   Lines not used as framers for design units.......................
   San Lorenzo Red-on-brown (p. 46)

SAN LORENZO RED-ON-BROWN

DESCRIBED BY: Haury, Q:1:14, p. 6.
NAMED BY: Haury, loc. cit.
ILLUSTRATIONS: Haury, loc. cit., Fig. 1.
TYPE SPECIMENS: Gila Pueblo, Globe, Arizona.
TYPE SITE: New Mexico Q:1:14 (Gila Pueblo Survey).
STAGE: San Francisco Phase (=Pueblo I).
TIME: Pre-900 A.D. (Haury, 1936, Fig. 9).

DESCRIPTION (revised):

Constructed: by coiling. *Fired:* in oxidizing atmosphere. *Core:* dark gray, changing to reddish brown near surfaces. *Temper:* predominantly white angular fragments (apparently crushed rock); rounded quartz, rare; size of particles, varies from minute to one-half thickness vessel wall. *Texture core:* fine to medium. *Fracture:* devious, ragged; not very friable. *Hardness:* 3.5 to 4.0. *Surface finish:* interior scraped (before entirely dry), rubbed (apparently by hand), finally polished; polishing considerably better in late examples; coated with thin, finely divided slip which extends over rim; lightly polished; exteriors, usually rough, dented; may be smoothed; polishing marks, appear as bright streaks against dull unpolished background; visible in hollows. *Surface color:* brownish (14C6, 15A5)*, light brown (12A5, 14A7) in later examples; slip reddish-brown (6D11). *Form:* bowls, mostly shallow, sometimes near plate-like; diameters range from 10 to 20 cm. *Rims:* IA3, IIIA1 (most frequent). *Recorded thickness vessel walls:* average, ca 5 mm. *Decoration:* painted. *Paint:* reddish-brown (of same material as slip); polished after application thus blurring outline of decoration resulting in streaks carried over on unpainted areas. *Decoration:* entire interior surface; not on exterior; carries to rim where slip (coming over from exterior)

* See Color charts, Maerz and Paul, 1930.

provides narrow framing stripe. *Elements:* narrow and wide straight lines, small solid isosceles triangles; usually set fairly far apart; usually in parallel series; often frames for triangles, used (1) as independent elements, pendent from rim and serving as nuclei for sets of framing lines, or (2) pendent from line, in closely set series producing barbed or serrated line; entire field divided into quadrants, design of each quadrant the same; brushwork, sloppy, lines frequently carry over at intersections; late examples lines generally narrower, brushwork improved, still lacking in precision.

COMPARISON: Mogollon Red-on-brown, temper somewhat finer, less abundant, quartz grains more frequent; bowl interiors coated with light brown or pinkish brown slip; decoration more complicated; execution better, more diversified, triangles more often approaching right triangles; jar forms occur.

RANGE:
Known to occur only at the type site and at Mogollon 1:15 (Gila Pueblo Survey).

REMARKS:
Chronologically and typologically precedent to Mogollon Red-on-brown.

MOGOLLON RED-ON-BROWN

DESCRIBED BY: Haury, 1936, p. 10.
NAMED BY: Haury, loc. cit.
ILLUSTRATIONS: Haury, loc. cit., Fig. 3–5.
TYPE SPECIMENS: Gila Pueblo, Globe, Arizona.
TYPE SITE: Mogollon 1:15 (Gila Pueblo Survey).
STAGE: San Francisco Phase (=Pueblo I ?).
TIME: Pre-900 A.D. (Haury, 1936, Fig. 9).

DESCRIPTION (revised):

Constructed: by coiling. *Fired:* in oxidizing atmosphere. *Core:* light gray, merging into thick reddish-brown near surfaces. *Temper:* opaque, moderately fine white angular fragments; quartz sand, occasional. *Texture core:* fine. *Fracture:* devious, ragged; not very friable. *Hardness:* 3.5 to 4.5. *Surface finish:* bowl interiors, scraped, not polished; coated with thin, finely divided slip; scraping marks visible where slip worn; jar interiors, usually heavily scored; occasionally smoothed; bowl exteriors, usually finger-dented; sometimes smoothed; coated with thin reddish-brown slip; polished; tool strokes parallel to rim; jar exteriors coated with slip like bowl interiors; polished. *Surface color:* light brown to pinkish brown (6A10, 12A5, 14A7); fire clouds, frequent. *Forms:* bowls (predominate), jars (rare); bowls usually have outcurving sides, range from 10 to

25 cm in diameter; occasionally plate-like and beaker-like; jars usually wide-mouthed; diameters probably not over 40 cm. *Rims:* bowls, IA3 (most frequent), IB3, IIIA1. *Wall thickness:* fairly uniform, average thickness ca 4.5 mm. *Decoration:* painted. *Paint:* reddish-brown (same as exterior slip); polished after application blurring edges of painted elements causing streaks to carry over on unpainted areas. *Decoration:* designs cover entire interior bowl surfaces; all but jar bottoms field, usually quartered, in one of three general ways, each related to solid isosceles triangles pendent from rims: (1) quartering lines intersect rim mid-way between isolated triangles, (2) extend from one triangle to one opposite, (3) no quartering lines but each quadrant filled by roughly rectangular panel, with fifth and similar panel in center of field, sometimes last scheme modified by use of five pentagonal panels with sixth and similar one in center. *Elements:* narrow and occasional wide straight lines and solid triangles; lines usually in series as frames for solid elements; sometimes framing lines form nests of concentric figures, sometimes develop continuously as rectangular spiral; short fringe-like lines pendent to longer lines; cross-hatching, and interlocking frets, rare; checkerboard motifs, rare; small triangles frequent as pendent from larger solid areas or lines, producing barbs or serrated effect; slight extension of one side of triangle beyond apex, frequent; curved lines rare.

COMPARISONS: San Lorenzo Red-on-brown, surfaces usually less well-finished; decoration much less diversified and complicated; solid triangles smaller, less nearly right triangles; jar forms absent.

RANGE:

San Francisco and Mimbres rivers and intervening territory, New Mexico.

REMARKS:

This type is the painted component for the San Francisco Phase. It is probably a derivative from San Lorenzo Red-on-brown, and ancestral in decorative style to Mimbres Black-on-white.

SAN FRANCISCO RED

DESCRIBED BY: Haury, 1936, p. 28.
NAMED BY: Haury, loc. cit.
ILLUSTRATIONS: Haury, loc. cit., Fig. 7; Pl. III.
TYPE SPECIMENS: Gila Pueblo, Globe, Arizona.
TYPE SITE: Mogollon 1:5 (Gila Pueblo Survey).
STAGES: Georgetown to Mimbres Phases (=Basket Maker III–Pueblo III).
TIME: Pre-700-ca 1100 A.D.

OXIDIZING ATMOSPHERE

DESCRIPTION (revised):
Constructed: by coiling. *Fired:* in oxidizing atmosphere. *Core:* gray, shading to brown near surfaces. *Temper:* predominantly opaque whitish angular fragments, some rounded sand. *Fracture:* devious; not friable. *Hardness:* 3.5 to 4.5. *Surface finish:* bowl interiors coated with thin but tenacious reddish-brown slip; well-polished; polishing marks usually parallel to rim; sometimes radiating from center toward rim; light smudging occasional in late examples; jar interiors, sometimes scored; usually smoothed; bowl exteriors usually smoothed, or finger-dented; scraping marks, occasionally noticeable; sometimes vertical fluting; sometimes original coils unmodified; occasionally scraped and incised in carelessly drawn isolated straight lines; frequently slipped and polished; jar exteriors, similar to bowl interiors; rarely banded about neck and finger-dented. *Surface color:* reddish-brown (5H11, 6I11). *Forms:* bowls, jars, seed-jars; bowls usually shallow; later examples, deeper; jars, relatively small, not over 30 cm in diameter; jar shapes, vary from large-mouthed without necks, vertical necks, to short flaring necks; handles and lugs, infrequent; handles perforated vertically when present. *Rims:* bowls IIIA3, IIIC3. *Recorded thickness bowl walls:* average ca 6 mm. *No painted decoration.*

RANGE:
San Francisco and Mimbres rivers and intervening territory, southeastern Arizona and southwestern New Mexico.

REMARKS:
This type is fundamental and long-lived, but decreases in quantity in later phases; color becomes less rich and execution less expert as time goes on.

WINONA SERIES

For several years past occasionally have been found red ware sherds that differ greatly from other red ware sherds found in and described from the San Francisco Mountain region of northern Arizona. These undescribed types are familiar to some students of Southwestern Pueblo Ceramics. Workers have heretofore hesitated to describe these sherds because they were too few in number to indicate more than a trade relation with a locality apparently as yet unstudied. Further, major objective characters showed them to be genetically related to described types south of the localities from which they have been found.

The number of individual type sherds in the types presented

in this series are few. The scarcity of type material should not however delay description. That any specified number of sherds of a proposed type be available before a type is described and named should not be considered essential since objective differences naturally are the result of a different group of factors. After all, our main interest is in the factors that have produced *change*, material results, in this case being objective differences existing between pottery types. In some cases a mass of sherds would be necessary to clearly define a consistent difference between types; in another, one sherd would be sufficient. But the value of a type, either as a time indicator or as evidence of cultural diffusion, does not depend upon the frequency of its occurrence. The value comes from recognizing the factors for which the type stands. Abundance indicates the *strength* of these factors.

The material in this series has not only been found in some quantity at a single site but it represents five distinct treatments of the basic paste. There is then a distinct series of pottery types from one region, the series at present being recognized because of objective and not time differences. Further, the site, from which three types of this series have been found, has been dated by tree-ring analysis (McGregor, 1937). These types herein presented for the first time may now be used as time correlators and as indicators of cultural diffusion, even though the area from which they may have been traded, or from which their makers may have come, is not known.

Further, of these types, four are variations of, or are developments from, a single type. These types all occur in the Walnut Creek drainage and neighboring localities of the San Francisco Mountains, Coconino County, Arizona. The locality from which most of the sherds came lies near the railway station of Winona. The site where time and cultural relations were determined is known as "Winona Village" (NA2134). The Series is named for the type locality.

The order of development of these types has not been determined so the order of presenting them is based upon variations of techniques of manufacture, each type being presented logically according to the technique separating that type from the other types in the series.

Most of the type material was excavated at Winona Village by Mr. John C. McGregor in charge of a joint expedition at that site for the Museum of Northern Arizona and the Arizona State Teachers College at Flagstaff; some material was collected by Hargrave at other sites.

OXIDIZING ATMOSPHERE

The principal known difference between types in the Winona and Woodruff series is in the temper used.

KEY b: WINONA SERIES

1. Surface altered... 2
   Surface not altered... 3
2. Corrugated; painted design................Walnut Corrugated (p. 56)
   Corrugated; no painted design.............Winona Corrugated (p. 55)
3. Painted... 4
   Not painted... 5
4. Black paint..........................Winona Black-on-red (p. 53)
   Red paint............................Winona Red-on-tan (p. 54)
5. Interior surface smudged....................Winona Smudged (p. 52)
   Interior surface not smudged...................Winona Red (p. 51)

WINONA RED: new type

TYPE SPECIMENS: Sherds numbers AT 4649–4699, 4710, and 4714 in the Type Collection of the Museum of Northern Arizona.
TYPE SITE: Winona Village (NA 2134), Walnut Creek drainage, San Francisco Mountains, Coconino County, Arizona.
STAGE: Between Pueblo II–III.
TIME: Probably in use between 1050–1150 A.D. (McGregor 1937).

DESCRIPTION:

Constructed: by coiling. *Fired:* in oxidizing atmosphere. *Core:* black to dark gray. *Temper:* predominantly minute (pinpoint-like) light-colored angular fragments, frequently some minute sand grains (seen as points of light), and occasionally minute black specks (basaltic sand?); light-colored angular fragments generally seen and frequently conspicuous on exterior (sometimes interior) surface. *Texture core:* fine; core nearly always shows diagonal laminations. *Vessel walls:* medium strong to strong; slightly friable to friable. *Fracture:* crumbling. *Surface finish:* both surfaces highly polished (sometimes appear to be slipped); exterior surface sometimes slightly bumpy, always shiny, generally with polishing marks (sometimes conspicuous); interior surface perfectly smooth, generally with faint (sometimes conspicuous) polishing marks. *Surface color:* bright red to dark brown; both surfaces generally about same shade of color; color surface and core, contrast; surface color sometimes grades into core color. *Fire clouds:* on almost all specimens. *Forms:* bowls, jars (rare). *Rims:* IA3 (tending to IA4). *Recorded range thickness bowl walls:* 5.6 to 6.2 mm; greatest individual range recorded, 0.4 mm (uniform thickness bowl walls); average thickness, 5.9 mm (based upon two measurements each of six sherds). *Not decorated.*

COMPARISONS: Differs from San Francisco Red as follows:—Not smudged, exterior surface not "finger-dented," no vertical flutings, original coils obliterated, not "scraped and incised" (see "San Francisco Red," Haury, 1936).
Similar to Woodruff Red but has different temper.
If there is doubt whether material is Winona Red or San Francisco Red, direct comparison with known material is advised since objective differences in some examples of each type are difficult to describe sufficiently clearly to be used in key identification.

RANGE:
Reported only from Walnut Creek drainage, San Francisco Mountains, Coconino County, Arizona, but it is believed to occur south and east of that region.

REMARKS:
Winona Red, as a type, may have been indigenous to the type locality since the black temper appears to be ground black volcanic temper.

WINONA SMUDGED: new type

TYPE SPECIMENS: Sherds numbers AT 4700–4709, 4711, 4713, and 4715 in the Type Collection of the Museum of Northern Arizona. Collected by McGregor.
TYPE SITE: Winona Village (NA 2134) as above located.
STAGE: Between Pueblo II-III.
TIME: Probably in use between 1050–1150 A.D.

DESCRIPTION:

Constructed: by coiling. *Fired:* in oxidizing atmosphere. *Core:* black to dark gray, or purplish. *Temper:* predominantly (pinpoint-like) light-colored angular fragments, frequently some minute sand grains (seen as points of light), and occasionally minute black specks (basaltic sand?), or predominantly minute black angular fragments; light-colored angular fragments generally seen and frequently conspicuous on exterior (sometimes interior) surface. *Texture core:* fine; core nearly always shows diagonal laminations. *Vessel walls:* medium strong to strong; slightly friable to friable. *Fracture:* crumbling. *Surface finish:* both surfaces highly polished (sometimes appears to be slipped); exterior surface sometimes slightly bumpy, always shiny, generally with polishing marks (sometimes conspicuous); interior surface perfectly smooth, generally with faint (sometimes conspicuous) polishing marks. *Surface color:* exterior surface bright red to dark brown; both surfaces not same shade of color; interior surface smudged, generally lustrous; color surface and core, contrast; color exterior surface sometimes grades into core color. *Fire clouds:* on almost all specimens. *Forms:* bowls, jars (rare). *Rims:* IA3, IA4. *Recorded range thick-*

ness bowl walls: 3.9 to 6.5 mm; greatest individual range recorded, 1.6 mm; average thickness, ca 5 mm. *Decoration:* smudged interior surface.

COMPARISONS: Differs from San Francisco Red as noted under "Winona Red." Differs from Winona Red by having a smudged interior surface. Woodruff Smudged has quartz-like sand temper.

RANGE:
San Francisco Mountains, Coconino County, Arizona. One sherd (AT 4636) from Chaco Canyon, New Mexico.

REMARKS:
Sherds that roughly fit the description of Winona Smudged have been reported from northern New Mexico. Two of these sherds (AT 4572 and 4573) have been donated to the Museum by Florence M. Hawley and are noted by her as "(11a) Chaco /G.R.," and "(11b) Chaco/G.R.", respectively. These sherds differ from Winona Smudged, as described above, only in having a quartz-like sand temper. There is probably an unrecognized series of types similar to the types in the Winona Series except for a change in temper.

Most of the type material used in the study of this series has been submitted to the Laboratory of Anthropology, Santa Fe, New Mexico, and to Gila Pueblo, Globe, Arizona, from which institutions has come assurance that the types are new and, further, that the area from which these types may have been traded is unknown.

WINONA BLACK-ON-RED: new type

TYPE SPECIMENS: Sherd number AT 4563 in the Type Collection of the Museum of Northern Arizona.
TYPE SITE: Pithouse NA 1653, Sunset Crater National Monument, Coconino County, Arizona.
STAGE: Pueblo I.
TIME: Pre-885 A.D. Site NA 1653 has not been dated but it was abandoned prior to the eruption of Sunset Crater.

DESCRIPTION:
Constructed: by coiling. *Fired:* in oxidizing atmosphere. *Core:* gray. *Temper:* predominantly minute (pinpoint-like) light-colored angular fragments. *Texture core:* fine; diagonal laminations. *Vessel walls:* strong; slightly friable. *Fracture:* crumbling. Surface finish: both surfaces highly polished, slipped; exterior surface slightly bumpy, shiny, polishing marks conspicuous; interior surface perfectly smooth. *Surface color:* exterior surface reddish-brown; interior surface brownish buff (abnormally fired); both surface same general shade of color;

color surface and core, contrast. *Form:* bowl. *Thickness bowl wall:* 6.1 mm. *Decoration:* painted. *Paint:* brownish. *Design:* narrow lines (3 mm wide).

RANGE:
Recorded only from the type site.

REMARKS:
There can be no question that the type sherd (AT 4563) belongs in Winona Series since all objective characters are typical. That there is only one available specimen does not void the recognition of the type since there are several sherds of another type in the series that have a black painted design. The type was postulated when the series was first recognized.

Of far greater importance is the occurrence of this sherd in a Pueblo I site since the occurrence strongly indicates that the series was developed earlier than indicated by the discovery of the series in a Pueblo II site. The sequential development of the Winona Series probably did not occur in the San Francisco Mountain region.

At one time this sherd (AT 4563) was thought to be Hohokam (Hargrave, 1932, p. 6–7).

WINONA RED-ON-TAN: new type

TYPE SPECIMEN: Sherd number AT 326 in the Type Collection of the Museum of Northern Arizona. Collected by Lyndon L. Hargrave in 1930.
TYPE SITE: Pithouse NA 2001, in upper Deadmans Flat, San Francisco Mountains, Coconino County, Arizona (Hargrave, 1930).
STAGE: Probably between Pueblo II–III.
TIME: Since 964 A.D. The pithouse from which the type sherd came has been dated by tree ring studies that show the structure to have been abandoned after the above date (McGregor, 1932).

DESCRIPTION:

Constructed: by coiling. *Fired:* in oxidizing atmosphere. *Core:* black to gray. *Temper:* predominantly minute (pinpoint-like) light-colored angular fragments; light-colored angular fragments rarely seen on surfaces (probably because of relatively heavy slip). *Texture core:* fine; diagonal laminations. *Vessel walls:* medium strong to strong; slightly friable. *Fracture:* crumbling. *Surface finish:* both surfaces highly polished, slipped; exterior surface slightly bumpy, shiny, with polishing marks conspicuous. *Surface color:* exterior surface bright red; both surfaces, in part, same color; color surface and core, contrast; surface color sometimes grades into core color; interior surface (bowl), buff. *Fire Clouds:* noted. *Form:* bowl. *Rim:* IA3. *Recorded range thickness bowl walls:* 6.0 to 6.7 mm; individual

OXIDIZING ATMOSPHERE 55

range recorded, 0.7 mm; average thickness, 6.3 mm. *Decoration:* painted. *Paint:* red (same shade as slip on exterior surface). *Design:* (type sherd) broad stripes (around rim and vertically up side walls); encircling stripe, 20 mm wide.

COMPARISONS: Differs from San Lorenzo Red-on-brown and Mogollon Red-on-brown in style of design. Other minor differences will be seen by comparing the descriptions of the three types.

RANGE:

Recorded only from the type site.

REMARKS:

Although the description of this type is based upon a single sherd, its genetic relation to other types in the Winona Series cannot be questioned when the description of Winona Red-on-tan is compared, point for point, with the description of any other type in the same series. Nor must the value of this type be overlooked since in the treatment of the decoration was employed a variation of decorative style not found upon other vessels known to occur in the region prior to the occurrence of this sherd of Winona Red-on-tan. Moreover, of equal importance is the similarity of this type, in many respects but particularly in the use of slip as paint for decoration of the interior surface, to three types of the Alma Series of Mogollon Brown Ware, from southwestern New Mexico (for descriptions of these types see Haury, 1936). The recognition of Winona Red-on-tan thus strengthens the belief that Winona Series not only belongs in Mogollon Brown Ware, but that Winona Series is close genetically to Alma Series, admitted to be the earliest known series in this ware.

WINONA CORRUGATED: new type

ILLUSTRATION: Fig. 7.
TYPE SPECIMENS: Sherds numbers AT 4717–4728 and 4737–4739 in the Type Collection of the Museum of Northern Arizona.
TYPE SITE: Winona Village (NA 2134) as above located.
STAGE: Between Pueblo II–III.
TIME: Probably in use between 1050–1150 A.D.

DESCRIPTION:

Constructed: by coiling. *Fired:* in oxidizing atmosphere. *Core:* black to dark gray. *Temper:* predominantly minute (pinpoint-like) light-colored angular fragments, frequently some minute specks (basaltic (?) sand); light-colored angular fragments generally seen and frequently conspicuous on exterior (sometimes interior) surface. *Texture core:* fine; core nearly always shows diagonal laminations. *Vessel walls:* medium strong to strong; slightly friable to friable. *Fracture:* crumbling. *Surface finish:* exterior surface corrugated; interior surface generally highly polished (sometimes appears to be slipped), perfectly smooth, generally with faint (sometimes conspicuous) polishing marks. *Surface color:* interior surface, black (generally), red, or brown (uncommon); smudged (black) interior surface frequently lustrous. *Forms:* bowls, jars (rare). *Rims:* IA3 (tending to IA4), IIIA3. *Recorded range thickness bowl walls:* 4.5 to 6.7 mm; greatest individual range recorded, 1.1 mm (uniform thickness of bowl walls); average thickness, 5.8 mm (based upon measurements of ten sherds). *Decoration:* exterior surface corrugated (not painted). *Designs:* smooth surface below lip of rim, 12 to 27 mm wide; frequently three or more straight or tooled (or both) coils between rim and corrugated body; corrugations Tusayan or Deadmans styles; corrugations very slightly altered by polishing *over* corrugations; polishing streaks generally conspicuous.

COMPARISONS: Differs from Linden Corrugated principally in having a bright, lively surface with polishing marks rather conspicuous over corrugations. Other differences will be seen if descriptions are compared. Differs also from Salado Red on these, as well as on other, points.

RANGE:

San Francisco Mountains, Coconino County, Arizona. One sherd (AT 4575), from Chaco Canyon, New Mexico, donated by F. M. Hawley, is noted by her as "Chaco, G. R., 11c."

REMARKS:

Although the slight bumpy areas (and slight depressions) sometimes seen on types in this series are slightly suggestive of the technique of construction when the paddle and the anvil were used, critical examination of some sherds shows the imprints of fingers. Further substantiation that the paddle and the anvil were not used is found in the occurrence of corrugated types. *Corrugated exteriors, such as on this type, could not be produced by the paddle and anvil.*

WALNUT CORRUGATED: new type

TYPE SPECIMENS: Sherds number AT 4729, and 4740 in the Type Collection of the Museum of Northern Arizona. Collected by Lyndon L. Hargrave in 1932.
TYPE SITE: Pithouse NA 2098 at Turkey Tanks, Walnut Creek drainage, San Francisco Mountains, Coconino County, Arizona.

STAGE: Between Pueblo II–III.
TIME: In use probably between 1130–1150 A.D. Since this type was not found in Winona Village, yet was found in the Turkey Tanks site where the pottery complex was essentially the same as the complex found at Winona Village, it may be that Walnut Corrugated is a few years later than Winona Corrugated. Site NA 2098 has not been dated by tree rings.

DESCRIPTION:

Constructed: by coiling. *Fired:* in oxidizing atmosphere. *Core:* black to dark gray, purplish, or pinkish. *Temper:* predominantly minute (pinpoint-like) light-colored angular fragments, frequently some minute specks (basaltic ? sand); light-colored angular fragments generally seen and frequently conspicuous on exterior surface. *Texture core:* fine; core nearly always shows diagonal laminations. *Vessel walls:* medium strong to strong; slightly friable. *Fracture:* crumbling. *Surface finish:* exterior surface corrugated; interior surface slipped (red), perfectly smooth, highly polished. *Surface color:* interior surface bright red; exterior surface shade of red or brown. *Forms:* bowls. Rims: IA3, IA4. *Recorded range thickness bowl walls:* 5.1 to 6.0 mm; greatest individual range recorded, 0.9 mm; average thickness (three sherds), 5.5 mm. *Decoration:* painted and corrugated. *Paint:* rich black (lively) or bluish black (dull). *Design:* pendent from rim or beneath narrow encircling line (ca 3 mm wide). *Elements:* solid triangles and narrow lines.

COMPARISONS: Differs from Wingate Corrugated and Showlow corrugated (Mera, 1934) by having "minute light-colored angular fragments" as temper, and in the occurrence of distinct polishing marks over the corrugations.

REMARKS:

These two sherds (particularly AT 4729) so strongly suggest Showlow Black-on-red that this black-on-red type probably has the same common ancestor as does Walnut Corrugated. There appears to be no conflicting characters in the description of the two types.

WOODRUFF SERIES

Probably represents a very early northern extension of influence, possibly from the Alma Series, or from some closely related series not yet described. The distinguishing characters of types within the Woodruff Series generally are clearly seen but some very small sherds individually are difficult to identify specifically. Types in this series differ from types in Winona Series by having quartz-like sand temper.

KEY: c WOODRUFF SERIES

1. Slipped... 2
   Not slipped............................Woodruff Brown (p. 58)
2. Decorated..............................Woodruff Incised (p. 59)
   Not decorated... 3
3. Smudged interior surface.............Woodruff Smudged (p. 59)
   No smudged surface.......................Woodruff Red (p. 58)

WOODRUFF BROWN

DESCRIBED BY: Mera, 1934, p. 6.
NAMED BY: Mera, loc. cit.
TYPE SPECIMENS: Laboratory of Anthropology, Santa Fe, New Mexico. Cotype sherds, numbers AT 798–799 in the Type Collection of the Museum of Northern Arizona, were collected, identified, and donated by Mera.
TYPE SITE: LA 1399, Woodruff Butte, Navajo County, Arizona (Mera, loc. cit.).
STAGE: Basket Maker III (Mera, loc. cit., opposite p. 24).
TIME: Probably pre-800 A.D.
DESCRIPTION (revised):

Constructed: by coiling. *Fired:* in oxidizing atmosphere. *Core:* black, gray, pinkish, or brown. *Temper:* coarse to fine quartz sand; not prominently noticeable on surfaces. *Texture core:* medium to coarse. *Fracture:* slightly crumbling to shattering. *Vessel walls:* medium strong. *Surface finish:* variable, usually fairly well-smoothed, slightly gritty; not slipped. *Surface color:* brick red to brown (5A11, 12B7, 13B6). *Forms:* jars, seed-jars, bowls. *Rims:* bowls, direct; jars, flared. *Recorded range thickness vessel walls:* ca 3 to 6 mm. *Undecorated.*

COMPARISONS: Rio de Flag Brown, core finer texture than Woodruff Brown; apparently less quartz sand. Surface sometimes moderately polished, usually smoother and less gritty; mica (?) moderately apparent on surface; frequently somewhat smoked.
Alma Plain, temper "heterogeneous."
Adamana Brown, paddled, mica (?) particles noticeable on surfaces.

RANGE:

Petrified Forest and surrounding country, Arizona. One broken vessel from Jeddito Valley, Navajo County, Arizona (Hargrave, 1935, a. p. 22).

WOODRUFF RED

DESCRIBED BY: Mera, 1934, p. 6.
NAMED BY: Mera, loc. cit.
TYPE SPECIMENS: Laboratory of Anthropology, Santa Fe, New Mexico.
TYPE SITE: LA 1399 (by inference).
STAGE: Basket Maker III (by inference from Woodruff Brown).
TIME: Probably Pre-800 A.D.
DESCRIPTION (revised):

Constructed: by coiling. *Fired:* in oxidizing atmosphere. *Core:*

OXIDIZING ATMOSPHERE 59

black, gray, or brown. *Temper:* coarse to medium fine quartz sand; not prominently noticeable on surfaces. *Texture core:* coarse to fine. *Fracture:* slightly crumbling. *Surface finish:* slipped; more or less polished. *Surface color:* dark red (6J10, 7H5, 7H10). *Form:* bowl. *Undecorated.*

RANGE:
Petrified Forest and surrounding country, Arizona.

WOODRUFF INCISED: new type

SYNONYM: Woodruff Brown, Mera, 1934, p. 6.
DESCRIBED BY: Mera, loc. cit., p. 6.
TYPE SPECIMENS: Laboratory of Anthropology, Santa Fe, New Mexico.
STAGE: Basket Maker III (Mera, loc. cit., p. 6, opposite p. 24, and diagram).
TIME: Probably pre-800 A.D.

DESCRIPTION (revised):
Constructed: by coiling. *Fired:* in oxidizing atmosphere. *Core:* black, gray, pinkish, or brown. *Temper:* coarse to fine quartz sand; not prominently noticeable on surfaces. *Texture core:* coarse to medium. *Fracture:* slightly crumbling to shattering. *Vessel walls:* medium strong. *Surface finish:* variable, usually fairly well-smoothed; somewhat gritty; slipped. *Surface color:* brick red to brown (inferred from Woodruff Brown). *Recorded range thickness vessel walls:* ca 3 to 6 mm (inferred). *Decoration:* incised lines.

RANGE:
Petrified Forest and surrounding country, Arizona.

REMARKS:
Recognition is based upon a statement by Mera that "the type (Woodruff Brown) is not decorated save a very rare attempt at what appears to be a variety of incising" (1934, p. 6).

WOODRUFF SMUDGED

DESCRIBED BY: Mera, 1934, p. 6.
NAMED BY: Mera, loc. cit.
TYPE SPECIMENS: Laboratory of Anthropology, Santa Fe, New Mexico. Cotype sherd No. AT 800, in the Type Collection of the Museum of Northern Arizona, was collected, identified, and donated by Mera.
TYPE SITE: LA 1399 (by inference).
STAGE: Basket Maker III (by inference from Woodruff Brown).
TIME: Probably pre-800 A.D.

DESCRIPTION (revised):
Constructed: by coiling. *Fired:* in oxidizing atmosphere. *Core:* black, gray, or brown, *Temper:* almost invisible even under

hand glass; quartz sand, rare; not prominently noticeable on surfaces. *Vessel walls:* medium strong. *Texture core:* fine. *Fracture:* slightly crumbling. *Surface finish:* variable; slipped; interior surface smudged. *Surface color:* exterior surface, red to brown (6J10, 7H5, 7H10 by inference); interior surface bowls, black. *Form:* bowls. *No painted decoration.*

COMPARISONS: Rio de Flag, constructed by paddling; temper less fine with feldspar (?) and quartz sand temper; exterior surface, impacted; interior polished.

RANGE:

Petrified Forest and surrounding country, Arizona.

LINDEN SERIES

The relation of this series to most other series within the ware has not yet been determined satisfactorily.

KEY d: LINDEN SERIES

1. Painted decoration.................McDonald Corrugated (p. 61)
   No painted decoration.. 2
2. Horizontal flutings or ribs (Fig. 00)....Silver Creek Corrugated (p. 62)
   No horizontal flutings or ribs.............Linden Corrugated (p. 60)

LINDEN CORRUGATED: new type

Fig. 8. (½ ×).

SYNONYMS: (a) Coiled Ware, Hough, 1903, Pl. 45; (b) Corrugated-indented, Schmidt, 1928, p. 298; (c) Lower-level corrugated ware, Haury, 1931, p. 30. Pl. 9, 1.
DESCRIBED BY: Haury, loc. cit., p. 30.
ILLUSTRATIONS: Hough, 1903, Pl. 45; Schmidt, 1928, Fig. 33; Haury, 1931, Pl. 9, 1; AT 493 (Fig. 8).
TYPE SPECIMENS: Sherds Nos. AT 791–794, 1095, 2785–2805 in the Type Collection of the Museum of Northern Arizona.
TYPE SITE: Pottery Hill Pueblo (NA 1013), Linden, Navajo County, Arizona.
STAGE: Pueblo III.
TIME: Probably between 1050–1250 A.D.

DESCRIPTION (revised):

Constructed: by coiling. *Fired:* in oxidizing atmosphere. *Core:* dark gray to light gray; tan, brownish, brick-red. *Temper:* very fine to coarse round or angular quartz; fragments crushed rock, rare. *Texture core:* usually medium; sometimes fine, rarely coarse. *Vessel walls:* weak to medium strong. *Fracture:* crumbling. *Surface finish:* coils unobliterated, usually fairly regular vertical indentations, height of indentations ca equal to width; other forms indentations, less frequent; sometimes no conspicuous indentations; coils almost always partly flattened, smoothed, or lightly polished; less frequently clapboard variety, not flattened, not polished; usually 3 to 4 mm in width, occasional variations up to 6 mm; interior surface smoothed, not polished, usually gritty, occasionally coarsely crazed; frequently smudged. *Surface color:* exterior surface orange, buff, tan, pinkish, brick-red; interior surfaces light gray, dark gray, black, tan, buff, orange, brick-red. *Forms:* jars (predominate), bowls; difficult to distinguish form from individual sherds. *Rims:* IA3, IIIA2, IIIA3, IB3, IIIB2. *Recorded range thickness vessel walls:* 5.5 to 10.7 mm; greatest individual range recorded, 2.7 mm; average thickness (53 sherds), ca 7.2 mm. *No painted decoration.*

COMPARISONS: Elden Corrugated, interiors more often smudged, frequently well-polished; exteriors usually somewhat better polished; width coils averages somewhat greater; temper, mostly black volcanic sand.

McDonald Corrugated, similar to Linden Corrugated with addition of white stripe decoration on exteriors; only bowls; interiors almost always smudged and well-polished.

Silver Creek Corrugated, similar to Linden Corrugated with indentations blurred, indistinct, leaving coils unobliterated giving effect of horizontal flutings or ribs.

RANGE:

White Mountain region, Arizona; abundant on Upper Silver Creek and nearby streams, and south to and including Tularosa Valley, New Mexico

McDONALD CORRUGATED: new type

SYNONYMS: (a) Rugose Redware, Hough, 1903, p. 287; (b) Coiled Ware, Hough, loc. cit., Pl. 45; (c) Corrugated-indented, Schmidt, 1928, p. 298; (d) Lower-level corrugated ware, Haury, 1931, Pl. 9, 1.
DESCRIBED BY: Haury, 1931, p. 30.
ILLUSTRATIONS: Hough, 1903, Plates 27, 28, 45; Schmidt, 1928, Fig. 33; Haury, 1931, Pl. 9, 1; Fig. 9.
TYPE SPECIMENS: Sherds Nos. AT 789–790, 2815–2830 in the Type Collection of the Museum of Northern Arizona.
TYPE SITE: Forestdale Pueblo (NA 999), near Showlow, Navajo County, Arizona.
STAGE: Pueblo III.
TIME: Probably between 1150–1250 A.D.

Fig. 9. ($\frac{1}{2}\times$).

DESCRIPTION (revised):

Constructed: by coiling. *Fired:* in oxidizing atmosphere. *Core:* dark gray to light gray; black, brownish, tan, brick-red. *Tem-*

per: very fine to coarse rounded or angular quartz sand; fragments crushed rock, rare. *Texture core:* usually medium; sometimes fine; rarely coarse. *Vessel walls:* weak to medium strong. *Fracture:* crumbling. *Surface finish:* corrugated usually fairly regular indentations, height of indentations ca equal to width; other forms of indentations less frequent; indentations sometimes conspicuous; coils almost always partly flattened, smoothed, or lightly polished; less frequently clapboard variety; not flattened; not polished; coils usually 3 to 4 mm wide, occasional variations to 6 mm; interior surfaces almost always smudged, well-polished. *Surface color:* exterior—orange, buff, tan, pinkish, brick-red; interior—black, occasionally reddish brown. *Form:* bowls. *Rims:* bowls, IA3, IA12, IIIA12, IB2. *Recorded range thickness bowl walls:* 4.6 to 8.5 mm; greatest individual range recorded, 2.1 mm; average thickness (33 sherds), ca 6 mm. *Paint:* white; partly fugitive. *Decoration:* confined to exterior; stripes, usually in diagonal parallel series, painted over corrugations; horizontal stripe frequently just below rim.

COMPARISONS: Linden Corrugated similar, without white painted decoration; usually not smudged; not polished on interior. Elden Corrugated temper mostly black volcanic sand.

RANGE:

White Mountain region, Arizona; abundant on upper Silver Creek and nearby streams. Trade pieces reported northwest to Flagstaff, Coconino County, Arizona.

REMARKS:

Haury (1931, p. 30) says: "This form is possibly best known from the Upper Gila. Its abundance at Showlow and at Pottery Hill (Linden, Arizona) suggests local manufacture and thus may indicate a direct link between the southeastern sub-culture."

SILVER CREEK CORRUGATED: new type

Fig. 10. ($\frac{1}{12}\times$).

SYNONYM: Upper-level corrugated ware, Haury, 1931, Pl. 9, 2.
DESCRIBED BY: Haury, loc. cit., p. 42.
ILLUSTRATIONS: Haury, loc. cit., Pl. 9, 2; AT 2826 (Fig. 10).
TYPE SPECIMENS: Gila Pueblo, Globe, Arizona. Cotype jar No. 393/1838 (Fig. 10) in the Type Collection of the Museum of Northern Arizona.
TYPE SITE: Showlow Pueblo (NA 1003), Silver Creek drainage, Navajo County, Arizona.
STAGE: Pueblo IV.
TIME: ca 1290–1400 A.D.
DESCRIPTION (revised):

Constructed: by coiling. *Fired:* in oxidizing atmosphere. *Core:* "gray." *Temper:* "quartz sand." *Fracture:* crumbling. *Surface finish:* exterior surfaces unobliterated coils, indistinct, blurred indentations; horizontal flutings or ribs. *Surface color:* brownish or reddish. *Form:* jars. *No painted decoration.*

COMPARISON: Linden Corrugated, indentations much more sharply marked, without effect of horizontal flutings or ribs. Salado Red, coated with purplish-red slip.

RANGE:
Recorded only from Pinedale and Showlow, Silver Creek drainage, Navajo County, Arizona.

REMARKS:
Although little attention has been paid to the utility types of the White Mountain region, it is indicated by the describer that this type is derived from Linden Corrugated (1931, p. 42). Although he does not expressly so state, the implication seems to be that this type is the same as Linden Corrugated in every objective characteristic except the manipulations of the coils, but that it represents a later horizon.

FLAGSTAFF SERIES

At present is represented by only one type but, although removed by many miles from reported foci of the Linden Series, this type, locally made, appears to be close genetically to the Linden Series.

ELDEN CORRUGATED

SYNONYM: Flagstaff Ware, Fewkes, 1927, p. 21.
DESCRIBED BY: Colton, 1932, p. 10.
NAMED BY: Colton, loc. cit.
ILLUSTRATION: Hargrave, 1932, Pl. IV, H; AT 2838 (Fig. 11).
TYPE SPECIMENS: Bowl No. 583-117T.9, and sherds Nos. AT 786, 2835-2844 in the Type Collection of the Museum of Northern Arizona.
TYPE SITE: Turkey Hill Pueblo (NA 660), Rio de Flag drainage, Flagstaff, Coconino County, Arizona.
STAGE: Pueblo III.
TIME: Probably between 1125-1225 A.D.
DESCRIPTION (revised):

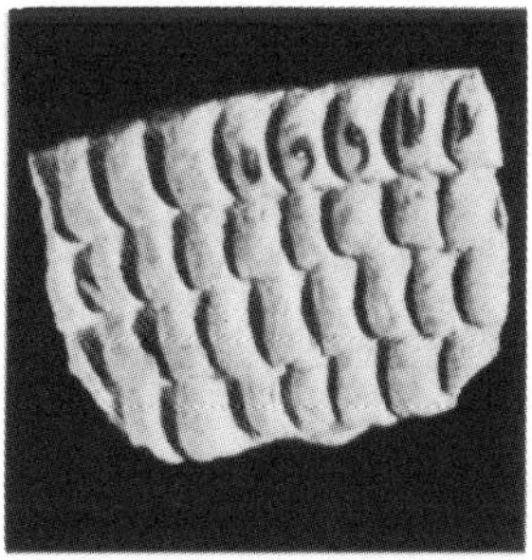

Fig. 11. ($\frac{1}{2}\times$).

Constructed: by coiling. *Fired:* in oxidizing atmosphere. *Core:*

black, brown, red. *Temper:* predominantly black volcanic sand, occasional grain quartz or feldspar (?); moderate amount opaque angular fragments, gray, tan, or brownish; often conspicuous on surfaces. *Texture core:* medium to fine. *Vessel walls:* medium strong. *Fracture:* crumbling. *Surface finish:* exterior surface corrugated; coils unobliterated, indented usually with vertical indentations; height of indentations ca half the width, width usually ca 5 to 8 mm; usually partly smoothed, flattened, sometimes polished; interior surfaces, smoothed, usually smudged; often polished or even burnished. *Surface color:* exteriors brown, pinkish, brick-red; interiors gray or black. *Forms:* bowls, jars; frequently difficult to distinguish forms from individual sherds. *Rims:* IB2, IB3. *Recorded range thickness vessel walls:* 5.5 to 8.1 mm; greatest individual range recorded, 2 mm; average thickness, ca 6.5 mm. *No painted decoration.*

COMPARISONS: Linden Corrugated, temper fine to fairly coarse quartz sand, no volcanic sand; interior surfaces usually gritty, only occasionally smudged; width coils averages less.
McDonald Corrugated, temper quartz sand; exteriors painted with white stripes.

RANGE:

Area east of San Francisco Mountains, Coconino County, Arizona, covered with black volcanic ash (cinders) from Sunset Crater.

REMARKS:

See Hargrave, 1932, p. 19.

SALADO SERIES

Is very distinct in objective characters yet even these characters compare closely with characters of the Linden Series. No direct areal trace between the known area of the Linden Series has been determined but there are pottery types of the upper Salt and Gila rivers, in Arizona, that, when properly described, will be seen to be close, objectively and genetically, to both the Linden and Salado Series.

KEY e: SALADO SERIES

With painted decoration.................Salado White-on-red (p. 65)
Without painted decoration....................Salado Red (p. 65)

OXIDIZING ATMOSPHERE 65

SALADO RED

SYNONYMS: (a) Corrugated-indented, Schmidt, 1928, p. 298; (b) Slightly indented, Schmidt, loc. cit.; (c) Salado Red Ware, Gladwin, W. & H. S., 1930b, p. 10.
DESCRIBED BY: Schmidt, loc. cit.
NAMED BY: Gladwin, W. & H. S., loc. cit. (N.B. The name originally used by the Gladwins has been abbreviated herein to "Salado Red").
ILLUSTRATIONS: Gladwin, W. & H. S., loc. cit., Pl. VIII.
TYPE SPECIMENS: Gila Pueblo, Globe, Arizona.
TYPE SITE: Roosevelt: 6:3, Gila County, Arizona.
STAGE: Pueblo III.
TIME: Probably between 1150–1250 A.D.
DESCRIPTION (revised):
Constructed: by coiling. *Fired:* in oxidizing atmosphere. *Core:* brick-red, tan, pinkish, dark gray. *Temper:* abundant waterworn sand; smaller amounts opaque angular fragments, tan, reddish, gray or black; occasionally flecks copper-colored mica. *Texture core:* medium to coarse. *Fracture:* crumbling, friable. *Surface finish:* bowl and jar exteriors corrugated; corrugations oblique; always smoothed over, sometimes almost obliterated, never polished; coated with powdery purplish-red or raspberry-colored wash; interiors, smudged; bowl interiors, polished, striations usually beginning at point on rim and carrying over to point opposite rim (as in a globe cut in half at the poles); jar interiors, rough; inside neck sometimes carelessly smoothed, slightly polished. *Surface color:* exteriors, purplish-red, or raspberry; interiors, generally black (smudged). *Fire clouds:* absent. *Forms:* bowls, jars, figurines, eccentric; bowls mostly shallow, sometimes hemispherical, sometimes rectangular; jars globular with short outflaring necks or squat with vertical necks, sometimes cylindrical; figurines (rare) usually well-made human and bird shapes. *Rims:* bowls, IA3, IA4, IB3, IB6, IE13; jars, IB3, IB13, IC3, IE13, IIIC3.
COMPARISONS: Showlow Corrugated, not slipped; coils horizontal flutings.
RANGE:
Roosevelt Basin, Gila County, Arizona.
REMARKS:
The original description of this type included also Salado White-on-red, herein separated on the basis of the white painted decoration.

SALADO WHITE-ON-RED: new type

SYNONYMS: (a) Corrugated-indented, Schmidt, 1928, p. 298; (b) Slightly indented, Schmidt, loc. cit.; (c) Salado Redware, Gladwin, W. & H. S., 1930b, p. 10.

DESCRIBED BY: Schmidt, loc. cit.
ILLUSTRATIONS: Schmidt, 11c. cit., Figs. 32, 33; Gladwin, W. & H. S., loc. cit., Plates VII, VIII.
TYPE SPECIMENS: Gila Pueblo, Globe, Arizona.
TYPE SITE: Roosevelt: 6:3, Gila County, Arizona.
STAGE: Pueblo III.
TIME: Probably between 1150–1250 A.D.
DESCRIPTION (revised):
Constructed: by coiling. *Fired:* in oxidizing atmosphere. *Core:* brick-red, tan, pinkish, dark gray. *Temper:* abundant water-worn sand, lesser amounts opaque angular fragments, tan, reddish, gray, or black; occasional flecks copper-colored mica. *Texture core:* medium to coarse. *Fracture:* crumbling, friable. *Surface finish:* bowl and jar exteriors corrugated; corrugations oblique, always smoothed over, sometimes almost obliterated, never polished; coated with powdery slip; interiors smudged; bowl interiors, polished, striations usually beginning at point on rim and carrying over to opposite point (as in a globe cut in half at the poles); jar interiors, rough, sides necks sometimes carelessly smoothed, slightly polished. *Surface color:* purplish-red, or raspberry. *Fire clouds:* absent. *Forms:* bowls, jars, figurines, eccentric; bowls mostly shallow, sometimes hemispherical, sometimes square; jars globular with short out-flaring necks, or squat with vertical necks, sometimes cylindrical; figurines (rare) usually well-made, human and bird shapes. *Rims:* bowls, IA3, IA4, IB3, IB6, IE13; jars, IB3, IB13, IC3, IE13, IIIC3. *Paint:* white or creamy white; thick, gritty, somewhat fugitive. *Decoration:* confined to exteriors; always consists of narrow straight or zigzag lines, often bordered with rows of dots or small pendent triangles; lines usually arranged in nests of triangles or chevrons pendent from rim.

RANGE:
Roosevelt Basin, Gila County, Arizona.

REMARKS:
This type originally was included by the Gladwins, (loc. cit., pp. 10–11) in their description of Salado Red; it has been separated herein solely on the basis of the presence of a white painted decoration. The decoration is somewhat similar to that appearing on Gila White-on-red.

OXIDIZING ATMOSPHERE

SAN JUAN RED WARE

The origin of this ware is unknown. Objective characters, however, are very similar to objective characters of Mogollon Brown Ware but all recognized types within San Juan Red ware occur far to the north of known foci of the Mogollon Brown Ware. Nor are there known service or utility types in the ware, a puzzling fact since the ware, in part, occurs consistently in a region where types consistently fired in a reducing atmosphere are dominant. Utility types may have been overlooked (Hargrave, 1936). On the basis of objective characters and techniques of manufacture, San Juan Red Ware and Mogollon Brown Ware have much in common.

White paint is a decorative character of one type in this ware and was used with black paint to produce a polychrome. The first use of white as paint greatly increased the possibilities for decorating pottery with color, because the pigments previously used as paint had all reacted in the same manner when fired in an oxidizing atmosphere. Clay used as paint on vessels to be fired in an oxidizing atmosphere had to be free of iron to remain white after firing. Two pigments, one with and one without an iron base were, therefore, necessary to the production of a polychrome.* These same two pigments, if fired in a reducing atmosphere, would produce only one paint color. We may say then, that, with the paint pigments used prior to knowledge of glaze paint, *a polychrome could be produced only in an oxidizing atmosphere.*

KEY 2: SAN JUAN RED WARE

1. Temper light-colored angular fragments; conspicious on surface..... 2
   Temper not light-colored angular fragments; not conspicious on surface................................Bluff Black-on-red (p. 69)
   Deadmans Black-on-red (p. 71)
2. Polychrome.........................Citadel Polychrome (p. 75)
   Not polychrome... 2
3. Always solid elements in design (other than lines).................
   ....Medicine Black-on-red (p. 72)
   Never solid elements in design (other than lines).................
   ....Tusayan Black-on-red (p. 74)

SAN JUAN RED WARE: new ware

STAGES: Pueblo I-early Pueblo III (?).
TIME: Pre-700-ca 1150 A.D.

* Glaze paints are not here considered.

DESCRIPTION:

Constructed: by coiling. *Fired:* in oxidizing atmosphere. *Core:* dark gray to gray, dark brown through brick-red to pink. *Carbon streak:* common. *Temper:* angular quartz sand or light-colored angular fragments with lesser amounts narrow black crystals, or basalt (?) sand; conspicuous in cross-section of reddish color; conspicuous on surfaces, except Deadmans Black-on-red and Bluff Black-on-red. *Texture core:* fine. *Vessel walls:* medium strong to strong. *Fracture:* slightly crumbling to shattering. *Surface finish:* bowls and decorative surface jar forms, smoothed, polished, impacted (two types) or slipped. *Surface color:* generally red; red and orange on Citadel Polychrome; interior jar surfaces generally gray; color surface and core do not contrast when color core reddish. *Fire clouds:* not uncommon. *Forms:* bowls, dippers, seed-jars, jars, pitchers, canteens (rare); bowls do not have horizontal handle. *Recorded range thickness bowl walls:* 2 to 8.9 mm; greatest individual range recorded, 2.4 mm; average thickness, ca 4.5 mm. *Recorded range thickness jar walls:* 2.3 to 7.2 mm; greatest individual range recorded, 3.4 mm; average thickness, ca 4.5 mm. *Recorded range thickness seed-jar walls:* 2.3 to 5.7 mm; greatest individual range recorded, 2.4 mm; average thickness, ca 4 mm. *Rims:* bowls, IA3, IA4, IIA3, IIIA3, IIIA4, IIIA11; seed-jars, IA3, IIIA3. *Decoration:* painted. *Paint:* black, red; color paint black, brown, purplish; dull or metallic; frequently polished after painting. *Pigment:* black, manganese; red, hematite. *Designs:* geometric.

RANGE:

San Francisco Mountains, Coconino County, Arizona (except Bluff Black-on-red) and about the Four-corners (except Deadmans Black-on-red). Traded to Chino Valley, Yavapai County, to Hopi Country, and Rainbow Plateau Area, northeastern Arizona and southeastern Utah.

BLUFF SERIES

Although normally a series name should not be given unless there are at least two related types from a given geographic region, there may be modifying circumstances. In the general neighborhood of Bluff, Utah, for instance, occur black-on-red sherds that, from a written description cannot be separated from Tusayan Black-on-red. Also, polychrome sherds from the same and from more eastern regions, i.e., Chaco Canyon, seem from published references to be the types described herein as Citadel Polychrome or a polychrome of Tsegi Orange Ware.

OXIDIZING ATMOSPHERE

Since Bluff and Chaco Canyon are widely separated from the San Francisco Mountains, Arizona, and since types similar to those mentioned above do not normally occur in the interlying country, it is probable that a series of red types, which paralleled in development and describable characters the Deadmans Series of the San Francisco Mountains, existed near Bluff. Critical examination of sherds similar to Tusayan Black-on-red and Citadel Polychrome from the Four-corners region may reveal differences sufficiently consistent in occurrence to warrant the describing and naming of other types related to Bluff Black-on-red. Since, at present, it seems inadvisable to separate types purely on the ground of geographic occurence, two other types of the San Juan Red Ware are postulated and in advance the series is here called "Bluff Series."

BLUFF BLACK-ON-RED

SYNONYMS: (a) Redware with shiny paint, in part, Kidder & Guernsey, 1919, p. 135; (b) Pueblo I Red Ware, in part, Guernsey, 1931, pl. 15; (c) Pueblo I Black-on-Red, in part, Guernsey, loc. cit., pl. 61.
DESCRIBED BY: Hargrave, 1936, pp. 29–34.
NAMED BY: Hargrave, loc. cit.
ILLUSTRATION: 23/257A (Fig. 12).
TYPE SPECIMENS: Bowl No. 23–243, jug No. 23–253 and sherds Nos. AT 2419, 2429, 2434, 2436, 2440, 2447, 2248, 2453, in the Type Collection of the Museum of Northern Arizona.
TYPE SITE: NA 2659, Bluff, San Juan County, Utah.
ILLUSTRATIONS: Guernsey, loc. cit., pl. 15, b, c, & d; pl. 61.
STAGES: Pueblo I–II (?).
TIME: Pre-1100 A.D.

Fig. 12. ($\frac{1}{5}\times$).

DESCRIPTION (revised):

Constructed: by coiling. *Fired:* in oxidizing atmosphere. *Core:* dark gray through pink to brick-red; carbon streak, occasional. *Temper:* predominantly coarse angular quartz sand, lesser amount light-colored angular fragments (crushed rock?), generally few grains basalt (?) sand; occasionally crushed rock, pinkish; temper generally conspicuous in cross-section of reddish color; not conspicuous on surfaces; glittering specks white or sometimes yellow (pyrite?), noticeable on surface. *Vessel walls:* strong. *Texture core:* medium to fine. *Fracture:* slightly crumbling to shattering. *Surface finish:* bowls generally bumpy, well-polished, crazed; polishing marks, horizontal, inconspicuous; exterior surface, generally pitted; both surfaces bowls and exterior surfaces jars, impacted. *Surface color:* reddish (3A10, 3B10, 4A10, 4B10, 4D11, 4E11, 11A8, 11A9, 11B8, 11B9, 11C8, 12A6, 12A7, 12A8, 13A9); color surface and core, do not contrast when color core reddish. *Fire clouds:* common. *Forms:* bowls, dippers (uncommon), jars, seed-jars, pitchers; bowl walls fairly uniform thickness. *Rims:* bowls IA3, IA4, IIIA3, IIIA4, IIIA11, IIIA14; jars, IA4, IIIA3 IIIA4; seed-jars, IA3. *Recorded range thickness bowl walls:* 2.9 to 8.1 mm; greatest individual range recorded, 2.8 mm; average thickness (114 sherds), 4.6 mm. *Recorded range thickness seed-jar walls:* 2.3 to 3.4 mm; greatest individual range recorded, 1.1 mm; average thickness, ca 3 mm. *Recorded range thickness jar walls:* 2.3 to 7.2 mm; greatest individual range recorded, 2.6 mm; average thickness (38 sherds), 4.5 mm. *Painted decoration. Color paint:* black, brown, purple; paint frequently reflects light; polished after painted; strong or weak, sometimes barely discernible; generally metallic sheen. *Decoration:* interior bowl surfaces, occasionally exterior surface; rim decoration, common; jar decoration, exterior surface only. *Designs:* geometric patterns crudely executed; arranged in circular order. *Motifs:* lines, solid triangles; lines narrow (rarely), broad (common), stripes (common); generally pendent from rim.

COMPARISONS: Deadmans Black-on-red, glittering particles more noticeable; slightly more highly polished; never bumpy; not pitted; rarely crazed; wall thickness less variable; bowls thinner; decoration more neatly executed; paint richer; narrow lines more frequent; hatching, lines in series, more frequent; usually one to four encircling lines below rim; solid elements generally smaller; elements usually arranged in angular patterns; curved lines and stripes, rare.

RANGE:

San Juan River drainage about the Four-corners; up Chinle Creek to Water Fall Pueblo, Nokito, Arizona. As trade (?), occurs westward sporadically to Nokai Canyon, Navajo County, Arizona.

REMARKS:

Trade specimens of Bluff Black-on-red from the Tsegi area and the Hopi Reservation can more certainly be distinguished from Deadmans Black-on-red by direct comparison.

DEADMANS SERIES

Types in this series, with the exception of known trade pieces, appear to be confined to the San Francisco Mountains Area. Companion types not only belong to other wares but were built by another technique of construction; the firing atmosphere used was the same, however. There is some doubt that types in the Deadmans Series actually were made in the San Francisco Mountains.

DEADMANS BLACK-ON-RED

SYNONYM: Redware with shiny paint, in part, Kidder & Guernsey, 1919, p. 135.
DESCRIBED BY: Colton, 1932, p. 11.
NAMED BY: Colton, loc. cit.
ILLUSTRATION: AT 2190 (Fig. 13).
TYPE SPECIMENS: Seed jar, No. 23–256; type sherd No. AT 1294; cotype sherds Nos. AT 1297, 2182–2218 in the Type Collection of the Museum of Northern Arizona.
TYPE SITE: Medicine Fort (NA 862), Deadmans Wash, San Francisco Mountains, Coconino County, Arizona.
ILLUSTRATIONS: Hargrave, 1932, loc. cit., Pl. IV, c; Bartlett, 1934, Fig. 35.
STAGES: Pueblo I–early Pueblo II.
TIME: ca 750–900 A.D.

Fig. 13. ($\frac{1}{2}$ X).

DESCRIPTION (revised):

Constructed: by coiling. *Fired:* in oxidizing atmosphere. *Core:* dark gray to gray; dark brown to brick-red. *Carbon streaks:* common. *Temper:* angular quartz sand, lesser amounts hornblende (?), or basalt (?); conspicuous in cross-section of reddish color; not conspicuous on surfaces; glittering specks white or yellow usually noticeable on surfaces. *Vessel walls:* medium strong to strong. *Texture core:* medium to fine. *Fracture:* slightly crumbling to shattering (uncommon). *Surface finish:* bowls not bumpy, highly polished; horizontal polishing marks frequently conspicuous; both surfaces bowls and exterior jar surfaces, impacted (seen best on seed-jars and jars). *Surface color:* red (3A11, 5A11, 5D11, 5E11, 6E10, 6E11); interior surface color seed-jars, 4A10, 4B11; jars, gray; color surface and core, do not contrast when color core reddish. *Fire clouds:* not uncommon. *Forms:* bowls, dippers (rare), seed-jars (uncommon), jars (rare). *Rims:* bowls IA3, IA4, IIA3, IIA11, IIIA3, IIIA4; seed-jars, IA3. *Recorded range thickness bowl walls:* 2 to 6.4 mm; greatest individual range recorded, 2.6 mm; average thickness (286 sherds), 3.8 mm; bowl walls uniform thickness. *Recorded range thickness seed-jar walls:* 2.4 to 5.4 mm; greatest individual range recorded, 2.4 mm; average thickness, ca 4 mm. *Recorded range thickness jar walls:* 3.2 to 6.7 mm; greatest individual range recorded, 3.4; average thickness, ca 5 mm. *Painted decoration. Color paint:* black, brown, purplish; polished after painting ("ghost pattern"); crystals in paint frequently show. *Pigment:* manganese (tests by Colton). *Decoration:* interior surface bowls, rarely exterior, rims occasionally painted; jars, exterior surface. *Patterns:* geometric, excellently executed. *Elements:* lines, stripes, solid triangles; lines 1 to 10 mm (rare); straight, wavy, singles, series, or hatchured in panels; occasionally running hatchure. *Patterns:* one to four encircling lines beginning at base of rim; occasionally motifs pendent from rim.

COMPARISON: Bluff Black-on-red, glittering particles less noticeable; slightly less highly polished; often somewhat bumpy; moderately pitted; often coarsely crazed; wall thickness more variable; bowl walls thicker; much more crudely executed; encircling line below rim absent; solid elements generally larger; elements often arranged in circular order; curved lines and stripes, frequent.

RANGE:

Center of abundance, San Francisco Mountains, Coconino County, Arizona. Trade Specimens recorded north to Hawks Nest Spring in Nokai drainage, and at mouth of Tsegi-ot-sosi, eighteen miles north of Kayenta, Navajo County, Arizona. Occurs sporadically from Polacca Wash west to and including Moenkopi Wash, Coconino County; also Chino Valley, Yavapai County, Arizona.

REMARKS:

Sherds of Deadmans Black-on-red from the Tsegi Canyons average lighter in color than sherds from the San Francisco Mountains. This may be because cotype sherds were recovered in excavating. This type is exceedingly common in the San Francisco Mountains, but is scarce in the Tsegi Canyons, rarely more than one or two sherds being found in a site collection. Rarely have red ware sherds been found at Pueblo I sites in the Tsegi region.

MEDICINE BLACK-ON-RED: new type

Fig. 14.($\frac{1}{5}$×).

SYNONYM: Tusayan Black-on-red, Colton, 1932, p. 11.

ILLUSTRATION: NA 1123.7 (Fig. 14).

TYPE SPECIMENS: Bowl No. NA 1123.7 and type sherds Nos. AT 1298, 2377–2388 in the Type Collection of the Museum of Northern Arizona.

TYPE SITE: NA 1653, Sunset National Monument, San Francisco Mountains, Coconino County, Arizona.

STAGES: Pueblo I–II.

TIME: Pre-800-ca 950 A.D.

OXIDIZING ATMOSPHERE

DESCRIPTION:

Constructed: by coiling. *Fired:* in oxidizing atmosphere. *Core:* black to gray; dark brown (rare) to brick red. *Carbon streak:* common. *Temper:* predominantly soft, light-colored (whitish or yellowish) angular fragments; usually lesser amount quartz sand; occasional isolated grain basalt (?); conspicuous in crosssection of reddish color; conspicuous on surfaces. *Vessel walls:* medium strong to strong. *Texture core:* medium to fine. *Fracture:* slightly crumbling to shattering. *Surface finish:* bowls sometimes bumpy; polished, horizontal polishing marks conspicuous around vessel; both surfaces bowls, exterior surfaces jar forms, slipped; slip (generally) thick with temper extruding; slip flakes off large areas of heavily weathered sherds leaving core mottled yellow with temper; generally coarsely crazed. *Surface color:* red (4B11, 5D10, 5F10, 5F11, 6A11); interior surface jar forms, tan; color surface and core, generally contrast. *Fire clouds:* common. *Forms:* bowls, jars. *Rims:* bowls, IA3, IA7, IIIA3; bowl walls uniform thickness. *Recorded range thickness bowl walls:* 2.7 to 6.3 mm; greatest individual range recorded, 2 mm; average thickness, ca 4.5 mm. *Recorded range thickness jar walls:* 3.7 to 5 mm; greatest individual range recorded, 1.3 mm; average thickness, ca 4.5 mm. *Decoration:* painted. *Paint:* black; generally dull, flat, lifeless; rarely metallic sheen, frequently reflects light; sometimes flakes off. *Pigment:* manganese (tests by Colton). *Decoration:* confined to interior surface bowls; exterior surface jar forms. *Patterns:* geometric; generally pendent from rim; rim sometimes decorated in part. *Elements:* narrow lines (uncommon), solid areas, broad lines, stripes, triangles.

COMPARISON: Tusayan Black-on-red, decoration mostly narrow or wide horizontal or diagonal hatching in rectangular or curved panels; never (?) solid elements; often one to four horizontal lines just below rim; Dogoszhi Style.

RANGE:

Deadmans Wash drainage from near its source to Wupatki National Monument; also Sunset Crater National Monument, San Francisco Mountains, Coconino County, Arizona.

REMARKS:

One jar sherd, AT 1298 from floor of Pueblo I pithouse, NA 1653, Sunset Crater National Monument, buried beneath cinder fall from Sunset Crater. This eruption has been dated at about 900 A.D. (McGregor, 1936, p. 15; 1936 a, p. 4).

TUSAYAN BLACK-ON-RED

SYNONYMS: (a) Redware with dull paint, in part, Kidder & Guernsey, 1919, p. 136; (b) Proto-Kayenta red, in part, Kidder, 1924, p. 22; (c) Proto-Kayenta (Tusayan) Black-on-red, in part, Gladwin, W. & H. S., 1931, p. 174; (d) Proto-Kayenta Black-on-red, in part, Morrs, 1931, p. 8; (e) Tusayan Black-on-red-plain-base, Hargrave, 1932, p. 22.
DESCRIBED BY: Kidder & Guernsey, loc. cit.
NAMED BY: Hargrave, loc. cit.
ILLUSTRATION: AT 2350 (Fig. 15).
TYPE SPECIMENS: Bowl No. NA 1123.6; type sherds Nos. AT 1957, 2319–2320; co-type sherds Nos. AT 2321–2356 in the Type Collection of the Museum of Northern Arizona.

Fig. 15. ($\frac{1}{2}$ ×).

TYPE SITE: NA 409, Medicine Valley, San Francisco Mountains, Coconino County, Arizona.
STAGES: Middle Pueblo II–early Pueblo III.
TIME: ca 850–ca 1125 A.D.

DESCRIPTION (revised):

Constructed: by coiling. *Fired:* in oxidizing atmosphere. *Core:* black to gray, dark brown (rare) to brick-red. *Carbon streaks:* common. *Temper:* predominantly soft, light-colored (whitish or yellowish) angular fragments; usually lesser amount quartz sand; occasional isolated grain basalt (?); conspicuous in cross-section of reddish color; conspicuous on surfaces. *Vessel walls:* medium strong to strong. *Texture core:* fine. *Fracture:* slightly crumbling to shattering. *Surface finish:* bowls sometimes slightly bumpy; sometimes highly polished; horizontal polishing marks conspicuous around vessel; both surfaces bowls, exterior surface jar forms, slipped; occasionally bottom or part of exterior surface, unslipped; slip generally thick with temper extruding; generally crazed; slip flakes off large areas heavily weathered sherds leaving core mottled with temper; frequently slip weathered away. *Surface color:* red (4A11, 5E11, 5H10, 5I9, 5J9, 5J10); interior jar surfaces, sometimes gray or tan; color surface and core, generally contrast. *Fire clouds:* common. *Forms:* bowls, canteens, seed-jars, jars (rare), dippers (?). *Rims:* bowls, IA3, IA4, IIIA3, IIIA4; seed-jars, IA3, IIIA3. *Recorded range thickness bowl walls:* 3.1 to 6.7 mm; greatest individual range recorded, 2.3 mm; average thickness (79 sherds), 5.0 mm; bowl walls uniform thickness. *Recorded range thickness seed-jar walls:* 2.7 to 5.7 mm; greatest individual range recorded, 2 mm; average thickness, ca 4.5 mm. *Recorded range*

OXIDIZING ATMOSPHERE

thickness jar walls: 3.7 mm to 5.4 mm; greatest individual range recorded, 1.7 mm; average thickness, ca 4.5 mm. *Decoration:* painted; color paint, black, occasionally reddish brown; generally dull, flat, lifeless; rarely metallic sheen, frequently reflects light; frequently flakes off; excessively weathered specimens, "ghost pattern"; polished after painted. *Pigment:* manganese (tests by Colton). *Decoration:* confined to interior surface bowls; exterior surface jar forms. *Patterns:* geometric; rarely encircling lines under rim; motifs generally pendent from rim; rim sometimes painted all around, sometimes only where motif is pendent. *Elements:* narrow and wide lines only element used; lines straight or wavy; horizontal or diagonal in squares, triangles (rare), or curved panels; horizontal encircling vertically or diagonally in series; hatchure and frame lines approximately same width.

COMPARISON: Medicine Black-on-red, decoration usually solid areas, triangles, broad lines, stripes; rarely narrow lines; never hatching; sometimes elements arranged in curved patterns.

RANGE:

San Francisco Mountains, Coconino County, Arizona, north to Navajo Mountain, San Juan County, Utah; east to Monument Valley, Navajo County, and south to Leupp, Coconino County, Arizona. Sporadic occurrences in Chino and Verde Valleys, Yavapai County, Arizona.

REMARKS:

Diagnostic characteristics are evidence of temper through slip and tendency of slip to flake off.

CITADEL POLYCHROME: new type

SYNONYM: Tusayan Polychrome, in part, Gladwin, W. & H. S., 1934, Fig. 1.
ILLUSTRATION: AT 2476 (Fig. 16).
TYPE SPECIMENS: Type sherds AT 2504–2508; cotype sherds AT 2474, 2476–2478, 2486, 2492–2500 in the Type Collection of the Museum of Northern Arizona.
TYPE SITE: Citadel Pueblo (NA 355), Wupatki National Monument, Coconino County, Arizona.
STAGES: Late Pueblo II–early Pueblo III (?).
TIME: ca 1115–ca 1150 A.D.

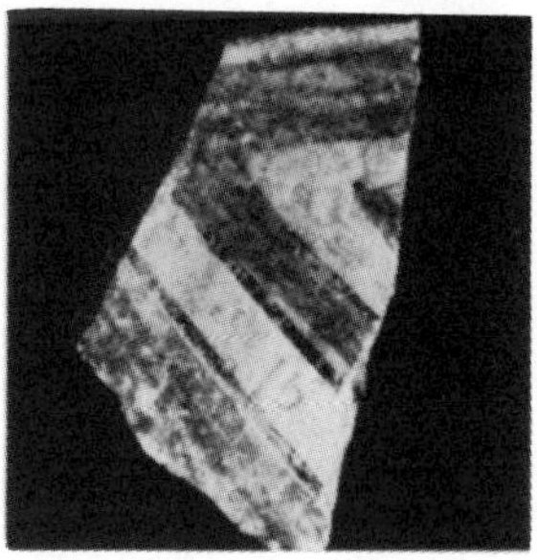

Fig. 16. ($\frac{1}{2}\times$).

DESCRIPTION:

Constructed: by coiling. *Fired:* in oxidizing atmosphere. *Core:*

black to gray, dark brown (rare) to brick-red. *Carbon streak:* common. *Temper:* predominantly soft, light-colored (whitish or yellowish) angular fragments; usually lesser amount quartz sand; occasionally isolated grain basalt (?); conspicuous in cross-section of reddish color; conspicuous on surfaces. *Vessel walls:* medium strong to strong. *Texture core:* fine. *Fracture:* slightly crumbling to shattering. *Surface finish:* bowls usually smooth; occasionally somewhat bumpy; polished; horizontal polishing marks conspicuous around sides; exterior bowl surfaces, slipped, except that broad unslipped stripe often occurs just below rim; base generally unslipped; slip generally thick with temper extruding; often crazed; slip flakes off large areas of heavily weathered sherds leaving core mottled with temper. *Surface color:* exterior, red; interior, orange; color interior surface and core do not generally contrast. *Form:* bowl; no record of horizontal handle. *Rims:* bowls, IA3, IA4, IIIA3. *Recorded range thickness bowl walls:* 2.6 to 7 mm; greatest individual range recorded, 2 mm; average thickness, ca 4.8 mm. *Decoration:* painted; color paint, black and red; confined to interior. *Red decoration:* horizontal and diagonal stripes and elongated triangles; sometimes stripe encircling vessel just below rim, no red stripes on exterior. *Black decoration:* narrow lines outlining red areas; diagonal hatching in areas between red elements; no staggered or solid black areas; rims slipped, partly slipped, or painted with black line.

COMPARISON: Tusayan Polychrome, bowls and jars; bowls generally have horizontal handle; decoration, same elements but sometimes additional narrow black horizontal lines in series, and staggered black lines or vertical black lines with staggered black squares between; exterior surface bowls, one to three stripes encircling vessel just below rim; exterior surface color, buff or orange; light-colored temper somewhat less abundant, less noticeable on surface.

RANGE:

San Francisco Mountain region (abundant), north to Tuba City (fairly common), Moenkopi Wash, Coconino County, Arizona; Tsegi Canyons (less common), Navajo County, Arizona.

REMARKS:

Polychrome sherds reported by Kidder from "the ruins of Grand Gulch and White Canyons; in the Chinle and Canyon de Chelly; and in sites along the San Juan from Bluff, Utah, nearly to the mouth of the McElmo" (1924, p. 73) and also those from Pueblo Bonito and Hungo Pavie in Chaco Canyon, in Cliff Palace on the Mesa Verde, and on Alkali Ridge in the

OXIDIZING ATMOSPHERE 77

Montezuma Creek drainage should closely be examined again to determine if Citadel Polychrome and not Tusayan Polychrome, since the time range of these two types is not the same.

ALAMEDA RED WARE

Recognition of this ware is made because a sequence of definitely related pottery types stands alone on the basis of some prominent objective and genetic characters. This sequence was recognized as a unit by Mera (1934) who gives his impression in a chart. Studies made at the Museum of Northern Arizona have supported Mera in his belief, except that Woodruff Brown is not admitted to be ancestral type of the sequence.

By recognizing Alameda Red Ware, another ware determinant is indicated. Since the types in this sequence are seen to be related and since no immediate ancestor for this sequence has been recognized, the sequence stands alone and is thus called a ware.

Although types in Alameda Red Ware have but recently been recognized, the value of the ware in the study of sub-culture areas is by no means lessened, but, rather, indications are that the ware exerted a profound influence over a wide area.

KEY 3: ALAMEDA RED WARE

1. Painted decoration..2
   No painted decoration........................Arauca Plain (p. 80)
2. Thin, watery red slip with base color showing through....Key g (p. 84)
   Red slip (?); base color does not show through...........Key f (p. 78)

ALAMEDA RED WARE: new ware

STAGES: Pueblo II (?)–IV.
TIME: Probably between 1150–1425 A.D.
DESCRIPTION:

Constructed: by coiling. *Fired:* in oxidizing atmosphere. *Core:* usually pinkish, brick-red, often gray, buff, or tan. *Temper:* fine grains quartz sand and fine opaque angular fragments, mostly reddish, black or gray, occasionally tan, or orange; sand usually predominant in several types; amounts of sand and opaque fragments about equal; frequently minute micaceous particles noticeable; temper usually not conspicuous on surfaces. *Texture core:* fine to coarse. *Vessel walls:* medium strong to strong. *Fractures:* crumbling. *Surface finish:* both surfaces bowls and jar exteriors, impacted; more frequently coated with thin, powdery slip; vessel exteriors usually moderately polished; gritty and pitted; frequently minutely crazed. *Surface color:* exteriors usually dull red or pinkish, sometimes orange; jar interiors often gray, tan, or pinkish. *Fire clouds:* fairly common. *Forms:* bowls in every type, except Arauca Plain; jars in every type, except Showlow Black-on-red, Chavez Pass Black-on-red, and Chavez Pass Polychrome; dippers in Homolovi Polychrome. *Recorded range thickness jar walls:* 4.6 to 9.1 mm; greatest individual range recorded, 2.5 mm; average thickness ca 6.2 mm. *Rims:* bowls, IA3, IA7, IIA3, IIA7, IIIA3, IIIA7; jars IB3, IC2. *Decoration:* painted. *Paint:* black, white; usually dull, powdery, often brownish; usually weak and thin, sometimes dense (in Homolovi Polychrome); decoration, bowl interiors and jar exteriors on all types, except Arauca Plain; sometimes also on bowl exteriors of Homolovi Black-on-red, Black Ax Polychrome, and Homolovi Polychrome. *White paint:* on polychrome types; usually powdery, sometimes fugitive; sometimes thick and granular (in Homolovi Polychrome).

RANGE:
Upper and middle Little Colorado River drainage, west to Canyon Diablo, and south to Mogollon Rim, with concentrations in the vicinity of Winslow, Navajo County, Arizona.

HOMOLOVI SERIES

The sequence recognized by Mera actually is a part of Homolovi Series that occurs in the immediate vicinity of Winslow and in the Petrified Forest National Monument.

KEY f: HOMOLOVI SERIES

1. Polychrome..2
   Not polychrome....................Showlow Black-on-red (p. 78)
                                    Homolovi Black-on-red (p. 80)
   Arauca Plain ....(p. 80)
2. White paint "blue"...................Black Ax Polychrome (p. 81)
   White paint "white"..................Homolovi Polychrome (p. 82)

SHOWLOW BLACK-ON-RED

DESCRIBED BY: Haury, 1931; p. 29.
NAMED BY: Haury, E. W. (Gladwin, W. & H. S., 1931, p. 27.
ILLUSTRATION: AT 1295 (Fig. 17).
TYPE SPECIMENS: Gila Pueblo, Globe, Arizona. Cotype sherds Nos. AT 1295 (identified by H. P. Mera), AT 1837–1838 (topotypes), AT 1296, and 1962 (identified by H. S. Gladwin) in the Type Collection of the Museum of Northern Arizona.

OXIDIZING ATMOSPHERE 79

TYPE SITE: Showlow Pueblo (NA 1003; Holbrook: 12:2), Showlow, Silver Creek, Navajo County, Arizona.
ILLUSTRATIONS: Gladwin, W. & H. S., loc. cit., Plate XXX (colored); Haury, loc. cit., Fig. 5.
STAGE: Pueblo II (?)–III.
TIME: Pre-1200 A.D.
DESCRIPTION (revised):
Constructed: by coiling. *Fired:* in oxidizing atmosphere. *Core:* gray to reddish. *Temper:* about equal amounts fairly fine quartz sand and fine angular fragments, usually tan or gray, sometimes black or red; temper not conspicuous in cross-section or on surfaces; glittering minute specks white or yellow usually noticeable on surfaces. *Carbon streak:* fairly frequent. *Texture core:* fine. *Vessel walls:* medium strong to strong; somewhat porous. *Fracture:* slightly crumbling to shattering (uncommon). *Surface finish:* bowls rarely bumpy; polished; horizontal polishing marks sometimes noticeable; both surfaces bowls, slipped; slip thin, frequently difficult to detect; often somewhat powdery. *Surface color:* red (D. C. pl. 7H5, 7H10; 6H10, 6J10; 5G10—Mera, 1934, p. 12). *Fire clouds:* common. *Forms:* bowls. *Recorded range thickness bowl walls:* 4.2 to 7 mm; greatest individual range recorded, 1.9 mm; average thickness, ca 6 mm; vessel walls, fairly uniform thickness. *Rims:* bowls, IA3, IIIA3. *Decoration:* painted; interior bowl surfaces only. *Paint:* black or brownish; dull, sometimes thin and watery; frequently partially obliterated. *Patterns:* geometric; "the decoration begins immediately below the rim, usually with a narrow band, and patterns are carried well down towards the center, in which a circular area is left unpainted; designs are almost exclusively rectilinear of broad lines or solid elements; crude hatching, keys, triangles, parallel sets of lines and stepped elements occur" (Gladwin, W. & H. S., loc. cit., p. 27).

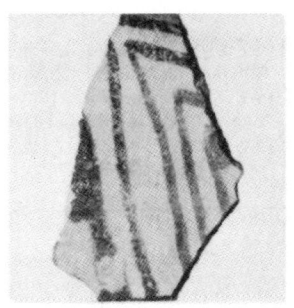

Fig. 17. ($\frac{1}{2}\times$).

RANGE:

Upper and middle Little Colorado River drainage, Arizona, south to the Mogollon Rim; sporadic pieces west to Canyon Diablo, Coconino County, Arizona.

REMARKS:

Showlow Black-on-red probably should be included in Mogollon Brown Ware.

ARAUCA PLAIN: new type

TYPE SPECIMENS: Sherds Nos. AT 4156–4160 in the Type Collection of the Museum of Northern Arizona.

TYPE SITE: Black Ax Pueblo (NA 1020), Petrified Forest National Monument, Apache County, Arizona.

STAGE: Late Pueblo III (?)–early Pueblo IV.

TIME: Probably between 1250–1400 A.D.

DESCRIPTION:

Constructed: by coiling. *Fired:* in oxidizing atmosphere. *Core:* gray to pinkish to brick-red. *Carbon streak:* occasional. *Temper:* predominantly fine grains quartz sand with lesser amounts fine angular fragments, usually black or red; white angular fragments, infrequent. *Vessel walls:* medium strong to strong; sometimes slightly porous. *Texture core:* fine. *Fracture:* crumbling. *Surface finish:* smoothed; frequently slightly bumpy; poorly polished, polishing marks, spotty, not conspicuous; exterior surfaces generally gritty; thickly pitted; impacted; surface and core do not contrast except in reduced portions; minute light-colored flakes sometimes seen on surface. *Surface color:* exteriors red, pinkish shades predominate; interiors jars gray, tan, or pink. *Form:* jars. *Recorded range thickness jar walls:* 5.3 to 9.1 mm; greatest individual range recorded, 2.1 mm; average thickness, ca 6.5 mm. *Rims:* jars IB3. Undecorated.

COMPARISON: Homolovi Black-on-red (unpainted sherds) but surface more poorly treated and more pink than red.

RANGE:

Petrified Forest National Monument, Arizona.

HOMOLOVI BLACK-ON-RED: new type

Fig. 18. (½×).

SYNONYMS: Red Ware, Hough, 1903.

NAMED BY: Mera, 1934, p. 19.

ILLUSTRATION: AT 2174 (Fig. 18).

TYPE SPECIMENS: Sherds Nos. AT 2171–2181, 2376 in the Type Collection of the Museum of Northern Arizona.

TYPE SITE: Homolovi Pueblo (NA 962), Winslow, Little Colorado River, Navajo County, Arizona.

STAGE: Pueblo IV.

TIME: Between 1300–1400 A.D.

OXIDIZING ATMOSPHERE 81

DESCRIPTION:

Constructed: by coiling. *Fired:* in oxidizing atmosphere. *Core:* pinkish, occasionally gray. *Temper:* predominantly fine grains quartz sand, lesser amounts fine angular fragments, mostly reddish, black or dark gray; whitish fragments, infrequent. *Vessel walls:* medium strong; frequently porous. *Texture core:* fine to medium. *Fracture:* crumbling. *Surface finish:* both surfaces bowls and jar exteriors well-polished, sometimes gritty and pitted, usually powdery; horizontal polishing marks noticeable; tiny light-colored flakes sometimes noticeable on surfaces; decorative surfaces impacted, possibly thinly slipped. *Surface color:* dull red; pinkish shades predominate. *Forms:* bowls, jars. *Recorded range thickness bowl walls:* 4.6 to 8.5 mm; greatest individual range recorded, 2.5 mm; average thickness, ca 6 mm. *Rims:* bowl, IA4; jar IC3. *Decoration:* painted. *Paint:* black; sometimes polished after painted (weak and faint, "ghost pattern"); often rich but dull black. *Designs:* on bowl interiors, rarely exteriors. *Patterns:* stripes, narrow and fine diagonal hatching in rectangular and stepped panels; wide staggered lines in series; occasionally opposed triangle-with-hooks in vertical bands; exterior jars, similar.

COMPARISON: Undecorated sherds similar to Arauca Plain but surfaces more finely treated and sometimes of redder color.

RANGE:

Petrified Forest National Monument (Mera, 1934) and Little Colorado River Valley (near Winslow), Arizona.

BLACK AX POLYCHROME: new type

TYPE SPECIMENS: Sherds Nos. AT 4165–4193 in the Type Collection of the Museum of Northern Arizona.
TYPE SITE: Stone Ax Pueblo (NA 1022), Petrified Forest National Monument, Apache County, Arizona.
STAGE: Pueblo IV.
TIME: Between 1300–1400 A.D.

DESCRIPTION:

Constructed: by coiling. *Fired:* in oxidizing atmosphere. *Temper:* somewhat variable; in most specimens medium fine quartz sand grains predominate; lesser amounts medium fine angular fragments, yellowish, red, dark gray; whitish fragments less frequent; in some specimens sand less frequent than angular fragments. *Carbon streak:* fairly frequent. *Vessel walls:* medium strong; frequently slightly porous. *Texture core:* fine. *Fracture:* generally crumbling. *Surface finish:* both surfaces bowls and jar exteriors, smoothed; frequently slightly bumpy; poorly polished, polishing marks spotty, not conspicuous; surfaces generally gritty and pitted; sometimes minutely crazed; minute light-colored flakes inconspicuous but frequent; surface and core do not contrast except in reduced portions; surfaces impacted but probably lightly slipped with same (?) material as basic clay; slip usually powdery. *Surface color:* jar exteriors reddish, pinkish shades predominate; interior surface gray, brick-red to pink; both surfaces bowls red, pinkish shades predominate. *Forms:* bowls (predominate), jars. *Recorded range thickness bowl walls:* 3.8 to 7.7 mm; greatest individual range recorded, 2.6 mm; average thickness (21 sherds), 5.8 mm. *Recorded thickness jar walls:* 4.6 to 8 mm; greatest individual range recorded, 1.5 mm. *Rims:* bowls, IA7, IIA7, IIIA7; bevelling of rims characteristic. *Decoration:* painted. *Paint:* black and white. *Pigments:* white, presumably kaolin, generally bluish tint, often crazed, frequently fugitive; black, weak and powdery, generally fugitive. *Designs:* on bowl interiors, rarely exteriors; jar exteriors. *Patterns:* generally black stripes and solid areas outlined with narrow white lines; occasionally isolated narrow white lines; generally black painted stripe immediately below rim, lower edge of stripe outlined with white; decorative band encircles bowl; occasionally panels hatchured with straight, wavy, or staggered black lines.

RANGE:

Recorded only from the Petrified Forest National Monument, Arizona.

REMARKS:

Under some conditions the red slip apparently breaks down into a brownish orange powder that can easily be rubbed off with the finger.

HOMOLOVI POLYCHROME

DESCRIBED BY: Mera, 1934, pp. 18–19.
NAMED BY: Mera, loc. cit.
TYPE SPECIMENS: Cotype sherds Nos. AT 1174–1175, AT 1189–1195 in the Type Collection of the Museum of Northern Arizona.
TYPE SITE: Homolovi II (NA 953), Winslow, Little Colorado River, Navajo County, Arizona.
STAGE: Pueblo IV.
TIME: Between 1300–1400 A.D.
DESCRIPTION (revised):

Constructed: by coiling. *Fired:* in oxidizing atmosphere. *Core:*

OXIDIZING ATMOSPHERE

normally pinkish to tan, occasionally shade of buff or gray. *Temper:* predominantly fine quartz sand with black or red angular fragments in lesser quantities; white angular fragments infrequent. *Vessel walls:* medium strong; friable and porous. *Texture core:* fine. *Fracture:* crumbling. *Surface finish:* usually gritty and pitted, often minutely crazed; tiny white flakes sometimes noticeable on surfaces; surfaces not bumpy; fairly well-polished; usually somewhat powdery; decorative surfaces impacted; not slipped. *Surface color:* variable; pink through red and orange to tan; sometimes slightly purplish tint. *Forms:* bowls, dippers, jars. *Recorded range thickness bowl walls:* 4 to 6.9. mm; greatest individual range recorded, 2.9 mm; average thickness, ca 6 mm. *Rims:* bowls, IA4, IA7, IIA3, IIA7, IIIA7. *Decoration:* painted. *Paint:* black and white; black paint often brownish, rich when black, may appear purplish; white paint presumably kaolin, frequently indistinct in spots, thick and granular in others. *Designs:* bowls—exterior and interior; black stripe just below rim, outlined with narrow white line, sometimes on both edges, sometimes on lower edge only; decorative band horizontal or solid black areas or panels containing hatching, straight or staggered lines; solid areas and panels outlined in narrow white lines; jars—exterior only, in same style as bowls.

COMPARISON: Elements and motifs in general same as on Winslow Polychrome although solid black areas are more frequent on Homolovi Polychrome.

RANGE:

Middle Little Colorado River near Winslow and on Clear Creek (Chavez Pass Pueblo), Navajo County; also Petrified Forest National Monument (see Mera, 1934, pp. 18–19).

REMARKS:

Styles of decoration for this type have not been determined and further separation may be expected. Homolovi Polychrome in style of decoration, is strongly suggestive of Fourmile Polychrome.

CHAVEZ PASS SERIES

Types in this series at present are recorded only from an area west of the range of Homolovi Series. Types in Chavez Pass Series objectively are easily distinguished from types of Homolovi Series.

KEY g: CHAVEZ PASS SERIES

Polychrome..................Chavez Pass Polychrome (p. 84)
                             Black Ax Polychrome (p. 81)
Not polychrome.............Chavez Pass Black-on-red (p. 84)

CHAVEZ PASS BLACK-ON-RED: new type

TYPE SPECIMENS: Sherds Nos. AT 1197–1198 and AT 1200 in the Type Collection of the Museum of Northern Arizona.
TYPE SITE: Chavez Pass Pueblo (NA 658), Clear Creek, Coconino County, Arizona.
STAGE: Pueblo IV.
TIME: Between 1300–1400 A.D.

DESCRIPTION:

Constructed: by coiling. *Fired:* in oxidizing atmosphere. *Core:* normally pinkish to tan. *Temper:* predominantly fine quartz sand with lesser amounts opaque fragments, mostly reddish, occasionally black or gray. *Texture core:* fine. *Vessel walls:* medium strong; slightly porous. *Fracture:* crumbling. *Surface finish:* fairly well-polished, horizontal polishing marks often noticeable; usually pitted; usually minutely crazed; tiny white flakes usually noticeable on surfaces; both surfaces bowls coated with thin watery slip. *Surface color:* red, sometimes orange tint. *Form:* bowls. *Recorded range thickness bowl walls:* 4.3 to 6.6 mm; greatest individual range recorded, 1 mm; average thickness, ca 5.5 mm. *Rims:* bowls, IA7, IIIA7. *Decoration:* painted. *Paint:* black; shade more often brownish; weak, frequently watery. *Design:* confined to interior surface; no rim decoration recorded; stripes; broad, narrow, and staggered lines; solid areas; broken line; unnamed style of decoration characteristic of Pueblo IV in the Hopi Country.

RANGE:

Recorded only from Chavez Pass Pueblo but should occur regularly in Pueblo IV sites of the middle Little Colorado River drainage near Winslow, Navajo County, Arizona.

CHAVEZ PASS POLYCHROME: new type

ILLUSTRATION: AT 1202 (Fig. 19).
TYPE SPECIMENS: Sherds Nos. AT 1199 and 1202–1203 in the Type Collection of the Museum of Northern Arizona.
TYPE SITE: Chavez Pass Pueblo (NA 658), Clear Creek, Navajo County, Arizona.
STAGE: Pueblo IV.
TIME: Between 1200–1400 A.D.

OXIDIZING ATMOSPHERE

DESCRIPTION:

Constructed: by coiling. *Fired:* in oxidizing atmosphere. *Core:* pinkish to tan. *Temper:* predominantly fine quartz sand with almost equal amount red angular fragments; black or gray fragments infrequent. *Texture core:* fine. *Vessel walls:* medium strong. *Fracture:* crumbling. *Surface finish:* smoothed; sometimes slightly bumpy; normally pitted; usually minutely crazed; scraped, scraping marks sometimes discernible; tiny white flakes usually noticeable on surfaces; interior and exterior surfaces bowls coated with thin watery slip. *Surface color:* reddish, sometimes with orange tint. *Form:* bowls. *Recorded range thickness bowl walls:* 3.2 to 5.6 mm; greatest individual range recorded, 1.5 mm; average thickness, ca 5 mm. *Rims:* bowls, IA3. *Decoration:* painted. *Paint:* black and white; black paint often brownish; white paint, presumably kaolin, powdery, fugitive used as narrow line bordering black stripes, solid black areas, or hatched panels. *Design:* patterns recorded only on interior surface bowls; no rim decoration recorded; elements and motifs in general same as on Chavez Pass Black-on-red.

Fig. 19. ($\frac{1}{2}$×).

RANGE:

Reported only from Chavez Pass Pueblo but should occur regularly in Pueblo IV sites of the middle Little Colorado River drainage near Winslow, Arizona.

ROOSEVELT RED WARE

At sometime during the development of a series there may appear a new type as a result of anyone of a number of type determinants. Some determinants have possibilities for even further change and thus are potential ancestors to new series, or even to new wares. The use of white as a background for a black painted decoration is the basis for the recognition of a new type, Showlow Polychrome, in the Fourmile Series of White Mountain Red Ware (p. 104). Had only one or two examples of "Showlow Polychrome" been found, most workers would have called it "aberrant" and immediately would have ignored it. But because specimens were relatively abundant it was given type recognition as a variant of a closely related companion type, Fourmile Polychrome. But had further type changes been recognized later, Showlow Polychrome (as described herein) would have been the first type in a new series, or, if influence from this type were strong enough to cause a radical change in pottery types over a large area, Showlow Polychrome probably would have been the first type in a new ware. Fourmile Polychrome would then be the ancestral type to the ware.

As has been said, the character that made Showlow Polychrome different from its immediate ancestor, Fourmile Polychrome, was the use of white paint as a *background* for a black painted decoration. This same use of white paint appeared on a type of Alameda Red Ware in a contiguous region. With the use of white in this manner, a new type was born. No description and name of this "new type" has been published, however, because of certain similarities to a well-known and long recognized type have not been analyzed. This suspected type is thought to be ancestral to Roosevelt Red Ware. In fact, Mera presented this theory when he graphically indicated that a type, Pinto Polychrome, in Roosevelt Red Ware, was derived from his Showlow Black-on-red—Homolovi Polychrome sequence (chart, 1934).

KEY 4: ROOSEVELT RED WARE

1. Red as integral part of design..............Tonto Polychrome (p. 90)
   No red as integral part of design................................ 2
2. Encircling stripe below rim.................Gila Polychrome (p. 88)
   No encircling stripe below rim..............Pinto Polychrome (p. 87)

ROOSEVELT RED WARE: new ware

SYNONYMS: (a) Polychrome Ware, Hough, 1903; (b) Red Ware, Hough, loc. cit.; (c) Gila Ware, Hough, loc. cit.
STAGES: Pueblo III–IV.
TIME: Probably between ca 1150–1400 A.D.

DESCRIPTION:

Constructed: by coiling. *Fired:* in oxidizing atmosphere. *Core:* gray to black, tan to brick-red. *Carbon streak:* common. *Temper:* moderately abundant fine water-worn sand. *Texture core:* medium to fine. *Fracture:* slightly crumbling; friable. *Surface finish:* smoothed, not highly polished; slipped; generally gritty;

OXIDIZING ATMOSPHERE

sometimes crazed. *Surface color:* red; sometimes white, in part. *Forms:* bowls, jars, eccentric. *Recorded range thickness bowl walls:* 3.9 to 7.1 mm; greatest individual range recorded, 2.4 mm; average thickness, ca 5.5 mm. *Recorded range thickness jar walls:* 4.0 to 7.4 mm; greatest individual range recorded, 1.1 mm; average thickness, ca 6 mm. *Rims:* bowls, IA4, IE4, IB2, IF3; jars, IB2, IB3, IB4, IC2, IC3. *Decoration:* painted. *Pigments:* black, carbon; red, hematite (?); white kaolin (?). *Designs:* interior surface all bowls, white; decoration, geometric; bold and free; decorative styles unnamed. *Elements:* solid or hatchured stripes, steps, keys, squares, triangles, scrolls, scrolls with scalloped or serrated edges.

RANGE:

South of the Mogollon Rim, with concentrations in Roosevelt Basin, Gila Basin, Verde Valley (trade ?), San Pedro Valley, and vicinities of Globe and Safford, Arizona. Occasionally found near Flagstaff, Winslow, Ajo, Gila Bend, and Nogales, Arizona; El Paso, Texas; and Casas Grandes, Mexico.

REMARKS:

In selecting a name for this ware "Salado" was considered since the Gladwins included these types in the Salado Culture (1930 b) but since there are types named "Salado," in this work, that are here assigned to another ware, it is thought best not to use "Salado" as a ware name that there may not be a type bearing the name of a ware to which it does not belong. Since these types occur commonly in the Roosevelt Basin, "Roosevelt" has, therefore, been selected as the geographic part of the ware name.

PINTO POLYCHROME

SYNONYMS: (a) Polychrome Red, Kidder, 1924, p. 107; (b) Polychrome Redware, Kidder, loc. cit., p. 109; (c) Lower Gila Polychrome, Kidder, 1924, p. 113; (d) Central Gila Polychrome, Schmidt, 1928, p. 289; (e) Early Middle Gila Polychrome, Hawley, 1929, p. 751; (f) Middle Gila Polychrome, Hawley, 1929; (g) Late Middle Gila Polychrome, Hawley, 1929.
DESCRIBED BY: Gladwin, W. & H. S., 1930b, pp. 4–5.
NAMED BY: Gladwin, W. & H. S., loc. cit.
ILLUSTRATIONS: Gladwin, W. & H. S., loc. cit., Plates II (colored), IV.
TYPE SPECIMENS: Gila Pueblo, Globe, Arizona.
TYPE SITE: Pinto Creek Pueblo (NA 1280; Roosevelt: 9:12), Roosevelt Lake, Gila County, Arizona.
STAGE: Late Pueblo III.
TIME: Probably between ca 1150–1250 A.D.

DESCRIPTION (revised):

Constructed: by coiling. *Fired:* in oxidizing atmosphere. *Core:* brick-red, tan, gray to black. *Carbon streak:* common. *Temper:*

moderately abundant fine water-worn sand. *Texture core:* medium to fine. *Fracture:* slightly crumbling; friable. *Surface finish:* interiors well-smoothed but not polished; coated allover with white slip, often thin and faded, occasionally pinkish or bluish-gray; gritty and usually minutely crazed; exteriors thinly slipped, fairly well-polished. *Surface color:* exteriors, red, on bases and other places from which slip has weathered, color dull brownish to brick-red; interiors, white. *Form:* bowl; bowl hemispherical, $5\frac{1}{2}$ to 13 inches in diameter. *Rims:* bowls, IA4, IE4, IB2, IF3. *Decoration:* painted. *Paint:* black, sometimes dense; often thin and watery. *Pigment:* carbon (test by Hawley). *Design:* interiors—usually completely covered with design carrying to rim without bordering line or stripe; occasionally lay-out horizontal band, leaving open circle in bottom; mostly balanced solid and hatchured elements, usually triangles, elongated rectangular panels, squares, stripes, interlocking scrolls; exteriors—usually unpainted, very rarely several panels wide horizontal black dashes.

COMPARISONS: Gila Polychrome, horizontal stripe or broken line always present; hatchuring very rare; decoration never carries to rim.
    Tonto Polychrome, horizontal stripe or broken line usually present; decoration employs red as integral part of design on one or both surfaces; brush work somewhat less well executed.

RANGE:
    Roosevelt Basin, east of Roosevelt Dam, Gila County, Arizona.

GILA POLYCHROME

SYNONYMS: (a) Polychrome Red, Kidder, 1924, p. 107; (b) Polychrome Redware, Kidder, 1924, p. 109; (c) Lower Gila Polychrome, Kidder, 1924, p. 113; (d) Central Gila Polychrome, Schmidt, 1928, p. 289; (e) Early Middle Gila Polychrome, Hawley, 1929, p. 751; (f) Middle Gila Polychrome, Hawley, 1929; (g) Late Middle Gila Polychrome, Hawley, 1929.
DESCRIBED BY: Kidder, 1924, p. 109.
NAMED BY: Kidder, 1924, p. 113 (abbreviated from Lower Gila Polychrome).
ILLUSTRATIONS: Gladwin, W. & H. S., 1930 b, Plate V (colored).
TYPE SPECIMENS: Gila Pueblo, Globe, Arizona. Cotype sherds Nos. AT 4254–4270 in the Type Collection of the Museum of Northern Arizona.
TYPE SITE: Gila Pueblo, Globe, Arizona.
STAGE: Pueblo IV.
TIME: ca 1300 A.D.

DESCRIPTION (revised):
    Constructed: by coiling. *Fired:* in oxidizing atmosphere. *Core:* brick-red, tan, gray to black. *Carbon streak:* common. *Temper:* moderately abundant fine water-worn sand. *Texture core:* medium to fine. *Fracture:* slightly crumbling. *Surface finish:* bowl

OXIDIZING ATMOSPHERE

interiors, well-smoothed and coated all-over with thick slip; usually crazed; slightly gritty; never polished; bowl exteriors coated with thin slip; usually well-polished, horizontal striations; occasionally also coated from rim downward about halfway to base with same slip as used on interiors; jar exteriors well-smoothed; coated with same slip as used on bowl interiors from (but not including) rim to point about midway between base and greatest body diameter; unpolished; usually gritty; crazed; inside necks and area below (white) slip, coated with thin (red) wash; well-polished. *Surface color:* bowl exteriors, red, sometimes white in part; bowl interiors, creamy-white; jar exteriors, red and white; bases and other areas from which wash has weathered, color dull brownish or brick-red. *Forms:* bowls, jars, figurines; bowls (predominate), usually hemispherical with incurved lip; jars, usually small and nearly globular with short, slightly flaring necks, sometimes with squat bodies and elongated tapering necks about equal in length to height of body; figurines usually bird form; rarely human. *Recorded range thickness jar walls:* 4 to 7.4 mm; greatest individual range recorded 1.1 mm; average thickness, ca 6 mm. *Rims:* bowls, IA4, IE4, IB2, IF3; jars. IB2, IB3. *Decoration:* painted. *Paint:* black, dense, carefully applied. *Pigment:* carbon (test by Hawley). *Design:* bowl interiors usually completely covered in all-over lay-out, frequently with fold design or horizontal band leaving open circle in bottom; decoration never carries to rim; rim, usually plain, occasionally ticked; bowl exteriors—usually unpainted; on bowls having exterior white slip appears decorative band similar to band on interiors, with horizontal stripe just below rim, stripe almost always broken; jar decoration—horizontal stripe, usually broken, encircles shoulder, dividing white slipped area into two zones, one around neck and one around body; zones painted in bands containing elements similar to elements on bowl exteriors; rarely horizontal stripe just below rim, leaving only one decorative zone on white slipped area. *Elements:* solid elements predominate, running largely to tapering triangles and scrolls with scalloped edges; also solid steps, keys, and small mazes; hatchuring in triangular panels fairly frequent; horizontal stripe always present, usually just below rim, sometimes one or two inches below rim, dividing surface into two areas, decorated with horizontal band above stripe and with all-over lay-out below; stripe, usually broken.

COMPARISONS: Pinto Polychrome, horizontal stripe or broken line absent; decoration carries to rim; use of balanced solid and hatchured elements, common.

Tonto Polychrome, decoration employs red as integral part of design on one or both surfaces; brush work somewhat less well-executed.

RANGE:

South of the Mogollon Rim, with concentrations in Roosevelt Basin, Tonto Basin, Gila Basin, Verde Valley (trade?), San Pedro Valley, vicinity of Globe and Safford, Arizona. Sherds found occasionally near Winslow, Ajo, Gila Bend, and Nogales, Arizona; El Paso, Texas; and Casas Grandes, Mexico.

REMARKS:

This name is here applied to that form of polychrome having the widest range in southern Arizona; it has been frequently used to refer to all polychromes in this area. The color combination and vessel shapes of Pinto Polychrome are retained in this type, but a marked change takes place in the character of the decoration, notably through the introduction of the broken line.

TONTO POLYCHROME

SYNONYMS: (a) Lower Gila Polychrome, Kidder, 1924, p. 113; (b) Central Gila Polychrome, Schmidt, 1928, p. 289; (c) Early Middle Gila Polychrome, Hawley, 1929, p. 751; (d) Late Middle Gila Polychrome, Hawley, 1929.
DESCRIBED BY: Gladwin, W. & H. S., 1930 b, pp. 8–9.
NAMED BY: Gladwin, W. & H. S., loc. cit.
ILLUSTRATIONS: Gladwin, W. & H. S., loc. cit., Plate VI (colored).
TYPE SPECIMENS: Gila Pueblo, Globe, Arizona.
TYPE SITE: Roosevelt: 9:11, Roosevelt Lake, Gila County, Arizona.
STAGE: Pueblo IV.
TIME: ca 1400 A.D.
DESCRIPTION (revised):

Constructed: by coiling. *Fired:* in oxidizing atmosphere. *Core:* brick-red, tan, gray to black. *Carbon streak:* common. *Temper:* moderately abundant fine water-worn sand. *Texture core:* medium to fine. *Fracture:* crumbling; slightly friable. *Surface finish:* bowl interiors—well-smoothed, coated (usually all-over) with thick (creamy-white) slip, unpolished, somewhat gritty, often crazed, rarely (white) slip only covers band extending from rim downward two or three inches, remainder area coated with (red) slip; bowl exteriors—coated in part with (white) slip, in part with (red) slip, latter usually fairly well-polished; jar interiors—well-smoothed; jar exteriors same as bowl interiors. *Surface color:* bowl and jar exteriors, red in part, white in part: bowl interiors, creamy-white. *Forms:* bowls, jars; bowls usually hemispherical; sometimes deep with vertical sides, sometimes small with flaring sides; jars small, squat, with elongated necks; large jars globular, well-shaped, with fairly short vertical or tapering necks. *Rims:* bowls, IA4, IE4, IB2, IF3; jars, IA2, IB4, IC2, IC3. *Decoration:* painted. *Paint:* black, dense, thick. *Pigments:* black, carbon (test by Hawley); red, hematite (?), bright, almost maroon, fairly thick; white, presumably kaolin, thick, dull, often creamy-white or light blue-gray, often flakes off. *Design:* usually completely covers bowl interiors and carries to rim, in few cases where white is applied only to portion of interior area, black decoration limited to white portion; very rarely red and white in combination on interiors in same manner as on exteriors; horizontal black stripe sometimes broken, frequently on bowl interiors, either at rim or about half way down side; bowl exteriors first painted in large irregular areas with white, then heavy black elements over white, leaving white visible around edged of black as outline; rest, red in areas not already covered with white; net effect balanced patterns of white and red, sometimes in angular masses, sometimes in scrolls, sometimes in panels or bands of one color separated by stripes of other color; black always used against white background, never against red background; pattern almost wholly of stripes and large solid elements, often with scalloped or serrated edges, sometimes producing almost negative effect; hatchuring rare; painted zone never extends much below greatest diameter of body; red below that point, where used as part of painted design; jar exteriors similar to bowl exteriors, red most frequently occurs in one or two encircling stripes, dividing surface into two or three bands of white on which is superimposed black decoration; brush work free, bold, and rather careless.

COMPARISONS: Pinto Polychrome, horizontal stripe or broken line never occurs, red never used as integral part of design. Gila Polychrome, red never used as integral part of design; brush work somewhat better executed.

RANGE:
Roosevelt Basin, and vicinity of Globe, Arizona.

REMARKS:
This is a late and highly specialized type.

TSEGI ORANGE WARE

Little is known about the early history of the development of Tsegi Orange Ware. The ware suddenly made an appearance in the Tsegi Canyons with the erection of the large cliff pueblos so it is presumed that the ware was brought into these canyons by the peoples who built the pueblos. Prior to the construction of the large pueblos (ca 1270 A.D.) the ware did not hold a prominent position in canyons as early as 1127 A.D. although it may have been commonly produced in Marsh Pass and the Kayenta Flats during early and middle Pueblo III, from about 1150 to 1250 A.D.

Many similarities in objective characters between Tsegi Orange Ware and Bluff Black-on-red indicate a genetic relationship between the two and also that Tsegi Orange Ware may be an outgrowth of a type yet to be discovered but belonging to the Bluff Series.

KEY 5: TSEGI ORANGE WARE

1. Painted decoration.. 2
   No painted decoration....................... Tsegi Orange (p. 93)
2. Polychrome.. 3
   Not Polychrome..................... Tsegi Red-on-orange (p. 94)
   Tsegi Black-on-orange (p. 95)
3. With red decorative base (slip)............................. 4
   Without red decorative base (slip)........................... 5
4. With white paint..................... Kiet Siel Polychrome (p. 100)
   Without white paint................... Dogoszhi Polychrome (p. 98)
5. With white paint..................... Kayenta Polychrome (p. 99)
   Without white paint.. 6
6. Interior decoration (bowls) black........... Tsegi Polychrome (p. 96)
   Interior decoration bowls; exterior decoration jars, black and red.....
   Tusayan Polychrome (p. 96)

TSEGI ORANGE WARE: new ware

SYNONYM: Plain Yellow Ware, Kidder & Guernsey, 1919, p. 141.
STAGE: Pueblo III.
TIME: ca 1150–1300 A.D.

DESCRIPTION:

Constructed: by coiling. *Fired:* in oxidizing atmosphere. *Core:* dark gray to light gray, brownish through brick-red to pink. *Temper:* about equal amounts quartz-like sand and angular light-colored fragments; frequently conspicuous on surfaces, in cross-section, and on worn surfaces. *Texture core:* fine. *Vessel walls:* medium strong to strong. *Fracture:* slightly crumbling to shattering. *Surface finish:* bowls, bumpy to smooth; polished; jar exteriors, bumpy to smooth; polished, polishing marks generally noticeable; surfaces impacted or slipped. *Surface color:* generally dull orange, except slipped portions; slip, maroon red; color surface and core generally do not contrast except when core is gray. *Fire clouds:* generally common. *Forms:* bowls, jars, seed-jars, dippers; bowls generally have single horizontal handle; vessel bases frequently depressed. *Recorded range thickness bowl walls:* 2.8 to 8.3 mm; greatest individual range recorded, 3.7 mm; average thickness, ca 5.5 mm. *Recorded range thickness jar walls:* 2.5 to 10.5 mm; greatest individual range recorded, 3.6 mm; average thickness, ca 5.5 mm. *Rims:* bowls, IA3, IA4, IA6, IA7, IIIA3, IIIA4, IB3, IB4, IIIB3; jars, IA3, IB3, IC3. *Painted decoration* (one type unpainted): black, red, white. *Pigments:* black, manganese; white, kaolin; red, hematite. *Decoration:* confined to interior surface bowls; red band or red stripe characteristically encircle exterior surface bowls (diagnostic); white paint as outliner for black design; rims, frequently solid painted line. *Patterns:* geometric. *Elements and motifs:* hatchured panels, series parallel lines, narrow lines, horizontal and diagonal hatchure in rectangular, circular, stepped, or triangular panels; staggered lines, vertical lines with staggered squares between; black stripes, solid stepped elements. *Decorative style:* Dogoszhi Style is the only style of decoration named.

RANGE:

Apparently indigenous in the Rainbow Plateau Area. Traded to the Hopi Country and to the San Francisco Mountain region, Arizona.

TSEGI ORANGE: new type

SYNONYM: Plain Yellow Ware, Kidder & Guernsey, 1919, p. 141.
DESCRIBED BY: Kidder & Guernsey, loc. cit.
ILLUSTRATION :259/1126 (Fig. 20).
TYPE SPECIMENS: Seed-jar No. 259–1126, Fig. 8 and type sherds Nos. AT 589, 2510–2534 in the Type Collection of the Museum of Northern Arizona.
TYPE SITE: Kiet Siel Pueblo (NA 2519), Tsegi Canyons, Navajo National Monument, Navajo County, Arizona.
STAGE: Pueblo III.
TIME: ca 1250–ca 1300 A.D.
DESCRIPTION (revised):

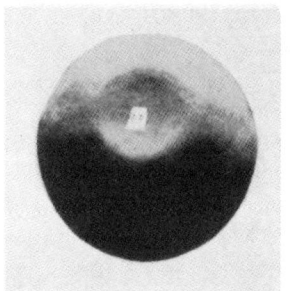

Fig. 20. (⅛×).

Constructed: by coiling. *Fired:* in oxidizing atmosphere. *Core:* gray, light brown to brick-red. *Carbon streak:* fairly common.

Temper: about equal amounts quartz sand and light-colored angular fragments; temper noticeable on surfaces, sometimes conspicuous, especially on worn or poorly polished surfaces. *Texture core:* medium. *Vessel walls:* medium strong to strong. *Fracture:* slightly crumbling to shattering. *Surface finish:* bowls, usually somewhat bumpy; sometimes polished; scraping and polishing marks often almost invisible but sometimes conspicuous; sometimes pitted; both surfaces bowls, impacted; exterior surfaces jars, sometimes impacted. *Surface color:* orange; color surface and core contrast when core is gray. *Fire clouds:* common. *Forms:* bowls, dippers, jars; bowls have single horizontal handle; jars have vertical handles; bases of vessels generally depressed (see Fig. 20). *Recorded range thickness bowl walls:* 3.7 to 6.8 mm; greatest individual range recorded, 3 mm; average thickness (14 sherds), 5.1 mm. *Recorded range thickness jar walls:* 2.5 to 10.5 mm; greatest individual range recorded, 3.6 mm; average thickness, ca 5.4 mm. *Rims:* bowls, IA4, IB4; jars, IB3, IC3. *Undecorated.*

RANGE:

Marsh Pass and the Tsegi Canyons, Navajo County, Arizona.

REMARKS:

This type was thought by Kidder and Guernsey to be unslipped red pottery (Deadmans, Bluff, and Tusayan black-on-red) but was recognized by them as being intentionally left undecorated as unslipped decorated vessels were also found (1919, loc. cit.).

TSEGI RED-ON-ORANGE: new type

ILLUSTRATION: AT 2537 (Fig. 21). Clarke, 1935, Pl. VII, (colored).

TYPE SPECIMENS: Sherds Nos. AT 2537–2542 in the Type Collection of the Museum of Northern Arizona.

TYPE SITE: Kiet Siel Pueblo (NA 2519), Navajo National Monument, Tsegi Canyons, Navajo County, Arizona.

STAGE: Pueblo III.

TIME: ca 1225–ca 1300 A.D.

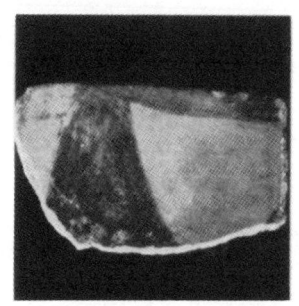

Fig. 21. ($\frac{1}{2}\times$).

DESCRIPTION:

Constructed: by coiling. *Fired:* in oxidizing atmosphere. *Core:* gray to brick-red. *Carbon streaks:* common. *Temper:* about equal amounts quartz sand and light-colored angular fragments; often noticeable on surfaces; sometimes conspicuous in cross-section and on worn surfaces. *Texture core:* medium. *Vessel walls:* medium strong. *Fracture:* slightly crumbling. *Surface finish:* sometimes slightly bumpy, impacted; frequently polished. *Surface color:* orange; color surface and core contrast when core is gray. *Fire clouds:* common. *Forms:* bowls. *Recorded range thickness bowl walls:* 4.6 to 8.3 mm; greatest individual range recorded, 3.7 mm; average thickness, ca 6 mm. *Rims:* bowls, IIIA3, IB3. *Painted decoration:* paint red. *Pigment:* probably hematite. *Decoration:* interior, solid red areas and broad stripes; exterior frequently red stripe (may be 70 mm wide) encircling vessel.

RANGE:

Klethla Valley, Tsegi Canyons, and Nokai Canyon, Navajo County, Arizona.

TSEGI BLACK-ON-ORANGE: new type

SYNONYM: Plain Yellow Ware, Kidder & Guernsey, 1919, p. 141.
DESCRIBED BY: Kidder & Guernsey, loc. cit.
ILLUSTRATION: AT 2559 (Fig. 22).
TYPE SPECIMENS: Sherds Nos. AT 2543–2563 in the Type Collection of the Museum of Northern Arizona.
TYPE SITE: Twin Caves Pueblo (NA 2536), Dogoszhi Biko, Tsegi Canyons, Navajo County, Arizona.
STAGE: Pueblo III.
TIME: ca 1225–ca 1300 A.D.
DESCRIPTION (revised):

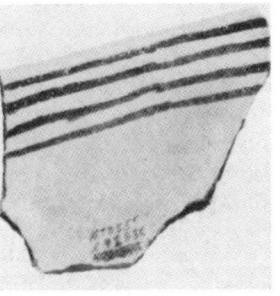

Fig. 22. ($\frac{1}{2}$ ×).

Constructed: by coiling. *Fired:* in oxidizing atmosphere. *Core:* black to gray; dark brown (rare) to brick-red. *Carbon streaks:* common. *Temper:* about equal amounts quartz sand and light-colored angular fragments; temper noticeable on surfaces, conspicuous in cross-section and on worn surfaces. *Texture core:* medium. *Vessel walls:* medium strong to strong. *Fracture:* slightly crumbling to shattering. *Surface finish:* bowl surfaces and exterior jar surfaces generally somewhat bumpy; scraping marks frequently conspicuous; surface often pitted; decorative surfaces, impacted. *Surface color:* orange; color surface and core generally do not contrast. *Fire clouds:* common. *Forms:* bowls (predominate), dippers (rare), jars (uncommon). *Recorded range thickness bowl walls:* 3.1 to 6.7 mm; greatest individual range recorded, 2.4 mm; average thickness (19 sherds), 4.8 mm. *Rims:* bowls, IA3, IA4, IA6, IIIA3, IB3, IB4; bowls generally have horizontal handle. *Painted decoration:* black. *Decoration:* bowls, two to five horizontal lines on interior surface just below rim; lines 1½ to 3 mm wide; occasionally one stripe (7 to 10 mm wide) below rim; occasionally pendent lines from rim; wall decoration scarce, occasionally hatchured panel or series of parallel lines; bowl bases, undecorated; frequently rim painted with wide line.

RANGE:
March Pass and the Tsegi Canyons, Navajo County, Arizona.

TSEGI POLYCHROME: new type

TYPE SPECIMENS: Sherds Nos. AT 2565, 4326–4327 in the Type Collection of the Museum of Northern Arizona.
TYPE SITE: NA 2512, Tsegi Canyon, Navajo County, Arizona.
STAGE: Pueblo III.
TIME: ca 1225–1300 A.D.

DESCRIPTION:
Constructed: by coiling. *Fired:* in oxidizing atmosphere. *Core:* gray to pinkish. *Temper:* about equal amounts quartz sand and light-colored angular fragments; temper noticeable on surfaces; conspicuous in cross-section and on worn surfaces. *Texture core:* medium. *Vessel walls:* medium strong. *Fracture:* slightly crumbling to shattering. *Surface finish:* bowls, sometimes somewhat bumpy; polishing marks noticeable; impacted or polished. *Surface color:* orange; color surface and core generally do not contrast. *Fire clouds:* common. *Form:* bowls. *Recorded range thickness bowl walls:* 4.3 to 5.9 mm; greatest individual range recorded, 1.6 mm. *Rims:* bowls, IA6. *Painted decoration:* black and red. *Pigment:* red, presumably hematite. *Decoration:* interior bowls, 4 narrow black lines (ca 2 mm wide) encircling vessel just below rim; exterior, red stripe (ca 30 mm wide) below rim; rim, red.

RANGE:
Recorded only from the Tsegi Canyons, Navajo County, Arizona.

TUSAYAN POLYCHROME

SYNONYMS: (a) Polychrome Ware, Kidder & Guernsey, 1919, p. 138; (b) Polychrome Redware, Kidder & Guernsey, loc. cit., Pl. 56; (c) Proto Kayenta Polychrome, Kidder, 1924, p. 73; (d) Kayenta Polychrome, Kidder, loc. cit., p. 71–73; (e) Proto-Kayenta (Tusayan) Polychrome Gladwin, W. & H. S., 1930 a, p. 174.
DESCRIBED BY: Kidder & Guernsey, loc. cit., p. 138–140.

OXIDIZING ATMOSPHERE

NAMED BY: Hargrave, 1932, p. 22.
ILLUSTRATIONS: Kidder & Guernsey, loc. cit., fig. 59–60, pl. 56; Clarke, 1935, Pl. VIII & IX, (colored); AT 2485 (Fig. 23).
TYPE SPECIMENS: Cotype sherds Nos. AT 2473, 2475, 2479, 2480–2485, 2487–2491, 2509 in the Type Collection of the Museum of Northern Arizona.
TYPE SITE: Po-ci-o-le-lena (NA 1603), sometimes called Whistling Quail Pueblo, Moenkopi Wash, Coconino County, Arizona.
STAGE: Pueblo III.
TIME: ca 1150–ca 1300 A.D.
DESCRIPTION (revised):

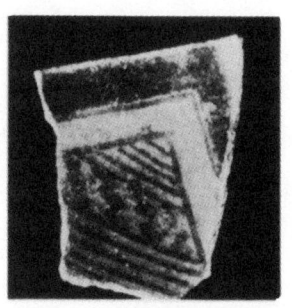

Fig. 23. ($\frac{1}{2} \times$).

Constructed: by coiling. *Fired:* in oxidizing atmosphere. *Core:* black to gray, dark brown (rare) to brick-red. *Carbon streaks:* common. *Temper:* about equal amounts quartz sand and light-colored angular fragments; temper somewhat noticeable on surfaces, conspicuous in cross-section and on worn surfaces. *Texture core:* fine to medium. *Vessel walls:* medium strong to strong. *Fracture:* slightly crumbling to shattering. *Surface finish:* bowl surfaces, sometimes bumpy; polished; scraping and polishing marks sometimes quite noticeable; decorative surfaces, impacted. *Surface color:* orange; color surface and core generally do not contrast. *Fire clouds:* common. *Forms:* bowls (predominate), dippers, jars (uncommon); bowls generally have horizontal handle. *Recorded range thickness bowl walls:* 2.8 to 7.7 mm; greatest individual range recorded, 2.7 mm; average thickness (13 sherds), 5.5 mm. *Recorded range thickness jar walls:* 3.7 to 5.2 mm; greatest individual range recorded, 1.5 mm; average thickness, ca 4.5 mm. *Rims:* bowls, IA3, IA4, IA6, IIIA3, IIIA4. *Painted decoration:* black and red. *Pigment:* red, probably hematite. *Decoration:* interior bowls, exterior jars; red decoration—vertical, horizontal, and diagonal stripes, often encircling stripe just below rim on bowl exteriors; black decoration—narrow lines outlining red areas on bowl interiors, horizontal and diagonal hatching in rectangular or triangular panels between red areas, narrow horizontal lines in series, wide staggered lines, vertical lines in series with staggered lines between; bowl exterior painted with one to three wide horizontal stripes just below rims; rims, usually painted red or black.

COMPARISON: Citadel Polychrome, only bowls; no handles; decoration, absence of staggered lines, lines in series, lines in series with staggered squares; exterior surface slipped with red, except that broad unslipped stripe often occurs just below rim and sometimes, possibly, base unslipped; small sherds of Tusayan Polychrome with part of exterior red stripe often closely resembles Citadel Polychrome; temper, light-colored angular fragments usually somewhat more abundant and more noticeable on surface.

RANGE:

Marsh Pass and the Tsegi Canyons, Navajo County, Arizona; generally distributed from Tuba City north to Utah, and from Navajo Mountain east to Chinle Creek. Fairly common trade type in the San Francisco Mountain region, Coconino County, Arizona.

DOGOSZHI POLYCHROME: new type

TYPE SPECIMENS: Bowl No. NA 3093.5 and sherds Nos. AT 4316–4325, 4431–4433 in the Type Collection of the Museum of Northern Arizona.
TYPE SITE: NA 2504, Tsegi Canyon, Navajo County, Arizona.
STAGE: Pueblo III.
TIME: ca 1250–ca 1300 A.D.

DESCRIPTION:

Constructed: by coiling. *Fired:* in oxidizing atmosphere. *Core:* black to gray, dark brown (rare) to brick-red. *Carbon streak:* common. *Temper:* about equal amounts quartz sand and light-colored angular fragments; somewhat noticeable on surfaces; conspicuous in cross-section and on worn surfaces. *Texture core:* fine. *Vessel walls:* medium strong to strong. *Fracture:* slightly crumbling to shattering. *Surface finish:* bowl forms, sometimes bumpy; polished; scraping and polishing marks sometimes quite noticeable; interior surface, slipped. *Surface color:* exteriors, orange; exterior surface jar forms, red, in part; interiors, gray or orange; color surface and core generally do not contrast, except with decorative surface. *Fire clouds:* common. *Forms:* bowls, dippers, jars; bowls generally have horizontal handle. *Recorded range thickness bowl walls:* 4.8 to 7.6 mm; greatest individual range recorded, 2.1 mm; average thickness, ca 5.5 mm. *Recorded range thickness dipper walls:* 6.6 to 8.5 mm; greatest individual range recorded, 1.9 mm; average thickness, ca 7.5 mm. *Recorded range thickness jar walls:* 5 to 8 mm; greatest individual range recorded, 3 mm; average thickness, ca 7 mm. *Rims:* bowls, IA3, IA7, IIIB3. *Painted decoration:* black and red. *Pigment:* red, hematite. *Decoration:* bowl forms—interior and exterior surfaces; jars—exterior surface. *Red decoration:* exterior surface only. *Black decoration:* interior surface bowl forms, exterior jars. *Patterns:* red, stripe or stripes, on exterior bowl forms; black, Dogoszhi Style, generally; rarely broad lines.

RANGE:

In the Tsegi drainage, recorded from the Main Tsegi and in

Kiet Siel Canyon and Dogoszhi Biko; also recorded from Nokai, Paiute, and Forbidding canyons. The type bowl is a trade product from Polacca Wash, Hopi Indian Reservation, Navajo County, Arizona.

KAYENTA POLYCHROME

SYNONYM: Polychrome Ware, Kidder & Guernsey, 1919, p. 138.
DESCRIBED BY: Kidder & Guernsey, loc. cit., pp. 138–139.
NAMED BY: Kidder, 1924, p. 71.
ILLUSTRATION: AT 2580 (Fig. 24).
TYPE SPECIMENS: Sherds Nos. AT 2566–2582 in the Type Collection of the Museum of Northern Arizona.
TYPE SITE: Kiet Siel Pueblo (NA 2519), Navajo National Monument, Tsegi Canyons, Navajo County, Arizona.
STAGE: Pueblo III.
TIME: ca 1250–ca 1300 A.D.
DESCRIPTION (revised):

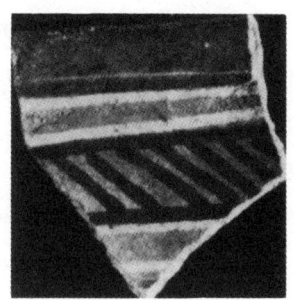

Fig. 24. ($\frac{1}{2}$×).

Constructed: by coiling. *Fired:* in oxidizing atmosphere. *Core:* dark gray to light gray, brownish to pink. *Temper:* about equal amounts quartz sand and light-colored angular fragments; temper frequently conspicuous on surfaces, especially in cross-section and on worn surfaces. *Texture core:* fine to medium. *Vessel walls:* medium strong to strong. *Fracture:* slightly crumbling to shattering. *Surface finish:* bowls usually somewhat bumpy; polished, polishing marks noticeable; sometimes impacted. *Surface color:* orange; color surface and core generally do not contrast except when core is gray. *Fire clouds:* common. *Forms:* bowls; have horizontal handle. *Recorded range thickness bowl walls:* 3.6 to 7.3 mm; greatest individual range recorded, 2.3 mm; average thickness, 5.3 mm. *Rims:* bowls, IA3, IA6, IA7, IIIA3. *Painted decoration:* black, red, and white. *Pigments:* white, kaolin; red, presumably hematite. *Red decoration:* interior—vertical, horizontal, diagonal stripes; often an encircling stripe just below rim. *Black decoration:* narrow lines outlining red areas; horizontal and diagonal hatching in rectangular or triangular panels between red areas; wide staggered lines between series of narrow lines. *White decoration:* usually narrow white lines outlining black lines; sometimes white outlines red areas; exterior—sometimes undecorated but usually one to three red stripes encircling vessel.

COMPARISON: Tusayan Polychrome which is essentially similar but without the white line decoration.

RANGE:

Center of production is Marsh Pass and the Tsegi Canyons, Navajo County, Arizona. Generally distributed from Tuba City, Coconino County to Utah, and from Navajo Mountain, Utah east to Chinle Creek. Occasionally traded to the San Francisco Mountains, Coconino County, Arizona.

KIET SIEL POLYCHROME: new type

SYNONYM: Kayenta Polychrome, Kidder, 1924.
ILLUSTRATIONS: Kidder, 1924, pl. 32; AT 2588 (Fig. 25).
TYPE SPECIMENS: Sherds Nos. AT 2583–2603 in the Type Collection of the Museum of Northern Arizona.
TYPE SITE: Kiet Siel Pueblo (NA 2519), Navajo National Monument, Tsegi Canyons, Navajo County, Arizona.
STATE: Pueblo III.
TIME: ca 1270–ca 1300 A.D.

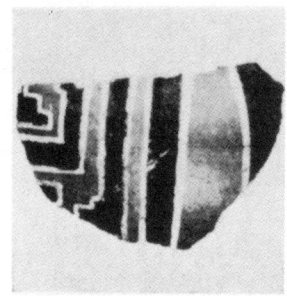

DESCRIPTION: Fig. 25. (½×).

Constructed: by coiling. *Fired:* in oxidizing atmosphere. *Core:* dark gray to light gray; brown to pink. *Temper:* generally about equal amounts quartz sand and light-colored angular fragments; temper frequently conspicuous on unslipped surface; conspicuous in cross-section and on worn surfaces. *Texture core:* fine. *Vessel walls:* medium strong to strong. *Fracture:* slightly crumbling to shattering. *Surface finish:* bowls, sometimes slightly bumpy; polished on interior, sometimes on exterior; scraping marks often conspicuous on exterior; interior always slipped all-over; exterior sometimes slipped; jars, sometimes slightly bumpy; exterior slipped, polished; interior not slipped, not polished; base frequently unslipped. *Surface color:* slip, maroon red; surface color and core contrast only where slipped. *Fire clouds:* common. *Forms:* jars (predominate), bowls (uncommon); bowls have horizontal handle. *Recorded range thickness bowl walls:* 6 mm. *Recorded range thickness jar walls:* 3.8 to 7.6 mm; greatest individual range recorded, 2.6 mm; average thickness, ca 5.5 mm. *Rims:* bowls, IIA3, IIIA3; jars, IA3, IB3, IC3. *Painted decoration:* black and white. *Pigments:* black, manganese (tests by Hawley and Colton); white, kaolin; red (slip), presumably hematite. *Decoration:* bowls—interior, black stripes and black hatching or rectangular cross-hatching in triangular or rectangular panels, stripes and panels outlined with narrow white line; exterior—if unslipped, sometimes horizontal red stripes encircling vessel just below rim; rim, usually black painted line; jar decoration—exterior only, black stripes, solid stepped elements, horizontal or diagonal hatching in rectangular, triangular, circular, or stepped panels; wide staggered lines in series in horizontal panels; hatched panels framed in black lines of about same width as hatchures; stripes, panels, solid elements outlined by narrow white lines; rims, usually black painted line.

COMPARISON: Pinedale Polychrome, black paint sometimes glaze; temper, almost entirely light-colored angular fragments; slip, brick-red to orange-yellow, occasionally tan; bowls always slipped on both surfaces; interior decoration uncommonly includes white; exterior decoration always black elements with white outline.

Fourmile Polychrome, black paint always glaze; temper mostly light-colored angular fragments; slip often not well-polished, frequently powdery; bowls always slipped on both surfaces; bowl exteriors decorated with horizontal band with principal elements white lines; solid white areas sometimes occur; also white lines with superimposed black dots; "centiform" element frequent; occasional life forms.

Showlow Polychrome, white slip on bowl interiors and on upper portion of jar exteriors.

RANGE:

Center of production is Marsh Pass and the Tsegi Canyons, Navajo County, Arizona.

WHITE MOUNTAIN RED WARE

The range of this ware for years has commonly been considered as centering in the Little Colorado River Valley. This impression probably was gained from the abundance of sherds of types in certain series, or because these types were conspicuous. The center of this ware area, when purity and density are considered, appears to be more restricted to the rough mountainous country of the southeastern part of the Mogollon Rim, or more specifically to the White Mountains Area, Arizona, from which mountains the ware name was taken.

Basic techniques of construction indicate that this ware is somehow related to the earlier Mogollon Brown Ware.

In this ware there appears a new principle in decorative technique. White paint in line decoration appears on nearly every type, and is thus one of the most conspicuous characters. During the latter part of the life of this ware, however, white paint was also commonly used as a base for black paint, giving a black-on-white-on-red effect. Solid white areas in decoration occurred rarely on St. Johns Polychrome but is a dominant character of Showlow Polychrome.

KEY 6: WHITE MOUNTAIN RED WARE

1. Exterior surface slipped.. 2
   Exterior surface corrugated............... Wingate Corrugated (p. 119)
   Exterior surface not slipped............... Houck Polychrome (p. 121)
2. Slip orange or yellow, thick, bright; temper inconspicuous on surface
   Key k (p. 123)
   Key h (p. 104)
   Slip brownish, less thick, bright; temper conspicuous on surface.......
   Key l (p. 125)
   Slip red... 3
   Slip white or cream.. 4
3. White line decoration more than 3 mm wide............. Key h (p. 104)
   White line decoration rarely 3 mm wide................. Key i (p. 113)
   No white line decoration..................................... 4
4. Both surfaces same color.................................... 5
   Both surfaces different color.......................... Key i (p. 113)
   Key j (p. 118)
   Showlow Polychrome (p. 111)
5. Exterior decoration black only........... Pinedale Black-on-red (p. 106)
   Exterior decoration black and white and red........... Key h (p. 104)
   No exterior decoration....................................... 6
6. Interior decoration glaze............... Pinnawa Black-on-red (p. 113)
   Interior decoration not glaze................................ 7
7. Surface color red..................... Wingate Black-on-red (p. 118)
   Puerco Black-on-red (p. 120)
   Surface color not red.. 8
8. Slip orange or yellow, thick, bright; temper inconspicuous on surface..
   Klageto Black-on-yellow (p. 123)
   Slip brownish, more thin, less bright; temper conspicuous on surface..
   Kintiel Black-on-orange (p. 125).

WHITE MOUNTAIN RED WARE: new ware

SYNONYMS: (a) Red Ware, Hough, 1903; (b) Little Colorado Ware, Schmidt, 1928, p. 289; (c) Little Colorado Red Ware, Hargrave, 1935, a, p. 22.
STAGES: Pueblo III–IV.
TIME: pre-1200–Post-1400 A.D.

DESCRIPTION:

Constructed: by coiling. *Fired:* in oxidizing atmosphere. *Core:* gray, black, cream, buff, pink, orange, brownish to brick-red. *Carbon streak:* occasional. *Temper:* light-colored angular fragments, mostly medium fine of fairly uniform size (occasionally varying in size to 2 mm in diameter), usually grayish in reduced, yellowish in oxidized portions; sometimes black, red, or pinkish fragments; quartz sand grains rare or absent, except in Fourmile Polychrome and Showlow Polychrome; temper usually conspicuous in cross-section and on worn surfaces; not conspicuous through slip. *Texture core:* medium; usually slightly crumbling; occasionally somewhat porous; occasionally shattering. *Vessel walls:* medium strong to strong. *Surface finish:* bowls, always slipped on both surfaces, except Houck Polychrome and Wingate Corrugated (which are slipped only on interior); jars, always slipped on exterior (only); slip usually heavy, usually well-polished, frequently powdery, occasionally flakes, occasionally crazed; sometimes slightly bumpy; Wingate Corrugated, exterior not smoothed. *Surface color:* red, pinkish, brownish, buff, cream (Querino Polychrome, exterior), orange, light yellow, rarely slate gray in part (Klageto Black-on-yellow, sometimes), in part white (some types); color core and surface, generally contrast. *Forms:* bowls (predominate), jars. *Recorded range thickness vessel walls:* 2.8 to 8.2 mm; greatest individual range recorded, 2.3 mm; average thickness, ca 5.5 mm. *Rims:* bowls, IA3, IA6, IA7, IA9, IA11, IB6, IB7, IIA3, IIA6, IIA7, IIB3, IIB6, IIIA1, IIIA3, IIIA7, IIIB7; jars, IIIA3. *Painted decoration:* black, white, red; black usually glaze, sometimes gritty, sometimes vitreous, occasionally weak and watery. *Pigments:* usually copper, lead, and some manganese; occasionally iron-carbon when non-glaze; white pigment, usually somewhat chalky and fugitive, presumably kaolin; red pigment, dull, thin, and watery, sometimes thick, almost like slip, probably hematite. *Decoration:* bowl interiors, usually black paint on red slip, sometimes black and black-and-red on white slip, sometimes black-and-white on red slip; exteriors, usually black, white or black-and-white on red slip, sometimes black on white slip; jar exteriors, same as bowl interiors.

COMPARISONS: San Juan Red Ware, surface never cream; carbon streak common; surface color and core rarely contrast; temper, about equal amounts opaque angular fragments and quartz sand, conspicuous through slip in some types; mica-like flakes fairly frequent in some types; slip always red when present, several types unslipped; jars fairly frequent, predominate in one type; black paint always non-glaze.

RANGE:

Zuni Indian Reservation in West-central New Mexico to Chaco Canyon; East-central Arizona from Springerville north to Ganado, Navajo County; west along Mogollon Rim to San Francisco Mountains; North-east from San Francisco Mountains to Ganado; also south of Mogollon Rim to Sierra Ancha and the Tonto Basin, Gila County, Arizona. Trade specimens have been reported from Casas Grandes, Chihuahua, Mexico, to Mesa Verde, Colorado, and from Casa Grande, Pinal County, Arizona, to Kwaituki Pueblo on Oraibi Wash, fourteen miles north of Oraibi Pueblo, Hopi Reservation, Navajo County, Arizona.

FOURMILE SERIES

A prominent group of types within this ware occurs in the neighborhood of Showlow where intensive studies of types in this group has been made (Haury, 1931; Gladwin, W. & H. S., 1931). This series represents types that were used as a basis for the study of the White Mountain Red Ware. Because Fourmile Series is best understood of all the series in this ware, it is, therefore, presented first.

The series name is taken from a prominent and well-known type, Fourmile Polychrome.

KEY h: FOURMILE SERIES

White as decorative base....................Showlow Polychrome (p. 111)
Exterior decoration black only..............Pinedale Black-on-red (p. 106)
Exterior decoration white only..............St. Johns Polychrome (p. 104)
Exterior decoration black and white; no massed white areas..........
            Pinedale Polychrome (p. 107)
Exterior and interior decoration black and white....................
            Fourmile Polychrome (p. 109)

ST. JOHNS POLYCHROME

SYNONYMS: (a) Black and white on red, Spier, 1917, p. 282; (b) Three Color painted ware, Spier, 1919, Table I; (c) Little Colorado redware, Hargrave, 1929, p. 3; (d) Little Colorado black-on-red, Hargrave, loc. cit.; (e) Chevlon Ware, Hough, 1930, p. 16; (f) Little Colorado Polychrome, Haury, 1931, p. 30; (g) Black-on-orange-red, Haury, loc. cit., p. 78.

DESCRIBED BY: Haury, loc. cit., p. 30.

NAMED BY: Gladwin, W. & H. S., 1931, pp. 36–37.

ILLUSTRATIONS: Haury, 1931, pl. 8, Nos. 1–4; Gladwin, W. & H. S., loc. cit., pl. XXXV (colored); AT 1831 (Fig. 26).

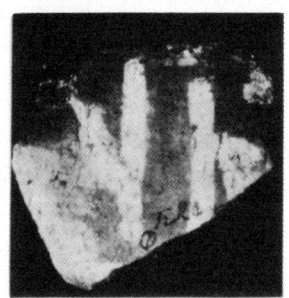

Fig. 26. (½×).

TYPE SPECIMENS: Gila Pueblo, Globe, Arizona. Cotype sherds Nos. AT 1216–1218, 1830, 1832–1833, 1844, 1846–1848 in the Type Collection of the Museum of Northern Arizona.

TYPE SITE: St. Johns: 4:1 (Gladwin, W. & H. S., loc. cit.).

STAGE: Pueblo III.
TIME: 1100–1200 A.D.

DESCRIPTION (revised):
Constructed: by coiling. *Fired:* in oxidizing atmosphere. *Core:* gray; frequently pinkish or tan. *Temper:* angular fragments greatly variable in size, many 2 mm or more, grayish in reduced, yellowish or tan in oxidized portions, rarely pinkish; grains quartz sand rare. *Texture core:* medium. *Vessel walls:* generally strong. *Fracture:* slightly crumbling; occasionally slightly friable. *Surface finish:* surfaces generally highly polished; usually bumpy and coarsely crazed; heavily slipped on both surfaces. *Surface color:* red to orange-red (according to Mera, shades are 4B11, 4C11, 4G11, 4G12; extreme variations, 3A10, 11E7, 12B7, 12C2—1934, p. 14); color core and surface contrast. *Form:* bowl. *Recorded range thickness bowl walls:* 4 to 7 mm; greatest individual range recorded, 1.2 mm; average thickness, ca 5 mm. *Rims:* bowls, IA3, IA6, IA7, IIA7, IIIA7. *Painted decoration:* black and white; black, weak brown to rich deep black; not glaze; white, chalky, sometimes fugitive. *Decoration:* interior, "mostly of repeated interlocking or opposed solid and hatched figures. These are confined in a broad horizontal zone by two narrow framing lines, one below the rim and the second toward the center" (Haury, 1931, p. 3C). "Often complicated and highly specialized. Hatched and solid patterns are the general rule, and the hatching is usually of the southern or longitudinal type" (Gladwin, W. & H. S., 1931, p. 37). "Exterior decoration is made up of broad, rudely drawn, white stepped lines or terraced figures. These are also limited to a horizontal zone below the rim but never as wide as the one on the interior" (Haury, 1931).

COMPARISON: Wingate Polychrome, has interior slip powdery; exterior decoration of narrow white lines. Heshotauthla Polychrome, has narrow narrow white lines on exterior but also black glaze paint on interior, not crazed.

RANGE:
"From Pecos to Casa Grande, from Mesa Verde to Casas Grandes, it occurs in the great ruins of the Classic Period. A definite focus lies within a radius of 50 miles of St. Johns" (Gladwin, W. & H. S., loc. cit., p. 37); northwest to the San Francisco Mountains, Coconino County, Arizona.

REMARKS:
Further separation from this type probably will be made when an adequate study has been made of St. Johns Polychrome

from the Tonto Basin, Gila County, Arizona. Cotype sherds AT 1830–1836 are from the 1204 A.D. horizon at Showlow Pueblo (NA 1003) and were collected by the National Geographic Society Beam Expedition. All were identified by Haury.

PINEDALE BLACK-ON-RED: new type

SYNONYM: Pinedale Polychrome, in part, Haury, 1932 a, p. 422.
DESCRIBED BY: Haury, loc. cit.
TYPE SPECIMENS: Sherds Nos. AT 1709–1710, 1713, 1715–1719, 1721, 1723–1725, 1729, 1839–1943 in the Type Collection of the Museum of Northern Arizona.
TYPE SITE: Pinedale Pueblo (NA 1069), Pinedale, Silver Creek drainage Navajo County, Arizona.
STAGE: Pueblo III.
TIME: Between 1200–1300 A.D.

DESCRIPTION:

Constructed: by coiling. *Fired:* in oxidizing atmosphere. *Core:* gray; sometimes pinkish. *Carbon streak:* occasional. *Temper:* small angular fragments nearly of uniform size, grayish in reduced, yellowish or tan in oxidized portions, rarely red or black; grains quartz sand rare; temper inconspicuous when core dark; occasionally conspicuous on worn surfaces. *Texture core:* fine. *Vessel walls:* medium strong. *Fracture:* slightly friable. *Surface finish:* both surfaces heavily slipped; slip frequently powdery; occasionally fairly well-polished; occasionally crazed. *Surface color:* maroon to reddish to orange yellow; color core and surface generally contrast. *Forms:* bowls. *Recorded range thickness bowl walls:* 3.2 to 6.7 mm; greatest individual range recorded, 2.1 mm; average thickness (15 sherds), 4.1 mm. *Rims:* bowls, IA3, IA6, IIIA7. *Painted decoration:* black glaze; paint sometimes dull, usually heavy and gritty. *Decoration:* interior and exterior surfaces; rarely exterior surface only; decorative treatment bold; interior decoration, frequently one encircling stripe, or one to four wide parallel lines just below rim, horizontal, diagonal, or vertical hatching of narrow lines in rectangular or triangular panels, occasionally staggered lines and ticked lines; exterior, often one stripe or 2 or 3 parallel wide lines just below rim, horizontal and diagonal stripes, occasionally staggered lines.

COMPARISON: Wingate Black-on-red has black decoration on interior surface only, more frequent hatching, hatchures usually fine, stripes and wide lines infrequent, designs usually crudely executed, paint never glaze.

RANGE:

Probably conterminous with Pinedale Polychrome. Sherds

have been examined from Pinedale, Showlow, and Fourmile pueblos, Navajo County, Arizona.

REMARKS:

Pinedale Black-on-red is included in Haury's second description of Pinedale Polychrome as he says "black decoration on vessel interiors; black and *usually* white on exteriors" (Gladwin, W. & H. S., 1931, p. 41). Pinedale Black-on-red is therefore characterized by a black painted decoration on both the interior and exterior surfaces of bowls. There is no white paint on either surface. Pinedale Polychrome has a black and white exterior decoration on bowls.

PINEDALE POLYCHROME

SYNONYMS: (a) Red Ware, Fewkes, 1904, p. 58; (b) Three color glazed and Painted Ware, Spier, 1919, Table I; (c) Chevlon Ware, Hough, 1930, p. 16; (d) Proto-Fourmile Polychrome, Haury, 1930, p. 4.

DESCRIBED BY: Haury, 1930, p. 4; 1931, pp. 64–68; Gladwin, W. & H. S., 1931, p. 41.

NAMED BY: Haury, 1931, p. 65.

ILLUSTRATION: AT 1742 (Fig. 27).

TYPE SPECIMENS: Gila Pueblo, Globe, Arizona. Cotype sherds Nos. AT 1712, 1714, 1722, 1726, 1728, 1730–1738, 1740–1748, 1750–1751, 1826–1827 in the Type Collection of the Museum of Northern Arizona.

TYPE SITE: Pinedale Pueblo (NA 1069; Holbrook: 12:11), Pinedale, Silver Creek drainage, Navajo County, Arizona.

STAGE: Pueblo III–IV.

TIME: ca 1250–1325 A.D.

Fig. 27. (½×).

DESCRIPTION (revised):

Constructed: by coiling. *Fired:* in oxidizing atmosphere. *Core:* gray or tan; sometimes slight pink tint. *Carbon streak:* occasional. *Temper:* small angular fragments (ground pot-sherds) nearly uniform size, grayish in reduced, yellowish or tan in oxidized portions; occasionally red or black angular fragments; grains quartz sand rare; temper conspicuous in cross-section when core and temper contrast; occasionally conspicuous on worn surfaces. *Texture core:* fine. *Vessel walls:* medium strong. *Fracture:* slightly friable, crumbling. *Surface finish:* both surfaces heavily slipped; slip thick, usually fairly well-polished, hard, rarely powdery. *Surface color:* brick-red to orange-yellow, occasionally tan (D.C. plates 5F12, 5G11—Mera, 1934, p. 16);

core and surface color generally contrast. *Forms:* bowls, jars (rare). *Recorded range thickness bowl walls:* 3.3 to 6.2 mm; greatest individual range recorded, 1.6 mm; average thickness (27 sherds), 4.8 mm. *Rims:* bowls, IA3, IA6, IA7, IA11, IIIA3. *Painted decoration:* black and white; glaze and non-glaze black and non-glaze white; dark paint dull black to distinct black glaze, generally lustrous, often in relief but nearly free of gritty particles, glaze paint frequently ran, black paint sometimes brownish and translucent, occasionally purple tint; white paint, chalky, often fugitive. *Pigments:* dark, combination lead, copper, manganese; white, presumably kaolin. *Decoration:* interior designs nearly always black, exterior design black and white; "considerable variation in interior bowl design; the area may be treated as a whole, divided into quadrants, or made to show a circular unpainted area in the bottom; patterns may be with or without borders at the rim. Balanced solid and hatched elements, areas filled with longitudinal hatching, and dotted lines predominate . . . Exterior designs may be narrow contiguous patterns, in a horizontal band, which is framed above and below with black stripes always outlined in white, the upper stripe being about 6 to 12 mm below rim but more often in disconnected panels, geometric figures and sometimes life forms, executed in black with white outlines" (Haury: Gladwin, W. & H. S., loc. cit., pp. 41–42).

COMPARISONS: Fourmile Polychrome, slip usually maroon red, usually not highly polished, often powdery; black paint always glaze, sometimes vitreous, usually in relief with brush marks evident; bowl interiors, always white decoration, interior rim stripe almost always present, main zone of decoration often separated from rim stripe by undecorated band; bowl exteriors, almost always decorated with horizontal band immediately below rim, upper black framing stripe outlined in white on lower edge only; designs within band usually formed of white lines, black elements less frequent; solid white masses and conventional life forms occasional on either surface; jar designs similar to bowls; in general, designs more bold, often arranged in contiguous non-repeating scheme rather than in symmetrical sectors or panels.

Kiet Siel Polychrome, temper mostly quartz sand; slip maroon red; bowl exteriors in some cases slipped but undecorated, in other cases unslipped and decorated only with horizontal red stripes below rim.

Showlow Polychrome has white slip on bowl interiors and on upper part of jar exteriors.

RANGE:

"Silver Creek drainage, south to the Salt River in Tonto Basin and east of Sierra Ancha" (Haury: Gladwin, W. & H. S., loc. cit., p. 42). Found also north to Fourmile Pueblo (NA 1055) near Taylor, Navajo County, Arizona. One sherd (AT 3012) from Turkey Hill Pueblo (NA 660), Flagstaff, Coconino County, Arizona.

OXIDIZING ATMOSPHERE

FOURMILE POLYCHROME

SYNONYMS: (a) Red Ware, Fewkes, 1904 p. 58; (b) Three color glazed and painted Ware, Spier, 1919, Table I; (c) White-bordered-Black-on-red, Schmidt, 1928, p. 294; (d) Chevlon Ware, Hough, 1930, p. 16.

DESCRIBED BY: Haury, 1930, p. 4; 1931, pp. 31–40; (Haury) Gladwin, W. & H. S., 1931, p. 43.

NAMED BY: Haury, 1930, p. 4.

ILLUSTRATIONS: Hough, 1903, Pl. 9 (colored); Haury, 1931, Figs. 7–10, pl. 11–12; Gladwin, W. & H. S., Pl. 12 (colored); Clarke, 1935, pl. XVII (colored); AT 1798 (Fig. 28).

Fig. 28. ($\frac{1}{2}$×).

TYPE SPECIMENS: Gila Pueblo, Globe, Arizona. Cotype sherds Nos. AT 1739, 1753, 1772–1778, 1780–1788, 1791–1804, 1828–1829, 1849–1856, 2389 in the Type Collection of the Museum of Northern Arizona.

TYPE SITE: Fourmile Pueblo (NA 1055; Holbrook: 12:2), Taylor, Navajo County, Arizona.

STAGE: Pueblo IV.

TIME: ca. 1350–1400 A.D.

DESCRIPTION (revised):

Constructed: by coiling. *Fired:* in oxidizing atmosphere. *Core:* gray, sometimes slight pink tint. *Carbon streak:* occasional. *Temper:* small angular fragments (ground pot-sherds) of nearly uniform size, grayish in reduced, yellowish or tan in oxidized portions; occasionally red or black fragments; grains quartz sand fairly frequent; temper inconspicuous in cross-section when core light-colored; conspicuous when core dark; temper occasionally conspicuous on worn surfaces. *Texture core:* fine. *Vessel walls:* medium strong to strong. *Fracture:* crumbling to shattering. *Surface finish:* heavily slipped and fairly well-polished often powdery, occasionally crazed; both surfaces bowls and exterior surface jars, slipped. *Surface color:* maroon red to dark brown, sometimes almost black in heavily over-fired specimens; core and surface color, generally contrast. *Forms:* bowls, pitchers (rare—see Fewkes, 1904, colored plate LIX d), jars. *Recorded range thickness bowl walls:* 3.7 to 7.6 mm; greatest individual range recorded, 1.9 mm; average thickness (64 sherds), 5.2 mm. *Rims:* bowls, IA3, IA4, IA6, IA7, IIA3, IIA4, IIA6, IIA7, IIIA3, IIIA7, also IA9 (Haury, 1931, p. 33, f). *Painted decoration:* black glaze and flat white; black paint dull, lustrous, sometimes vitreous, sometimes gritty, permanent; white paint, soft and chalky, frequently fugitive. *Pigments:* dark, combination lead, copper, and manganese; white, presumably kaolin. *Decoration:* free and bold; geometric and occasionally conventional life forms; decoration bowls—interior, black stripe 6 to 12 mm wide just below rim, bordered by narrow white line on lower side only, occasionally no other interior decoration, usually undecorated band is decorated zone covering entire central part of interior, includes hatching in triangular, rectangular, and curved panels framed with wide black lines or black stripes outlined with narrow white lines, sometimes ticked in white; also solid black stepped areas and stripes, outlined in white; horizontal or diagonal white lines occasionally with black dots superimposed, occasionally massed white areas; sometimes staggered lines; rims usually plain, rarely painted with white stripe with black ticks or dots superimposed; exterior—confined to band beginning immediately below rim, band 35 to 80 mm wide, framed by black stripes, upper stripe outlined in white on lower side only; lower stripe outlined in white on both sides; decoration within band mostly white horizontal and diagonal narrow or wide lines, white open stepped elements, frets, "centiform" elements; sometimes black dots superimposed on white lines; sometimes solid black triangles and stepped elements outlined in white; small jars—rims are sometimes painted white and embellished with simple black patterns; main body of jar treated with triangles, stepped figures and frets in black and white over a red background (Gladwin, W. & H. S., loc. cit.).

COMPARISONS: Pinedale Polychrome, color slip usually brick-red, orange, or occasionally tan; slip almost always well-polished, hard; black paint sometimes non-glaze, occasionally dull brown; glaze usually more lustrous, sometimes brownish, purplish or greenish; rim stripe in only about 50% of cases, main zone of decoration usually covers nearly entire area: bowl exteriors, usually decorated with isolated black elements outlined in white; when continuous band occurs, upper black framing line, 6 to 12 mm below rim, is outlined in white on both edges; use of white lines as outliners for black areas, rare; never solid white masses or conventional life forms on either surface; in general designs less bold and decorative field on interiors almost always divided into symmetrical sectors or panels, never continuous, non-repeating design.

Kiet Siel Polychrome, temper mostly quartz sand; slip darker red, well-polished and hard; black paint always non-glaze; bowl exteriors slipped but undecorated or unslipped and decorated only with horizontal red encircling stripes below rim; white lines never used except as outliners for black elements; black dots superimposed on white lines not recorded; "dentiform" element not recorded.

Showlow Polychrome, white slip on bowl interiors and upper part of jar exteriors.

RANGE:

"The major concentration lies east of the Sierra Ancha in an area that can be defined on the west by Cherry Creek, on the east by White River, on the south by Salt River, and extending almost to the Little Colorado on the north. The focal point, on the basis of the size and density of the ruins, is located below the Mogollon Rim . . . " (Haury, 1934, pp. 130–131). Fourmile Polychrome has been reported only from Arizona. For detailed distribution of the type see Haury, 1934, p. 129, fig. 23.

SHOWLOW POLYCHROME: new type

SYNONYM: Fourmile Polychrome, in part, Haury, 1931, p. 35.
DESCRIBED BY: Haury, loc. cit.
ILLUSTRATIONS: Fewkes, 1904, Fig. 98, colored plates XXI, XXII, XXXVIII b, XLI, XLII b, LIX a, and LXII d; Haury, 1931, fig. 7, pl. 11; Clarke, 1935, pl. XXIII; (Fig. 29).
TYPE SPECIMENS: Type jar No. 393/1837 and sherds Nos. AT 1896–1909, 1911–1928 in the Type Collection of the Museum of Northern Arizona.
TYPE SITE: Showlow Pueblo (NA 1003), Showlow, Navajo County, Arizona.
STAGE: Pueblo IV.
TIME: 1375–ca 1400 A.D.

Fig. 29. ($\frac{1}{6}$×).

DESCRIPTION (revised):

Constructed: by coiling. *Fired:* in oxidizing atmosphere. *Core:* gray, sometimes slight pink tint. *Carbon streak:* occasional. *Temper:* small angular fragments (ground pot-sherds) nearly uniform size, grayish in reduced, yellowish or tan in oxidized portions; occasionally red or black fragments; grains quartz sand fairly frequent; temper inconspicuous in cross-section when core light-colored, conspicuous when core dark, occasionally conspicuous on worn surfaces. *Texture core:* fine. *Vessel walls:* medium strong. *Fracture:* slightly crumbling to slightly shattering. *Surface finish:* surface heavily slipped, frequently crazed; surface bowls heavily slipped (with red) on exterior and (with white) on interior; white slip rough, often coarsely crazed; exterior surface jars, body and base slipped with red, neck with white; red slip rarely yellowish or tan; on both bowls and jars, red slip polished and hard, white slip usually unpolished and powdery; rarely polished. *Surface color:* in part red to orange-yellow; in part gray to white; core and surface color generally contrast in part. *Forms:* jars (predominate), bowls. *Recorded range thickness bowl walls:* 3.9 to 6.9 mm; greatest individual range recorded, 1.5 mm; average thickness, ca 5 mm. *Rims:* bowls, IA4, IA6, IA7, IIA3, IIA7; jars, IA3, IA7, IIIA3.

Painted decoration: black and white; black generally lustrous, often in relief; glaze paint sometimes ran; black paint sometimes brownish and translucent; occasionally purplish or greenish tint; white paint, chalky, sometimes fugitive. *Pigments:* black, combination lead, copper, and manganese; white, presumably kaolin. *Decoration:* free and bold; geometric, sometimes conventional life forms; jars—neck and small part of upper body covered with white slip, carried well down on neck interior; white zone painted in black, usually with simple independent elements such as crosses, turkey tracks, dots, stepped lines or paired vertical bars; sometimes three or more narrow or wide horizontal lines around neck; often wide stripe just below rim on both exterior and interior with elements pendent from exterior stripe; entire exterior surface below white zone slipped in red; on red field, broad horizontal band framed by black stripes, upper stripe painted over junction of white lines; stripes sometimes outlined in white lines; band usually divided into panels, contains solid triangles, stepped elements, hatching in black frets, often outlined in white; occasionally solid white panels; bowls—interior, covered with heavy white slip, surface often pitted; encircling stripe black glaze paint just below rim; main design area in center of vessel in black, composed of bands framed by two parallel narrow lines on each side with interlocking serrated stripes of black and white within; rectangular panels with diagonal hatching, sometimes with staggered lines; bowl exteriors—slipped with red; horizontal band black and white decoration, essentially same as on exterior Fourmile Polychrome, or occasionally same as exterior Pinedale Polychrome; rims, red or white.

COMPARISONS: Fourmile Polychrome, Pinedale Polychrome, Kiet Siel Polychrome, do not have white slip; jar sherds from red-slipped portions of vessels may be sometimes indistinguishable from Fourmile and Pinedale polychromes.

RANGE:

Silver Creek drainage, Navajo County and Canyon Creek, Sierra Ancha, Gila County, Arizona.

REMARKS:

This type is recognized because it has both bowl and jar forms showing influence from factors that resulted in the use of a white slipped decorative base that became of prominence in another region (see Roosevelt Red Ware). In all other characters it is White Mountain Red Ware.

OXIDIZING ATMOSPHERE 113

HAWIKUH SERIES

In general this series is characterized by the occurrence of glaze paint.

KEY i: HAWIKUH SERIES

Red paint, not glaze, on white slip...........Adamana Polychrome (p. 117)
White slip interior only; no red paint..........Wallace Polychrome (p. 114)
White slip exterior only; no red paint..........Pinnawa Polychrome (p. 115)
No white slip; no white decoration..........Pinnawa Black-on-red (p. 113)
No white slip; white line decoration......Heshotauthla Polychrome (p. 113)

PINNAWA BLACK-ON-RED: new type

SYNONYMS: (a) Black or green glaze on red or orange red, Hodge, 1923 p. 29; (b) Zuni Glazed Ware, Gladwin, W. & H. S., 1934, fig. 3.

DESCRIBED BY: Hodge, loc. cit.

TYPE SPECIMENS: Cotype sherds Nos. AT 2159–2160 in the Type Collection of the Museum of Northern Arizona.

TYPE SITE: Pinnawa Pueblo (NA 793), Zuni Indian Reservation, New Mexico.

STAGE: Pueblo III.

TIME: ca 1200–1250 A.D.

DESCRIPTION (revised):

Constructed: by coiling. *Fired:* in oxidizing atmosphere. *Core:* gray to black. *Temper:* angular fragments varying size, to 2 mm but vast majority much smaller; grayish in reduced, light-yellowish or tan in oxidized portions, occasionally pinkish; no quartz sand. *Texture core:* fine. *Vessel walls:* strong. *Fracture:* shattering. *Surface finish:* exterior vessel surface and interior surface jar neck, heavily slipped, slip highly polished; occasionally flakes. *Surface color:* red or orange-red; color surface and core, contrast. *Forms:* bowls, jars. *Recorded range thickness jar walls:* 5.1 to 6.8 mm; greatest individual range recorded, 1.7 mm; average thickness, ca 6 mm. *Recorded range thickness bowl walls:* 4.8 to 6 mm; greatest individual range recorded, 1.2 mm; average thickness, ca 5.5 mm. *Rims:* jars, IIIA3. *Painted decoration:* black glaze paint, sometimes greenish. *Decoration:* interior bowls only, narrow and wide horizontal lines; exterior jars only, wide diagonal lines.

RANGE:

Zuni Indian Reservation, New Mexico.

HESHOTAUTHLA POLYCHROME

SYNONYMS: (a) Black or green glaze on red or orange-red, Hodge, 1923, p. 29; (b) Zuni Glazed Ware, Gladwin, W. & H. S., 1934, fig. 3.

DESCRIBED BY: Hodge, loc. cit.

NAMED BY: Kidder, A. V. (Kidder & Shepard, 1936, pp. 363–366).

TYPE SPECIMENS: Cotype sherds Nos. AT 1356, 2154–2158, 2161–2163 in the Type Collection of the Museum of Northern Arizona.

TYPE SITE: Pinnawa Pueblo (NA 973), Zuni Indian Reservation, New Mexico.

STAGE: Pueblo III.

TIME: ca 1200–1250 A.D.

DESCRIPTION (revised):
Constructed: by coiling. *Fired:* in oxidizing atmosphere. *Core:* gray, pinkish to buff. *Temper:* angular fragments greatly variable size, to 2 mm but vast majority much smaller; grayish in reduced, light yellowish or tan in oxidized portion, rarely pinkish; no quartz sand. *Texture core:* fine. *Vessel walls:* medium strong to strong. *Fracture:* slightly crumbling. *Surface finish:* interior and exterior bowl surfaces heavily slipped; slip highly polished, occasionally flakes off; exterior surface jars, heavily slipped. *Surface color:* red; color surface and core usually contrast. *Forms:* bowls (predominate), jars. *Recorded range thickness bowl walls:* 3.4 mm to 6.3 mm; greatest individual range recorded, 1.4 mm; average thickness, ca 5.5 mm. *Rims:* bowls, IA3, IA7, IIIA1, IIIA7. *Painted decoration:* black or greenish glaze and white non-glaze paint. *Pigments:* dark, some copper and lead (tests by F. G. Hawley); white pigment, presumably kaolin. *Decoration:* bowls—interior, black paint, narrow and wide lines, stripes; usually one or more stripes just below rim; carelessly executed; paint usually ran; exterior, white decoration of fine narrow and wide lines, usually one to three lines just below rim; diagonal lines, open diamonds, or stepped panels.

COMPARISON: St. Johns Polychrome, no black glaze paint; stripes or wide line decoration on exterior.

RANGE:
Zuni Indian Reservation, New Mexico.

WALLACE POLYCHROME: new type

SYNONYMS: (a) Red Ware, Green Decoration, Hough, 1903, p. 74; (b) Polychrome Ware, Hough, loc. cit., pl. 75; (c) Glazed Ware, Spier, 1917, p. 312; (d) Three Color Glazed and Painted Ware, Spier, 1919, Table I; (e) Black, green, or purplish glaze on white or cream slip, Hodge, 1923, p. 29; (f) Zuni Glazed Ware, Gladwin, W. & H. S., 1934, fig. 3.

DESCRIBED BY: Hodge, loc. cit.

TYPE SPECIMENS: Cotype sherds Nos. AT 1353, 1934–1938, 1940–1946 in the Type Collection of the Museum of Northern Arizona.

TYPE SITE: Pinnawa Pueblo (NA 973), Zuni Indian Reservation, New Mexico.

OXIDIZING ATMOSPHERE 115

STAGES: Pueblo III (?)–Pueblo IV.
TIME: ca 1300–1400 A.D.
DESCRIPTION (revised):
   Constructed: by coiling. *Fired:* in oxidizing atmosphere. *Core:* dark gray to cream, sometimes pink tint. *Temper:* medium fine angular fragments fairly uniform size, grayish in reduced, yellowish or orange in oxidized portions, occasionally pinkish or red; grains quartz sand rare. *Texture core:* fine. *Vessel walls:* medium strong to strong. *Fracture:* slightly crumbling to shattering. *Surface finish:* surfaces heavily slipped; generally highly polished; scraping and temper scars frequently noticeable; slips frequently powdery, occasionally crazed. *Surface color:* brownish through red to buff on exterior, white or cream on interior; color surface and core, contrast. *Form:* bowl. *Recorded range thickness bowl walls:* 3.4 to 5.7 mm; greatest individual range recorded, 1.2 mm; average thickness (22 sherds), 4.8 mm. *Rims:* bowls, IA7, IB7. *Painted decoration:* black, green, or purplish glaze; flat white paint; dark paints weak and watery, sometimes gritty; white paint, chalky, frequently partially obliterated, fugitive. *Pigments:* glaze—lead, copper and manganese (tests by F. G. Hawley); white pigment, presumably kaolin. *Designs:* interior—black, green, or purplish on white slip; narrow and wide lines, mostly horizontal, usually horizontal stripe just below rim; solid stepped masses, series opposed solid diamonds, sometimes narrow horizontal bands of four narrow lines in series, staggered squares or rectangles between; exterior—horizontal and diagonal narrow white lines, sometimes one line just below rim, on red slip; red slip covers rim and extends down interior surface about 5 mm.

COMPARISONS: Adamana Polychrome, interior decoration both red and black (or greenish) lines. Pinnawa Polychrome, red slip on bowl interior and exterior, in part; white on bowl and jar exteriors, in part.

RANGE:
   In general, Petrified Forest National Monument, Arizona, and contiguous localities; east to and including the western part of the Zuni Indian Reservation, New Mexico.

REMARKS:
   There is no exterior glaze decoration on this type.

PINNAWA POLYCHROME: new type

SYNONYMS: (a) Red Ware, Green Decoration, Hough, 1903, pl. 74; (b) Polychrome Ware, Hough, loc. cit., pl. 75; (c) Glazed Ware, Spier, 1917, p. 312; (d) Three color glazed and painted Ware, Spier, 1919, Table I; (e) Black, green, or purplish glaze on white or cream slip, Hodge, 1923, p.

29; (f) Zuni Glaze, Haury, 1931, p. 76; (g) Zuni Glazed Ware, Gladwin, W. & H. S., 1934, fig. 3.

TYPE SPECIMENS: Cotype sherds Nos. AT 1948–1949, 1951 in the Type Collection of the Museum of Northern Arizona.

TYPE SITE: Heshotauthla Pueblo, Zuni Indian Reservation, New Mexico.

STAGE: Pueblo IV.

TIME: ca 1300–1400 A.D.

DESCRIPTION (revised):

Constructed: by coiling. *Fired:* in oxidizing atmosphere. *Core:* dark gray to cream, or yellowish, sometimes pink tint. *Temper:* medium size angular fragments, fairly uniform size, grayish in reduced, yellowish or orange in oxidized portions, occasionally pink or red; occasional grains quartz sand. *Texture core:* fine. *Vessel walls:* medium strong to strong. *Fracture:* slightly crumbling to shattering. *Surface finish:* bowl surfaces heavily slipped on both surfaces; jars slipped on exterior surface; generally polished; scraping marks fairly noticeable. *Surface color:* brownish through red to dull orange, in part; white in part; color core and surface contrast; slips, red on bowl interior and exterior, in part, white on bowl and jar exteriors, in part; frequently powdery; occasionally crazed. *Forms:* bowls, dippers, jars. *Recorded range thickness bowl walls:* 3.6 to 6.6 mm; greatest individual range recorded, 1.1 mm; average thickness, ca 5 mm. *Rims:* bowls, IIIA3. *Painted decoration:* black, green, or purplish glaze; flat white; dark paints weak and watery, sometimes gritty; white paint chalky, frequently partially obliterated. *Decoration:* bowls, interior, black hatching or narrow lines in rectangular or triangular panels on white slip, or black stripes, narrow lines and solid elements on red slip; exterior bowls, black wide lines and stripes on white slip, or black stripes outlined in narrow white lines on red slip; slip never same color on both surfaces; jars—exterior, black and white stripes on red slip.

COMPARISONS: Adamana Polychrome, has white slip on interior only; decoration in red, black, and white paint; exterior decoration white or black-and-white.

Wallace Polychrome has white slip in interiors; no black decoration on exterior; no flat red decoration on bowl interiors.

RANGE:

Apparently center in the Zuni Indian Reservation, New Mexico, but occurs commonly in the Petrified Forest National Monument, Arizona. Kidder found this type at, and in, the neighborhood of Pecos Pueblo, New Mexico (Kidder, 1936, p. 363).

ADAMANA POLYCHROME: new type

SYNONYMS: (a) Red Ware, Green Decoration, Hough, 1903; (b) Polychrome, Ware, Hough, loc. cit.; (c) Glazed Ware, Spier, 1917, p. 312; (d) Three color glazed and painted Ware, Spier, 1919, Table I; (e) Black, green, or purplish glaze on white or cream, with non-glaze, Hodge, 1923, p. 76; (f) Zuni Glazed Ware, Gladwin, W. & H. S., 1934, fig. 3.

TYPE SPECIMENS: Sherds Nos. AT 1952–1956 in the Type Collection of the Museum of Northern Arizona.

TYPE SITE: Stone Ax Pueblo (NA 1023), Petrified Forest National Monument, Arizona.

STAGE: Pueblo IV.

TIME: ca 1300–1400 A.D.

DESCRIPTION:

Constructed: by coiling. *Fired:* in oxidizing atmosphere. *Core:* dark gray to cream, or yellowish; sometimes pink tint. *Temper:* medium fine angular fragments, fairly uniform size, grayish in reduced, yellowish or orange in oxidized portions; occasionally pinkish; occasional grains quartz sand. *Texture core:* fine. *Vessel walls:* medium strong to strong. *Fracture:* slightly crumbling to shattering. *Surface finish:* surfaces heavily slipped, generally highly polished; slips, red on exterior, white on interior, frequently powdery, occasionally crazed. *Surface color:* exterior surface brownish through red to maroon, interior white; color core and surface contrast. *Form:* bowl. *Recorded range thickness bowl walls:* 2.8 to 5.3 mm; greatest individual range recorded, 1.6 mm; average thickness, ca 4.5 mm. *Rim:* bowl, IA7. *Painted decoration:* black, green, or purplish glaze; flat white and brownish red; dark paints, weak and watery, sometimes gritty; white and red paint, chalky, frequently partially obliterated (fugitive). *Pigments:* glaze—lead, copper, and manganese (tests by F. G. Hawley); nonglaze—white presumably kaolin, red presumably hematite. *Decoration:* interior—horizontal and diagonal narrow and wide lines, usually in series and alternately black (or greenish) and red, sometimes isolated dots; exterior—narrow white line band decoration, sometimes wide black framing lines bordered by narrow white line.

COMPARISONS: Wallace Polychrome has white slip on interior; no black decoration on exterior; no flat red decoration on bowl interiors.
   Pinnawa Polychrome, red slip on bowl interior and exterior, in part; white on bowl and jar exteriors, in part.

RANGE:

Recorded only from the Petrified Forest National Monument, Arizona.

HOUCK SERIES

Types in this series are distinct as compared to types in other series of White Mountain Red Ware. So far as known they occur indigenously only in the neighborhood of Houck, Arizona, near the northern boundary of the ware.

KEY j: HOUCK SERIES

1. Exterior, slipped... 2
   Exterior not slipped..................... Houck Polychrome (p. 121)
2. Corrugated........................... Wingate Corrugated (p. 119)
   Not corrugated... 3
3. Polychrome......................... Querino Polychrome (p. 122)
   Not polychrome...................... Wingate Black-on-red (p. 118)
   Puerco Black-on-red (p. 120)

WINGATE BLACK-ON-RED

SYNONYMS: (a) Two color painted ware, Spier, 1919, Table I; (b) Little Colorado Black-on-red Ware, Hawley, 1929, p. 734.
DESCRIBED BY: Gladwin, W. & H. S., 1931, p. 29.
NAMED BY: Gladwin, W. & H. S., loc. cit.
ILLUSTRATIONS: Gladwin, W. & H. S., loc. cit., Pl. XXXII (colored), Pl. XXXIII a; 23/255 (Fig. 30).
TYPE SPECIMENS: Gila Pueblo, Globe, Arizona. Cotype sherds Nos. AT 1273–1275, 1277–1279 in the Type Collection of the Museum of Northern Arizona.
TYPE SITE: St. Johns 11:1 (Gladwin, W. & H. S., loc. cit.).
STAGE: Late Pueblo II.
TIME: ca 950 A.D.

Fig. 30. ($\frac{1}{4}\times$).

DESCRIPTION (revised):

Constructed: by coiling. *Fired:* in oxidizing atmosphere. *Core:* gray, cream, or pink. *Temper:* light-colored angular fragments variable size, usually grayish in unoxidized, yellowish, tan, or pinkish in oxidized portions; quartz sand grains, rare; temper generally conspicuous on worn surfaces and in cross-section. *Texture core:* fine to medium. *Vessel walls:* medium strong. *Fracture:* slightly crumbling. *Surface finish:* interior and exterior bowl surfaces heavily slipped; slip frequently turns to powder and wears off easily, sometimes flakes; surface occasionally crazed. *Surface color:* red, maroon red (no suggestion orange—Gladwin, W. & H. S., loc. cit.); surface color as given by Mera (1934, p. 11), D.C. plates 4I11, 5I10, 6K10; color core and surface, usually contrast. *Forms:* bowls, jars (rare); bowl walls fairly uniform thickness. *Recorded range thickness bowl walls:* 5.9 to 8.2 mm; greatest individual range recorded, 1.6 mm; average thickness, ca 6.5 mm. *Painted decoration:* black; dull, heavy. *Pigment:* iron carbon (Hawley, loc. cit.). *Decoration:* bowls, confined to interior surface. *Designs:* balance hatchured panels and solid elements; hatchures vary in width; sometimes carelessly drawn and overlap at intersections with lines.

RANGE:

"The general eastern section of the basin of the Little Colorado. The western boundary follows the 110th meridian; Springerville marks the southern boundary; numerous instances have appeared as far north as Fort Defiance; the eastern extension has not been defined, but this ware (type) is the prevailing type in the valley of the Rio Puerco as far east as Mt. Taylor" (Gladwin, W. & H. S., loc. cit.).

WINGATE CORRUGATED

DESCRIBED BY: Mera, 1934, p. 11.
NAMED BY: Mera, loc. cit.
TYPE SPECIMENS: Laboratory of Anthropology, Santa Fe, New Mexico.
STAGE: Pueblo III (?).
TIME: ca 1050 A.D.

DESCRIPTION (revised):

Constructed: by coiling. *Fired:* oxidizing atmosphere. *Core:* gray, cream, or pink. *Temper:* light-colored angular fragments, possibly some quartz sand; temper generally conspicuous in cross-section and on worn surfaces. *Texture core:* fine. *Fracture:* slightly crumbling. *Surface finish:* interior surface slipped, slip may be powdery, may flake, may be crazed; exterior surface corrugated. *Surface color:* red to maroon-red. *Form:* bowl. *Painted interior decoration:* black paint. *Decoration:* interior similar to decoration Wingate Black-on-red; exterior corrugated, not painted.

RANGE:

Reported from Petrified Forest National Monument, Arizona.

REMARKS:

Wingate Corrugated is placed in Hawikuh Series rather than Fourmile Series since geographically it occurs in the region where Hawikuh Series predominates.

PUERCO BLACK-ON-RED

DESCRIBED BY: Hawley, 1934, pp. 43–44.
NAMED BY: Gladwin, W. & H. S., 1934, Fig. 4.
ILLUSTRATION: AT 4621 (Fig. 31).
TYPE SPECIMENS: Gila Pueblo, Globe, Arizona. Cotype sherds Nos. AT 1960, 4621 in the Type Collection of the Museum of Northern Arizona.
TYPE SITE: NA 933, Cottonwood Seep, Rio Puerco, Navajo County, Arizona.
STAGE: Pueblo III (?).
TIME: post 950–pre 1150 A.D.

DESCRIPTION (revised):

Fig. 31. ($\frac{1}{2}\times$).

Constructed: by coiling. *Fired:* in oxidizing atmosphere. *Core:* tan, or pink to red. *Temper:* light colored angular fragments of variable size, grayish, yellowish, tan, or pinkish; rarely grain quartz sand; sometimes dark-colored angular fragments; temper generally conspicuous on worn surfaces and in cross-section. *Texture core:* fine to medium. *Vessel walls:* medium strong. *Fracture:* slightly crumbling to shattering. *Surface finish:* interior and exterior surface bowls, heavily slipped (with red); slip frequently turns to powder and wears off easily; sometimes flakes off. *Surface color:* reddish (D.C. plate 4I10, 4I11). *Form:* bowls; bowl walls fairly uniform thickness. *Recorded range thickness bowl walls:* 5.9 to 7.9 mm; greatest individual range recorded, 1.2 mm; average thickness, ca 7 mm. *Rims:* bowls, IA4, IIIA3. *Painted decoration:* black. *Decoration:* confined to interior surface bowls. *Designs:* broad lines, stripes; pattern starts at rim; rims, undecorated. (Hawley says: "Designs: wide bands of diagonal hatching: border lines of same narrowness. Solid lines. Opposed solid and hatched figures."—1936, p. 47.)

RANGE:

"Arizona Puerco east into New Mexico, north into the Chaco" (Hawley, loc. cit.).

REMARKS:

Some confusion exists regarding the use of the name Puerco Black-on-red since the characters that constitute the type have never been clearly defined, at least by the Gladwins who were first to use the name but without definition. The Gladwins state that Puerco Black-on-red is "intermediate between Wingate Black-on-red and St. Johns Polychrome" (1934, p. 20). Hawley first coupled the name to a description (1936, p. 47),

OXIDIZING ATMOSPHERE

she assigning a previous description (1934, pp. 43–44) of an unnamed type found by her in Chaco Canyon to the Gladwin name, Puerco Black-on-red. Hawley's description does apply to a sherd (AT 1960) identified by H. S. Gladwin and donated by him to the Museum of Northern Arizona, although Hawley's full description of the design of Puerco Black-on-red reads as though she has included a part of the description of Wingate Black-on-red, which she says Puerco Black-on-red resembles. Since her description fits the sherd identified by the originator of the name, Hawley's description is here accepted until such time as the Gladwins elaborate or restrict Hawley's description according to the objective characters of the material upon which they first recognized the type.

HOUCK POLYCHROME

DESCRIBED BY: Roberts, 1932, pp. 111–112.
NAMED BY: Roberts, loc. cit.
ILLUSTRATIONS: Roberts, loc. cit., Pl. 31 c.
TYPE SPECIMENS: Cotype sherds Nos. AT 1214–1215, 1269–1270 in the Type Collection of the Museum of Northern Arizona.
TYPE SITE: Village of the Great Kivas, Zuni Reservation, New Mexico.
STAGE: Pueblo III.
TIME: ca 1200–1250 A.D.

DESCRIPTION (revised):

Constructed: by coiling. *Fired:* in oxidizing atmosphere. *Core:* pink to salmon to cream, heavily over-fired specimens gray. *Temper:* medium fine angular fragments fairly uniform size, grayish in reduced, yellowish or tan in oxidized portions; red or pink and black fragments rare; occasional grain quartz sand, usually noticeable on surfaces. *Texture core:* fine. *Vessel walls:* medium strong. *Fracture:* slightly crumbling. *Surface finish:* interior surface bowls slipped with red; exterior surface bowl unslipped (diagnostic); slip bright, dull, or powdery; surface usually crazed. *Surface color:* interior surface red; exterior, cream or buff. *Form:* bowl. *Recorded range thickness bowl walls:* 3.9 to 7 mm; greatest individual range recorded, 1.4 mm; average thickness, ca 6 mm. *Rims:* bowl, IA6. *Painted decoration:* interior, black; exterior, designs in red slip paint; red interior slip extends over rim and forms a stripe around exterior surface bowl. *Design:* interior similar to Wingate Black-on-red, black horizontal and diagonal hatching narrow lines in rectangular or triangular panels; sometimes narrow lines in series; diagonal or horizontal stripes; black stripe around inner edge of rim; exterior design—broad red stripes, background and design about equally balanced; red slip-paint horizontal, diagonal, and sometimes curved stripes.

COMPARISON: Querino Polychrome, cream-colored slip on exterior.

RANGE:

Nutria Canyon, New Mexico; Rio Puerco and upper Cottonwood Wash, Navajo County, and Petrified Forest National Monument, Arizona.

QUERINO POLYCHROME

SYNONYM: Polychrome—three-color, Roberts, 1932, p. 111.
DESCRIBED BY: Roberts, loc. cit.
NAMED BY: Hargrave, (Mera, 1934, p. 11).
ILLUSTRATIONS: Roberts, loc. cit., pl. 27 a, b.
TYPE SPECIMENS: Cotype sherds Nos. AT 1206–1213 in the Type Collection of the Museum of Northern Arizona.
TYPE SITE: Village of the Great Kivas, Zuni Reservation, New Mexico.
STAGE: Pueblo III.
TIME: ca 1250–1300 A.D.

DESCRIPTION (revised):

Constructed: by coiling. *Fired:* in oxidizing atmosphere. *Core:* pink to salmon to cream, heavily over-fired specimens gray. *Temper:* medium fine angular fragments fairly uniform size, grayish in reduced, yellowish or tan in oxidized portions; red or pinkish and black fragments, rare; occasional grain quartz sand; temper noticeable only on worn surface. *Texture core:* fine. *Vessel walls:* medium strong. *Fracture:* slightly crumbling. *Surface finish:* bumpy, usually well-polished; interior surface slipped with red; exterior heavily slipped with cream; both surfaces usually crazed. *Surface color:* interior, red, usually dull, lifeless and powdery; frequently weathers badly, sometimes hard, bright (nearly glossy), and reflects light; color core and surface contrast. *Form:* bowls. *Recorded range thickness bowl walls:* 4.8 to 7.3 mm; greatest individual range recorded, 1.7 mm; average thickness, ca 6 mm. *Rims:* bowls, IA6, IA7, IB6, IB7, IIIB7. *Painted decoration:* black and red. *Pigments:* black —some copper, iron-carbon, and manganese (tests by F. G. Hawley); flat black; no brown tones recorded; paint frequently crazed; sometimes in relief (harder than slip and sometimes intact even when undecorated portions of slip have badly weathered); red paint—presumably hematite; usually thicker than slip. *Designs:* interior—begins just below rim, usually with encircling narrow line (1 to 2 mm wide), occasionally wide line (ca 4 mm) wide; rarely no encircling line; exterior—heavy coarse red slip-paint upon creamy slipped surface; encircling

OXIDIZING ATMOSPHERE

red stripe (8 to 18 mm wide) around outside, includes rim; red stripes both horizontal and diagonal, occasionally curved, with solid stepped elements and triangles in band extending just above base; rarely exterior decoration repeated red zoomorphic figures in band around bowl (Roberts, loc. cit., pl. 27, b). *Elements:* diagonal or horizontal hatchures in curved rectangular or triangular panels; solid triangles often in stepped series.

COMPARISONS: St. Johns Polychrome, exterior decoration white stripes on red slip; interior similar but more carelessly and crudely executed.

Houck Polychrome, no exterior slip but red stripes painted directly on unslipped surface.

RANGE:

Nutria Canyon, New Mexico, to head of Rio Pueblo Colorado in northeastern Arizona. Abundant along northern tributaries of Rio Puerco, Navajo County, Arizona.

KLAGETO SERIES

Recognition of this series is based upon a distinct color tone of the slip that occurs consistently in another geographic division of the ware range. Only a limited amount of research has been done in this areal division about Klageto Trading Post, Apache County, Arizona. Much still is to be learned about the types in this series.

KEY k: KLAGETO SERIES

White line exterior decoration . . . . Klageto Polychrome (p. 124)
No white line exterior decoration . . . . Klageto Black-on-yellow (p. 123)

KLAGETO BLACK-ON-YELLOW: new type

NAMED BY: Colton, 1932, p. 11.
TYPE SPECIMENS: Sherds Nos. AT 1106–1114, 1354–1355, 1932 in the Type Collection of the Museum of Northern Arizona.
TYPE SITE: NA 954, Rio Puerco, Navajo County, Arizona.
STAGE: Pueblo III.
TIME: ca 1250 A.D.
DESCRIPTION:

Constructed: by coiling. *Fired:* in oxidizing atmosphere. *Core:* gray, sometimes brownish to brick-red. *Temper:* small angular fragments, grayish in reduced, yellowish or orange in oxidized portions; occasional grain quartz sand; porosity variable, usually much greater in oxidized portions; temper conspicuous in cross-section and on worn surfaces; mica-like flakes rarely seen on surface. *Texture core:* fine. *Vessel walls:* medium strong to strong. *Fracture:* crumbling to shattering. *Surface finish:* frequently bumpy but well-polished, horizontal polishing marks usually visible; both surfaces slipped. *Surface color:* orange to light yellow; occasionally slate gray (on partly reduced surface); color core and surface contrast. *Form:* bowls. *Recorded range thickness bowl walls:* 4.2 to 6.1 mm; greatest individual range recorded, 0.6 mm; average thickness, ca 5 mm. *Rims:* bowls, IIA3, IIA7, IB7. *Painted decoration:* black, weak brown, dull or glossy black; frequently glaze paint; confined to interior surface. *Pigment:* some copper, iron-carbon, and manganese (tests by F. G. Hawley). *Decoration:* interior—usually wide stripe just below rim with 4 or 5 narrow or wide encircling lines below stripe; frequently horizontal bands containing staggered lines in series and outlined by single wide lines; occasionally solid stepped elements, and narrow or wide lines in series, always horizontal; exterior—decoration rare; horizontal and diagonal black stripes.

COMPARISON: Kintiel Black-on-orange, very thinly slipped; usually thin, brownish paint (polished after painted), never glaze, minute mica-like particles apparent on surface, temper abundant yellowish or brownish angular fragments; fracture crumbling.

RANGE:

Rio Puerco and its northern tributaries. Reported from Petrified Forest National Monument (Mera, 1934); one sherd from Tuzigoot Pueblo, Verde Valley, Yavapai County; and one sherd from Turkey Hill Pueblo, Flagstaff. Has not been reported outside Arizona.

REMARKS:

Two sherds, Nos. AT 1354–1355, from NA 1169 in Oraibi Valley, Hopi Indian Reservation, show minor variations, having a core of orange with almost no contrast between the core and the surface color. These sherds are highly polished but have an extremely thin slip, if any, and grains of quartz sand are fairly frequent. These two examples probably represent trade vessels from near the northwestern periphery of the type.

KLAGETO POLYCHROME: new type

TYPE SPECIMENS: Sherd No. AT 1115 in the Type Collection of the Museum of Northern Arizona.
TYPE SITE: Not designated.
STAGE: Pueblo III.
TIME: ca 1250 A.D.

DESCRIPTION:

Constructed: by coiling. *Fired:* in oxidizing atmosphere. *Core:*

OXIDIZING ATMOSPHERE

light gray. *Temper:* small angular fragments, grayish in reduced, tan in oxidized portions; quartz sand, occasional. *Texture core:* fine. *Vessel walls:* strong. *Fracture:* shattering. *Surface finish:* slipped and well-polished. *Surface color:* buff or slate-gray; color surface and core contrast in part. *Form:* bowl. *Thickness bowl wall:* 4.7 mm. *Rim:* bowl, IIA7. *Painted decoration:* dull black and white. *Pigment:* white—presumably kaolin. *Decoration:* interior surface, black stripe just below rim with series narrow black lines encircling bowl below stripe; exterior, white diagonal stripes.

RANGE:

Locality of manufacture unknown; should be same as Klageto Black-on-yellow. The type sherd is from Kwaituki Pueblo (NA 849), upper Oraibi wash, Hopi Reservation, Arizona. Is trade product.

REMARKS:

Although it would not be advisable to describe a new type from one sherd in every instance, the objective character, namely, a white exterior decoration, of Klageto Polychrome that differs from Klageto Black-on-yellow, not only is striking but would have been postulated had this sherd not been found. Not only will more examples probably be found but descriptive characters eventually may cover the same range as Klageto Black-on-yellow once comparative material is available.

KINTIEL SERIES

The space range of the two preceding series are not far removed from the space range of Kintiel Series and when better understood these three ranges may overlap in part. Kintiel Series is now composed of pottery types developed very late in the history of the White Mountain Red Ware. Stratigraphy probably would show types of Kintiel Series to be a late development from an earlier, possibly Klageto Series.

KEY 1: KINTIEL SERIES

White line exterior decoration.................Kintiel Polychrome (p. 126)
No white line exterior decoration..........Kintiel Black-on-orange (p. 125)

KINTIEL BLACK-ON-ORANGE: new type

TYPE SPECIMENS: Sherds Nos. AT 1242–1250, 1259 in the Type Collection of the Museum of Northern Arizona.

TYPE SITE: Kintiel Pueblo (NA 1015) Leroux Wash, Navajo County, Arizona.

STAGE: Pueblo III.
TIME: ca 1275–1300 A.D.

DESCRIPTION:
Constructed: by coiling. *Fired:* in oxidizing atmosphere. *Core:* brownish to orange, frequently pinkish. *Temper:* small angular fragments fairly uniform size, yellowish or orange; occasional grain quartz sand; temper conspicuous in cross-section and on worn surfaces; mica-like particles almost always present, seen only on surface. *Texture core:* fine. *Vessel walls:* medium strong. *Fracture:* crumbling. *Surface finish:* surfaces thinly but obviously slipped with same (?) material as core clay; surfaces not bumpy, fairly well-polished after application of paint; polishing marks, frequent. *Surface color:* light brown to yellowish through orange; color surface and core vary together. *Forms:* bowls. *Recorded range thickness bowl walls:* 4.2 to 6.9 mm; greatest individual range recorded, 2.3 mm; average thickness (22 sherds), 4.7 mm. *Rims:* bowls, IA7, IIA3, IIB6. *Painted decoration:* dull black, reddish brown; sometimes fairly thick, usually thin. *Pigment:* iron-carbon, some copper (tests by F. G. Hawley; H. S. Colton). *Decoration:* interior bowl surfaces only; usually horizontal band framed with one to five narrow or wide lines; top and bottom lines nearly always broader than others; sometimes wide lines and stripes in diagonal series; bottom bowls, undecorated; wide top line sometimes wide bottom line has gap (so-called life line); decorative style characteristic of Pueblo IV in the Little Colorado River Valley and in the Hopi Country.

COMPARISON: Klageto Black-on-yellow, usually more heavily slipped, usually thicker and richer paint (sometimes slightly glazed), paint never brownish, color core usually gray, surface frequently somewhat bumpy, no glittering mica-like particles apparent on surface; temper not conspicuous.

RANGE:
Leroux and Rio Puerco washes in northeastern Arizona.

REMARKS:
Kintiel Black-on-orange is abundant at the type site where sherds of the type were found on top of timbers from a kiva (KT-I) giving a late date of 1276 A.D. (Hargrave, 1931, p. 94).

KINTIEL POLYCHROME: new type

TYPE SPECIMENS: Sherds Nos. AT 1248, 1265–1268 in the Type Collection of the Museum of Northern Arizona.
TYPE SITE: Kintiel Pueblo (NA 1015), Leroux Wash, Navajo County, Arizona.
STAGE: Pueblo III.
TIME: ca 1250–1300 A.D.

OXIDIZING ATMOSPHERE 127

DESCRIPTION:
Constructed: by coiling. *Fired:* oxidizing atmosphere. *Core:* brownish to orange, occasionally pinkish. *Temper:* small angular fragments fairly uniform size, yellowish or orange; occasionally grain quartz sand; temper conspicuous in cross-section and on worn surfaces; minute mica-like particles almost always present, seen only on vessel surface. *Texture core:* fine. *Vessel walls:* medium strong. *Fracture:* crumbling. *Surface finish:* surfaces very thinly but obviously slipped with same (?) material as core clay; fairly well-polished, apparently after application of paint; polishing marks frequent. *Surface color:* light brown through orange to yellowish; color surface and core vary together. *Form:* bowls. *Recorded range thickness bowl walls:* 4.1 to 6.4 mm; greatest individual range recorded, 1.2 mm; average thickness, ca 5 mm. *Rims:* bowls, IA7. *Painted decoration:* dull black and white; black paint often weak brown shade. *Pigments:* black presumably same as Kintiel Black-on-orange; white, presumably kaolin. *Decoration:* interior—black only; encircling stripe just below rim; beneath stripe is wide horizontal band framed by single stripe or by 3 to 5 narrow lines in series; band contains diagonal stripes, staggered lines in horizontal or diagonal panels, solid rectangles, sometimes nests of open rectangles formed of narrow lines; exterior decoration—diagonal and horizontal white stripes; sometimes white stepped areas; no exterior black decoration.

RANGE:
Leroux and Rio Pueblo Colorado washes in north-eastern Arizona.

ZUNI WHITE WARE

In the three preceding wares is seen first, how white (iron-free clay) was used in line decoration, and second, how white was later used to cover areas as a background for a dark painted design. In Zuni White Ware the white covers the *entire* decorative surfaces of all vessel forms, thus producing a wholly white vessel even though the vessel generally was fired in an oxidizing atmosphere as was its *red* progenitor. The principal difference between Zuni White Ware and White Mountain Red Ware is in the material used as a slip.

Recognition of this ware is for convenience in study because of radical differences in the appearance of some objective characters.

KEY 7: ZUNI WHITE WARE

Non-glaze red paint only................Pinnawa Red-on-white (p. 129)
Dark colored glaze and non-glaze red paint.....Arauca Polychrome (p. 131)
Black, green, or purplish glaze paint only..Hawikuh Glaze-on-white (p. 130)

ZUNI WHITE WARE: new type

SYNONYMS: (a) White Ware, Hough, 1903, p. 324; (b) White and Green Ware, Fewkes, 1904, p. 61; (c) Buff Ware, Spier, 1917, p. 255; (d) Zuni Ware, Hargrave, 1931, p. 119; (e) Zuni Glazed Ware, Gladwin, W. & H. S., 1934, fig. 3.
STAGE: Pueblo IV.
TIME: ca 1350–1400 A.D.

DESCRIPTION:

Constructed: by coiling. *Fired:* in oxidizing atmosphere. *Core:* gray, brown through brick-red to salmon pink. *Temper:* predominantly opaque light-colored angular fragments, occasionally some quartz sand or black fragments, or both. *Carbon streak:* common. *Texture core:* fine to medium. *Vessel walls:* medium strong to strong. *Fracture:* crumbling to shattering. *Surface finish:* both surfaces bowls and exterior surface jars coated with heavy white or light cream slip; slip generally highly polished; occasionally scraping marks discernible through slip; frequently crazed; slip chalky and powdery, sometimes flakes off. *Surface color:* white; color core and surface, generally contrast. *Forms:* bowls (predominate), jars (uncommon). *Recorded range thickness bowl walls:* 3.1 to 6.8 mm; greatest individual range recorded, 2 mm; average thickness, ca 5 mm. *Recorded range thickness jar walls:* 4.1 to 6.6 mm; greatest individual range recorded, 1.5 mm; average thickness ca 5 mm. *Rims:* bowls, IA3, IA4, IA6, IA7, IA12, IIA4, IIA12, IIIA7, IIIA12. *Painted decoration:* on all types; black, purplish, or green glaze, or red or brown nonglaze, or both. *Pigments:* glaze —copper, lead and manganese; nonglaze, presumably an iron. *Decoration:* jar exteriors; interiors and usually also on bowl exteriors.

RANGE:

Zuni Reservation in west-central New Mexico to and including the Petrified Forest National Monument, Arizona. Intrusive at Showlow, Silver Creek drainage, Navajo County to the southwest and in the Hopi Reservation, Navajo County, to the northwest.

OXIDIZING ATMOSPHERE

PINNAWA RED-ON-WHITE: new type

SYNONYM: (a) White Ware, Hough, 1904; (b) Red-on-white Ware, Spier, 1919, p. 369.

TYPE SPECIMENS: Sherds Nos. AT 2037–2039 in the Type Collection of the Museum of Northern Arizona.

TYPE SITE: Pinnawa Pueblo (NA 973), Zuni Reservation, New Mexico.

STAGE: Pueblo IV.

TIME: Probably between 1350–1400 A.D.

DESCRIPTION:

Constructed: by coiling. *Fired:* in oxidizing atmosphere. *Core:* dark gray; pinkish tint toward surfaces. *Temper:* predominantly opaque light-colored angular fragments; occasionally some black fragments. *Carbon streak:* common. *Texture core:* fine. *Vessel walls:* medium strong. *Fracture:* slightly crumbling. *Surface finish:* both surfaces bowls and exterior surface jars heavily coated with white or light cream slip; slip highly polished; occasionally scraping marks discernible through slip; frequently faintly crazed. *Surface color:* white; color surface and core contrast. *Forms:* bowls (predominate), jars. *Recorded range thickness bowl walls:* 3.5 to 5.4 mm; greatest individual range recorded, 1.8 mm; average thickness, ca 5 mm. *Recorded range thickness jar walls:* 4.7 to 5.4 mm; greatest individual range recorded, 0.7 mm; average thickness, ca 5 mm. *Rims:* bowls, IA6, IA12. *Painted decoration:* reddish brown; usually powdery or chalky; frequently partially worn off. *Decoration:* interior, exterior, or both surfaces bowls; exterior surface jars; rims unpainted. *Elements:* stripes, wide lines, solid areas.

RANGE:

Recorded from Zuni Indian Reservation in New Mexico and the Petrified Forest National Monument, Arizona. One sherd (trade) from Machonpi Pueblo (NA 835), one half mile north of Hotevilla, Hopi Reservation, Navajo County, Arizona.

REMARKS:

Although no whole vessels of this type are available the use of red paint on this type is identical to the use of the dark glaze paint on other types in the same ware and thus is strongly suggestive of a one color decoration. Also, on other types this red occurs with the dark glaze paints and eventually becomes prominent with another flat color on Pinnawa Polychrome. Its use clearly shows the genetic relationship of otherwise greatly differing types in this ware. It is given specific rank for that reason. The occurrence of Pinnawa Red-on-white at Machonpi Pueblo is suggestive of the late Pueblo III or early Pueblo IV stages.

HAWIKUH GLAZE-ON-WHITE: new type

SYNONYMS: (a) White Ware, Hough, 1904, pl. 74; (b) White and Green Ware, Fewkes, 1904, p. 61; (c) Black, green, or purplish glaze on white or cream slip, Hodge, 1923, p. 29; (d) Zuni Glazed Ware, Gladwin, W. & H. S., 1934, fig. 3.

DESCRIBED BY: Hodge, loc. cit.

ILLUSTRATION: Hough, loc. cit., colored pl. 74.

TYPE SPECIMENS: Cotype sherds Nos. AT 1358, 1988–2025 in the Type Collection of the Museum of Northern Arizona.

TYPE SITE: Stone Ax Pueblo (NA 1023), Petrified Forest National Monument, Arizona.

STAGE: Pueblo IV.

TIME: Probably between 1350–1425 A.D.

DESCRIPTION (revised):

Constructed: by coiling. *Fired:* in oxidizing atmosphere. *Core:* gray, brown through brick-red to salmon pink. *Temper:* predominantly opaque light-colored angular fragments; occasionally some quartz sand and black fragments. *Carbon streak:* common. *Texture core:* fine to medium. *Vessel walls:* medium strong to strong. *Fracture:* crumbling to shattering. *Surface finish:* both surfaces bowls and exterior surface jars coated with heavy white or light cream slip; slip generally highly polished; often minutely crazed; occasionally scraping marks discernible through slip. *Surface color:* white; color surface and core generally contrast. *Forms:* bowls (predominate), jars. *Recorded range thickness bowl walls:* 3.3 to 6.7 mm; greatest individual range recorded, 2 mm; average thickness (67 sherds), 5 mm. *Recorded range thickness jar walls:* 4.1 to 6.2 mm; greatest individual range recorded, 1.5 mm; average thickness, ca 5 mm. *Rims:* bowls, IA3, IA6, IA7, IA12, IIA4, IIA12, IIIA7. *Painted decoration:* glaze—purplish-black through purple, dark green to light green. *Pigments:* copper, lead, and manganese (tests by F. G. Hawley). *Decoration:* interior and frequently exterior surface bowls: exterior surface jars; rims, unpainted. *Elements:* narrow and wide lines, solid triangles, solid stepped elements, often interlocking; isolated dots and staggered lines, occasional; horizontal or diagonal narrow-line hatching (uncommon) in rectangular panels.

RANGE:

Recorded as common at Hawikuh Pueblo, Zuni Reservation, west-central New Mexico (Hodge, loc. cit.); also common in Petrified Forest National Monument, Arizona. Intrusive at Showlow Pueblo, and in the Hopi Reservation, Arizona.

ARAUCA POLYCHROME: new type

SYNONYMS: (a) White Ware, Hough, 1904; (b) White and Green Ware, Fewkes, 1904; (c) Red-on-white Ware, Spier, 1919, p. 369; (d) Black, or green glaze on white or cream with non-glaze colors, Hodge, 1923, p. 29; (e) Zuni Glazed Ware, Gladwin, W. & H. S., 1934, fig. 3.

DESCRIBED BY: Hodge, loc. cit.

TYPE SPECIMENS: Cotype sherds Nos. AT 2040–2075 in the Type Collection of the Museum of Northern Arizona.

TYPE SITE: Stone Ax Pueblo (NA 1023), Petrified Forest National Monument, Arizona.

STAGE: Pueblo IV.

TIME: Probably between 1350–1425 A.D.

DESCRIPTION (revised):

Constructed: by coiling. *Fired:* in oxidizing atmosphere. *Core:* gray, brown through brick-red to salmon pink. *Temper:* predominantly opaque light-colored angular fragments; occasionally some quartz sand or black fragments. *Carbon streak:* common. *Texture core:* fine to medium. *Vessel walls:* medium strong to strong. *Fracture:* crumbling to shattering. *Surface finish:* both surfaces bowls and exterior surface jars coated with heavy white or light cream slip; slip generally highly polished; occasionally scraping marks discernible through slip; frequently crazed; chalky and powdery, sometimes flakes off. *Surface color:* white; color surface and core generally contrast. *Forms:* bowls (predominate), jars (rare). *Recorded range thickness bowl walls:* 3.1 to 6.8 mm; greatest individual range recorded, 1.6 mm; average thickness (34 sherds), 4.9 mm. *Recorded range thickness jar walls:* 4.1 to 6.6 mm; greatest individual range recorded, 1.3 mm; average thickness, ca 5 mm. *Rims:* bowls, IA3, IA4, IA6, IA7, IA12, IIIA2. *Painted decoration:* glaze and nonglaze; glaze varies from purplish-black through purple, dark green to light green; nonglaze varies from brown to reddish. *Decoration:* exterior jars, usually both surfaces bowls; rims not painted. *Elements:* horizontal narrow to wide lines and stripes, in series, usually with black, purplish, or green glaze alternating with reddish or brown nonglaze; solid triangles, solid stepped elements (sometimes interlocking) in either color, often outlined with narrow lines of other color, fairly common; diagonal narrow-line hatching rare.

RANGE:

Zuni Reservation, New Mexico; also Petrified Forest National Monument, Arizona. Intrusive in Hopi Reservation, Navajo County, Arizona.

REMARKS:
Because there are so few local geographic names in some sections of the country it frequently is difficult to select an appropriate name for a pottery type. The name "Arauca Polychrome" is derived from Araucarioxylon arizonicum, the scientific name of most of the petrified trees in the Petrified Forest National Monument, Arizona.

HOMOLOVI ORANGE WARE

Only utility types are known to occur in this ware. It is admitted that types in Winslow Orange Ware, a companion ware, and types in Homolovi Orange Ware, genetically, should be in the same ware since evidence tends to prove that the two wares were made by the same people. But even in the face of this admission, it is advantageous to separate these wares on the basis of objective characters in order to facilitate identification through use of the Key. As has already been said, the authors recognize that, generally, two indigenous wares, as companion wares, occur in nearly every major geographic division of the Southwestern Pueblo Area. But by stating that two companion wares in an area are genetically related and that the two wares are contemporaneous in time, a misunderstanding as a result of the separation purely on the basis of objective characters should be avoided.

Homolovi Orange Ware at present is known to occur only in Pueblo IV sites in the Little Colorado River Valley, especially in the Homolovi group, from which group the ware name is taken.

KEY 8: HOMOLOVI ORANGE WARE

Surface corrugated.........................Homolovi Corrugated (p. 134)
Surface not corrugated.......................Homolovi Plain (p. 133)

HOMOLOVI ORANGE WARE: new type

STAGE: Pueblo IV.
TIME: Between 1300–1400 A.D.

DESCRIPTION:
Constructed: by coiling. *Fired:* in oxidizing atmosphere. *Core:* pinkish to tan, sometimes gray or buff. *Temper:* variable; quartz sand with smaller amounts angular fragments black, white,

gray, red, or orange; gray or white in reduced portions, buff, red, or orange in oxidized portions; temper noticeable but not conspicuous on surfaces. *Carbon streak:* occasional. *Vessel walls:* medium strong; friable; porous. *Texture core:* medium to coarse. *Fracture:* slightly crumbling to crumbling. *Surface finish:* rough and gritty, or corrugated. *Surface color:* pinkish to tan to orange; color rarely uniform through vessel wall although core and surface colors do not vary greatly. *Form:* jars. *Recorded range thickness jar walls:* 4.6 to 7.8 mm; greatest individual range recorded, 1.4 mm; average thickness, ca 5.5 mm. *Decoration:* undecorated or corrugated.

RANGE:
 Middle Little Colorado River Valley near Winslow, Navajo County, Arizona.

HOMOLOVI PLAIN

DESCRIBED BY: Hargrave, 1932, p. 24.
NAMED BY: Hargrave, loc. cit.
TYPE SPECIMENS: Type sherd lost. Cotype sherd No. AT 1116 in the Type Collection of the Museum of Northern Arizona.
STAGE: Pueblo IV.
TIME: Between 1300–1400 A.D.

DESCRIPTION (revised):
 Constructed: by coiling. *Fired:* in oxidizing atmosphere. *Core:* pinkish. *Temper:* predominantly quartz sand with smaller amounts black and white angular fragments; noticeable but not conspicuous on surfaces. *Vessel walls:* medium strong; porous; friable. *Surface finish:* rough and gritty. *Surface color:* orange with pinkish tint. *Forms:* jar. *Thickness:* 4 mm. *Undecorated.*

COMPARISON: Tuwiuca Orange, moderately polished on one surface, polished surface often minutely crazed, sometimes tiny white mica-like flakes on surface.

RANGE:
 Reported only from the Type Site and Homolovi Pueblo (NA 952) at Winslow, Navajo County, Arizona.

REMARKS:
 Homolovi Plain is rare in surface collections probably because of its inconspicuousness. Since this type indicates a change in decorative technique at a time when change is not conspicuous in painted types, Homolovi Plain may become a valuable criterion after a detailed study has been made of pottery types of Pueblo IV sites near Winslow.

HOMOLOVI CORRUGATED

DESCRIBED BY: Hargrave, 1932, p. 25.
NAMED BY: Hargrave, loc. cit.
TYPE SPECIMENS: Type sherds Nos. AT 1117–1130 in the Type Collection of the Museum of Northern Arizona.
TYPE SITE: Moquaki Pueblo (NA 926), Cottonwood Wash, six miles east of Winslow, Navajo County, Arizona.
STAGE: Pueblo IV.
TIME: Between 1300–1425 A.D.

DESCRIPTION (revised):

Constructed: by coiling. *Fired:* in oxidizing atmosphere. *Core:* pinkish to tan, sometimes gray, or buff. *Temper:* variable; moderately coarse quartz sand predominated in some specimens, with smaller amounts of angular fragments; fragments gray or white in reduced portions, red or orange in oxidized portions; in some specimens angular fragments predominate with quartz sand infrequent; temper noticeable on surfaces but not conspicuous. *Carbon streak:* occasional. *Vessel walls:* medium strong, friable, porous. *Texture core:* medium. *Fracture:* crumbling. *Surface finish:* exterior surface corrugated and indented in moderately low relief. *Surface color:* pinkish to tan to orange; color never uniform through vessel wall although core and surface colors do not vary greatly. *Form:* jars. *Recorded range thickness jar walls:* 4.6 to 7.8 mm; greatest individual range recorded, 1.4 mm; average thickness, ca 5.5 mm. *Decoration:* plain and indented corrugations, usually partly flattened.

RANGE:

Middle Little Colorado River Valley near Winslow, Navajo County, Arizona.

WINSLOW ORANGE WARE

In this ware are the table types, companion types to types of Homolovi Orange Ware. The relation of these two wares to each other is discussed under "Homolovi Orange Ware."

Because of the relative abundance of sherds of this ware near Winslow, which seems to be the focus for the ware, this geographical name has been chosen for the ware. "Orange" was selected for the descriptive term since it is the predominating surface shade.

OXIDIZING ATMOSPHERE 135

KEY 9: WINSLOW ORANGE WARE

1. Painted decoration... 2
   No painted decoration...................... Tuwiuca Orange (p. 136)
2. Black painted decoration only........ Tuwiuca Black-on-orange (p. 137)
   Jeddito Black-on-orange (p. 141)
   Polychrome... 3
3. Exterior decoration white only........... Tuwiuca Polychrome (p. 138)
   Jeddito Polychrome (p. 142)
   Decoration black and white together...... Winslow Polychrome (p. 139)

WINSLOW ORANGE WARE: new ware

SYNONYM: Buff Ware, Spier, 1919, p. 369, Table II.
STAGE: Pueblo III (?)–Pueblo IV.
TIME: Between 1300–1400 A.D.
DESCRIPTION:

Constructed: by coiling. *Fired:* in oxidizing atmosphere. *Core:* Pinkish, tan, or orange, sometimes buff or gray, occasionally brick-red (in Jeddito Series). *Temper:* variable in most types, some specimens predominantly quartz sand with lesser amounts soft angular fragments yellow, gray, black, or red; some specimens relatively small quantity quartz sand with abundant angular fragments; some types about equal amounts quartz sand and angular fragments; temper usually noticeable but not conspicuous on surface; tiny white mica-like flakes on surfaces some types. *Carbon streaks:* uncommon. *Vessel walls:* medium strong to strong; porous; slightly friable to friable. *Texture core:* medium to fine. *Fracture:* slightly crumbling to crumbling, except in Jeddito Series which is shattering. *Surface finish:* gritty and pitted, except in Jeddito Series which is smooth and sometimes slick; in some types surface minutely crazed; impacted or polished on both surfaces bowls, exterior surface jars. *Surface color:* orange through ochre to tan, sometimes pinkish to light brick-red; color surface and core rarely vary greatly. *Forms:* bowls, jars; vessel walls usually fairly uniform thickness. *Recorded range thickness bowl walls:* 3.5 to 7.1 mm; greatest individual range recorded, 2 mm; average thickness, ca 5.5 mm. *Recorded range thickness jar walls:* 3.4 to 7.1 mm; greatest individual range recorded, 2.2 mm; average thickness, ca 5.5 mm. *Decoration:* undecorated; painted. *Paint:* black—usually weak and flat, occasionally rich and dense (in Jeddito Series); white— usually somewhat fugitive, sometimes fairly thick. *Pigments:* black—manganese or iron-carbon, occasionally some copper; white—presumably kaolin. *Designs:* bowls—one or both surfaces; exterior usually white only (black and white rarely on Winslow Polychrome); interior usually black only, black and white occasionally on Winslow Polychrome and Jeddito Polychrome; jars—on exterior only; no rim decoration recorded. *Designs:* Pueblo IV style.

RANGE:

Middle Little Colorado River, Winslow, Arizona and Chavez Pass Pueblo on Clear Creek, Navajo County, Arizona. Common trade material in the Verde Valley, Yavapai County, Arizona.

WINSLOW SERIES

This is apparently the basic series of Winslow Orange Ware, the early types in the series probably being ancestral to the later. No stratigraphic work has been done in the region since the recognition of these types so that the order of presenting the types in this work is based upon the results of other methods of study.

Differences in many of these types, as well as some major objective characters, indicate that the peoples manufacturing these types were subject to the same, or to many similar, factors that affected the Hopis to the north. Because of these similarities and of the abundance of trade vessels of Jeddito Yellow Ware associated in sites where the Winslow Series is indigenous, these sites have generally been considered as Hopi.

TUWIUCA ORANGE: new type

TYPE SPECIMENS: Type sherds Nos. AT 1139–1142 in the Type Collection of the Museum of Northern Arizona.

TYPE SITE: Tuwiuca Pueblo (NA 2212), Little Colorado River, Winslow, Navajo County, Arizona.

STAGE: Pueblo III.

TIME: Probably between 1250–1300 A.D.

DESCRIPTION:

Constructed: by coiling. *Fired:* in oxidizing atmosphere. *Core:* pinkish to tan, occasionally buff or gray. *Temper:* predominantly quartz sand, small grains fairly uniform size; angular fragments relatively infrequent, white, red, yellowish, or black; temper noticeable on surface. *Texture core:* fine to medium. *Vessel walls:* medium strong to strong. *Fracture:* generally crumbling. *Surface finish:* surfaces normally gritty and pitted, faint minute crazing on polished surfaces; tiny light-colored mica like flakes sometimes on surface (not seen in core); exterior surface polished, always smoother than interior surface; exterior jar surface, impacted; not slipped; polishing marks usually often faintly detected horizontally around vessel. *Surface color:*

OXIDIZING ATMOSPHERE 137

orange, through ochre to tan; color surface and core do not vary greatly. *Forms:* jars, jar walls uniform thickness. *Recorded range thickness jar walls:* 4 to 7.1 mm; greatest individual range recorded, 1.6 mm; average thickness, ca 5 mm. *Undecorated.*

COMPARISON: Homolovi Plain, not polished on either surface; no mica-like flakes on surface.

RANGE:

Restricted, so far as known, to sites on the Little Colorado River, near Winslow, Arizona.

REMARKS:

Name abbreviated from Tsuerca-tuwiuca, Hopi for "muddy point."

TUWIUCA BLACK-ON-ORANGE: new type

TYPE SPECIMENS: Type sherds Nos. AT 1150–1158 in the Type Collection of the Museum of Northern Arizona.
TYPE SITE: Tuwiuca Pueblo (NA 2212), Little Colorado River, Winslow, Navajo County, Arizona.
STAGE: Pueblo III.
TIME: Probably between 1250–1300 A.D.

DESCRIPTION:

Constructed: by coiling. *Fired:* in oxidizing atmosphere. *Core:* pinkish to tan to orange, occasionally buff. *Temper:* variable; predominantly fine grains quartz sand; fairly abundant amounts angular fragments, mostly red, but also gray, yellowish, and black; temper noticeable on most surfaces; tiny white mica-like flakes sometimes seen on surface (not seen in core). *Texture core:* fine to medium. *Vessel walls:* medium strong to strong. *Fracture:* crumbling. *Surface finish:* surfaces usually gritty and pitted although not conspicuous; minutely crazed; exterior surface jars polished, always smoother than interior surface; little difference between interior and exterior surface finish bowls; decorative surface impacted; not slipped; polishing marks usually faintly detected horizontally around vessel. *Surface color:* orange through ochre to tan; color surface and core do not vary greatly. *Forms:* jars, bowls: vessel walls fairly uniform thickness. *Recorded range thickness jar walls:* 4.3 to 7 mm; greatest individual range recorded, 1.6 mm; average thickness, ca 5.5 mm. *Recorded range thickness bowl walls:* 3.5 to 5.9 mm; greatest individual range recorded, 2 mm; average thickness, ca 4.7 mm. *Decoration:* painted. *Paint:* black—nearly always dull, weak. *Pigment:* black—manganese, iron-carbon (test by F. G. Hawley). *Designs:* exterior surface jars, interior surface bowls; usually stripe just below rim and band around bowl sides; motifs in band usually join line framing band and are composed of parallel narrow lines, broad lines, and stripes; panels of diagonal lines or hatchure; solid areas massed black; rarely narrow line between band and rim stripe; another stripe below band; bowl bottoms undecorated; decorative patterns on jar exteriors of same elements as on bowl interiors; brush work bold, often sloppy.

RANGE:
Middle Little Colorado River Valley, near Winslow, Navajo County, Arizona. One sherd from Kwaituki Pueblo (NA 849), upper Oraibi Wash, Hopi Reservation, Navajo County, Arizona; one sherd (AT 2114) from Hawikuh Pueblo (NA 960), Zuni Reservation, New Mexico.

REMARKS:
Tuwiuca Black-on-orange reflects the same characters of form, and style of design as occur at other late Pueblo III or early Pueblo IV sites of the general region on the plateau, north and southwest of the Little Colorado. Also, it is so similar to Jeddito Black-on-orange, from a distant region, that comparison with known material is advisable when questionable material is from other regions.

TUWIUCA POLYCHROME: new type

TYPE SPECIMENS: Type sherds Nos. AT 2170 and 1149 in the Type Collection of the Museum of Northern Arizona.
TYPE SITE: Tuwiuca Pueblo (NA 2212), Little Colorado River Valley, near Winslow, Navajo County, Arizona.
STAGE: Pueblo III.
TIME: Probably between 1200–1300 A.D.

DESCRIPTION:

Constructed: by coiling. *Fired:* in oxidizing atmosphere. *Core:* pinkish to buff to orange. *Temper:* about equal amounts quartz sand and angular fragments, gray, yellowish, or black; temper noticeable on surfaces. *Texture core:* fine to medium. *Vessel walls:* medium strong. *Fracture:* slightly crumbling. *Surface finish:* surfaces gritty and pitted; impacted, not slipped; both surfaces bowls and jar exteriors polished; polishing marks faintly detected horizontally around vessel. *Surface color:* orange to tan; color surface and core blend. *Forms:* bowls, jars; vessel walls fairly uniform thickness. *Recorded range thickness bowl walls:* 4.6 to 5.9 mm; greatest individual range recorded, 1.3 mm; average thickness, ca 5.5 mm. *Recorded range thickness jar*

OXIDIZING ATMOSPHERE

walls: 4.7 mm. *Rims:* bowls, IA12; jars, IB3. *Decoration:* painted. *Paints:* black and white; black—weak and watery, brownish tint; white—sometimes watery, generally chalky. *Design:* bowl—black geometric pattern on interior, white rim stripe with pendent diagonal stripes on exterior; jar designs, narrow white lines on exterior.

RANGE:

Reported only from Tuwiuca Pueblo, Little Colorado River Valley, near Winslow, Navajo County, Arizona.

REMARKS:

Among the sherds of this type is one jar sherd (AT 1149) that shows only white painted decoration. Since the sherd is from the neck of a vessel and believing that body sherds probably would show a black painted design, this sherd has been included in the description of this type to avoid useless synonymy.

WINSLOW POLYCHROME: new type

ILLUSTRATION: AT 1170 (Fig. 32).
TYPE SPECIMENS: Type sherds, Nos. AT 1167–1176 in the Type Collection of the Museum of Northern Arizona.
TYPE SITE: Homolovi Pueblo (NA 952), Little Colorado River Valley, Winslow, Navajo County, Arizona.
STAGE: Pueblo IV.
TIME: ca 1350–1400 A.D.

DESCRIPTION:

Constructed: by coiling. *Fired:* in oxidizing atmosphere. *Core:* pinkish to tan; occasionally buff or gray; yel-

Fig. 32. ($\frac{1}{2}$×).

lowish or gray in partly reduced, red or orange in oxidized portions. *Temper:* variable; moderately fine quartz sand with lesser amounts angular fragments; or predominance of angular fragments with lesser amounts quartz sand; temper sometimes noticeable on surface. *Texture core:* fine to medium. *Vessel walls:* medium strong. *Fracture:* crumbling. *Surface finish:* surfaces gritty and pitted, or smooth to slick; usually minutely crazed; sometimes powdery; exterior surface jars, polished; little difference between interior and exterior finish bowl surfaces. *Surface color:* orange through ochre to tan; sometimes decidedly pinkish; color surface and core do not vary greatly. *Forms:* jars, bowls;

vessel walls fairly uniform thickness. *Recorded range thickness bowl walls:* 4.5 to 6.6 mm; average thickness, ca 5 mm. *Rims:* bowls, IA4, IA7 (common), IB3, IB7, IIA3, IIA4, IIA7, IIIA4 (common), IIIA7 (common). *Decoration:* painted. *Paint:* black and white; black more often brown, sometimes weak (nearly same shade as surface color), when dark is rich purplish; white paint, less permanent, frequently indistinct in spots, thick and granular in other places. *Pigment:* white, presumably kaolin. *Designs:* bowls, usually interiors, sometimes both surfaces; jars, on exteriors only; no rim decoration recorded; patterns usually a broad black stripe immediately below rim bordered on lower side only by narrow white line; black stripes bordered with white; rectangular panels with diagonal hatching in black; solid black stepped elements; wide staggered lines; triangles, zigzag lines; generally narrow white lines as borders to black patterns.

RANGE:

Middle Little Colorado River Valley, near Winslow, and on Clear Creek (Chavez Pass Pueblo); trade vessels have been found at Tuzigoot Pueblo, Verde River Valley, Yavapai County, Arizona.

KWAITUKI SERIES

With the exception of this series, no types in Winslow Orange Ware are known to occur indigenously anywhere within the Jeddito drainage. But because a black-on-orange first recognized in or near this drainage subsequently was described and named "Jeddito Black-on-orange," the type name must be retained, according to Rules of Naming and Rules of Priority.

Kwaituki Series is important in the study of later developed types in Jeddito Yellow Ware of the Hopi Country since a type in this series seems to have been the first type, in the Hopi Country, to have a predominance of southern characters.

Although the accepted practice in this work has been to use the geographic part of one of the type names as the geographic part of the series name, an exception is here made because of the dominance of Jeddito Yellow Ware in the area occupied by the types Jeddito Black-on-orange and Jeddito Polychrome. Ideally, the geographic part of a type or series name should not be used in more than one ware, nor, for that matter, in more than one series. But because so many type names have been in use for sometime, and also because geographic names have not always been available, geographic names, in some cases, obviously are not appropriate. With gross inconsistencies apparent in the present use of Southwestern ceramic terms, care should hereafter be taken in the selection of a new type or series name. In this connection, when selecting these names it is advisable not to consider any name that has once appeared in print and that later has been discarded.

JEDDITO BLACK-ON-ORANGE

SYNONYMS: (a) Buffware, Spier, 1917, p. 256; (b) Hopi Black-on-orange, Gladwin, W. & H. S., 1934, Fig. 7.
DESCRIBED BY: Hargrave, 1931, p. 118.
NAMED BY: Hargrave, loc. cit.
TYPE SPECIMENS: Dipper, No. NA 1019R14.1, and sherds Nos. AT 1083–1100 in the Type Collection of the Museum of Northern Arizona.
TYPE SITE: Kwaituki Pueblo (NA 849), upper Oraibi Wash, Hopi Reservation, Navajo County, Arizona (Hargrave, 1932, p. 27).
STAGE: Pueblo III.
TIME: Probably between 1200–1300 A.D.
DESCRIPTION (revised):

Constructed: by coiling. *Fired:* in oxidizing atmosphere. *Core:* light brick-red to pinkish to dark orange. *Temper:* variable; in most specimens, angular fragments, medium fine of fairly uniform size, yellowish, gray, black, or red, lesser amounts fine quartz sand; sometimes sand and angular fragments about equal amounts; sometimes sand predominates; temper conspicuous in cross-section and on worn surfaces. *Texture core:* fine to medium. *Vessel walls:* strong. *Fracture:* shattering. *Surface finish:* surfaces impacted; polished, polishing marks often conspicuous around vessel; polished after painted. *Surface color:* dull orange-red to orange; color surface and core vary together; do not contrast. *Forms:* bowls, jars (rare). *Recorded range thickness bowl walls:* 3.7 to 6.7 mm; greatest individual range recorded, 2 mm; average thickness (24 sherds), 5 mm. *Rims:* bowls, IA3, IA7, IA8, IIA7, IIIA3, IIIA4, IIIA7. *Decoration:* painted. *Paint:* black; usually dark brown or light black; usually weak and flat, occasionally rich and dense; often more dense at ends of brush stroke. *Pigment:* manganese (test by Colton). *Designs:* bowls—interior surface only; usually stripe immediately beneath rim; decorative band around vessel sides; motifs of band often join narrow or wide line framing band; below band, stripe as below rim; top and bottom lines occasionally broken (life line); band composed of narrow diagonal or horizontal hatching, rectangular panels with series of wide staggered lines; sometimes small squares pendent from narrow lines; long solid triangles with hooks; interlocking scrolls; occasionally wide-line cross-hatchings.

RANGE:

The Jeddito, Polacca, Wepo, and Oraibi drainages; also Little Colorado River near Winslow, and Clear Creek, Navajo County, Arizona.

REMARKS:

This type is so similar to Tuwiuca Black-on-orange that trade specimens from the interlying area may need to be compared directly with known material for safe identification.

JEDDITO POLYCHROME: new type

TYPE SPECIMENS: Type sherds Nos. AT 1227, 1229–1231, 1237–1239 in the Type Collection of the Museum of Northern Arizona.

TYPE SITE: Kwaituki Pueblo (NA 849), upper Oraibi Wash, Hopi Reservation, Navajo County, Arizona.

STAGE: Pueblo III.

TIME: Probably between 1250–1300 A.D.

DESCRIPTION:

Constructed: by coiling. *Fired:* in oxidizing atmosphere. *Core:* light brick-red to dark orange, frequently pink, sometimes gray. *Temper:* variable; in most specimens, angular fragments, medium fine of fairly uniform size, yellowish, gray, black, or red, lesser amounts fine quartz sand; sometimes sand and angular fragments about equal amounts; sometimes sand predominates; temper conspicuous in cross-section and on worn surfaces. *Texture core:* fine to medium. *Vessel walls:* generally strong. *Fracture:* slightly crumbling to shattering. *Surface finish:* surfaces generally impacted, or possibly lightly slipped or washed with same (?) material as paste clay; polishing marks generally noticeable; surface occasionally crazed; usually fairly smooth. *Surface color:* orange-red to buff; color surface and core generally vary together. *Forms:* bowls. *Recorded range thickness bowl walls:* 3.7 to 7.1 mm; greatest individual range recorded, 1.6 mm; average thickness, ca 6 mm. *Rims:* bowls, IA3, IA4, IA6, IA7. *Decoration:* painted. *Paint:* black and white; black paint, generally light brown to black, usually weak and flat (polished after painted), occasionally rich and dense. *Pigments:* black—manganese, iron-carbon, some copper (tests by F. G. Hawley; H. S. Colton); white pigment—presumably kaolin. *Designs:* bowls—interior and exterior surfaces; interior, predominantly black, occasionally black outlined in white; exterior design, white; usually stripe immediately beneath rim; decorative band around vessel sides; motifs of band often join line framing band; exterior, one or more stripes or wide lines, often almost obliterated. *Style of Design:* early Pueblo IV.

RANGE:

Abundant in the Hopi Reservation; recorded also from Little Colorado River (NA 2212), and from Clear Creek (Chavez Pass Pueblo). Recorded only from Navajo County, Arizona.

AWATOBI YELLOW WARE

The recognition of this ware is made principally for convenience in study for the same reasons as those already given for Homolovi Orange Ware. Because Awatobi Yellow Ware is presented before Jeddito Yellow Ware does not mean that a type in Awatobi Yellow Ware was the first type to show characters common only to these two wares. If a ware includes only utility types it is presented before the companion ware of table types to more forcefully stress the indigenous character of the utility types.

KEY 10: AWATOBI YELLOW WARE

Surface corrugated..........................Jeddito Corrugated (p. 144)
Surface tooled................................Jeddito Tooled (p. 145)
Surface not altered..........................Jeddito Plain (p. 144)

AWATOBI YELLOW WARE: new ware

SYNONYM: Hopi Yellow Ware, Hough, 1903.
STAGE: Pueblo IV.
TIME: Between 1300–1700 A.D.

DESCRIPTION:

Constructed: by coiling. *Fired:* in oxidizing atmosphere. *Core:* normally yellow; black in some specimens. *Temper:* fine to coarse quartz sand; occasionally reddish angular fragments; temper generally conspicuous in cross-section and on surfaces. *Texture core:* medium to very coarse. *Fracture:* crumbling or shattering. *Vessel walls:* medium strong to strong. *Surface finish:* never slipped, never polished (diagnostic). *Surface color:* normally yellow; over-fired specimens pinkish or blackish but some yellow usually present; surface and core do not contrast. *Fire clouds:* common. *Forms:* jars, plates, bowls. *Jar rims:* IA2, IIIA2, IIIA3, IB2, IIIB3, IC2. *Recorded range thickness jar walls:* 3.2 to 10.3 mm; greatest individual range recorded, 5.3 mm; average thickness, ca 7 mm. *Decoration:* no painted decoration; plain, corrugated, or tooled surfaces; base of vessels sometimes have basket imprint.

RANGE:
Hopi Indian Reservation, Navajo County, Arizona.

REMARKS:
Named for Awatobi Mesa. Apparently this ware includes utility types only.

JEDDITO CORRUGATED

DESCRIBED BY: Hargrave, 1932, p. 26.
NAMED BY: Hargrave, loc. cit.
TYPE SPECIMENS: Type sherds Nos. 2632–2646, 2660–2662, 4060 in the Type Collection of the Museum of Northern Arizona.
STAGE: Pueblo IV.
TIME: Between 1300–1625 A.D.

DESCRIPTION (revised):
Constructed: by coiling. *Fired:* in oxidizing atmosphere. *Core:* normally yellow; blackish in some specimens. *Temper:* coarse quartz sand; conspicuous in cross-section and on surfaces; occasionally reddish angular fragments. *Texture core:* medium to coarse. *Fracture:* crumbling or shattering. *Vessel walls:* strong. *Surface finish:* interior surface, scraped, not polished; exterior surface, corrugated; coils unobliterated on surfaces; manipulated in various ways—sometimes indented, sometimes flattened. *Surface color:* yellow to cream; overfired specimens, blackish or pinkish but some yellow usually present; surface and core do not contrast. *Fire clouds:* common. *Forms:* jars, plates. *Rims:* jars, IIIA2; plain; sometimes flattened coils. *Decoration:* Deadmans, Tusayan, and Moenkopi styles of corrugating; sometimes basket imprint.

RANGE:
Hopi Indian Reservation, Navajo County, Arizona. One sherd of small trade (?) vessel (AT 2660) from Homolovi Pueblo (NA 952), Winslow, Navajo County, Arizona.

REMARKS:
For detailed distribution see Hargrave, 1932, pp. 26–27.

JEDDITO PLAIN

DESCRIBED BY: Hargrave, 1932, p. 25.
NAMED BY: Hargrave, loc. cit.

OXIDIZING ATMOSPHERE

TYPE SPECIMENS: Jar No. 257/1118, and sherds Nos. AT 2607–2620, 2631 in the Type Collection of the Museum of Northern Arizona.
TYPE SITE: Kokopnyama Pueblo (NA 1019), Jeddito Valley, Navajo County, Arizona.
STAGE: Pueblo IV.
TIME: Between 1300–1625 A.D.

DESCRIPTION (revised):
Constructed: by coiling. *Fired:* in oxidizing atmosphere. *Core:* normally yellow; blackish in some specimens. *Temper:* generally coarse quartz sand; conspicuous in cross-section and on surfaces. *Texture core:* medium to very coarse. *Fracture:* crumbling to shattering. *Vessel walls:* strong. *Surface finish:* scraped, not corrugated. *Surface color:* yellowish to cream; surface and core do not contrast. *Fire clouds:* common. *Forms:* jars, plates. *Rims:* jars, IIIA3, IB2, IIIB3, IC2; jar rims plain, sometimes flattened coil; plate rim: IA3. *Decoration:* undecorated except that bases sometimes have basket imprint.

RANGE:
Hopi Indian Reservation, Navajo County, Arizona.

JEDDITO TOOLED

DESCRIBED BY: Hargrave, 1932, p. 27.
NAMED BY: Hargrave, loc. cit.
ILLUSTRATED: Fig. 7, P. 38.
TYPE SPECIMENS: Jar No. 627–A185 and type sherds Nos. AT 2663–2681 in the Type Collection of the Museum of Northern Arizona.
TYPE SITE: Kokopnyama Pueblo (NA 1019), Jeddito Valley, Navajo County, Arizona.
STAGE: Pueblo IV.
TIME: Between 1300–1625 A.D.

DESCRIPTION (revised):
Constructed: by coiling. *Fired:* in oxidizing atmosphere. *Core:* normally yellow; blackish in some specimens. *Temper:* generally coarse quartz sand; conspicuous in cross-section and on surfaces. *Texture core:* fine to very coarse. *Fracture:* crumbling to shattering. *Vessel walls:* strong. *Surface finish:* interiors scraped, not polished; exterior surface, scraped and tooled. *Surface color:* yellow to cream; over-fired specimens pinkish to blackish but some yellow usually present; surface and core do not contrast. *Fire clouds:* common. *Form:* jars. *Rims:* jars, IA2, IIIA3. *Recorded range thickness jar walls:* 5.4 to 9.5 mm; greatest individual range recorded, 3.3 mm; average thickness (21 sherds), 7.2 mm. *Decoration:* various imprints made with tools; base of vessels sometimes have basket imprint.

RANGE:
Hopi Indian Reservation, Navajo County, Arizona.
REMARKS:
For detailed distribution see Hargrave, 1932, p. 27.

JEDDITO YELLOW WARE

Probably no ware of Pueblo Pottery is admired as much as is Jeddito Yellow Ware. Not only are vessels of this ware conspicuous for beauty of form and for elaborate designs, but probably are admired as much for the clear, bright yellow tones of the vessel surface. The vessels of gold that lured the early Spanish explorers into the Southwest, easily could have been pottery vessels of Jeddito Yellow Ware that were commonly traded throughout the Southwest. To natives who did not refine metals, "gold" would refer to color (Hargrave, 1935, a, p. 20).

The ware developed late. Its appearance does not mark a great change or special advancement in techniques since examples of this ware do not differ greatly in form or finish from vessels made long before. Perfection in techniques of constructing and finishing pottery vessels seems to have been reached before the appearance even of the oldest pottery types of the culture. But the appearance of this, and of its companion ware, Awatobi Yellow Ware, does mark the adoption of a new technique in firing—or possibly indicates the arrival of peoples using a different technique of firing—into a region where this new technique was known only from trade vessels. Prior to the birth of these two yellow wares, the reducing atmosphere was used exclusively in the region where these yellow wares are indigenous. The same materials used in manufacturing vessels of Awatobi Yellow and Jeddito Yellow wares were used in vessels of the earlier gray and white wares of the same region. Where vessels once were white, later they were shades of yellow.

KEY 11: JEDDITO YELLOW WARE

Slipped...Key m (p. 148)
Not slipped..Key n (p. 150)

JEDDITO YELLOW WARE: new ware

SYNONYMS: (a) Hopi Yellow Ware, Hough, 1903; (b) Bluff Ware, Spier, 1917, p. 255.

STAGES: Pueblo III (?)–Pueblo IV.

TIME: Probably between 1250–1937 A.D.

DESCRIPTION:
Constructed: by coiling. *Fired:* in oxidizing atmosphere. *Core:* creamy yellow or tan, occasionally pinkish or brownish. *Carbon streak:* absent. *Temper:* predominantly quartz sand; rarely visible without glass to naked eye; occasionally reddish angular fragments; rarely visible without glass either in cross-section or on vessel surfaces. *Texture core:* fine to very fine. *Vessel walls:* strong. *Fracture:* shattering. *Surface finish:* both surfaces bowls, exterior surfaces jars, impacted in all types except in Kokop Series which are slipped; surfaces all types well-polished; interior jars, scraped, frequently well-smoothed. *Surface color:* orange through yellow to cream; impacted surfaces, usually cream, yellow, sometimes light orange or brownish yellow. *Fire clouds:* absent. *Forms:* bowls, dippers. *Recorded range thickness bowl walls:* 3 to 10 mm; greatest individual range recorded, 3.9 mm; average thickness, ca 6.4 mm. *Recorded range thickness jar walls:* 4.1 to 9.8 mm; greatest individual range recorded, 2.7 mm; average thickness, ca 6.7 mm. *Rims:* bowls, IA3, IA4, IA6, IB2, IIB2, IIIB2, ID2, VB2; jars, IIIA2, IB2, IIB2, IC2, ID3. *Decoration:* painted; black—on every type, often brownish; white—on some types, usually somewhat fugitive. *Pigment:* black—manganese, iron, copper; white—presumably kaolin; red—in combination with black on some types, red in combination with black and white on Kawaioku Polychrome. *Designs:* usually well executed; always on bowl interiors and jar exteriors; less frequently on bowl exteriors; stippling on Jeddito Stippled and Awatobi Polychrome; engraving through paint on Jeddito Engraved and Awatobi Polychrome.

RANGE:
Southern part of Hopi Indian Reservation, Arizona. Widely traded.

KOKOP SERIES

There are early types of Jeddito Yellow Ware that differ in some minor process of finishing the vessel surface. Objectively this difference is conspicuous because the surface color is *red* and not *yellow* as in the later types. *Kokop Series is characterized by a thin reddish slip on a yellow base.* Beneath this slip the surface of the vessel, as also is the cross-section of the vessel, does not materially differ from other types of Jeddito Yellow Ware. In form and design, these early types clearly evidence strong influence from regions further south (Hargrave, 1935 a, p. 22).

KEY m: KOKOP SERIES

1. Polychrome.. 2
   Not polychrome.....................Kokop Black-on-orange (p. 149)
2. Temper visible to naked eye.............Kwaituki Polychrome (p. 148)
   Temper not visible to naked eye...........Kokop Polychrome (p. 149)

KWAITUKI POLYCHROME: new type

TYPE SPECIMENS: Type sherds Nos. AT 1233 and 4272 in the Type Collection of the Museum of Northern Arizona.

TYPE SITE: Kwaituki Pueblo (NA 894), upper Oraibi Wash, Hopi Indian Reservation, Navajo County, Arizona.

STAGE: Pueblo III.

TIME: Probably between 1250–1300 A.D.

DESCRIPTION:

Constructed: by coiling. *Fired:* in oxidizing atmosphere. *Core:* yellow. *Temper:* predominantly quartz sand; rarely visible without glass either in cross-section or on vessel surfaces. *Texture core:* fine to very fine. *Fracture:* generally shattering. *Vessel walls:* strong. *Surface finish:* surfaces smoothed, polished, slipped; slip thin. *Surface color:* orange-red to red; surface and core contrast; base color frequently seen beneath slip; occasionally few minute whitish or yellowish flakes visible on surface. *Forms:* bowls. *Rims:* bowls IA6, IA7. *Recorded range thickness bowl walls:* 4.9 to 6.7 mm; greatest individual range recorded, 1.7 mm; average thickness, ca 6 mm. *Decoration:* painted black and white. *Pigment:* black—manganese, iron, copper (test by F. G. Hawley); white—presumably kaolin. *Designs:* geometric; black decoration, only on interior bowl surfaces; white decoration, confined to exterior surface. *Decorative Style:* St. Johns Style.

RANGE:

Recorded only from Kwaituki Pueblo, Oraibi Wash, and Kokopnyama Pueblo, Jeddito Valley, Hopi Indian Reservation, Navajo County, Arizona.

REMARKS:

Named for Kwaituki Pueblo, the Type Site. A basic type in the origin of Jeddito Yellow Ware.

KOKOP BLACK-ON-ORANGE

DESCRIBED BY: Hargrave, 1932, p. 28.
NAMED BY: Hargrave, loc. cit.
TYPE SPECIMENS: Type sherds Nos. AT 922–924, 1044, 1046, 1071, 2709 in the Type Collection of the Museum of Northern Arizona.
TYPE SITE: Kokopnyama Pueblo (NA 1019), Jeddito Valley, Hopi Indian Reservation, Navajo County, Arizona.
STAGE: Pueblo III.
TIME: Probably between 1250–1325 A.D.

DESCRIPTION (revised):
Constructed: by coiling. *Fired:* in oxidizing atmosphere. *Core:* creamy-yellow to yellow. *Temper:* predominantly fine quartz sand rarely visible to naked eye; occasionally reddish angular fragments; rarely visible without glass either in cross-section or on vessel surfaces. *Texture core:* very fine. *Fracture:* shattering. *Vessel walls:* strong. *Surface finish:* surfaces smoothed, generally highly polished; slipped. *Surface color:* reddish; surface and core, contrast; base color generally seen beneath thin slip; occasionally few minute whitish or yellowish flakes visible on surface. *Forms:* bowls, dippers, jars; bowl sometimes has single horizontal handle. *Rims:* bowls, IA3, IA4; jars, IIIA2. *Recorded range thickness bowl walls:* 4.8 to 6.7 mm; greatest individual range recorded, 1.9 mm; average thickness, ca 6 mm. *Recorded range thickness jar walls:* 6.2 to 9.8 mm; greatest individual range recorded, 1.6 mm; average thickness, ca 7 mm. *Decoration:* painted black. *Designs:* geometric; decoration on interior surface bowls; exterior surface jars.

RANGE:
Hopi Indian Reservation, Navajo County, Arizona. Trade specimens, AT 1044 and 1046, recorded from Cakwabayaki Pueblo (NA 1026), Bidahochi Pueblo (NA 1054), upper Cottonwood Wash, Moqui Butte section, Navajo County, Arizona; also, sherd No. AT 2709 from Walker Canyon, Verde River Valley, Yavapai County, Arizona.

REMARKS:
For further details see Hargrave, 1932, pp. 28–29.

KOKOP POLYCHROME: new type

TYPE SPECIMENS: Type sherds Nos. AT 298, 2710, and 4273 in the Type Collection of the Museum of Northern Arizona.
TYPE SITE: Kokopnyama Pueblo (NA 1019), Jeddito Valley, Hopi Indian Reservation, Navajo County, Arizona.
STAGE: Pueblo III or (early) Pueblo IV.
TIME: Probably between 1250–1325 A.D.

DESCRIPTION:

Constructed: by coiling. *Fired:* in oxidizing atmosphere. *Core:* creamy-yellow to yellow. *Temper:* predominantly fine quartz sand, rarely visible to naked eye; occasional reddish angular fragment; rarely visible without glass either in cross-section or on vessel surfaces. *Texture core:* very fine. *Fracture:* shattering. *Vessel walls:* strong. *Surface finish:* surfaces smoothed, highly polished; slipped. *Surface color:* reddish; surface and core, contrast; base color generally seen beneath thin slip; occasionally few minute whitish or yellowish flakes visible on surface. *Forms:* bowls. *Rim:* bowls, IA7. *Recorded range thickness bowl walls:* 6.1 to 7.6 mm; greatest individual range recorded, 0.8 mm; average thickness, ca 6.5 mm. *Decoration:* painted black and white; black decoration only on interior surface bowls; white decoration, generally confined to interior surface. *Pigment:* white, presumably kaolin.

RANGE:

Jeddito Valley, Hopi Indian Reservation, Navajo County, Arizona.

JEDDITO SERIES

Characterized by yellow core, polished and unslipped yellow surface.

KEY n: JEDDITO SERIES

Black painted decoration only.............Jeddito Black-on-yellow (p. 150)
Stippled.......................................Jeddito Stippled (p. 153)
Engraved (in paint).........................Jeddito Engraved (p. 154)
Black design outlined with white............Bidahochi Polychrome (p. 151)
White filled areas.........................Kawaioku Polychrome (p. 156)
Black or brown and red painted design........Sikyatki Polychrome (p. 152)
Black or brown and red painted design; engraved....................
 Awatobi Polychrome (p. 155)

JEDDITO BLACK-ON-YELLOW

SYNONYMS: (a) Polished decorated Ware, Fewkes, 1898, p. 652; (b) Yellow Ware, Fewkes, loc. cit.; (c) Buff Ware, Spier, 1918, p. 339; (d) Jeddito Yellow, Kidder, 1924, p. 93; pl. 42, e; (e) Jeddito Yellow Ware, Hawley, 1929, p. 748; (f) Jeddito Brown-on-yellow, Gladwin, W. & H. S., 1930 a, p. 177.
DESCRIBED BY: Fewkes, 1898, p. 652.
NAMED BY: Hargrave, 1931, p. 118.
ILLUSTRATIONS: Fewkes, 1898, colored plates Nos. LX, CXLV; 1904, XXVI b, XLII; Hough, 1903, colored plated Nos. 59, 68, 69, upper plate 70 (except cat. no. 212333), 94, 99, 101; 258/1121 (Fig. 33).

Fig. 33. ($\frac{1}{6}\times$).

TYPE SPECIMENS: Bowl No. 243–940, jar No. 147–579; sherds Nos. AT 2727–2768, AT 3061–3063 in the Type Collection of the Museum of Northern Arizona.

TYPE SITE: Kokopnyama Pueblo (NA 1019), Jeddito Valley, Navajo County, Arizona.

STAGE: Pueblo IV.

TIME: Probably between 1325–1600 A.D.

DESCRIPTION (revised):
Constructed: by coiling. *Fired:* in oxidizing atmosphere. *Core:* generally yellow; pinkish in some specimens. *Temper:* fine quartz sand rarely visible to naked eye; occasionally reddish angular fragments; sand temper rarely visible without glass either in cross-section or on vessel surfaces. *Texture core:* very fine to fine. *Vessel walls:* strong. *Fracture:* shattering. *Surface finish:* smooth, highly polished, impacted; occasionally few minute whitish or yellowish flakes visible on surface (not seen in cross-section). *Surface color:* cream to bright yellow (yellow predominates); over-fired specimens orange or metallic; surface and core do not contrast. *Forms:* bowls, jars, dippers. *Recorded range thickness bowl walls:* 3.7 to 10 mm; greatest individual range recorded, 3.9 mm; average thickness (56 sherds), 6.1 mm. *Recorded range thickness jar walls:* 4.3 to 9 mm; greatest individual range recorded, 2.7 mm; average thickness, ca 6.5 mm. *Rims:* bowls, IA3, IA6, IIIA6, IB2, IIB2, IIIB2, ID2, VB2; jars, IIIA2, IB2, IC2. *Painted decoration:* black or brown. *Pigments:* manganese (test by Colton). *Designs:* geometric; occasionally life forms.

RANGE:
Center of production, Hopi Reservation. Generally distributed as trade in Pueblo IV sites over nearly the whole of the Pueblo Area.

BIDAHOCHI POLYCHROME

DESCRIBED BY: Hargrave, 1932, p. 30.

NAMED BY: Hargrave, loc. cit.

ILLUSTRATIONS: Hough, 1903, pl. 70, cat. No. 212333; Fewkes, 1904, colored plate LVI b; 20/235 (Fig. 34).

TYPE SPECIMENS: Jar No. 20–235 and sherds Nos. AT 1047–1060, 2834 in the Type Collection of the Museum of Northern Arizona.

TYPE SITE: Bidahochi Pueblo (NA 1054), upper Cottonwood Wash, north of Holbrook, Navajo County, Arizona.

STAGE: Pueblo IV.

TIME: Probably between 1320–1400 A.D.

Fig. 34. ($\frac{1}{6}\times$).

DESCRIPTION (revised):

Constructed: by coiling. *Fired:* in oxidizing atmosphere. *Core:* yellow, pinkish in some specimens. *Temper:* fine quartz sand, rarely visible to naked eye; occasionally reddish angular fragments; sand temper rarely visible without glasses either in cross-section or on vessel surfaces. *Texture core:* very fine to fine. *Vessel walls:* strong. *Fracture:* shattering. *Surface finish:* highly polished, impacted; occasionally few whitish or yellowish flakes visible on surface. *Surface color:* yellow, some vessels orange or metallic (if over-fired); surface and core do not contrast, except in over-fired specimens. *Forms:* bowls, jars. *Recorded range thickness bowl walls:* 3 to 7.4 mm; greatest individual range recorded, 2.2 mm; average thickness, ca 6 mm. *Recorded range thickness jar walls:* 5 to 8.3 mm; greatest individual range recorded, 2.2 mm; average thickness, ca 6.5 mm. *Rims:* bowls, IA3, IIA7. *Painted decoration:* black and white; white paint always used in outlining black paint. *Designs:* geometric. *Patterns:* on exterior surface jars; interior and sometimes exterior surface bowls.

RANGE:

Center of manufacture, Hopi Reservation, Navajo County, Arizona. Widely traded to early Pueblo IV sites.

SIKYATKI POLYCHROME

SYNONYMS: (a) Polished decorated ware, Fewkes, 1898, p. 652; (b) Yellow Ware, Fewkes, loc. cit.; (c) Buff Ware, Spier, 1918, p. 339; (d) Sikyatki Ware, Kidder, 1924, p. 93.
DESCRIBED BY: Fewkes, 1898.
NAMED BY: Hargrave, 1931, p. 118.
ILLUSTRATIONS: Fewkes, 1898, colored plates Nos. CXXI, CXXII, CXXIV, CXXV b, CXXVI, CXXXVII, CXXXIX, CXLIII, CXLIV, and CXLVIII; 1904, colored plates Nos. XXVII a, LI, LVI a; Hough, 1903, colored plate No. 98.
TYPE SPECIMENS: Cotype jar No. 302–1599 and cotype sherds Nos. AT 2769–2782, 2064 in the Type Collection of the Museum of Northern Arizona.
TYPE SITE: Sikyatki Pueblo (NA 814), upper Polacca Wash, Hopi Reservation, Navajo County, Arizona.
STAGE: Pueblo IV.
TIME: Probably between 1400–1625 A.D.

DESCRIPTION (revised):

Constructed: by coiling. *Fired:* in oxidizing atmosphere. *Core:* cream to yellow, brownish, pinkish in some specimens. *Temper:* fine quartz sand rarely visible to naked eye; occasionally reddish angular fragments; sand temper rarely visible without glass either in cross-section or on vessel surfaces. *Texture core:* very fine to fine. *Vessel walls:* strong. *Fracture:* shattering. *Surface finish:* impacted, highly polished; occasionally few minute whitish or yellowish flakes visible on surface. *Surface color:* creamy yellow to bright yellow; yellow predominates; over-fired specimens usually orange; surface and core do not contrast, except in over-fired specimens. *Forms:* bowls, jars, dippers. *Recorded range thickness bowl walls:* 4.2 to 8.6 mm; greatest individual range recorded, 0.9 mm. *Recorded range thickness jar walls:* 4.1 to 8.2 mm; greatest individual range recorded, 2.4 mm. *Painted decoration* (never engraved): black or brown and red. *Designs:* geometric; occasionally life forms; characterized by black and red and yellow (base).

RANGE:

Center of production, Hopi Reservation. Two trade sherds from Homolovi (NA 953), Little Colorado River Valley, near Winslow, Navajo County, Arizona.

JEDDITO STIPPLED: new type

SYNONYM: Jeddito Black-on-yellow-stippled, Hargrave, 1932, p. 30.
DESCRIBED BY: Hargrave, loc. cit.
ILLUSTRATION: AT 2725 (Fig. 35).
TYPE SPECIMENS: Sherds Nos. AT 2725 in the Type Collection of the Museum of Northern Arizona.
TYPE SITE: Kawaioku Pueblo (NA 1001), Jeddito Valley, Hopi Reservation, Navajo County, Arizona.
STAGE: Pueblo IV.
TIME: Probably between 1350–1600 A.D.
DESCRIPTION (revised):

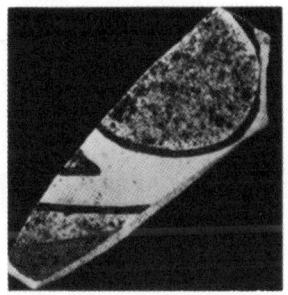

Fig. 35. (½ ×).

Constructed: by coiling. *Fired:* in oxidizing atmosphere. *Core:* generally yellow, pinkish in some specimens. *Temper:* fine quartz sand rarely visible to naked eye; occasionally reddish angular fragments; sand temper rarely visible without glass either in cross-section or on vessel surfaces. *Texture core:* very fine to fine. *Vessel walls:* strong. *Fracture:* shattering. *Surface finish:* impacted, highly polished; occasionally few minute whitish or yellowish flakes visible on surface. *Surface color:* cream to bright yellow; yellow predominates; over-fired specimens, usually orange. *Forms:* bowls. *Recorded range thickness bowl walls:* 5 to 6 mm; greatest individual range recorded, 1 mm; average thickness, ca 5.5 mm. *Painted decoration:* black or brown. *Design:* geometric; always characterized by stippled areas in design.

COMPARISON: Distinguished from other types of Jeddito Series by use of one decorative color and employment of stippling.

RANGE:

Recorded only from the Hopi Reservation, Navajo County, Arizona.

REMARKS:

The recognition of this type is based entirely upon the appearance of a new variation in decorative technique, namely, stippling. Normally this type would be included with Jeddito Black-on-yellow but there is a definite time interval between the first appearance of Jeddito Black-on-yellow and of Jeddito Stippled. The long time range of Jeddito Black-on-yellow makes the recognition of Jeddito Stippled convenient since the time range of Jeddito Stippled is shorter than, although concurrent in part with, Jeddito Black-on-yellow.

JEDDITO ENGRAVED: new type

SYNONYM: Jeddito Black-on-yellow-engraved, Hargrave, 1932, p. 30.
DESCRIBED BY: Hargrave, loc. cit.
TYPE SPECIMENS: Sherds Nos. AT 2722–2724, 2726 in the Type Collection of the Museum of Northern Arizona.
TYPE SITE: Kawaioku Pueblo (NA 1001), Jeddito Valley, Hopi Reservation, Navajo County, Arizona.
STAGE: Pueblo IV.
TIME: Probably between 1350–1600 A.D.

DESCRIPTION (revised):

Constructed: by coiling. *Fired:* in oxidizing atmosphere. *Core:* generally yellow, pinkish in some specimens. *Temper:* fine quartz sand rarely visible to naked eye; occasionally reddish angular fragments; sand temper rarely visible without glass either in cross-section or on vessel surfaces. *Texture core:* very fine to fine. *Vessel walls:* strong. *Fracture:* shattering. *Surface finish:* impacted, highly polished. *Surface color:* creamy yellow to bright yellow; yellow predominates; over-fired specimens usually orange; surface and core do not contrast; occasionally few minute whitish or yellowish flakes visible on surface. *Forms:* bowls, jars. *Recorded range thickness bowl walls:* 5.2 to 7 mm; greatest individual range recorded, 1.8 mm; average thickness, ca 6.5 mm. *Recorded range thickness jar walls:* 5 to 7.5 mm; greatest individual range recorded, 2.2 mm; average thickness, ca 6.5 mm. *Decoration:* painted and engraved; paint black. *Designs:* geometric; always characterized by engravings in paint; engravings simple geometric designs or elements.

OXIDIZING ATMOSPHERE

COMPARISON: Distinguished from other types of Jeddito Series by use of one decorative color and employment of engraving.

RANGE:

Recorded only from the Hopi Reservation, Navajo County, Arizona.

REMARKS:

The recognition of this type is based entirely upon the appearance of a new variation in decorative technique, namely, engraving. Like Jeddito Stippled, the recognition of Jeddito Engraved is a convenience in recognizing short time periods since the appearance of Jeddito Engraved is later than some other types in the Jeddito Series.

AWATOBI POLYCHROME: new type

SYNONYM: Sikyatki Polychrome, in part, Hargrave, 1932, p. 30.

TYPE SPECIMENS: Sherds Nos. AT 2065, 2783 in the Type Collection of the Museum of Northern Arizona.

TYPE SITE: Awatobi Pueblo (NA 820), Jeddito Valley, Navajo County, Arizona.

STAGE: Pueblo IV.

TIME: Probably between 1400–1625 A.D.

DESCRIPTION:

Constructed: by coiling. *Fired:* in oxidizing atmosphere. *Core:* cream to yellow, brownish (rarely). *Temper:* fine quartz sand rarely visible to naked eye; occasionally reddish angular fragments; sand temper rarely visible without glass either in cross section or on vessel surfaces. *Texture core:* very fine to fine. *Vessel walls:* strong. *Fracture:* shattering. *Surface finish:* impacted, highly polished. *Surface color:* creamy yellow to bright yellow; yellow predominates; surface color and core do not contrast; occasionally few minute whitish or yellowish flakes visible on surface. *Forms:* bowls, jars. *Recorded range thickness bowl walls:* 6 to 7.6 mm; greatest individual range recorded, 1.6 mm. *Recorded range thickness jar walls:* 6.6 mm; greatest individual range recorded, 1.7 mm. *Decoration:* painted and engraved; paint, black or brown and red. *Designs:* geometric; characterized by patterns in black and red on yellow (base) with engravings in black paint; sometimes stippled also.

RANGE:

Recorded only from the upper Jeddito Valley, Navajo County, Arizona.

KAWAIOKU POLYCHROME

SYNONYMS: (a) Polished decorated ware, Fewkes, 1898, p. 652; (b) Yellow Ware, Fewkes, loc. cit.; (c) Sikyatki Ware, Kidder, 1924, p. 93.
DESCRIBED BY: Hargrave, 1932, p. 31.
NAMED BY: Hargrave, loc. cit.
ILLUSTRATIONS: Fewkes, 1898, colored plate CXXIV.
TYPE SPECIMENS: Jar No. 378–1820 and sherds Nos. AT 2711–2721 in the Type Collection of the Museum of Northern Arizona.
TYPE SITE: Kawaioku Pueblo (NA 1001), Jeddito Valley, Navajo County, Arizona.
STAGE: Pueblo IV.
TIME: Probably between 1450–1625 A.D.
DESCRIPTION (revised):

Constructed: by coiling. *Fired:* in oxidizing atmosphere. *Core:* cream to yellow; pinkish in some specimens. *Temper:* fine quartz sand rarely visible to naked eye; occasionally reddish angular fragments; sand temper rarely visible without glass either in cross section or on vessel surfaces. *Texture core:* very fine to fine. *Vessel walls:* strong. *Fracture:* shattering. *Surface finish:* impacted, highly polished. *Surface color:* creamy yellow to bright yellow; yellow predominates; surface color and core do not contrast; occasionally few minute whitish or yellowish flakes visible on surface. *Forms:* bowls, jars. *Recorded range thickness bowl walls:* 4.1 to 9.2 mm; greatest individual range recorded, 2.6 mm; average thickness, ca 7 mm. *Recorded range thickness jar walls:* 4.9 to 8.1 mm; greatest individual range recorded, 1.7 mm; average thickness, ca 6.5 mm. *Rims:* jars, IIA2, ID3. *Painted decoration:* black and white on yellow (base) or black, red, and white on yellow (base). *Designs:* geometric; characterized by white in massed areas outlined with another painted color.

COMPARISONS: Differs from other types in the Jeddito Series in the use of white paint in solid massed areas.

RANGE:

Jeddito Valley and Polacca Wash (Sikyatki Pueblo), Navajo County, Arizona.

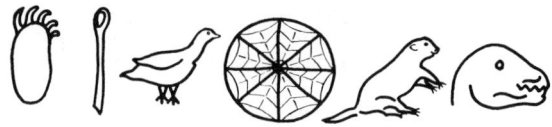

B: POTTERY CONSTRUCTED BY PADDLING

Gifford (1928) has presented evidence to prove that the method of constructing pottery vessels with the assistance of an anvil and a paddle is an advanced technique over constructing vessels by "coiling." Regardless of which of these two methods actually is the more recently developed, the fact remains that both methods appeared in southern Arizona before fired pottery appeared in northern Arizona. Further, the earliest known examples of Arizona pottery made by paddling, like the earliest examples of "coiling" are perfect when techniques of construction only are considered. The point of origin has no specific bearing on this work.

The oldest known paddle-and-anvil pottery of Arizona is of the Hohokam Culture of the southern desert. Hohokam wares are not included in this handbook because the Hohokam Culture is distinct from the Basket Maker—Pueblo Culture. This southern culture cannot lightly be passed by, however, because apparently influence from the Hohokam Culture was felt far to the north. Whereas, ceramic knowledge of the true Basket Maker—Pueblo Culture seems to have come from peoples producing Mogollon Brown Ware, ceramic knowledge of peoples in the San Francisco Mountain region, from the west and south, possibly was derived from Hohokam peoples. Few examples of Hohokam Buff Ware have been found on the plateaus of northern Arizona but techniques of construction, and a number of other cultural characters, are dominant in some northern localities south of the Little Colorado River.

Because of the strength of Hohokam influence in a large part of the area covered by this handbook we find several wares and numerous types.

ALAMEDA BROWN WARE

At an early date this ware was parallel in time and contiguous in area to Mogollon Brown Ware of the eastern strip of the Pueblo area. Alameda Brown Ware is the dominant ware north of the Hohokam Country and south of the Little Colorado River. The ware name is taken from an early Spanish name for the Little Colorado River.

Because both table and utility types occur in all types of this ware, and also because painted decoration is rare, trade pieces of Alameda Brown Ware would not be expected to commonly occur.

KEY 12: ALAMEDA BROWN WARE

1. Temper predominantly black volcanic sand............Key p (p. 161)
    Temper not black volcanic sand................................ 2
2. Temper predominantly mica.........................Key r (p. 173)
    Temper mica, but not predominant...................Key o (p. 159)
    Temper (in part) red angular fragments...............Key q (p. 167)
    Temper predominantly light-colored angular fragments....Key p (p. 161)
                     Tonto Red (p. 166)
    Temper not predominantly light-colored angular fragments........
                            Key p (p. 161)

ALAMEDA BROWN WARE: new ware

STAGES: Basket Maker III–Pueblo IV.
TIME: pre-700 (?)–ca 1400 A.D.
DESCRIPTION:

Constructed: by paddling. *Fired:* in oxidizing atmosphere. *Core:* usually brick-red, brown, buff, orange, yellowish; less frequently gray or black. *Temper:* variable; in Adamana Series and Tonto Red, mostly quartz sand with small amounts opaque angular fragments; in Verde Series, usually about equal amounts quartz or feldspar (?) sand and opaque angular fragments; in some types of Rio de Flag and Tonto Series (except Tonto Red), mostly opaque fragments; in some types of Rio de Flag Series, mostly black volcanic sand. *Texture core:* usually medium to fine in most types; coarse to very coarse in Tonto Series. *Vessel walls:* usually medium strong to strong; sometimes weak in some types. *Fracture:* usually crumbling; occasionally shattering in Rio de Flag Series. *Surface finish:* always smoothed; frequently well-polished; sometimes gritty; never corrugated or indented; in Tonto, Verde, and Rio de Flag Series, several types impacted or thinly slipped; in most types smudged surfaces frequent or predominant; sometimes burnished; anvil marks on jar interiors, usually conspicuous. *Surface color:* exteriors usually red, tan, buff; occasionally grayish, as in Adamana Brown and Tuzigoot Black-on-gray; interiors (bowls), frequently black (smudged). *Forms:* bowls, jars; often difficult to distinguish form from individual sherds. *Rims:* IA3, IIA3, IA4, IIIA3, IIIA7, IB3, IIIB3. *Recorded range thickness vessel walls:* 3.8 to 13.8 mm; greatest individual range recorded, 9.9 mm; average thickness, ca 6.7 mm. *Paint:* black or red, white; both white and black paints, frequently somewhat fugitive.

OXIDIZING ATMOSPHERE

Decoration: painted; confined to exteriors of those types on which white or black paint occur; confined to bowl interiors of Tuzigoot Red-on-black.

RANGE:

Petrified Forest, Apache County; San Francisco Mountains, Coconino County; Verde Valley, Yavapai County; Tonto and Roosevelt basins, Gila County; Upper Gila River drainage, Arizona.

ADAMANA SERIES

The region about the Petrified Forest National Monument appears to be the focus for types of this series.

KEY o: ADAMANA SERIES

Exterior surface brown..........................Adamana Brown (p. 159)
Exterior surface red....................Adamana Fugitive Red (p. 160)

ADAMANA BROWN

DESCRIBED BY: Mera, 1934, pp. 4–5.

NAMED BY: Mera, loc. cit.

TYPE SPECIMENS: Laboratory of Anthropology, Santa Fe, New Mexico.

TYPE SITE: LA 1318, Petrified Forest National Monument, Apache County, Arizona.

STAGE: Basket Maker III (Mera, loc. cit., p. 5).

TIME: Pre-700 A.D.

DESCRIPTION (revised):

Constructed: by paddling. *Fired:* in oxidizing atmosphere. *Core:* gray through tan to light red. *Temper:* predominantly coarse water-worn quartz sand containing numerous flakes mica-like particles ("micaceous cast strikingly resembling fragments of mussel shell") and moderate amounts opaque angular fragments, gray or black; temper conspicuous on surfaces. *Texture core:* medium. *Vessel walls:* weak to medium strong. *Fracture:* slightly crumbling. *Surface finish:* "exterior surfaces of jars and both surfaces bowls are usually well smoothed but show little attempt to produce a polish. The interiors of jars, especially present on uneven appearance like that produced by the paddle and anvil process of shaping . . . " (Mera, loc. cit.). *Surface color:* "a light warm gray, through a tan to a light red" (Mera, loc. cit.); Dictionary of Color, 4B10, 13A1, 14E7. *Forms:* bowls, jars. *Rims:* "direct with no flaring." *Recorded range thickness vessel walls:* ca 4 mm to ca 6 mm. *Undecorated.*

COMPARISON: Rio de Flag, lesser amounts quartz sand; mica-like particles, not conspicuous on surfaces; surface color, brown. Woodruff Brown, constructed by coiling; no mica-like particles.

RANGE:
Petrified Forest National Monument, Arizona.

REMARKS:
See Mera, loc. cit., for further details.

ADAMANA FUGITIVE RED: new type

DESCRIBED BY: Mera, 1934 p. 4.
TYPE SPECIMENS: Laboratory of Anthropology, Santa Fe, New Mexico.
TYPE SITE: LA 1318, Petrified Forest National Monument, Arizona.
STAGE: Basket Maker III (Mera, loc. cit., p. 5).
TIME: Pre-700 (?)–ca 800 A.D.

DESCRIPTION (revised):

Constructed: by paddling. *Fired:* in oxidizing atmosphere. *Core:* gray through tan to light red. *Temper:* predominantly coarse water-worn quartz sand containing numerous flecks mica-like particles (micaceous cast strikingly resembling fragments of "mussel shell") and moderate amounts opaque angular fragments, gray or black; temper conspicuous on surfaces. *Texture core:* medium. *Vessel walls:* weak to medium strong. *Fracture:* slightly crumbling. *Surface finish:* "exterior surfaces of jars and both surfaces bowls are usually well smoothed but show little attempt to produce a polish. The interiors of jars, especially, present an uneven appearance like that produced by the paddle and anvil process of shaping . . . " (Mera, loc. cit.). *Surface color:* red (fugitive); pinkish when weathered; beneath red, color surface is gray through tan to light red. *Forms:* bowls, jars. *Recorded range thickness vessel walls:* ca 4 mm to ca 6 mm. *Decoration:* "fugitive red wash still adhering to their surfaces" (Mera, loc. cit.).

RANGE:
This type is included by Mera in the original description of Adamana Brown. See Mera, loc. cit., for further details.

RIO DE FLAG SERIES

The San Francisco Mountain Region is the focus of types in this series. Rio de Flag Series has a time range from Pueblo I to about the end of Pueblo III. At one time, near the beginning of Pueblo III, there was a change in the tempering material used. Other basic characters remained constant, however, and,

OXIDIZING ATMOSPHERE

although the new temper is conspicuous, other objective characters are readily recognized.

KEY p: RIO DE FLAG SERIES

1. Temper predominantly black volcanic sand.........Sunset Red (p. 163)
   Temper not predominantly black volcanic sand................... 2
2. Slipped................................Turkey Hill Red (p. 165)
   Not slipped... 3
3. Temper coarse light-colored angular fragments...Winona Brown (p. 162)
   Temper not coarse, but light-colored angular fragments; interior not smudged..............................Rio de Flag Brown (p. 161)
   Temper not light-colored angular fragments; interior surface smudged
   Rio de Flag Smudged (p. 162)

RIO DE FLAG BROWN

DESCRIBED BY: Colton, 1932, p. 9.
NAMED BY: Colton, loc. cit.
ILLUSTRATION: Jar 41/26a and bowl 41/26b (Fig. 36).
TYPE SPECIMENS: Jar No. 41/26a, bowl No. 41/26b, and sherds Nos. AT 448–449, 4152 in the Type Collection of the Museum of Northern Arizona.
TYPE SITE: Medicine Fort (NA 862), Medicine Valley, San Francisco Mountain region, Coconino County, Arizona.
STAGES: Pueblo I–II.
TIME: Pre-700–ca 1050 A.D.

DESCRIPTION (revised):

Fig. 36. (1/12×).

Constructed: by paddling. *Fired:* in oxidizing atmosphere. *Core:* gray to black; brick-red to brown to buff. *Carbon streak:* common. *Temper:* predominantly opaque angular fragments, gray, tan, or black; occasional grain quartz or feldspar (?). *Texture core:* medium to fine. *Vessel walls:* medium strong. *Fracture:* slightly crumbling to shattering. *Surface finish:* usually bumpy, impacted; sometimes polished; anvil marks, often conspicuous. *Surface color:* jar exteriors and both surfaces bowls, reddish-brown to rich brown; jar interiors, brown to brownish-gray. *Fire clouds:* common. *Forms:* bowls, jars (predominate). *Recorded range thickness vessel walls:* 4.7 to 8.5 mm; greatest individual range recorded, 3 mm; average thickness, ca 6 mm. *Undecorated.*

COMPARISONS: Woodruff Brown, temper abundant fine grains quartz sand; surface color dull red to light brown; interiors frequently slate gray; surface finish gritty but fairly uniform; constructed by coiling.
Adamana Brown, temper mostly quartz sand; flakes mica-like particles conspicuous on surfaces.

RANGE:
Recorded only from the San Francisco Mountains, Coconino County, Arizona.

REMARKS:
For further details see Hargrave, 1932, p. 17.

RIO DE FLAG SMUDGED: new type

TYPE SPECIMENS: Type sherds Nos. AT 904–912 in the Type Collection of the Museum of Northern Arizona.
TYPE SITE: NA 1653, Sunset Crater National Monument, Coconino County, Arizona.
STAGE: Pueblo I–II.
TIME: ca 850–1050 A.D.

DESCRIPTION:
Constructed: by paddling. *Fired:* in oxidizing atmosphere. *Core:* gray to black; brown to buff. *Carbon streak:* common. *Temper:* about equal amounts opaque angular fragments, gray or tan, and feldspar (?) sand; occasionally some quartz sand. *Texture core:* medium to fine. *Vessel walls:* medium strong. *Fracture:* slightly crumbling. *Surface finish:* smoothed but often bumpy; frequently highly polished or burnished; anvil marks usually conspicuous; impacted interior smudged. *Surface color:* exterior—brownish; interior, black (smudged). *Fire clouds:* common. *Forms:* bowls. *Recorded range thickness bowl walls:* 3.5 to 6 mm; greatest individual range recorded, 2.2 mm; average thickness, ca 4 mm. *Rims:* bowls, IIIA3. *No painted decoration.*

COMPARISON: Woodruff Smudged, temper almost invisible, sand grains rare; texture core, fine; lightly slipped on exterior.

RANGE:
Recorded only from the San Francisco Mountains, Coconino County, Arizona.

WINONA BROWN: new type

Fig. 37. ($\frac{1}{6}$×).

SYNONYM: *Flagstaff Ware*, Fewkes. 1927, p. 221.
ILLUSTRATION: AT (Fig. 37).
TYPE SPECIMENS: Jar No. NA 2134T.110 and sherds Nos. AT 4514–4516 in the Type Collection of the Museum of Northern Arizona.
TYPE SITE: Winona Village (NA 2134 A), Walnut Creek drainage, San Francisco Mountains, Coconino County, Arizona.
STAGES: Pueblo II–III.
TIME: ca 1000–1150 A.D.

OXIDIZING ATMOSPHERE

DESCRIPTION:
Constructed: by paddling. *Fired:* in oxidizing atmosphere. *Core:* gray to dark brown (usually well-fired through). *Temper:* abundant very coarse angular fragments crushed rock, gray, white, buff, or reddish; occasional minute quartz crystals, sometimes few grains volcanic sand. *Texture core:* coarse. *Vessel walls:* weak to medium strong. *Fracture:* ragged, seldom crumbling. *Surface finish:* outsides smoothed, impacted, never slipped, wiping marks often prominent; interiors almost never polished or finished, anvil marks conspicuous even in bowls. *Surface color:* exterior and interior bowls and jars, buff, orange, to dark brown to dark gray (near black); interiors very rarely carelessly smudged, thus black. *Fire clouds:* common. *Forms:* jars (predominate), bowls, shallow plates, odd forms (as rectangular bowls) rare; Gila shoulder present in many vessels. *Recorded range thickness vessel walls:* 3 to 15 mm; greatest individual range recorded, 3 mm; average thickness (100 sherds), 6.5 mm. *Rims:* bowls, IA4 (common), IA6, IB3 (rare); jars, IA4, IB3, IB4 (common), IC4 (common). *Decoration:* none.

COMPARISONS: Winona Brown Differs from Rio de Flag Brown by having much coarser temper and in being more buff or orange than brown.
    Sunset Red has predominance of cinder temper, and is predominantly red in color; Winona Brown is never red.
    Turkey Hill Red, has very smooth slipped surface, generally of pronounced red color.

RANGE:
Walnut Creek drainage and adjacent localities, San Francisco Mountains, Coconino County, Arizona.

REMARKS:
On the basis of physical characters Winona Brown intergrades with Rio de Flag Brown, Sunset Red, and Turkey Hill Red.

SUNSET RED

SYNONYMS: (a) Dark Red Ware, Fewkes, 1926, p. 3; (b) Undecorated red Ware, Fewkes, loc. cit., p. 8; (c) Redware with glossy black interior, Fewkes, loc. cit.; (d) Flagstaff Ware, Fewkes, 1927, p. 221; (e) Flagstaff Red, Colton, 1932, p. 10.
DESCRIBED BY: Colton, 1932, p. 9.
NAMED BY: Colton, loc. cit.
ILLUSTRATIONS: Hargrave, 1932, Pl. IV, D, E, F.
TYPE SPECIMENS: Bowl No. NA 1139.1 and type sherds Nos. AT 2901–2818, 2926–2945 in the Type Collection of the Museum of Northern Arizona.
TYPE SITE: Two Kivas Pueblo (NA 700), Walnut Creek, San Francisco Mountains, Coconino County, Arizona.
STAGES: Pueblo II–III.
TIME: ca 1050–ca 1200 A.D.

DESCRIPTION (revised):
Constructed: by paddling. *Fired:* in oxidizing atmosphere. *Core:* black to light gray (rare). *Temper:* predominantly black volcanic sand; occasional grain quartz sand; some angular fragments, usually reddish or tan, sometimes angular fragments almost as abundant as volcanic sand; temper particles often visible on surfaces. *Texture core:* fine to medium. *Vessel walls:* medium strong to strong. *Fracture:* usually crumbling; occasionally shattering. *Surface finish:* exterior bowl and jar surfaces impacted or coated with (red) slip; scraped, smoothed, sometimes highly polished, polishing marks frequently conspicuous; sometimes pitted, frequently bumpy; interior bowl surfaces smoothed; almost always smudged and polished; sometimes coarsely crazed; interior jar surfaces scraped, pitted; anvil marks generally conspicuous on jar interiors. *Surface color:* exteriors—brown, or brick-red to orange-red; interiors—gray, black, brown, or red. *Fire clouds:* common. *Forms:* bowls, jars. *Recorded range thickness bowl walls:* 5.5 to 7.4 mm; greatest individual range recorded, 1.8 mm; average thickness, ca 6.5 mm. *Recorded range thickness jar walls:* 3.8 to 8.3 mm; greatest individual range recorded, 2.5 mm; average thickness, ca 6 mm. *Rims:* bowls, IA3, IA4, IIA3, IIIA3, IIIA7; jars, IB3. *No painted decoration.*

COMPARISONS: Winona Brown, Turkey Hill Red, Tonto Red, Tuzigoot Red, all lack black volcanic sand temper.

RANGE:
That portion of the San Francisco Mountain region covered with Black volcanic ash from Sunset Crater. Greatest abundance in Walnut Creek drainage, Coconino County, Arizona. Reported as traded to Lowry Ruin, Montezuma County, Colorado (Martin, 1936 m, p. 80).

REMARKS:
Objective characters of sherds of Sunset Red and "Flagstaff Red," as described by Colton (1932, loc. cit.), show there are distinctions between the two types. Examination of a number of complete vessels, however, has demonstrated that the characters of each type, as presented, often may be found on a single vessel. Although there are recorded a large number of late Pueblo II and early Pueblo III sites at which Sunset Red (as first described), and not "Flagstaff Red," sherds were found, the authors now feel there is no real justification for the recognition of these two types since obviously one is a more finished product, in time occurring so close to the cruder that no time

difference of value can be stated. It has, therefore, been deemed advisable to combine the two types under the name of Sunset Red.

TURKEY HILL RED: new type

SYNONYMS: (a) Dark red ware, Fewkes, 1926, p. 3; (b) Undecorated red ware, Fewkes, loc. cit.; (c) Red ware with glossy black interior, Fewkes, loc. cit.; (d) Flagstaff Ware, Fewkes, 1927, p. 221; (e) Gila Red Ware, Gladwin, W. & H. S., 1930 b, p. 12.

TYPE SPECIMENS: Jar No. NA 1139.5; also type sherds Nos AT 2980–2987, 2990–2996, 2998–3001 in the Type Collection of the Museum of Northern Arizona.

TYPE SITE: Turkey Hill Pueblo (NA 660) Rio de Flag drainage, San Francisco Mountans, Coconino County, Arizona.

STAGES: Pueblo III–IV.

TIME: ca 1150–ca 1275 A.D.

DESCRIPTION:

Constructed: by paddling. *Fired:* in oxidizing atmosphere. *Core:* black, gray, dark brown to brick-red. *Temper:* abundant; predominantly opaque angular fragments variable size, gray, white, or reddish; frequently also some black volcanic sand; occasional isolated grain quartz sand. *Texture core:* medium to coarse. *Vessel walls:* weak to medium strong. *Fracture:* crumbling. *Surface finish:* exterior bowl and jar surfaces smoothed, impacted or coated with thin slip; slip sometimes slightly powdery; usually well-polished, polishing marks often conspicuous; interior bowl surfaces nearly always smudged; well-polished or burnished; interior jar surfaces frequently not smoothed; anvil marks conspicuous. *Surface color:* exterior bowls and jars red, maroon, or brown; interiors bowls black, red, brown; interiors jars, gray, or brick-red; color core and surface do not contrast except smudged, and exterior slipped portions. *Fire clouds:* common. *Forms:* bowls, jars (predominate); often difficult to distinguish form from individual sherds. *Recorded range thickness vessel walls:* 3.9 to 13.8 mm; greatest individual range recorded, 4.2 mm; average thickness (42 sherds), 7.7 mm. *Rims:* IB3, IIIB3. *No painted decoration.*

COMPARISONS: Tonto Red, temper usually more abundant, predominantly coarse feldspar (?) particles and quartz sand; anvil marks usually more conspicuous; surfaces usually less well-polished with temper often very conspicuous on worn surfaces.
    Tuzigoot Red, temper finer with smaller proportions opaque angular fragments; texture core, medium to fine; surfaces usually fairly well-polished, not powdery; mica-like particles sometimes apparent in temper; vessel walls average somewhat thinner.

RANGE:

San Francisco Mountain region, Coconino County, Arizona.

TONTO SERIES

There is only one type in this series which occurs from Payson, Gila County, south to Roosevelt Lake. A review of material from this area probably would reveal the existence of other types belonging to Tonto Series.

TONTO RED: new type

SYNONYMS: (a) Plain Ware, Schmidt, 1928, p. 298; (b) Gila Redware, in part, Gladwin, W. & H. S., 1930 b, pl. 12.

TYPE SPECIMENS: Sherds Nos. 449–503, 2949–2970 in the Type Collection of the Museum of Northern Arizona.

TYPE SITE: NA 779, Reiser Ranch, Near Payson, East Verde River, Gila County, Arizona.

STAGE: Pueblo III.

TIME: Probably between 1150–1275 A.D.

DESCRIPTION:

Constructed: by paddling. *Fired:* in oxidizing atmosphere. *Core:* gray, dark brown to brick red. *Temper:* very abundant; predominantly large grains quartz sand and crushed feldspar (?), with smaller amounts opaque angular fragments, gray, reddish, black or whitish; temper always conspicuous on worn surfaces; frequently on unworn surfaces. *Texture core:* coarse to very coarse. *Vessel walls:* weak to medium strong. *Fracture:* crumbling. *Surface finish:* exteriors, bumpy; sometimes moderately polished; usually gritty; sometimes lightly coated with thin wash, often fugitive; generally impacted; occasionally lightly polished; interior surfaces, often lightly polished, often smudged; anvil marks usually conspicuous. *Surface color:* exteriors—usually dull brick-red; interiors—black, brown, gray, or buff; color core and surfaces do not contrast except smudged interiors and slipped exteriors. *Fire clouds:* uncommon. *Forms:* bowls, jars (predominate); often difficult to distinguish form from individual sherds. *Recorded range thickness vessel walls:* 4.2 to 12.1 mm; greatest individual range recorded, 3.8 mm; average thickness (160 sherds), 7.8 mm. *Rims:* bowls, IIIA3; jars, IB3. *No painted decoration.*

COMPARISONS: Turkey Hill Red, usually more evenly finished, often fairly highly polished expecially on bowl interiors; temper somewhat less abundant, less coarse, with larger proportion opaque angular fragments; anvil marks somewhat less conspicuous.

Tuzigoot Red, temper about equal amounts medium fine quartz or feldspar (?) sand and opaque angular fragments, with micaceus particles occasionally present; texture core usually medium to fine; anvil marks less noticeable; vessel walls average somewhat thinner.

Flagstaff Red and Sunset Red, temper mostly black volcanic sand.

RANGE:

Tonto Basin, Gila County, Arizona.

OXIDIZING ATMOSPHERE

VERDE SERIES

Much variability exists among types in this series that is indigenous in the Verde River Valley, Yavapai County. The extent of this variability might, in part, be recognized as a result from a relatively intensive study of ceramic material found there. Basic factors that effected change in the Verde Series, however, seem to have come from Prescott Gray Ware, an indigenous ware companion to the Verde Series.

KEY q: VERDE SERIES

Painted design, red.........................Verde Red-on-buff (p. 168)
Painted design black.....................Tuzigoot Black-on-red (p. 170)
Painted design white....................Tuzigoot White-on-red (p. 171)
Painted design red (on smudged bowl interiors)......................
                                                    Tuzigoot Red-on-black (p. 171)
Painted design black-on-gray..............Tuzigoot Black-on-gray (p. 172)
No painted design..............................Tuzigoot Red (p. 169)
                                                               Verde Brown (p. 167)

VERDE BROWN

SYNONYM: Verde Brown Ware, Caywood and Spicer, 1935, p. 42.
DESCRIBED BY: Caywood and Spicer, loc. cit.
NAMED BY: Caywood and Spicer, loc. cit.
ILLUSTRATION: Caywood and Spicer, loc. cit., Pl. VIII.
TYPE SITE: Tuzigoot Pueblo (NA 1261), Verde Valley, Yavapai County, Arizona.
STAGES: Pueblo II (?)–III.
TIME: Possibly between 1000–1300 A.D.
DESCRIPTION (revised):

Constructed: by paddling. *Fired:* in oxidizing atmosphere. *Core:* black to gray, red-brown to dark brown (usually), sometimes glowing red-brown or metallic copper color. *Temper:* "consists of thirty to fifty per cent of coarse particles of feldspar, sometimes angular, but more generally round sand grains"; occasionally some micaceous particles; "temper varies from fine to extremely coarse"; "temper does not show on surface except for an occasional flake of mica." *Fracture:* crumbling. *Vessel walls:* medium weak to medium strong; porous. *Surface finish:* both surfaces bowls, exterior surfaces jars, "smoothed but not polished; irregular but not lumpy"; scraping marks generally apparent on exteriors, particularly near rim where generally rough and unsmoothed; irregular depressions, frequent; interiors, scraped; exterior surface, impacted. *Surface color:* red-brown. *Forms:* jars (predominate), bowls. *Rims:* rounded, direct, or outflared, out-bevelled, flaring, flat, and direct (rare). *Handles:* lugs on either side jars (rare). *Average thickness:* jar walls, ca 13 mm; bowl walls, ca 5 mm. *Undecorated.*

RANGE:
Recorded from Tuzigoot Pueblo, Verde Valley, Yavapai County, Arizona.

REMARKS:
For further details see Caywood and Spicer, loc. cit. Descriptive characters of types in the Verde Series probably were included by Gila Pueblo in "An Archaeological Survey of Verde Valley" (Gladwin, W. & H. S., 1930) but individual types are not clearly distinguished.

VERDE RED-ON-BUFF

DESCRIBED BY: Caywood and Spicer, 1935, p. 52.
NAMED BY: Caywood and Spicer, loc. cit.
TYPE SITE: Tuzigoot Pueblo (NA 1261), Verde Valley, Yavapai County, Arizona.
STAGES: Pueblo III–IV.
TIME: Probably between 1150–ca 1425 A.D.

DESCRIPTION (revised):

Constructed: by paddling. *Fired:* in oxidizing atmosphere. *Core:* "gray to buff." *Temper:* variable proportions medium fine quartz sand and opaque angular fragments, usually reddish or tan, occasionally gray or black; occasionally micaceous particles. *Texture:* medium to fine. *Fracture:* slightly crumbling. *Surface finish:* bowls—smoothed, often impacted and polished; horizontal scraping marks visible but not conspicuous; surface sometimes gritty; interior surface bowls occasionally smudged and burnished; jars—exteriors occasionally coated (?) with thick slip; jar interiors, not smoothed; irregular anvil and scraping marks conspicuous. *Surface color:* both surfaces bowls and exterior surfaces jars, buff; interior surface bowls, occasionally black; exteriors jars, occasionally, cream-colored. *Forms:* bowls (rare), jars. *Rims:* bowls—"rounded, flat, or out-bevelled and most commonly direct or recurved, but sometimes incurving or flaring"; jars—"necks are most commonly recurved with out-bevelled rims, but sometimes are vertical or inclined inward with direct or recurved rounded or out-bevelled rims." *Decoration:* painted. *Paint:* red. *Design:* "crudely applied to the interiors of bowls and the exteriors of jars. Design elements are parallel chevrons, interlocked angular scrolls, triangles with single hooks, lines with short pendent lines or blunt barbs, solid triangles pendent from broad lines. Only rarely are the elements

OXIDIZING ATMOSPHERE

intergraded into systematic designs. One bowl . . . had on the exterior large figures of crudely made cornstalks repeated about the surface."

RANGE:

"Seems to extend at least as far south as West Clear Creek northward throughout the upper Verde drainage to King's Ruins on Chino Creek" (Caywood and Spicer, loc. cit.).

REMARKS:

The describers imply that this type is closely allied with Tuzigoot Red, and further state that, on the authority of Dr. Emil Haury of Gila Pueblo, that it is not a Hohokam type.

TUZIGOOT RED

DESCRIBED BY: Caywood and Spicer, 1935, p. 44.

NAMED BY: Caywood and Spicer, loc. cit.

ILLUSTRATIONS: Caywood and Spicer, loc. cit., Plates IX, X.

TYPE SPECIMENS: Cotype sherds Nos. AT 504–506, 4153–4155 in the Type Collection of the Museum of Northern Arizona.

TYPE SITE: Tuzigoot Pueblo (NA 1261), Verde Valley, Yavapai County, Arizona.

STAGES: Pueblo III–IV.

TIME: Probably between 1150–1400 A.D.

DESCRIPTION (revised):

Constructed: by paddling. *Fired:* in oxidizing atmosphere. *Core:* reddish, pinkish, yellowish-buff. *Carbon streak:* occasional. *Temper:* variable proportions medium fine quartz or feldspar (?) sands and opaque angular fragments, usually reddish or tan, occasionally gray or black; also occasional micaceous particles. *Texture core:* medium to fine; porous. *Vessel walls:* medium strong. *Fracture:* slightly crumbling. *Surface finish:* smoothed; often impacted and polished; often smudged; sometimes gritty; horizontal scraping marks visible but not conspicuous; exterior surfaces jars sometimes coated (?) with thin slip; interior surfaces jars, not smoothed; anvil and scraping marks conspicuous. *Surface color:* both surfaces bowls and exterior surfaces jars, usually brick-red, or black; exteriors jars, brown or brick-red; jar interiors, gray, purplish, tan, or reddish. *Fire clouds:* frequent, usually black but "often with yellow and gray gradations from the black cloud to the red surface." *Forms:* bowls, jars; jars frequently have Gila Shoulder. *Rims:* bowl rims, "rounded, flat, out-bevelled; most commonly direct or recurved; sometimes incurved or flared"; jar rims, "out-bevelled, direct, recurved, rounded." *No painted decoration.*

COMPARISONS: Turkey Hill Red, temper predominantly opaque angular fragments very little quartz sand; texture core, usually coarse; interior bowl surfaces nearly always smudged and well-polished; vessel walls average thicker.

Tonto Red, temper very abundant coarse feldspar (?) and quartz sand; texture core coarse to very coarse; anvil marks usually more conspicuous; vessel walls average thicker.

RANGE:
Reported only from type site.

TUZIGOOT BLACK-ON-RED

SYNONYM: Tuzigoot Fugitive Black-on-red (Caywood and Spicer, 1935, p. 54).
DESCRIBED BY: Caywood and Spicer, loc. cit.
NAMED BY: Caywood and Spicer, loc. cit.
TYPE SITE: Tuzigoot Pueblo (NA 1261), Verde Valley, Yavapai County, Arizona.
STAGE: Pueblo IV.
TIME: Probably between 1300–1425 A.D.

DESCRIPTION (revised):
Constructed: by paddling. *Fired:* in oxidizing atmosphere. *Core:* reddish, pinkish, yellowish-buff. *Carbon streak:* occasional. *Temper:* variable proportions medium fine quartz or feldspar (?) sands and opaque angular fragments, usually reddish or tan, occasionally gray or black; occasional micaceous particles. *Texture core:* medium to fine; porous. *Vessel walls:* medium strong. *Fracture:* slightly crumbling. *Surface finish:* smoothed; often impacted and polished; often smudged; sometimes gritty; horizontal scraping marks visible but not conspicuous; exterior surfaces jars sometimes coated (?) with thin slip; interior surfaces jars, not smoothed; anvil and scraping marks conspicuous. *Surface color:* both surfaces bowls and exterior surfaces jars, brick-red, or black; exteriors jars, brown, or purplish, tan, or reddish. *Fire clouds:* frequent; usually black but "often with yellow and gray gradations from the black cloud to the red surface." *Forms:* bowls, jars. *Decoration:* painted. *Paint:* black; partly fugitive. *Design:* "crude broad lines."

RANGE:
Verde Valley, Yavapai County, Arizona.

REMARKS:
The describers say that "the decoration is suggestive of that on the exterior surfaces of Prescott Polychrome."

OXIDIZING ATMOSPHERE

TUZIGOOT WHITE-ON-RED

DESCRIBED BY: Caywood and Spicer, 1935, p. 50.
NAMED BY: Caywood and Spicer, loc. cit.
TYPE SITE: Tuzigoot Pueblo (NA 1261), Verde Valley, Yavapai County, Arizona.
STAGE: Pueblo IV.
TIME: Probably between 1300–1425 A.D.

DESCRIPTION (revised):
Constructed: by paddling. *Fired:* in oxidizing atmosphere. *Core:* reddish, pinkish, yellowish-buff. *Carbon streak:* occasional. *Temper:* variable proportions medium fine quartz or feldspar (?) sands and opaque angular fragments, usually reddish or tan, occasionally gray or black; occasional micaceous particles. *Texture core:* medium to fine; porous. *Vessel walls:* medium strong. *Fracture:* slightly crumbling. *Surface finish:* smoothed; often impacted and polished; often smudged; sometimes gritty; horizontal scraping marks visible but not conspicuous; exterior surfaces jars sometimes coated (?) with thin slip; interior surfaces jars, not smoothed; anvil and scraping marks conspicuous. *Surface color:* both surfaces bowls and exterior surfaces jars, brick-red, or black; exteriors jars, brown, or brick-red; jar interiors, gray, purplish, tan, or reddish. *Fire clouds:* frequent, usually black but "often with yellow and gray gradations from the black cloud to the red surface." *Forms:* bowls, jars; jars frequently have Gila Shoulder. *Rims:* bowls, "rounded, flat, out-bevelled; most commonly direct or recurved; sometimes incurved or flared"; jars, "out-bevelled, direct, recurved, rounded." *Decoration:* painted. *Paint:* white; thick but fugitive. *Design:* confined to bowl and jar interiors; "elements are broad lines with pendent dots, groups of large dots, irregular meanders, and zigzags. The execution . . . is always crude and lines are characterized by messiness. The elements are rarely intergraded into symmetrical designs."

RANGE:
"The Upper Verde River drainage, from Beaver Creek to at least Sycamore Canyon. Has been found also at Fitzmaurice Ruin, near Prescott" (Caywood and Spicer, 1935, p. 51).

TUZIGOOT RED-ON-BLACK

DESCRIBED BY: Caywood and Spicer, 1935, p. 54.
NAMED BY: Caywood and Spicer, loc. cit.
TYPE SITE: Tuzigoot Pueblo (NA 1261), Verde Valley, Yavapai County, Arizona.
STAGE: Pueblo IV.
TIME: Probably between 1300–1425 A.D.

DESCRIPTION (revised):

Constructed: by paddling. *Fired:* in oxidizing atmosphere. *Core:* reddish, pinkish, yellowish-buff. *Carbon streak:* occasional. *Temper:* variable proportions medium to fine quartz or feldspar (?) sands and opaque angular fragments, usually reddish or tan, occasionally gray or black; occasional micaceous particles. *Texture core:* medium to fine; porous. *Vessel walls:* medium strong. *Fracture:* slightly crumbling. *Surface finish:* smoothed and often impacted; sometimes gritty; horizontal scraping marks visible but not conspicuous; interior surfaces smudged; not polished. *Surface color:* exteriors brick-red; interiors black. *Fire clouds:* frequent. *Decoration:* painted. *Paint:* "very bright red." *Design:* confined to interior surfaces; red "narrow barbed lines" over smudged surface.

RANGE:

Reported only from Tuzigoot Pueblo.

REMARKS:

The describers state that the shade of red used in the paint of this type is "not comparable" with that used on Verde Red-on-buff.

TUZIGOOT BLACK-ON-GRAY

DESCRIBED BY: Caywood and Spicer, 1935, p. 51.
NAMED BY: Caywood and Spicer, loc. cit.
ILLUSTRATIONS: Caywood and Spicer, loc. cit., Pl. XI, D.
TYPE SITE: Tuzigoot Pueblo (NA 1261), Verde Valley, Yavapai County, Arizona.
STAGES: Pueblo III (?)–IV.
TIME: Probably between 1150–1425 A.D.

DESCRIPTION (revised):

Constructed: by paddling. *Fired:* in oxidizing atmosphere; in part reducing. *Core:* reddish, pinkish, orange, yellowish-buff; sometimes "grey or dirty buff." *Carbon streak:* occasional. *Temper:* "fine and entirely lacking in mica, usually fine feldspar sand." *Texture core:* "moderately fine, but variable to coarse." *Fracture:* slightly crumbling. *Surface finish:* interior surfaces smoothed, rarely polished; exterior surfaces smoothed, often polished with scraping marks rarely visible "as wide smooth bands with a higher luster than the rest of the surface"; never slipped. *Surface color:* gray. *Form:* bowls. *Rims:* bowls, "direct and rounded or flat." *Decoration:* painted. *Paint:* black, thin. *Design:* "angular scrolls, isolated swastikas, crosses and dots, . . . one bowl utilizes fine lines and solid triangles . . . elements are grouped in unframed or, rarely, framed bands on the in-

OXIDIZING ATMOSPHERE 173

teriors of bowls. Sometimes an isolated element, such as a swastika, occurs in the bottom of the bowls."

COMPARISON: Prescott Black-on-gray, similar in decoration but temper usually coarse and contains mica which is apparent on both surface.

RANGE:
Reported only from Tuzigoot Pueblo and "large valley pueblos nearby" in the Verde Valley, Yavapai County, Arizona.

REMARKS:
Although frequently gray in color, examination of sherds shows that they were fired in an oxidizing atmosphere. The describers say: "It is definitely a carrying over of the Prescott Black-on-gray decorative technique to a finer type of basic pottery and by potters who were more accomplished workers with the paint brush. It appears to have developed fairly early in the history of Tuzigoot and was made occasionally during a great part of the existence of the Pueblo."

Although no specimens have been examined by the reviser, from the published description, this type probably belongs to Alameda Brown Ware and not to Prescott Gray Ware.

GILA SERIES

Types in this series seem to be nearer Hohokam types in character than do types in other series in Alameda Brown Ware. With the exception of the Gila Series, all other series presented herein in Alameda Brown Ware are believed to have resulted from a northern extension of Hohokam influence. As the central focus for this diffused influence is approached, more and more similarity to the parent stock might be expected to be seen. There possibly is an area south of Payson where Alameda Brown Ware and a Hohokam ware intergrade. Types presented in Alameda Brown do not seem to have been derived directly from a type in Hohokam Buff Ware. Investigation probably would show an indigenous Hohokam ware companion to Hohokam Buff Ware. It is even probable that types in this unrecognized and unnamed Hohokam *ware* probably already have been described and named. As has been said, it is not a purpose of this Handbook to deal in detail with wares of the Hohokam Culture.

KEY r: GILA SERIES

Slipped, painted design........................Gila White-on-red (p. 177)
Slipped, no painted design...........................Gila Red (p. 176)
Not slipped...Gila Plain (p. 174)
                                                Santan Red (p. 175)

GILA PLAIN

DESCRIBED BY: Gladwin, W. & H. S., 1933, pp. 26–27.
NAMED BY: Gladwin, W. & H. S., loc. cit.
ILLUSTRATIONS: Gladwin, loc. cit., Plate IX; Haury, 1932, Plate XX, Figs. 17, 18, & 19.
TYPE SPECIMENS: Gila Pueblo, Globe, Arizona.
TYPE SITE: Roosevelt: 9:6, Gila County, Arizona.
STAGE: Colonial and Sedentary Hohokam.
TIME: ca 700–1100 A.D.

DESCRIPTION (revised):
Constructed: by paddling. *Fired:* in oxidizing atmosphere. *Core:* brick-red, pinkish, brown, gray to nearly black. *Carbon streak:* absent. *Temper:* abundant opaque angular fragments, gray, whitish, or tan, with individual particles sometimes 1/8 inch diameter; smaller quantities water-worn sand; large proportions mica; mica conspicuous on surfaces. *Texture core:* usually coarse, sometimes medium. *Fracture:* crumbling. *Surface finish:* usually well-smoothed (perhaps with hand or cloth (?); polishing stone may sometimes have been used); striated— striations appear to have been made while surface was wet, often broad and carelessly applied, direction fairly regular; striations, bowl exteriors narrow band just below rim, vertical over balance of surface; on jars at right angles to rim; surfaces impacted; never slipped; jar interiors sometimes moderately smoothed, anvil marks usually noticeable; bowl interiors sometimes smudged, never polished; all surfaces moderately pitted. *Surface color:* soft russet brown, light brick-red, pinkish, buff, sometimes slatey-gray. *Forms:* bowls, dippers, jars, spindle whorls, figurines; bowls, usually hemispherical or globular, sometimes deep with vertical sides, usually not over 9 inches diameter; shallow plate-like bowls with slightly out-curved lips, rare; shallow trays, usually on four legs, rare; dippers, either scoop-shaped or oval, extremities of long diameter higher than those of short diameter, always without handles; jars, globular with short necks and slightly out-curved lips, 6 to 25 inches diameter, or egg-shaped with full rounded underbodies and sloping upper bodies, 5 to 6 inches diameter; figurines, usually human, extremely variable. *Rims:* bowls, IB12, IE3, IE9; jars, IE6, IE12. *Fire clouds:* common. *No painted decoration.*

RANGE:
Gila and Tonto basins, Santa Cruz Valley as far south as Tucson, east to Safford, Arizona, and as far south as the Sonora, Mexico, line.

OXIDIZING ATMOSPHERE 175

REMARKS:

This type is always the companion type of Santa Cruz Red-on-buff in Hohokam sites (for description of Santa Cruz Red-on-buff see Gladwin, W. & H. S., 1933, p. 8). Gila Plain apparently is the ancestor of Santan Red and Gila Red, in which the peculiar striations were more fully developed. It is often impossible to assign individual vessels or sherds to Gila Plain as distinguished from Santan Red. Gila Plain was apparently intrusive in the Hohokam area, but it became very widespread there in the Colonial and Sedentary stages. "Texture core" as used in the above description is not made by standard comparisons but is from the original description.

SANTAN RED

DESCRIBED BY: Gladwin, W. & H. S., 1933, p. 28.
NAMED BY: Gladwin, W. & H. S., loc. cit.
ILLUSTRATIONS: Gladwin, W. & H. S., loc. cit., Plate XI.
TYPE SPECIMENS: Gila Pueblo, Globe, Arizona.
TYPE SITE: Florence: 7:6, Adamsville, Pinal County, Arizona.
STAGE: Pueblo II–III; sedentary Hohokam (?).
TIME: ca 900–1100 A.D.

DESCRIPTION (revised):

Constructed: by paddling. *Fired:* in oxidizing atmosphere. *Core:* brick-red, pinkish, brown, dark gray. *Carbon streak:* absent. *Temper:* abundant opaque angular fragments, smaller quantities water-worn sand, heavy proportions mica; mica noticeable, sometimes conspicuous, on both surfaces. *Texture core:* crumbling. *Surface finish:* smoothed; striated—striations usually apparent, producing irregular high-lights with dull interspaces, striations vertical; smoothed surfaces, impacted; bowl interiors, smudged; not polished; not smoothed; anvil marks apparent. *Surface color:* exteriors light terra cotta or light brick-red; dull and somewhat chalky. *Forms:* bowls, jars; bowls usually shallow, from 10 to 18 inches diameter; jars usually globular with very long vertical or slightly tapering necks, entire vessel usually not over 10 inches in height. *Fire clouds:* common. *No painted decoration.*

RANGE:

On the basis of reported finds, apparently restricted to Casa Grande and the Phoenix area.

REMARKS:

This type is intermediate between Gila Plain and Gila Red. There is a continuous intergradation from Gila Plain through

Santan Red to Gila Red so it is impossible accurately to place many individual vessels and sherds. In general the development displays a progressive heightening of the polishing and a deepening of surface color from the light brownish, pinkish or buff of Gila Plain through the dull but deeper brick-red or pinkish-red of Santan Red to the rich, lustrous orange-red of Gila Red. The proportions of mica in the temper seems to decline chronologically and the texture of the core to change from coarse to medium.

GILA RED

SYNONYMS: (a) Plain Red, Kidder, 1924, p. 107; (b) Flagstaff Ware, Fewkes, 1927, p. 221; (c) Plain Ware, Schmidt, 1928, p. 298; (d) Smooth Redware, Schmidt, loc. cit.; (e) Onionware, Schmidt, loc. cit., Fig. 36; (f) Gila Redware, Gladwin, W. & H. S., 1930 b, p. 12.
DESCRIBED BY: Schmidt, loc. cit.; also by Gladwin, loc. cit.
NAMED BY: Gladwin, W. & H. S., 1930 b, p. 12. (N. B.: The name originally used by the Gladwins was "Gila Redware.")
ILLUSTRATIONS: Schmidt, 1928, Fig. 36; Gladwin, W. & H. S., 1930 b, Plates IX, X.
TYPE SPECIMENS: Gila Pueblo, Globe, Arizona.
TYPE SITE: Casa Grande National Monument, Pinal County, Arizona.
STAGES: Pueblo IV; Classic Hohokam.
TIME: ca 1200–1400 A.D.

DESCRIPTION (revised):

Constructed: by paddling. *Fired:* in oxidizing atmosphere. *Core:* brick-red, tan, pinkish, gray. *Carbon streak:* absent. *Temper:* abundant water-worn sand; also in some specimens moderate amounts opaque angular fragments, usually gray or white; varying quantities copper-colored mica, mica noticeable, not conspicuous on all surfaces. *Texture core:* medium. *Surface finish:* exteriors bowls and jars, slipped; exteriors, highly polished; bowls striated usually in one of two manners: (A) striations start at center and carry to rim (as in globe cut in half at the poles at the equator); (B) striations start at point on the rim and pass over the surface to an opposite point; interiors, smudged, either polished or left dull, when polished striations of "B" style; jar exteriors highly polished, usually "A" style above shoulder, "B" style below shoulder; other striation arrangements occur also on both bowls and jars; always evident an attempt to produce some sort of pattern; interiors jars and pitchers, usually not scraped; anvil marks apparent; insides of necks often roughly smoothed; usually smudged. *Surface color:* bright orange-red or terra cotta, in spots worn away showing brownish-orange. *Forms:* bowls, dishes, jars, dippers, figurines, eccentric; bowls, square and round, the latter varying in shape

OXIDIZING ATMOSPHERE

from shallow dishes to deep hemispherical vessels, holding up to eight quarts; dishes up to 20 inches diameter occur in southern part of range; jars, various shapes, some with small round bodies and almost no necks, others with necks "out of all proportion to the size of the body," usually "well-balanced ... with well shaped bodies, cylindrical necks," "frequently made in such a way as to leave a pronounced angle around the body" (=Gila Shoulder); pitchers, usually globular, similar to jars with addition of one vertical handle, usually small with round or elliptical cross-section. *Rims:* IA3, IA6, IB4, IB6, IB12. *Fire clouds:* common. *No painted decoration.*

RANGE:
Gila Basin, Roosevelt Basin, Tonto Basin, Verde Valley, Arizona.

REMARKS:
The characteristic striations and the presence of mica in large quantities are most noticeable in the Roosevelt and Gila basins. For further details see Gladwin, W. & H. S., 1930 b, pp. 14–15. See also REMARKS under Santan Red herein.
Gila Red apparently is intrusive in the Hohokam area.

GILA WHITE-ON-RED

SYNONYM: Gila Redware, Gladwin, W. & H. S., 1930 b, p. 12.
DESCRIBED BY: Gladwin, W. & H. S., loc. cit.
TYPE SPECIMENS: Gila Pueblo, Globe, Arizona.
STAGE: Pueblo III–IV; Classic Hohokam.
TIME: Probably between 1200–1400 A.D.

DESCRIPTION (revised):
Constructed: by paddling. *Fired:* in oxidizing atmosphere. *Core:* brick-red, tan, pinkish, gray. *Carbon streak:* absent. *Temper:* abundant water-worn sand; also in some specimens moderate amounts opaque angular fragments, usually gray or white; varying quantities copper-colored mica, mica noticeable, not conspicuous on all surfaces. *Texture core:* medium. *Surface finish:* exteriors bowls and jars, slipped; exteriors, highly polished; bowls striated usually in one of two manners, A or B (see description of Gila Red); other striation arrangements occur also on both bowls and jars; always evident an attempt to produce some sort of pattern; interiors jars and pitchers, usually not scraped; anvil marks apparent; insides of necks often roughly smoothed; sometimes smudged; bowls well-polished with striations of "B" style; jar exteriors highly polished, striations of "A" style above shoulder, "B" style below;

interiors jars and pitchers, usually not scraped; anvil marks apparent; insides of necks often carelessly smoothed; usually smudged. *Surface color:* bright orange-red or terra cotta, where worn away shows brownish orange. *Forms:* bowls, dishes, jars, pitchers, figurines, eccentric; bowls, square and round, the latter varying in shape from shallow dishes to deep hemispherical vessels holding up to eight quarts; dishes up to 20 inches diameter; jars, various shapes, some with small round bodies and almost no neck, others with necks out of proportion to body size, usually "well-balanced . . . with well-shaped bodies, cylindrical necks"; Gila shoulder frequent on jars; pitchers, usually globular, similar to jars but with addition of one vertical handle, usually small with round or elliptical cross-section. *Decoration:* painted. *Paint:* white; thin powdery, fugitive. *Design:* exteriors bowls and jars usually with narrow straight lines in nests of squares, diamonds, chevrons, interlocking rectangular scrolls; lines often bordered with rows of pendent dots or short fringe-like dashes.

RANGE:
Not clearly defined; probably same as range of Gila Red.

REMARKS:
Gila White-on-red was originally included by the Gladwins (1930 b, pp. 12–15) in their description of Gila Red; it has been separated herein solely on the basis of the presence of white painted decoration. In all other respects it is apparently the same as Gila Red, except that it occasionally has bowls which are not smudged on the interiors. The decoration is very similar to that appearing on Salado White-on-red.

COCONINO BUFF WARE

The occurrence in the San Francisco Mountains of northern Arizona of a buff ware of undoubted affinity with Hohokam Buff Ware of southern Arizona, yet distinct in several basic characters, has been known for several years. Also, sherds of true Hohokam Buff Ware have been found in the same site with sherds of Coconino Buff Ware. The strong influence of the Hohokam Culture upon the local culture of the San Francisco Mountains cannot be doubted.

The strength of this influence is clearly seen in the similarity of types of the new buff ware to contemporary types of the Hohokam Buff Ware. Differences existing between these two wares are distinct, however, and because of these distinctions a new ware is recognized. Moreover, a distinguishing ware character of this proposed ware is a basic character in the identification of types in Rio de Flag Series of Alameda Brown Ware, the dominant ware in the San Francisco Mountain region throughout its known archaeological history.

Indigenous buff ware seems to have appeared rather suddenly in the area. Examination of sherds shows that basically many sherds of types in Coconino Buff Ware are the same as Winona Brown or as Sunset Red. By "basically" is meant that types in the buff ware and the two types of Alameda Brown Ware were constructed by the same techniques and that the material used in the construction of vessels were the same. Thus, Coconino Buff Ware objectively is derived (jointly?) from Winona Brown and Sunset Red.

Objective traits characteristic of Coconino Buff Ware are sufficiently distinctive for type and ware recognition, irrespective of the number of sherds used in the study. Moreover, all of these sherds have been examined by Dr. Emil W. Haury who stated positively that they were not types found in the true Hohokam Culture.

KEY 13: COCONINO BUFF WARE

1. Painted design.. 2
   No painted design...........................Walnut Wiped (p. 180)
2. Decorative surface slipped..............Coconino Red-on-buff (p. 182)
   Decorative surface not slipped...........Winona Red-on-buff (p. 181)

COCONINO BUFF WARE: new ware

STAGE: At present assigned to the transition between Pueblo II–III.
TIME: Known to have been in use between 1050–1150 A.D. A previous reference to a sherd of Colonial Hohokam in the region has been proved erroneous (p. 54).

DESCRIPTION:

Constructed: by paddling. *Fired:* in oxidizing atmosphere. *Core:* black, gray, white, or buff tending to brick-red at one or both surfaces, or brick-red. *Temper:* predominantly black volcanic sand, or light-colored angular fragments, or both. *Texture core:* fine to medium; does not show laminations. *Vessel walls:* medium strong. *Fracture:* crumbling to slightly shattering. *Surface finish:* impacted, slipped, wiped, or not smoothed (interior jars). *Surface color* (except jar interiors): reddish-brown, buff, or cream. *Fire clouds:* common on unpainted type. *Forms:* bowls (uncommon), jars. *Rims:* IA3. *Recorded range thickness vessel walls:* 4.8 to 9.2 mm; greatest individual range recorded, 2.5 mm; average thickness, ca 6 mm. *Decoration:* painted, wiped.

RANGE:

Walnut Creek drainage, San Francisco Mountains, Coconino County, Arizona; possibly indigenous in the Verde Valley, Yavapai County, Arizona.

REMARKS:

Although this ware is believed to be directly derived from types in Alameda Brown Ware, decorative treatment, style of design, color combinations, and vessel forms all indicate strong Hohokam influence. From sites where Coconino Buff Ware has occurred, have been found other material objects that have been attributed solely to the Hohokam Culture.

WALNUT WIPED: new type

Fig. 38. (⅓×).

ILLUSTRATION: AT 4552, (Fig. 38).

TYPE SPECIMENS: Sherds numbers AT 4552 and 4555 in the Type Collection of the Museum of Northern Arizona.

TYPE SITE: Pithouse NA 2098 above Turkey Tanks, Walnut Creek drainage, San Francisco Mountains, Coconino County, Arizona.

STAGE: Between Pueblo II–III.

TIME: Probably between 1050–1150 A.D. Wood specimens from NA 2098 have not been dated. The probable time is estimated from the occurrence at this site of dated pottery types.

DESCRIPTION:

Constructed: by paddling. *Fired:* in oxidizing atmosphere. *Core:* predominantly black; brick-red toward outside surface. *Temper:* predominantly black volcanic sand; occasionally (accidental?) inclusion light-colored angular fragment; temper not commonly seen on polished surface, except on worn parts. *Texture core:* fine; does not show laminations. *Vessel walls:*

medium strong. *Fracture:* crumbling to slightly shattering. *Surface finish:* interior surface generally anvil marked and unpolished; occasionally poorly smoothed and *wiped:* exterior surface fairly well smoothed (slight irregularities seen), scraping marks occasional, and coated with buff-colored wash, *wiped* horizontally or occasionally wiped diagonally and horizontally on same vessel. *Surface color:* interior surface (jars only) brownish, black, or grayish (if wiped); exterior surface streaked buff with reddish base color showing through; color exterior surface and core, contrast. *Fire clouds:* on almost all specimens. *Forms:* jars. *Recorded range thickness jar walls:* 4.8 to 6.8 mm; greatest individual range recorded, 2 mm; average thickness (two sherds), 5.7 mm. *Decoration:* wiping marks.

COMPARISON: Same as Sunset Red except there has been added a buff wash that has been wiped.

RANGE:

Recorded only from Walnut Creek drainage, San Francisco Mountains, Coconino County, Arizona.

REMARKS:

Walnut Wiped is expected to be found in some numbers when several thousand sherds from the type site have been examined. This type with a different temper probably will be found.

WINONA RED-ON-BUFF: new type

TYPE SPECIMENS: Sherds numbers AT 4550, 4551, 4553, 4561, 4562, 4564, and 4730–4732 in the Type Collection of the Museum of Northern Arizona.
TYPE SITE: Pithouse NA 2098, above Turkey Tanks, Walnut Creek, San Francisco Mountains, Coconino County, Arizona.
STAGE: Between Pueblo II–III.
TIME: Probably in use between 1050–1150 A.D. Sherds of this type were found at Winona Village by McGregor. Dated timbers have given the above estimate of time.

DESCRIPTION:

Constructed: by paddling. *Fired:* in oxidizing atmosphere. *Core:* black, gray, or buff tending to brick-red near the outer surface (jars), or brick-red. *Temper:* (variety 1) predominantly abundant coarse light-colored angular fragments, gray, white, or buff; or (variety 2) predominantly abundant grains black volcanic sand. *Texture core:* fine to medium. *Vessel walls:* medium strong. *Fracture:* crumbling to slightly shattering. *Surface finish:* interior surface generally anvil marked and unpolished; exterior surface, impacted; sometimes scraping, and frequently wiping marks noticeable. *Surface color:* exterior (jars), reddish-brown to light buff; interior (jars), dark gray, buff, or reddish-brown; exterior surface color and core, contrast. *Fire clouds:* occasional. *Forms:* jars. Rims: IA3. *Recorded range thickness jar walls:* 4.9 to 9.2 mm; greatest individual range recorded, 2.5 mm; average thickness (ten sherds), 6.5 mm (sherds with "variety 2" temper are thinner than sherds of "variety 1"). *Decoration:* painted. *Paint:* bright red, dull red, or purplish red. *Designs:* apparently cover vessel from rim to near base; background and design about equally balances. *Elements:* lines and (occasionally) solid areas.

COMPARISON: Types of Hohokam Buff Ware all have different temper. Coconino Red-on-buff differs in that it definitely has a slip.

RANGE:

Recorded from several sites in Walnut Creek drainage below Walnut Canyon National Monument, Coconino County, Arizona.

REMARKS:

Vessels of this type having black volcanic sand temper, structurally and on the basis of basic material used, are identical to Sunset Red; on the same basis of comparison, those specimens having light-colored angular temper essentially are Winona Brown. Sunset Red and Winona Brown overlap in time so that these two types are here considered the immediate ancestors of the corresponding varieties of Winona Red-on-buff.

Also, since the essential difference between these two varieties is a difference in materials and since these materials are of local occurrence, further type separation is deemed unnecessary unless one of these varieties is later proved older than the other.

There is at hand a single sherd (AT 4089), from Tuzigoot Pueblo, in the Verde Valley, Yavapai County, Arizona, that differs from Winona Red-on-Buff in the kind of temper used; minor objective differences, as a result of this temper, are also seen. It is thus possible to postulate the occurrence of a locality where there are undescribed types of red-on-buff that belong to the same group as these red-on-buffs presented herein.

COCONINO RED-ON-BUFF: new type

ILLUSTRATION: AT 4546 (Fig. 39).

TYPE SPECIMENS: Sherds Nos. AT 4546–4549, 4554, 4733–4734, and 4741 in the Type Collection of the Museum of Northern Arizona.

TYPE SITE: Pithouse NA 2098, above Turkey Tanks, Walnut Creek, San Francisco Mountains, Coconino County, Arizona.

STAGE: Probably in use between 1050–1150 A.D.

Constructed: by paddling. *Fired:* in oxidizing atmosphere. *Core:* black, gray, or buff tending to brick-red near the outer surface (jars), or brick-red. *Temper:* (variety 1) predominantly abundant coarse light-colored angular fragments, gray, white, or buff; or (variety 2) predominantly abundant grains black volcanic sand. *Texture core:* fine to medium. *Vessel walls:* medium strong. *Fracture:* crumbling to slightly shattering. *Surface finish:* exterior surface (jars), slipped with buff wash or creamy slip, interior surfaces generally coated with thin buff wash and wiped; exterior surface (bowls), coated with thin buff wash and wiped, interior surfaces slipped with buff or creamy slip. *Surface color:* buff, cream. *Forms:* jars (predominate), bowls. *Recorded range thickness jar walls:* 4.1 to 7.1 mm; greatest individual range recorded, 1.4 mm; average thickness (six sherds), 5.5 mm. *Recorded range thickness bowl walls:* 6.0 to 7.9 mm; greatest individual range recorded, 1.9 mm; average thickness (two sherds), 6.8 mm. *Decoration:* painted. *Designs:* same as on Winona Red-on-buff.

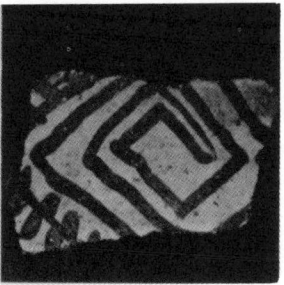

Fig. 39. ($\frac{1}{2}\times$).

COMPARISON: Types of Hohokam Buff Ware all have different temper. Winona Red-on-buff differs in that it definitely is not slipped.

RANGE:

Recorded only from NA 2098, 2132, and 2134, in Walnut Creek drainage below Walnut Canyon National Monument, Coconino County, Arizona.

PRESCOTT GRAY WARE

It is not clear where this ware fits into the picture of ceramic expansion in the Southwest. Although the area occupied by Prescott Gray Ware is roughly known, nothing definite is known about its origin. Ware characters are stable, however, and some types in the ware are so distinctive that their ware affinity cannot be doubted.

KEY 14: PRESCOTT GRAY WARE

1. Temper, "quartz, feldspar, and mica"............................
   Prescott Black-on-brown (p. 186)
   Temper not "quartz, feldspar, and mica"....................... 2
2. Polychrome............................Verde Polychrome (p. 186)
   Not polychrome.......................Verde Black-on-gray (p. 184)

PRESCOTT GRAY WARE

DESCRIBED BY: Caywood and Spicer, 1935, p. 42.
NAMED BY: Caywood and Spicer, 1935, loc. cit.
STAGES: Pueblo III–IV.
TIME: Probably between 1150–1400 A.D.
DESCRIPTION (revised):

Constructed: by paddling. *Fired:* in oxidizing atmosphere, partly reducing. *Core:* generally reddish in part. *Temper:* quartz sand, crushed rock and mica; mica flakes always show on both surfaces; temper more than 50% of core. *Texture core:* coarse. *Fracture:* crumbling. *Surface finish:* interior, "irregular and bumpy"; exteriors, smoothed; impacted. *Surface color:* exteriors jars brown or red; interior jars, generally gray, occasionally red; interiors bowls, gray; exteriors bowls gray, frequently pinkish, or reddish tint. *Forms:* bowls, jars, dippers, scoops. *Recorded range thickness bowl walls:* 5.1 to 8 mm; greatest individual range recorded, 2.9 mm; average thickness, ca 6.5 mm. *Recorded range thickness jar walls:* 8.9 to 10.6 mm; greatest individual range recorded, 1 mm; average thickness, ca 10 mm. *Decoration:* painted.

RANGE:

San Francisco Mountains, Coconino County, and Verde Valley, Yavapai County west to the Colorado River; Bradshaw Mountains, Yavapai County north to the Grand Canyon.

REMARKS:

"Prescott Gray Ware is the basis for such types as Prescott Black-on-gray, Prescott Black-on-brown, and Prescott Polychrome" (Caywood and Spicer, loc. cit.).

VERDE BLACK-ON-GRAY

SYNONYMS: (a) Verde Black-on-white, Gladwin, W. & H. S., 1930 c, p. 140;
(b) Prescott Black-on-gray, Caywood and Spicer, loc. cit.
DESCRIBED BY: Gladwin, W. & H. S., 1930 c, p. 140; also Caywood and Spicer, loc. cit.
NAMED BY: Gladwin, W. & H. S., 1930 a, p. 176.

OXIDIZING ATMOSPHERE 185

ILLUSTRATIONS: Gladwin, W. & H. S., 1930 c, Plate XX (colored).

TYPE SPECIMENS: Gila Pueblo, Globe, Arizona. Cotype sherds Nos. AT 496–498, 507–511, and 4094 in the Type Collection of the Museum of Northern Arizona.

TYPE SITE: King's Ruin, Chino Valley, Yavapai County, Arizona (Caywood and Spicer, loc. cit.).

STAGE: Pueblo III–IV.

TIME: Probably between 1150–1400 A.D.

DESCRIPTION (revised):

Constructed: by paddling. *Fired:* in oxidizing atmosphere, in part reducing. *Core:* dark gray, brownish. *Carbon streak:* absent. *Temper:* very abundant opaque angular fragments, gray, withish or tan, with smaller quantities water-worn sand; variable quantities mica, usually minute particles; temper particles frequently noticeable on surfaces; mica conspicuous on all surfaces. *Texture core:* medium to coarse. *Fracture:* crumbling; friable. *Surface finish:* both surfaces bowls and exterior surfaces jars well-smoothed, perhaps impacted; not polished. *Surface color:* vessel interiors usually dirty dark gray, sometimes with faint pinkish, tan or creamy tint; vessel exteriors dark gray, often oxidized in part to grayish brown or even metallic copper color. *Forms:* bowls, jars. *Recorded range thickness bowl walls:* 5.1 to 8 mm; greatest individual range recorded, 2.9 mm; average thickness, ca 6.5 mm. *Recorded range thickness jar walls:* 8.9 to 10.6 mm; greatest individual range recorded, 1 mm; average thickness, ca 10 mm. *Rims:* bowls, IA3, IA4. *Decoration:* painted. *Paint:* black, dull, usually fairly dense; sometimes thin. *Pigment:* carbon (test by Colton). *Design:* confined to bowl interiors and interiors of jar necks; bowls—mostly straight wide lines or stripes, in wide horizontal band or all-over lay-out, usually arranged in nests of open triangles, squares or chevrons; sometimes large solid triangles, often with pendent dots along one edge; rows of small equilateral solid triangles, contiguous at bases or pendent from wide lines; frequently in parallel series; execution careless and sloppy; unintentional splashes paint sometimes occur; darker colored surfaces painted decoration almost indistinguishable.

RANGE:

San Francisco Mountain region, Coconino County, and Verde Valley, Yavapai County, west to the Colorado River; also Bradshaw Mountains, Yavapai County, north to the Grand Canyon, Arizona.

REMARKS:

Although great variation occurs in surface color, particularly between jar forms on the one hand and bowl forms on the other, such variation is believed to be the result of the method of firing.

It is probably that eventually this type may be subdivided into two or more types on the basis of differences in decoration, but as yet not sufficient study has been given to warrant a division.

VERDE POLYCHROME: new type

SYNONYM: Prescott Black-on-gray, Caywood and Spicer, 1935, p. 54.
DESCRIBED BY: Caywood and Spicer, loc. cit.
TYPE SPECIMENS: Excavated at Tuzigoot Pueblo by Caywood and Spicer. Disposition not given.
TYPE SITE: Tuzigoot Pueblo (NA 1261), Verde Valley, Yavapai County, Arizona.
STAGE: Pueblo IV (?).
TIME: Probably between 1250–1400 A.D.

DESCRIPTION:

"The paste is identical with that of Prescott Gray Ware as is the temper and finish. The interior surface is gray, the exterior brown. The interior is decorated in black with typical Prescott Black-on-gray (=Verde Black-on-gray) motifs, repeated interlocking keys; the exterior was covered with a thick wash and over this was painted in red a design consisting of solid traingles pendent from narrow parallel lines" (Caywood and Spicer, loc. cit.).

RANGE:

Tuzigoot Pueblo, Verde Valley and Fitzmaurice Ruin, east of Prescott, Arizona.

REMARKS:

Although only one sherd was found at Tuzigoot Pueblo, "a somewhat similar type has been found to be of extremely rare occurrence at Fitzmaruice Ruin" (Caywood and Spicer, loc. cit.). The occurrence at two widely separated sites of sherds of what may here be considered the same type and the great difference in appearance between Verde Polychrome and Verde Black-on-gray, its nearest apparent relative, seems sufficient reason for the recognition of Verde Polychrome as a valid type.

PRESCOTT BLACK-ON-BROWN

DESCRIBED BY: Caywood, 1936, p. 103.
NAMED BY: Caywood, loc. cit.

OXIDIZING ATMOSPHERE

TYPE SITE: Fitzmaurice Ruin, Lynx Creek, Aqua Fria drainage, 7 miles east of Prescott, Yavapai County, Arizona.
STAGE: Possibly Pueblo II–III.
TIME: Probably between 1050–1300 A.D.

DESCRIPTION (revised):
Constructed: by paddling. *Fired:* in oxidizing atmosphere. *Temper:* mica schist. *Decoration:* painted. *Paint:* black.

COMPARISON: Verde Black-on-gray temper is "quartz, feldspar, and mica (Caywood, loc. cit., p. 102).

RANGE:
Reported only from the type site.

REMARKS:

It is assumed that Prescott Black-on-brown is similar to Verde Black-on-gray (=Prescott Black-on-gray) in surface treatment and decorative technique, although the describer does not say so. The pottery from the Fitzmaurice Ruin is described collectively, leaving much to the imagination, when thinking of types, although the types are definitely named according to the accepted standard. Had each type been treated as a unit this confusion would not exist.

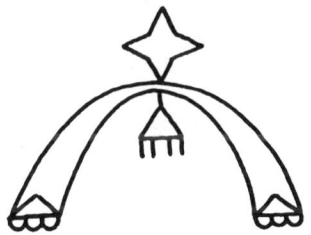

CHAPTER XI

REDUCING ATMOSPHERE

FREQUENTLY remarks and references have been made to the reducing atmosphere and to the effect it has had upon certain pottery wares of the Basket Maker–Pueblo Culture. This method of firing pottery is unique because apparently it was used only in a limited area of North America. The physical principle of the effect of a reducing atmosphere upon clays is well known, but the application and control of this atmosphere by primitive peoples is not known. Nor is it probable that the stages in the use of this method by these peoples can ever be determined since the method is not known to have been used in historic time. Theories there are and the Museum of Northern Arizona has and is still conducting experiments in firing with this method in an effort to learn how and why it was used in so limited an area.

The principal objective character of vessels fired in a reducing atmosphere is color. All normal vessels fired by this method are gray or white. This identifying character is infallible, although the inverse is not true of vessels fired in an oxidizing atmosphere. Moreover, vessels fired in a reducing atmosphere are one or two-color; never more. With the knowledge and materials used in the manufacture and in the decorating of vessels fired in this atmosphere in northern Arizona, a vessel with more than one applied color, i.e., a polychrome, could not be produced. Other than the limitations imposed by the use of a reducing atmosphere, wares of the Basket Maker–Pueblo Culture do not greatly differ from some wares of the south, from which probably came the impetus for ceramic development and expansion in the north.

KEY D: SURFACE NOT ALTERED

EXTERIOR SURFACE GRAY OR WHITE

1. Polished surface... 3
    No polished surface.. 2
2. Painted design........................Lino Black-on-gray (p. 194)
    No painted design................................Key 15 (p. 190)
3. Temper apparent.. 4
    Temper not apparent..............Bidahochi Black-on-white (p. 245)
    Key 16 (p. 203)
4. Temper, mica...................................Key 14 (p. 184)
    Temper, not mica... 5

5. Temper light-colored angular fragments; conspicious lenses in core....
   Key 18 (p. 234)
   Temper light-colored angular fragments; no lenses in core........... 8
   Temper not light-colored angular fragments..................... 6
6. Grayish or whitish; not noticeably slipped............. Key 16 (p. 203)
   Definitely gray; not noticeably slipped................ Key 19 (p. 251)
   Grayish or whitish; definitely slipped............................ 7
7. Pinedale Style of Design............. Wide Ruin Black-on-white (p. 249)
   Kayenta Style of Design............... Jeddito Black-on-white (p. 247)
   Otherwise......................... Kokop Black-on-white (p. 248)
8. Glaze paint.. 9
   Not glaze paint; paint red.............. Pinnawa Red-on-white (p. 129)
                                           Showlow Polychrome (p. 111)
   Not glaze paint; paint not red........................ Key 17 (p. 229)
                                           Hawikuh Glaze-on-white (p. 130)
9. Surface jar forms bumpy................ Showlow Polychrome (p. 111)
   Surface any form not bumpy........................ Key 7 (p. 128)

A: CONSTRUCTED BY COILING

With one exception all known wares, from northern Arizona, fired in a reducing atmosphere were constructed by coiling.

TUSAYAN GRAY WARE

There are two dominant wares in northern Arizona that appeared at an early date and that continued to be dominant until the end of Pueblo III (ca 1300 A.D.). Genetically these two wares might be considered one, since the most conspicuous difference is a minor character. Both wares were made of the same materials, by the same techniques of construction, in the same region, and by the same peoples. Separation of these two wares, one from the other, admittedly is for convenience in study and treatment.

Tusayan Gray Ware is presented first because the oldest known type in the two wares objectively belongs to Tusayan Gray Ware. This ware, with the exception of one type, is a ware of utility types. Moreover, each of the utility types has a companion type in the companion ware, Tusayan White Ware.

Tusayan Gray Ware had an early beginning. How, where, and why it was originated is not yet clearly known, but, as has been already inferred, it may have been a result of a contact between northern non-pottery-making people and southern pottery-making people. Regardless of the incidents of its beginning, the earliest known type in this ware was perfectly constructed when it first appeared. Since that date no improved stages in the construction of vessels of this ware are in evidence.

Methods of decorating and styles of decoration, i.e., incising, corrugating, painting, etc., appear in this new ware, or in its companion ware, Tusayan White Ware, even as they occurred on types of an older ware to the south, although some styles of decoration were not employed so frequently.

KEY 15: TUSAYAN GRAY WARE

1. Painted decoration...................Lino Black-on-gray (p. 194)
   No painted decoration.. 2
2. Surface altered... 4
   Surface not altered.. 3
3. Thick, bumpy; structural coils generally noticeable...............
   Kiet Siel Gray (p 198)
   Thin, not bumpy; structural coils not evident.......Lino Gray (p. 191)
4. Tooled... 5
   Corrugated... 6
   Neck coils not tooled.........................Kana-a Gray (p. 195)
5. Neck coils trimmed with tool.................Coconino Gray (p. 201)
   Tool marks as isolated punchings.............O'Leary Tooled (p. 200)
   Tool marks as series of lines..................Honani Tooled (p. 202)
6. Neck corrugations only.....................Medicine Gray (p. 199)
   Body corrugations.. 7
7. Corrugations flattened and partially obliterated..................
   Moenkopi Corrugated (p. 197)
   Corrugated not flattened and not partially obliterated............
   Tusayan Corrugated (p. 196)

TUSAYAN GRAY WARE: new ware

SYNONYMS: Gray Ware, Hough, 1903.
STAGES: Basket Maker III–Pueblo III.
TIME: ca 600–1300 A.D.

DESCRIPTION:

Constructed: by coiling. *Fired:* in reducing atmosphere. *Core:* dark gray (sometimes almost black) to light gray. *Carbon streak:* fairly frequent in some types, not generally characteristic. *Temper:* abundant quartz sand, from medium fine to coarse; coarse to very coarse quartz sand with occasional opaque fragment, gray or tan; occasional feldspar (?) grains in some types; temper usually conspicuous. *Texture core:* fine to very coarse. *Vessel walls:* medium strong to weak. *Fracture:* crumbling. *Surface finish:* most types roughly scraped, not smoothed, not polished; usually pitted; scraping marks conspicuous; exterior surface, plain, corrugated, tooled; no true slip on any type but fugitive red wash on one (Lino Fugitive Red). *Surface color:* gray, black (smoked), part red one type. *Fire clouds:* common only in Kiet Siel Gray. *Forms:* jars, bowls, pitchers, dippers. *Recorded range thickness bowl walls:* 2.5 to 9.7 mm; greatest individual range recorded, 3.5 mm; average thickness, ca 5 mm. *Recorded range thickness jar walls:* 2.5 to 9.7 mm; greatest indi-

REDUCING ATMOSPHERE

vidual range recorded, 3.5 mm; average thickness, ca 5.2 mm. *Rims:* bowls, IIIA3; jars, IA3, IB3, IIIB3, IC2. *Decorative techniques:* manipulation of surface clay or paint applied to surface. *Decoration:* painted on Lino Black-on-gray only. *Paint:* dull black, occasionally brownish if thin. *Pigment:* carbon. *Pattern:* narrow lines, often ticked, isolated dots between narrow framing lines; crudely applied.

RANGE:

In general most types occur over a relatively large area, the exact boundaries of which have not been determined, but which includes southwestern Colorado; northwestern New Mexico; and northeastern Arizona north of the Mogollon Rim and west to Havasupai Canyon. A few types, however, are localized within this area.

TSEGI SERIES

The name for this series was chosen because the earliest types in Tusayan Gray Ware in Arizona were first recorded from the Tsegi region.

LINO GRAY

SYNONYMS: (a) *Blackware*, Kidder & Guernsey, 1919, p. 153; (b) *Post Basket Maker Pottery*, Kidder, 1924, p. 76; (c) *Post Basket Maker Ware*, Morris, 1927, p. 161; (d) *Plain Gray Ware*, Colton, 1932, p. 9; (e) *Lino Gray Ware*, Gladwin, W. & H. S., 1934, Fig. 3.
DESCRIBED BY: Kidder & Guernsey, loc. cit.
NAMED BY: Hargrave, 1932, p. 11.
ILLUSTRATIONS: Roberts, 1929, Pl. 11, a, b; Pl. 17 a; AT 2 (Fig. 40).
TYPE SPECIMENS: Cotype Canteen, NA 1600.98, and AT 1, 2, 383–393 in the Type Collection of the Museum of Northern Arizona.

Fig. 40. ($\frac{1}{2}$×).

TYPE SITE: Fluteplayer House (= Ruin 5), Hagoe Canyon, Monument Valley, Navajo County, Arizona (see Kidder & Guernsey, 1919, p. 41).
STAGE: Basket Baker III–Pueblo I.
TIME: Pre-750 A.D.

DESCRIPTION (revised):

Constructed: by coiling. *Fired:* in reducing atmosphere. *Core:* usually dark gray or almost black, sometimes light gray. *Temper:* abundant medium-fine to coarse quartz sand; temper conspicuous on surface. *Vessell walls:* medium strong. *Texture core:* fine to coarse. *Fracture:* crumbling. *Surface finish:* very roughly finished; scraped and occasionally lightly smoothed in spots; never slipped; usually deeply pitted; scraping marks very conspicious. *Surface color:* normally gray. *Carbon streak:* common. *Forms:* bowls, jars (predominate), pitchers, dippers, canteens (rare); often difficult to distinguish jar sherds from bowl sherds; vessel walls usually of fairly uniform thickness in individual vessels but wide variation between vessels. *Rims:* bowls, IIIA3; jars, IA3. *Recorded range thickness vessel walls:* 2.5 to 9.7 mm; greatest individual range recorded, 3.5 mm; average thickness, 4.9 mm. *No painted decoration:* one sherd in the type collection has three small conical bases (applique) arranged in a triangle.

COMPARISONS: Kana Gray, exterior surfaces jar necks unobliterated wide and flattened coils; body sherds scraped; generally indistinguishable.

Coconino Gray, exterior jar necks unobliterated coils, emphasized with horizontal tooling, creating channels of roughly semi-circular section; fluted effect; body and base sherds scraped; indistinguishable.

Medicine Gray, exteriors of jar necks unobliterated coils, relatively narrow and usually slightly finger-dented; body and base sherds scraped; indistinguishable.

Honani Tooled, exterior jar necks decorated with vertical or diagonal tooling; body and base sherds scraped; indistinguishable.

O'Leary Tooled, exterior jar necks decorated with rows of indentations or punches; body and base sherds indistinguishable.

Kiet Siel Gray, frequently somewhat coarser sand temper including also small amounts of opaque angular fragments; surfaces even less well-smoothed usually bumpy; coils often not quite obliterated; vessel walls somewhat thicker; generally fillet rim.

Deadmans Gray, constructed by paddling; temper contains micaceous particles; texture core, fine; surfaces well-smoothed, not noticeably scored or pitted.

RANGE:

Southwestern Colorado, northwestern New Mexico, northern Arizona north of the Mogollon Rim, southern Utah including the Virgin Valley (probably trade) west to Havasupai Canyon, Arizona.

REMARKS:

Lino Gray is the earliest known pottery type of northern Arizona with inorganic temper. It is a stage criterion for Basket Maker III but exists also in Pueblo I where it is later replaced by Kana-a Gray. Local variations occur in fineness and quantity of temper, a condition that greatly influences the smoothness of vessel surfaces. Peripheral occurrences of this type may eventually prove to be indicative of trade relations rather than of indigenous creation. Additional descriptive details are given by Morris, 1927, p. 163, and Roberts, 1929.

LINO FUGITIVE RED: new type

DESCRIBED BY: Morris, 1927, p. 176.

TYPE SPECIMENS: Cotype pitcher No. 147-577 and cotype sherds Nos AT 294, 395, and 577 in the Type Collection of the Museum of Northern Arizona.

TYPE SITE: Shabik'eschee Village, Chaco Canyon, New Mexico (see Roberts, 1929, p. 110).

STAGE: Basket Maker III.

TIME: Pre-750 A.D.

DESCRIPTION (revised):

Constructed: by coiling. *Fired:* in reducing atmosphere. *Core:* generally dark gray, sometimes light gray. *Temper:* abundant medium fine to coarse quartz sand; conspicuous on both surfaces *Vessel walls:* medium strong. *Texture core:* fine to coarse. *Fracture:* crumbling. *Surface finish:* very rough; scraped and occasionally lightly smoothed in spots; upper parts of exterior jar surfaces and interior bowl surfaces coated with thin (red) wash; wash almost completely weathers away or rubs off easily on unweathered specimens; usually deeply pitted; scraping marks very conspicuous. *Forms:* jars, bowls, pitchers. *Wall thickness:* walls fairly uniform thickness in individual vessels.

RANGE:

Probably corresponds with the range of Lino Gray. Known to occur in Chaco Canyon, New Mexico; in the Jeddito Valley, Navajo County, and in the San Francisco Mountain region, Arizona.

REMARKS:

Lino Fugitive Red is a variation of Lino Gray and may represent an early attempt to produce a pottery vessel of the color of vessels fired in an oxidizing atmosphere. The only way this red color could be produced on vessels fired in a reducing atmosphere would be by *painting the vessel after firing* since the paint would turn gray if fired. This theory is opposed to that offered by Roberts (1929, p. 9, 10). Relatively few specimens of Lino Fugitive Red are recognized because of the custom of washing vessels and sherds before studying them. Also, sherds exposed to weather lose most of the red wash but may sometimes be identified by a consistent pinkish tint with an accumulation of pigment in pitted and scraped areas.

LINO BLACK-ON-GRAY

Fig. 41. ($\frac{1}{2}\times$).

STAGE: Basket Maker III.
TIME: Pre-750 A.D.

SYNONYMS: (a) Post Basket Maker Ware, Kidder, 1924, p. 76; (b) Post Basket Maker Pottery, Morris, 1927, p. 175; (c) Basket Maker Black-on-white, Colton, 1932, p. 13; (d) Lino Black-on-white, Gladwin, W. & H. S., 1932, fig. 6.
DESCRIBED BY: Morris, 1927.
NAMED BY: Hargrave, 1932, p. 12.
ILLUSTRATIONS: Morris, 1927; Roberts, 1929; AT 9 (Fig. 41).
TYPE SPECIMENS: Cotype bowl No. NA 3093.3 and sherds Nos. AT 8, 9, 4313, in the Type Collection of the Museum of Northern Arizona.
TYPE SITE: Shabik'eschee Village, Chaco Canyon, New Mexico (Roberts, 1929).

DESCRIPTION (revised):

Constructed: by coiling. *Fired:* in reducing atmosphere. *Core:* usually dark gray or almost black; sometimes light gray. *Temper:* abundant medium fine to coarse quartz sand; fairly conspicuous on both surfaces; less so on painted surfaces. *Vessels walls:* medium strong. *Texture core:* fine to coarse. *Fracture:* crumbling. *Surface finish:* rough; scraped; occasionally lightly smoothed in spots on unpainted surfaces; almost always moderately smoothed on painted surfaces; not polished; never slipped; unpainted surfaces usually pitted; scraping marks conspicuous. *Surface color:* normally gray. *Fire clouds:* common. *Forms:* bowls, jars. *Wall thickness:* vessel walls fairly uniform thickness. *Decoration:* painted. *Paint:* black, occasionally slightly brownish where thin. *Pigment:* carbon (test by Colton). *Design:* narrow lines, frequently ticked or fringed; often narrow bands framed by narrow lines containing two or more rows of small isolated dots (1 to 2 mm in diameter); designs crudely executed.

COMPARISONS: Kana-a Black-on-white, coated with moderately heavy white slip; decoration employs essentially the same elements plus small solid triangles, lines in series; generally somewhat better executed.
    Deadmans Black-on-gray, constructed by paddling; temper contains mica-like particles; surfaces well-smoothed; not noticeably pitted or scored.

RANGE:

Widespread. Southwestern Colorado, northwestern New Mexico, northern Arizona north of the Mogollon Rim, and southern Utah east of the Colorado River.

KANA-A GRAY

REMARKS:

Lino Black-on-gray is the common table type for Basket Maker III for which it is a stage criterion.

KANA-A GRAY

SYNONYMS: (a) Slab House Corrugated, Spier, 1917, p. 306; (b) Blackware, Kidder & Guernsey, 1919, p. 153; (c) Pre-pueblo Pottery, Kidder, 1924, Pl. 34, g, h; Pl. 35; (d) Banded Neck Culinary, Roberts, 1931, p. 121; (e) Plain Gray-Coil Neck, Colton, 1932, p. 10; (f) Kana-a Gray Ware, Gladwin, W. & H. S., 1934, Fig. 4.
DESCRIBED BY: Kidder & Guernsey, 1919, pp. 42, 153.
NAMED BY: Hargrave, 1932, p. 11.
ILLUSTRATIONS: Kidder, 1924, Pl. 34, g, h; Morris, 1927, Figs. 26a, b; AT 454 (Fig. 42).
TYPE SPECIMENS: Cotype sherds Nos. AT 3, 450–454 in the Type Collection of the Musuem of Northern Arizona.

Fig. 42. ($\frac{1}{3}$×).

TYPE SITE: Fluteplayer House (= Ruin 5), Hagoe Canyon, Monument Valley, Navajo County, Arizona (see Kidder & Guernsey, 1919).
STAGE: Pueblo I.
TIME: ca 700–ca 875 A.D.

DESCRIPTION (revised):

Constructed: by coiling. *Fired:* in reducing atmosphere. *Core:* dark gray to light gray. *Temper:* abundant medium fine to coarse quartz sand; temper conspicuous on both surfaces. *Vessel walls:* medium strong. *Texture core:* fine to coarse. *Fracture:* crumbling. *Surface finish:* very rough; scraped, occasionally lightly smoothed in spots; never polished; coils unobliterated but flattened on exterior surfaces of necks from rim to shoulder, coils usually fairly wide (from 8 to 14 mm wide; sometimes not over 5 mm); usually deeply pitted; scraping marks very conspicuous. *Surface color:* normally gray. *Carbon streak:* common. *Forms:* jars. *Recorded range thickness vessel walls:* 2.5 to 9.7 mm; greatest individual range recorded, 3.5 mm; average thickness, ca 4.9 mm. *No painted decoration.*

COMPARISONS: Lino Gray, coils always obliterated over entire vessel surface; body and base sherds indistinguishable. Coconino Gray, Honani Tooled, O'leary Tooled, exterior surfaces necks decorated with tooling marks; body and base sherds indistinguishable.

Medicine Gray, exterior surfaces necks show unobliterated coils, usually narrower, and slightly finger-dented; body and base sherds indistinguishable.

Kiet Siel Gray, temper includes small amounts of opaque angular fragments, usually somewhat coarser temper, surfaces even less well-smoothed, usually bumpy, coils sometimes not quite obliterated; vessel walls average considerably thicker.

RANGE:

Southwestern Colorado, northwestern New Mexico, northern Arizona north of the Mogollon Rim and west to Havasupai Canyon; also Virgin River Valley, Utah (possibly trade).

REMARKS:

Kana-a Gray essentially is the same as Lino Gray but is later in time. Kana-a Gray is the common utility type for Pueblo I.

TUSAYAN CORRUGATED

SYNONYMS: (a) Corrugated Ware, Cushing, 1886, p. 490; (b) Gray Corrugated, Colton, 1932, p. 10; (c) Deadmans Corrugated, Hargrave, 1932, p. 13.
DESCRIBED BY: Hargrave, 1932, p. 13.
NAMED BY: Hargrave, loc. cit.
ILLUSTRATIONS: Fig. 43, A (Tusayan Corrugated); Fig. 43, B ("Deadmans Corrugated").
TYPE SPECIMENS: Type sherds Nos. AT 5, 6, 469–475, 554, 555, 557, and cotype sherds Nos. AT 476–479, 482–487 in the Type Collection of the Museum of Northern Arizona.
TYPE SITE: Medicine Fort (NA 862), Medicine Valley, San Francisco Mountains, Coconino County, Arizona.
STAGE: Pueblo II–III.
TIME: 925–1275 A.D.

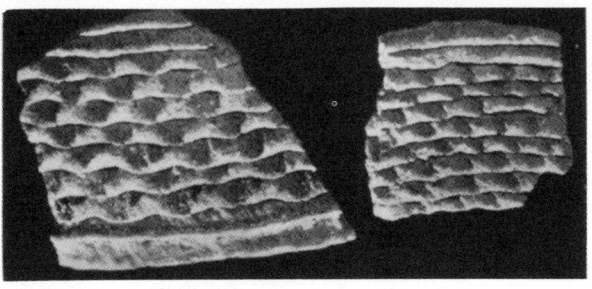

Fig. 43. (½ ×).

DESCRIPTION (revised):

Constructed: by coiling. *Fired:* in reducing atmosphere. *Core:* light gray to dark gray, sometimes almost black. *Carbon streak:* fairly frequent. *Temper:* abundant moderately coarse quartz sand; temper fairly conspicuous on both surfaces. *Vessel walls:* medium strong. *Texture core:* fine to coarse. *Fracture:* slightly crumbling. *Surface finish:* rough; interiors scraped; exteriors usually moderately well-smoothed; not polished; coils unobliterated on exterior surfaces; usually deeply finger-dented in fairly regular and carefully executed pattern; many minor variations; occasionally series contiguous non-dented coils; width of coils and depth and size of indentations vary widely; coils from ca 3 to 8 mm in width, most frequent width being between 5 and 7 mm; coils cover all or nearly all of exterior surfaces. *Surface color:* gray. *Forms:* jars, bowls, jugs. *Rims:* jars, IB3. *Recorded range thickness vessel walls:* 3.8 to 7.1 mm; greatest individual range recorded, 1.4 mm; average thickness, ca .5 mm. *No painted decoration.*

RANGE:

Undertermined. Known to occur in the San Francisco Mountains, Coconino County, Arizona; the Hopi Indian Reservation and the Tsegi drainage, Navajo County, Arizona; reported also from the Virgin River Valley, Utah.

MOENKOPI CORRUGATED

SYNONYM: Gray Corrugated, Colton, 1932, p. 10.
DESCRIBED BY: Hargrave, 1932, p. 14.
NAMED BY: Hargrave, loc. cit.
ILLUSTRATION: Hargrave, loc. cit., Pl. III, F; AT 493 (Fig. 44).
TYPE SPECIMENS: Type sherd No. AT 7 and cotype sherds Nos. AT 489–494, and 556 in the Type Collection of the Museum of Northern Arizona.
TYPE SITE: Po-ci-o-le-lena Pueblo (NA 1603 (=Whistling Quail Pueblo), Moenkopi Wash, near Tuba City, Coconino County, Arizona.
STAGE: Pueblo II–III.
TIME: ca 1075–ca 1275 A.D.

Fig. 44. ($\frac{1}{2}\times$).

DESCRIPTION (revised):

Constructed: by coiling. *Fired:* in reducing atmosphere. *Core:* light gray to dark gray; sometimes black. *Carbon streak:* frequent. *Temper:* abundant moderately coarse quartz sand; conspicuous on both surfaces. *Vessel walls:* medium strong. *Texture core:* fine to coarse. *Fracture:* slightly crumbling. *Surface finish:* rough; interior surfaces scraped and often fairly well-smoothed; not polished; coils partly obliterated by flattening, sometimes almost to a uniform surface; finger indentations sometimes noticeable, apparently not intentionally a part of decorative scheme; coils fairly wide, usually from 6 to 8 mm, often varying between 4 and 10 mm at extremes, and cover all or nearly all of the exterior surfaces. *Surface color:* normally gray. *Forms:* jars, bowls, jugs. *Recorded range thickness vessel walls:* 3.5 to 6.6 mm; greatest individual range recorded, 1.5

mm; average thickness, ca 4.7 mm; walls usually relatively thin. *No painted decoration.*

RANGE:

From the Hopi Indian Reservation, Navajo County, and the San Francisco Mountains, Coconino County, Arizona, north into southern Utah; east and west limits undetermined.

KIET SIEL GRAY: new type

TYPE SPECIMENS: Jar No. NA 2501.1, pitcher No. NA 2501.2 and sherds Nos. AT 576, 578–588, 590, 592, 595, 597–598, 601 in the Type Collection of the Museum of Northern Arizona.
TYPE SITE: Betatakin Pueblo (NA 2515), Tsegi drainage, Navajo National Monument, Navajo County, Arizona.
STAGE: Pueblo III.
TIME: ca 1274–1300 A.D.

DESCRIPTION:

Constructed: by coiling. *Fired:* in reducing atmosphere. *Core:* light gray to dark gray, sometimes black. *Carbon streak:* common. *Temper:* abundant opaque angular fragments, gray, tan; conspicuous on both surfaces but not so noticeable as other surface irregularities. *Vessel walls:* weak. *Texture core:* very coarse. *Fracture:* crumbling. *Surface finish:* very rough; scraped, often with structural coils not completely obliterated; often bumpy; surfaces deeply pitted; scraping marks conspicuous; often very coarsely crazed. *Surface color:* gray. *Fire clouds:* common. *Forms:* jars. *Rims:* jars, IA3, IC3; frequently single very wide coil, flattened but not obliterated (fillet). *Recorded range thickness jar walls:* 5 to 8.7 mm; walls usually relatively thick. *No painted decoration.*

COMPARISONS: Lino Gray, considerably finer temper composed entirely of quartz sand, surfaces little better smoothed, not bumpy, coils always completely obliterated, walls considerably thinner.
Kana-a Gray, considerably finer temper, composed entirely of quartz sand, surfaces a little better smoothed, not bumpy coils on exterior surfaces necks flattened but not obliterated.
Coconino Gray, Honani Tooled, O'Leary Tooled, exterior surfaces necks decorated with tooling marks, considerably finer temper, composed entirely of quartz sand, scraped surfaces little better smoothed, not bumpy, coils completely obliterated on body and base sherds, walls considerably thinner.
Medicine Gray, exterior surfaces necks decorated with unobliterated coils, slightly finger-dented, temper considerably finer; composed entirely of quartz sand; coils always completely obliterated on body and base sherds; scraped surfaces little better smoothed, not bumpy; walls considerably thinner.

RANGE:

Known to occur only in the Tsegi drainage, Navajo County, Arizona.

REMARKS:

Kiet Siel Gray resembles a revival of the surface treatment characteristic of Lino Gray but its time position and association with late black-on-white types lessens the probability of confusing it with Lino Gray, which occurs in the same region but only in Basket Maker or early Pueblo sites. The beginning of Kiet Siel Gray has erroneously been reported as late Pueblo II (Hargrave, 1935, p. 47), and as Pueblo II–III (Hargrave loc. cit., Tabular Results No. 36).

MEDICINE GRAY: new type

SYNONYM: Coconino Gray, in part, Hargrave, 1932, p. 12.

ILLUSTRATION: AT 461 (Fig. 45).

TYPE SPECIMENS: Jar No. 41/28 and sherds Nos. AT 4, 458/465 in the Type Collection of the Museum of Northern Arizona.

TYPE SITE: Medicine Fort (NA 862), Medicine Valley, San Francisco Mountains, Coconino County, Arizona.

STAGE: Pueblo II.

TIME: ca 875–925 A.D.

Fig. 45. ($\frac{1}{3}\times$).

DESCRIPTION:

Constructed: by coiling. *Fired:* in reducing atmosphere. *Core:* dark gray to light gray. *Temper:* abundant medium fine to coarse quartz sand, sometimes also feldspar (?); temper conspicuous on both surfaces. *Vessel walls:* medium strong. *Texture core:* fine to coarse. *Fracture:* crumbling. *Surface finish:* very rough; scraped; not smoothed; not polished; deeply pitted; scraping marks conspicuous; coils unobliterated on exterior surfaces of necks only; usually slightly finger-dented; usually varies from about 3 to 5 mm in width. *Surface color:* gray. *Forms:* jars. *Recorded range thickness jar walls:* 2.5 to 6.4 mm; greatest individual range recorded, 2.8 mm; average thickness, ca 4.3 mm. *No painted decoration.*

COMPARISONS: Lino Gray, coils always obliterated over entire surface; body and base sherds indistinguishable.

Kana-a Gray, exterior surfaces necks unobliterated coils without finger-indentations, usually somewhat wider; body and base sherds indistinguishable.

Coconino Gray, Honani Tooled, O'Leary Tooled, exterior surfaces necks decorated with tooling marks; body and base sherds indistinguishable.

Kiet Siel Gray, usually somewhat coarser temper, includes small quantities opaque angular fragments, surfaces even less well-smoothed, usually bumpy, coils sometimes not quite obliterated, vessel walls average somewhat thicker.

RANGE:

San Francisco Mountains, Coconino County, Arizona. Should be expected in early Pueblo II sites over the greater part of northern Arizona and southern Utah. Two sherds, Nos. AT 706 and 707, from Virgin Valley, near St. George, Utah.

REMARKS:

Medicine Gray is a late stage in the manipulation of the coils as decoration before corrugating became general in the Basket Maker–Pueblo Culture. Medicine Gray is a utility type of early Pueblo II in the San Francisco Mountains, Arizona.

O'LEARY TOOLED: new type

ILLUSTRATION: Fig. 7.
TYPE SPECIMENS: Sherds Nos. AT 4007–4018 and 4027 in the Type Collection of the Museum of Northern Arizona.
TYPE SITE: NA 1570, Bonito Park, Sunset Crater National Monument Coconino County, Arizona.
STAGE: Pueblo II.
TIME: ca 850–900 A.D.

DESCRIPTION:

Constructed: by coiling. *Fired:* in reducing atmosphere. *Core:* black to gray. *Temper:* abundant medium fine to medium coarse quartz sand. *Carbon streak:* usual and conspicuous. *Vessel walls:* medium strong. *Texture core:* fine to coarse. *Fracture:* crumbling. *Surface finish:* moderately well-smoothed; not polished; exterior surface necks, beginning about one inch below rim, decorated by vertical indentations ca 4 to 5 mm long by ca 2 mm wide, arranged in closely set horizontal rows. *Surface color:* gray. *Fire clouds:* occasional. *Forms:* jars. *Rims:* jars, IIIB2. *Recorded range thickness jar walls:* 4.7 to 8.9 mm; greatest individual range recorded, 2.5 mm; average thickness, 6.6 mm. *No painted decoration.*

COMPARISONS: Lino Gray, Kana-a Gray, are not tooled; body and base sherds indistinguishable.
  Coconino Gray, exterior surfaces necks unobliterated coils with horizontal tooling marks; body and base sherds indistinguishable.
  Medicine Gray, exterior surfaces necks unobliterated coils with slight finger-indentations; body and base sherds indistinguishable.
  Kiet Siel Gray, somewhat coarser temper, includes small quantities opaque angular fragments, never tooled.
  Honani Tooled, exterior surfaces necks decorated with vertical or diagonal tooling marks in series; body and base sherds indistinguishable.

RANGE:

Recorded only from the San Francisco Mountains, Coconino County, Arizona.

COCONINO GRAY

DESCRIBED BY: Hargrave, 1932, p. 12.
NAMED BY: Hargrave, loc. cit.
ILLUSTRATION: AT 565 (Fig. 46).
TYPE SPECIMENS: Sherds Nos. AT 455–457, 564–566 in the Type Collection of the Museum of Northern Arizona.
TYPE SITE: Medicine Fort (NA 862), Medicine Valley, Coconino County, Arizona.
STAGE: Pueblo II.
TIME: ca 850–900 A.D.

Fig. 46. ($\frac{1}{2}$×).

DESCRIPTION (revised):
Constructed: by coiling. *Fired:* in reducing atmosphere. *Core:* light gray. *Carbon streak:* rare. *Temper:* abundant medium fine to coarse quartz sand: occasionally some feldspar (?); conspicuous on both surfaces. *Vessel walls:* medium strong. *Texture core:* fine to coarse. *Fracture:* crumbling. *Surface finish:* very rough; scraped; not smoothed; not polished; often deeply pitted; scraping marks conspicuous; neck coils unobliterated on exterior surfaces, emphasized by horizontal tooling marks creating channels of roughly semi-circular section and producing fluted effect; coils vary from 1.5 to 6 mm in width; body and base, plain. *Surface color:* gray. *Forms:* jars. *Recorded range thickness jar walls:* 2.9 to 6 mm; greatest individual range recorded, 2.2 mm; average thickness, 4.3 mm. *No painted decoration.*

COMPARISONS: Lino Gray, Kana-a Gray, Medicine Gray, never tooled; body and base sherds indistinguishable.
  Honani Tooled, exterior surfaces necks decorated with vertical or diagonal tooling marks in series; body and base sherds indistinguishable.
  O'Leary Tooled, exterior surfaces necks decorated with indentations or punchings; no tooled channels; body and base sherds indistinguishable.
  Kiet Siel Gray, usually somewhat coarser temper including small quantities opaque angular fragments, surfaces even less well-smoothed, usually bumpy, coils generally not quite obliterated, vessel walls average considerably thicker.

RANGE:
San Francisco Mountains, Coconino County, Arizona, and sparingly in the Rainbow Plateau Area; should be expected in early Pueblo II sites over the greater part of northern Arizona and southern Utah.

REMARKS:
Coconino gray represents an early stage in the manipulation of coils in decoration. In part this type is believed to be con-

temporaneous with Kana-a Gray, Medicine Gray, and possibly with Tusayan Corrugated. The original description made no distinction between corrugations and indented corrugations. Coconino Gray is a Utility type.

HONANI SERIES

So little attention has been paid to utility types that much information frequently is needed before a proper placement of the type can be made. The type at present comprising Honani Series is in this category.

HONANI TOOLED: new type

ILLUSTRATIONS: Fig. 7, p. 38.
TYPE SPECIMENS: Sherds Nos. AT 467–468, 4070–4072, 4511–4512 in the Type Collection of the Museum of Northern Arizona.
TYPE SITE: NA 853, near Honani Spring, lower Oraibi Wash, Hopi Indian Reservation, Navajo County, Arizona.
STAGE: Pueblo II.
TIME: ca 900 A.D.

DESCRIPTION:

Constructed: by coiling. *Fired:* in reducing atmosphere. *Core:* dark gray to light gray. *Temper:* medium fine to medium coarse quartz sand; temper noticeable on surfaces. *Vessel walls:* medium strong. *Texture core:* fine to coarse. *Fracture:* crumbling *Surface fiinish:* rough; interiors scraped, moderately well smoothed; not polished; exterior surfaces necks tooled in parallel vertical or diagonal series of channels of roughly semicircular section, producing fluted effect, often in herringbone pattern; original coils sometimes obliterated, sometimes only flattened with tooling marks superimposed, sometimes emphasized by horizontal tooling with vertical or diagonal tooling superimposed; body sherds apparently not tooled. *Surface color:* gray. *Forms:* jars. Rims: jars, IC3. *Recorded range thickness jar walls:* 5.4 to 7 mm. *No painted decoration.*

COMPARISONS: Lino Gray, Kana-a Gray, not tooled; body sherds indistinguishable.
    Coconino Gray, exterior surfaces necks unobliterated coils with horizontal tooling marks; body and base sherds indistinguishable.
    Medicine Gray, exterior surfaces necks unobliterated coils with slight finger-indentations; body and base sherds indistinguishable.
    Kiet Siel Gray, somewhat coarser temper including small quantities opaque angular fragments, never tooled, interior surfaces less well-smoothed, somewhat bumpy, vessel walls average thicker.
    O'Leary Tooled, surfaces smoothed, necks decorated on exterior surfaces with indentations or punchings; no tooled channels; body and base sherds indistinguishable.

REDUCING ATMOSPHERE

REMARKS:

Drainages in the Hopi Indian Reservation, Navajo County, Arizona. One sherd from the San Francisco Mountains, Coconino County, Arizona. Probably occurs regularly in early Pueblo II sites in this area.

TUSAYAN WHITE WARE

The principal difference between Tusayan Gray Ware and Tusayan White Ware is that in types of the latter ware vessels have a smoothed surface as a base for a black painted decoration. Indigenously, this ware is companion in time and space to Tusayan Gray Ware. Tusayan White Ware is composed entirely of decorated types. Rarely, one surface of a bowl with a painted design may also be corrugated.

KEY 16: TUSAYAN WHITE WARE

1. Kana-a Style of Design................Kana-a Black-on-white (p. 205)
   Deadmans Style of Design..........Deadmans Black-on-white (p. 208)
   Dogoszhi Style of Design............Dogoszhi Black-on-white (p. 209)
   Sosi Style of Design....................Sosi Black-on-white (p. 211)
   ....Kia-ko Black-on-white (p. 219)
   Polacca Style of Design..............Polacca Black-on-white (p. 220)
   Flagstaff Style of Design... 2
   Kayenta Style of Design... 3
2. Temper noticeable; scraping marks generally conspicious on undecorated surface....................Flagstaff Black-on-white (p. 225)
   Temper not noticeable; scraping marks not noticeable.............
   ....Tusayan Black-on-white (p. 213)
3. Temper, not apparent... 4
   Temper, apparent.................Wupatki Black-on-white (p. 227)
4. Open work of cross hatchure.........Betatakin Black-on-white (p. 215)
   Negative design, highly polished.......Kayenta Black-on-white (p. 217)
   Negative design, rough surface.........Hoyapi Black-on-white (p. 222)

TUSAYAN WHITE WARE: new ware

SYNONYMS: (a) White Ware, Holmes, 1886, p. 305; (b) Black-and-white Ware, Fewkes, 1904.
STAGES: Pueblo I–IV.
TIME: ca 700–ca 1350 A.D.

DESCRIPTION:

Constructed: by coiling. *Fired:* in reducing atmosphere. *Core:*

usually light gray, dark gray occurs in most types, occasionally black. *Carbon streak:* absent or infrequent. *Temper:* in most types fine quartz sand, often almost invisible, but usually abundant in quantity; in several types also occasional dark colored opaque angular fragments; quartz grains less fine in Kana-a Black-on-white; in general temper becomes finer and less abundant in later types. *Vessel walls:* in most types strong or medium strong; decided ring in Hoyapi Black-on-white and Kayenta Black-on-white. *Surface finish:* exterior jar surfaces and interior bowl surfaces usually impacted or coated with thin slip or wash; exterior bowl surfaces also impacted or coated with thin slip on several types; slip usually very thin; on some types (Kana-a Black-on-white, Deadmans Black-on-white), moderately heavy; decorative surfaces moderately or well-polished; scraping marks infrequent; surfaces Flagstaff Black-on-white usually pitted; undecorated surfaces usually fairly well scraped or smoothed; scraping marks noticeable though not usually conspicuous; on Betatakin Black-on-white, Kayenta Black-on-white, scraping marks barely discernible. *Surface color:* bluish white, pearl gray or dead white. *Forms:* bowls, jars, dippers, colanders, mugs. *Rims:* bowls, IA2, IA3 (very frequent), IA4 (very frequent), IIA2 (infrequent), IIIA3 (infrequent); Jars, IA2, IA3, IA4, IIA3, IIIA3, IB3, IIB3, IIIB3, IIIB4, IC2, IC3, IIC2, IID3. *Recorded range thickness bowl walls:* 2 to 6.9 mm; greatest individual range recorded, 3.3 mm; average thickness, ca 4.5 mm; thickness individual bowl walls usually varies only slightly—generally not over 2 mm. *Recorded range thickness jar walls:* 1.8 to 8.6 mm; greatest individual range recorded, 2.6 mm; average thickness, ca 4.3 mm. *Decoration:* painted. *Paint:* always black. usually fairly dense and dull; often somewhat watery with tendency toward brownish or purplish tint in thin spots; often gritty in some types; rarely almost vitreous. *Pigment:* usually carbon, sometimes with traces of iron. *Designs:* present in all types; usually confined to exterior jar surfaces, interior bowl surfaces, although in Kia-ko Black-on-white exterior decoration on bowl forms occurs rarely. *Elements and motives:* almost exclusively geometric and angular, with curved figures on Deadmans Black-on-white; open-work style in Wupatki Black-on-white. Betatakin Black-on-white, frequent; negative style usual on Kayenta Black-on-white, Hoyapi Black-on white.

RANGE:

Generally all over northeastern Arizona from the Petrified Forest National Monument to the region of the San Francisco Mountains, north to the San Juan River between Chinle Creek and the Colorado River, south to the Little Colorado River; occasional intrusions in the Chino and Verde Valleys, Arizona.

KAYENTA SERIES

This series is companion to Tsegi Series in areas where the Kayenta Series is indigenous although this series is more restricted geographically than is Tsegi Series.

KEY S: Kayenta Series

1. Kana-a Style of Design (Fig. 00).......Kana-a Black-on-white (p. 205)
Deadmans Style of Design (Fig. 00)..Deadmans Black-on-white (p. 208)
Dogoszhi Style of Design (Fig. 00)....Dogoszhi Black-on-white (p. 209)
Sosi Style of Design (Fig. 00).............Sosi Black-on-white (p. 211)
Flagstaff Style of Design (Fig. 00).....Tusayan Black-on-white (p. 213)
Kayenta Style of Design (Fig. 00)............................. 2
2. Open work of cross hatchure........Betatakin Black-on-white (p. 215)
Negative design, highly polished.......Kayenta Black-on-white (p. 217)

KANA-A BLACK-ON-WHITE

SYNONYMS: (a) Slab-house Black-on-white Ware, Kidder & Guernsey, 1919, p. 152; (b) Pre-Pueblo Black-on-white, Kidder, 1924, p. 75; (c) Pueblo I Black-on-white, Gladwin, W. & H. S., 1930 a, p. 174; (d) 1st Tusayan, Gladwin, W. & H. S., loc. cit., p. 181; (e) Western Pueblo I Black-on-white, Morss, 1931, p. 2.
DESCRIBED BY: Kidder & Guernsey, loc. cit.
NAMED BY: Hargrave, 1932, p. 15.
ILLUSTRATIONS: Kidder & Guernsey, loc. cit., Pl. 63; Kidder, 1924, Pl. 24, 35; Colton, 1932, Pl. 1; (drawing) AT 42 (Fig. 47).
TYPE SPECIMENS: Cotype sherds Nos. AT 35–47, 4150, in the Type Collection of the Museum of Northern Arizona.

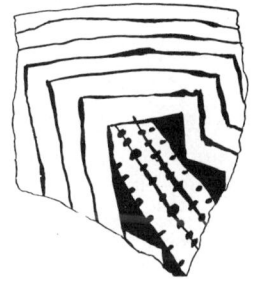

Fig. 47. (½×).

TYPE SITE: Fluteplayer House (=Ruin 5, as designated by Kidder & Guernsey, 1919, p. 41), Hagoe Canyon, Monument Valley, Navajo County, Arizona.
STAGE: Pueblo I.
TIME: ca 700–ca 850 A.D.

DESCRIPTION (revised):

Constructed: by coiling. *Fired:* in reducing atmosphere. *Core:* light gray. *Carbon streak:* usual. *Temper:* fairly abundant quartz sand; sometimes conspicuous on undecorated surfaces. *Vessel walls:* strong. *Texture core:* medium to fine. *Fracture:* crumbling or (rarely) shattering. *Surface finish:* bowl exteriors scraped, scraping marks usually discernible; interiors bowls and exteriors jars polished; somewhat bumpy; both surfaces bowls and exterior surfaces jars, slipped (white); slipped surfaces frequently coarsely crazed; slip line visible in cross-section of heavily slipped sherds. *Surface color:* bluish white, creamy white, or dead white. *Fire clouds:* occasional. *Forms:* bowls, jars, seed jars, pitchers. *Recorded range thickness bowl walls:* 2.7 to 5.9 mm; greatest individual range recorded, 2 mm; average thickness (34 sherds), 4.38 mm. *Recorded range thickness jar walls:* 2.1 to 6.2 mm; greatest individual range recorded, 1.4 mm; average thickness, ca 4.8 mm. *Rims:* bowls, IA3, IA4, IIA2, IIIA2, (abundant) IIIA4 (common). *Decoration:* painted. *Paint:* black, usually fairly dense, often watery, sometimes with brownish or purplish tint. *Pigment:* carbon (test by Colton). *Designs:* bowl interiors and jar exteriors only; fine straight lines, sometimes singly, more often parallel series of 3 to 10 lines, about 4 to 10 mm apart; lines almost always carry over slightly at junctions; small solid triangles, either isosceles or elongated, sometimes with hooks; pendent dots and ticked or pinnate lines frequent; characterized by marked crudity of brushwork.

COMPARISON: Lino Black-on-gray, never slipped nor polished; gritty surface; gray color.

RANGE:

Known to occur over the greater part of northeastern Arizona. On the Plateau, about San Francisco Mountains to Petrified Forest National Monument, north to San Juan River, to Colorado River, to junction of Little Colorado River. Intrusive in Colonial Hohokam site at Roosevelt Lake, Gila County, Arizona (Haury, 1932, p. 91, plate XXIV).

REMARKS:

Found principally in sherd areas. Sherds of Kana-a Black-on-white from the Tsegi Canyons (Hargrave, 1935), Navajo County (collection of the Rainbow Bridge-Monument Valley Expedition), the Hopi country, and the San Francisco Mountains are essentially the same although many sherds of this type from the San Francisco Mountains may average more friable than sherds from other regions. At Comar Springs, lower Jeddito Valley, north of Winslow, Navajo County, sherds of Kana-a Black-on-white are not finished as well as are sherds from other localities studied; nor do they appear to have been slipped. Kana-a Black-on-white is the common table type for Pueblo I.

Fig. 48. Deadmans Black-on-white ($\frac{1}{4} \times$).

DEADMANS BLACK-ON-WHITE

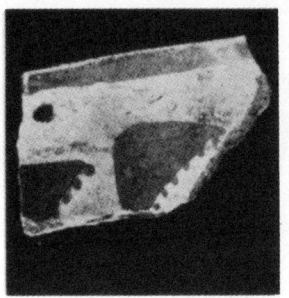

Fig. 49. (½×).

SYNONYMS: (a) Black-on-white Ware, Fewkes, 1921, p. 27; (b) 2nd Tusayan, Gladwin, W. & H. S., 1930 a, p. 181; (c) Black Mesa Pueblo II, Morss, 1931, p. 4; (d) Black Mesa Black-on-white, Gladwin, & H. S., 1934, Fig. 1.

[DESC]RIBED BY: Colton, 1932, p. 10.

[NAM]ED BY: Colton, loc. cit.

[ILLU]STRATIONS: Fewkes, 1911, Pl. 16, b; [Ki]dder & Guernsey, 1919, Pl. 54, d; Harve, 1932, Pl. VII, c; Colton, 1933, Fig. 1; [Gla]dwin, W. & H. S., 1934, Fig. 1; AT 1032 (Fig. 49).

TYPE SPECIMENS: Bowl No. NA 1123.5 and sherd No. AT 48; cotype sherds Nos. AT 1029–1032 in the Type Collection of the Museum of Northern Arizona.

TYPE SITE: Medicine Fort (NA 862), Medicine Valley, Deadmans Wash, San Francisco Mountains, Coconino County, Arizona.

STAGE: Pueblo II.
TIME: ca 875–ca 1100 A.D.

DESCRIPTION:

Constructed: by coiling. *Fired:* in reducing atmosphere. *Core:* dark gray to light gray. *Carbon streak:* common. *Temper:* fairly abundant quartz sand; sometimes noticeable on undecorated surfaces. *Vessel walls:* strong. *Texture core:* fine to medium. *Fracture:* slightly crumbling. *Surface finish:* interior surface bowls, exterior surface jars, polished sometimes somewhat bumpy; both surfaces bowls, exterior surface jars, coated with (white) slip; slip line visible in cross-section of heavily slipped specimens; scraping marks barely noticeable on unpainted surfaces. *Surface color:* dead white; sometimes with bluish tint. *Fire clouds:* occasional. *Forms:* bowls, dippers (rare), jars, jugs. *Recorded range thickness bowl walls:* 3 to 6 mm; greatest individual range recorded, 1.7 mm; average thickness, ca 4.8 mm. *Recorded range thickness jar walls:* 3 to 7.3 mm; average thickness, ca 4.7 mm. *Rims:* bowls, IA3 (abundant), IA4, IIA3, IIIA3; jars, IA3, IA4, IC2, IIB3, IIIA3. *Decoration:* painted. *Paint:* dull black, usually fairly dense, occasionally slightly watery with slight brownish tint. *Pigment:* carbon (test by Colton). *Designs:* bowl interiors, jar exteriors, only; bowl bottoms undecorated; jar bases undecorated; rims unpainted; stripes and wide straight horizontal lines, rarely curved lines, large solid triangles, isosceles and elongated; triangles sometimes in opposed series forming rows of open diamonds; stepped elements (rare), solid squares (rare); solid areas with large pendent dots; interlocking scrolls.

COMPARISONS: Kia-ko Black-on-white, paint usually less dense and rich, stripes and lines in general narrower, solid triangles infrequent, pendent dots absent; small sherds sometimes indistinguishable.
Sosi Black-on-white, treatment bolder and execution more precise; elements less closely massed; pendent dots absent; triangles, either isolated or contiguous, infrequent.

RANGE:
Regularly over greater part of northeastern Arizona. Northern tributaries of the Little Colorado River below Holbrook; along an east-west line following the Santa Fe railroad to Williams; north to, and along, the Colorado River to Navajo Mountain; southern tributaries of the San Juan River below Chinle Creek; and interlying area. Also, has been found in Chinle, Chino and Verde valleys.

REMARKS:
Deadmans style of design is more widespread than the known range of Deadmans Black-on-white (Colton, 1933).

DOGOSZHI BLACK-ON-WHITE: new type

SYNONYMS: (a) Black-on-white Ware, Kidder & Guernsey, 1919, pp. 130–134; (b) Proto-Kayenta Black-on-white, Morss, 1931, p. 10, Pl. 6, lower right hand corner; (c) Black Mesa Pueblo II Black-on-white, Morss, 1931, pl. 2; (d) Virgin Black-on-white, Spencer, 1934, p. 75, Pl. 1.
ILLUSTRATIONS: Kidder & Guernsey, loc. cit., Pl. 55; Morss, loc. cit., Pl. 2, Pl. 6; Spencer, loc. cit. (Drawing Fig. 50).
TYPE SITE: Len-a Ki (NA 2630), at head of Dogoszhi Biko, Tsegi drainage, Navajo County, Arizona.
STAGE: Pueblo II–III.
TIME: ca 875–ca 1150 A.D.

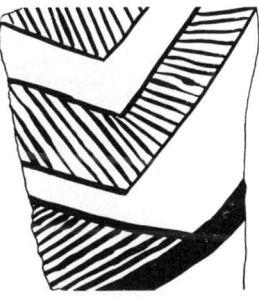

Fig. 50. ($\frac{1}{2}$×).

DESCRIPTION:

Constructed: by coiling. *Fired:* in reducing atmosphere. *Core:* dark gray to light gray. *Carbon streak:* usual. *Temper:* abundant fine quartz sand, rarely also dark opaque angular fragments. *Vessel walls:* strong. *Texture core:* fine. *Fracture:* shattering to slightly crumbling. *Surface finish:* exterior bowls, scraped, usually scraping marks very noticeable; sometimes polished; interior bowls and exterior jars, usually more smoothly polished than exterior surface bowls; interior surface jars, scraped; surfaces almost always impacted; rarely thinly slipped. *Surface color:* white, usually with slight bluish-gray tint. *Forms:* bowls, jars. *Recorded range thickness bowl walls:* 3.6 to 5.8 mm; greatest individual range recorded, 2 mm; average thickness, ca 4.8 mm. *Recorded range thickness jar walls:* 3.5 to 5.8 mm; greatest individual range recorded, 2.1 mm; average thickness, ca 4.6 mm. *Rims:* bowls, IA2, IA3, IA4; jars, IIIA2, IB3, IIIB3, IIIB4. *Decoration:* painted. *Paint:* black. *Pigment:* carbon (test by Colton). *Designs:* confined to bowl interiors; jar exteriors; no rim decoration; bowl bottoms and jar bases, undecorated. *Patterns:* rectangular, triangular, rarely curved panels containing diagonal or vertical narrow-line hatching; rectangular panels almost always much greater in one direction than in other; diagonal hatching predominates, width of hatchures and framing lines approximately same, varying from 1 to 3 mm, framing lines occasionally as wide as 4.5 mm; individual hatchures vary considerably in width, spaces between hatchures about equal to width of hatchures; hatchures occasionally wavy, apparently unintentional; design often begins just below rim with narrow border line; panels may begin at rim or be pendent from connecting line just below rim; rarely any other motif in design; treatment bold, uneven, often sloppy with intersecting lines overcarrying as in Kana-a Black-on-white.

COMPARISONS: Polacca Black-on-white, hatching bolder, less regular in execution, panels cover larger areas, less elongated in band form; spaces between hatchures wider than hatchures themselves; hatching usually combined with solid elements; framing lines usually wider than hatchures.

Padre Black-on-white, heavily slipped, well-polished; paint usually somewhat denser; hatchures slightly wider with interspaces about same width as hatchures; panels generally larger; temper mostly fine opaque angular fragments.

RANGE:

Recorded from the main Tsegi, Betatakin, Kiet Siel, and Long canyons, Dogoszhi Biko and Tsegi-ot-sosi, and the San Francisco Mountains in northeastern Arizona; also, Virgin Valley, Utah (Spencer, 1934). Fairly common at NA 1712, a Pueblo II pithouse site in upper Oraibi Wash, Hopi Indian Reservation, Navajo County, Arizona.

REMARKS:

Dogoszhi Black-on-white is named for the eastern drainage of the Tsegi system, Dogoszhi Biko, where the type is common. The type site is a small late Pueblo II or early Pueblo III cliff pueblo. Important information has already been secured from this site which has given the dates 1124 and 1127 A.D. (Hargrave, 1935). Recognition of the Dogoszhi Style of Design was made some time ago but the designation as a style was determined only after much study of material collected by the Rainbow Bridge—Monument Valley Expedition of 1933 and 1934. Sherds of Dogoszhi Black-on-white from the San Francisco Mountains appear to be slightly different from others of the type and it is thus probable that the type will eventually be broken up into several additional types. The widespread distribution of the Dogoszhi Style is just being recognized and because of its occurrence in some peripheral areas, and also because of striking resemblances to an early black-on-white from sherd areas of the Chinle Valley, this style seems destined to become important in the study of Pueblo ceramics of the extreme northeastern part of Arizona.

Spencer (loc. cit.) appears to have found this style to be fairly common in the Virgin Valley, Utah.

SOSI BLACK-ON-WHITE: new type

SYNONYMS: (a) Black-on-white Ware, Kidder & Guernsey, 1919, p. 130; (b) Proto-Kayenta Black-on-white, Kidder, 1924, p. 72; (c) 3rd Tusayan, Gladwin, W. & H. S., 1930 a, pp. 180–191; (d) Tusayan Black-on-white, Hargrave, 1932, p. 23; (e) Black Mesa Pueblo II Black-on-white, Morss, 1931, Pl. 2.

ILLUSTRATIONS: Morss, loc. cit., lower right hand corner; Fig. 51.

TYPE SPECIMENS: Sherds Nos. AT 62–72 in the Type Collection of the Museum of Northern Arizona.

TYPE SITE: Len-a Ki (NA 2630), head of Dogoszhi Biko, Tsegi drainage, Navajo County, Arizona.

STAGE: Late Pueblo II–early Pueblo III.

TIME: ca 1120–ca 1150 A.D. (McGregor, 1934, p. 8; Hargrave, 1935).

DESCRIPTION:

Constructed: by coiling. *Fired:* in reducing atmosphere. *Core:* light gray to dark gray. *Carbon streak:* fairly common. *Temper:* abundant fine quartz sand. *Vessel walls:* strong. *Texture core:* fine. *Fracture:* shattering to slightly crumbling. *Surface finish:* both surfaces bowls, exterior surfaces jars, impacted, or coated with thin (white) slip; bowl interiors, jar exteriors moderately polished; scraping marks visible on unpolished, sometimes on polished surfaces. *Surface color:* bluish white or pearl gray. *Fire clouds:* occasional. *Forms:* bowls, jars, dippers (rare). *Recorded range thickness bowl walls:* 3.2 to 6.7 mm; greatest individual range recorded, 1.5 mm; average thickness ca 4.5 mm. *Rims:* bowls, IA2, IA3 (abundant), IA4 (common), IB3, IIIB3; jars, IA3 (abundant), IIIA3, IB3. *Decoration:* painted. *Paint:* black sometimes brownish. *Pigment:* carbon (test by

212 NORTHERN ARIZONA POTTERY WARES

Colton). *Design:* bold and free, suggestive of Deadmans Style; two general styles, Style 1 (predominates): horizontal stripes make up major part of design, with large solid areas, triangles (frequent), stepped elements; interlocking scrolls (rare); Style

Fig. 51. Sosi Black-on-white ($\frac{1}{2} \times$).

II: stripes or wide lines with large solid traingles, singly or in series, strongly suggestive of the barbed lines on Flagstaff Black-on-white but heavier and bolder; decoration both styles covers most of bowl interior; bowl exteriors, undecorated; rims, undecorated; decoration jars, confined to neck and upper body.

COMPARISONS: Flagstaff Black-on-white, somewhat less bold in treatment, stripes and lines narrower, solid elements smaller; barbed lines very frequent; pinnate lines and coarse cross-hatching frequent; often rather less well-polished.

Kia-ko Black-on-white, somewhat less bold in treatment, stripes and lines narrower, solid elements smaller; small sherds often indistinguishable by description (doubtful material should be compared with identified specimens).

Deadmans Black-on-white, treatment somewhat less bold and execution less precise; elements more closely massed; pendent dots and continuous rows of solid triangles, frequent.

RANGE:

Tsegi drainage, Navajo County, Arizona as follows: lower main Tsegi, Kiet Siel and Long canyons, and Dogoszhi Biko to its head.

REMARKS:

At many sites in the Tsegi region are frequently found sherds which usually have so little individual character in decoration that it is difficult to place them in time and stage. In the past, all that could be said of this group of sherds was that a broad line decoration was characteristic. This characteristic has made for confusion because of a similarity to Deadmans Black-on-white (Morss, 1931). To avoid further confusion a detailed study was recently made of a large number of sherds from 53 sites, recorded by the Rainbow Bridge—Monument Valley Expedition in 1933. Although the exact time and stage is still unknown, it seems fairly obvious from this study that this new type is later than Deadman's Black-on-white and further that Sosi Black-on-white may have had a strong influence upon the decorative styles of Pueblo III in the region.

Though occurring commonly in the general region where Kidder and Guernsey worked, Sosi Black-on-white appears not to have been recognized by them since the paste makeup does not fit their description given for black-on-white pottery in the Tsegi, nor is there more than one illustration in their report (Pl. 54, j) that appears to be of this type. Morss did not recognize the type. But that it probably occurs in the area studied by him is shown by the illustration of a sherd grouped with "Black Mesa Pueblo II Black-on-white Sherds" (lower right hand corner of plate 2). The type is abundant in early Pueblo III sites. The name is derived from Tsegi-ot-sosi, a canyon draining a part of the Tsegi Mesas on the east.

TUSAYAN BLACK-ON-WHITE

SYNONYMS: (a) Pottery from Tusayan, Holmes, 1886; (b) Tusayan Pottery, Mason, Figs. 44, 45; (c) Black-and-white Ware, Kidder & Guernsey, 1919, pp. 130–134; (d) Proto-Kayenta Black-on-white, Kidder, 1924, p. 72; (e) 3rd Tusayan, Gladwin, W. & H. S., 1930 a, pp. 180–191.

DESCRIBED BY: Kidder & Guernsey, loc. cit.
NAMED BY: Hargrave, 1932, p. 2.
ILLUSTRATIONS: Holmes, 1886, figs. 302–305; Mason, 1898, loc. cit.; Kidder & Guernsey, loc. cit., Fig. 55; Kidder, loc. cit., fig. 14, C; Morss, 1931, Pl. 5–6.
TYPE SPECIMENS: Cotype sherds Nos. AT 10 and 750 in the Type Collection of the Museum of Northern Arizona.
TYPE SITE: Long House Pueblo (Fewkes, 1911) or Ruin A (Kidder & Guernsey, 1919, equals NA 897), Marsh Pass, Navajo County, Arizona.
STAGE: Pueblo III.
TIME: ca 1225–1300 A.D.

DESCRIPTION (revised):

Constructed: by coiling. *Fired:* in reducing atmosphere. *Carbon streak:* occasional. *Temper:* not very abundant fine quartz sand, sometimes almost invisible. *Vessel walls:* strong. *Texture core:* fine. *Fracture:* shattering to slightly crumbling. *Surface finish:* interior bowl surfaces, exterior jar surfaces, smoothed; not slipped; slightly polished; scraping marks noticeable on undecorated surfaces. *Surface color:* dead white to light pearl gray. *Forms:* jars, seed jars, colanders, jugs, canteens, dippers, bowls. *Recorded range thickness bowl walls:* 2.5 to 5.6 mm; greatest individual range recorded, 2.3 mm; average thickness, ca 4 mm. *Recorded range thickness jar walls:* 3.1 to 5.9 mm; greatest individual range recorded, 1.6 mm; average thickness, ca 4.5 mm. *Rims:* bowls, IA4. *Decoration:* painted. *Paint:* black, usually dense and sometimes gritty. *Designs:* "Most characteristic . . . is the lavish use of series of small ranking triangles set along straight lines in a sort of sawtooth edge and opposed by like series running in the opposite direction. Very commonly there is introduced between the two a line sawtoothed on both sides. . . . Opposed sets of isosceles triangles with their points touching, thus leaving diamond-shaped interspaces, each one of which is occupied by a single dot, are also abundant; interlocking scrolls . . . are common" (Kidder & Guernsey, 1919, p. 134); large solid areas with serrated edges are fairly common, and a rather coarse cross-hatching sometimes occurs as a background for the series of triangles.

COMPARISON: Flagstaff Black-on-white, temper abundant fine quartz sand; texture core, fine; decorated surfaces well-smoothed but slightly gritty; undecorated surfaces scraped with scraping marks generally conspicuous; not well-smoothed and usually badly pitted; paint somewhat thinner; elements in design bolder and larger, with white areas very slightly in excess of painted areas.

RANGE:

Northeastern Arizona. Sherds have been obtained from Kiet Siel Pueblo (NA 2519) Betatakin Pueblo (NA 2515), and Bat

Woman Pueblo (NA 2531), in the Tsegi Canyons; NA 2658 in Forbidding Canyon; NA 842 at Oraibi, Hopi Indian Reservation; and NA 2709 and 2727 in Tsegi-ot-sosi.

REMARKS:
Apparently a rare type. Since 1924 this type has been used as a criterion for Pueblo III in many parts of northeastern Arizona, but in this usage STYLE of design alone was usually considered. The name thus has inadvertently been applied to other types which exhibited the same or a similar style of design although possessing other and different characteristics. Great care must therefore be exercised in interpretating the use of the name Tusayan Black-on-white in the earlier publications to determine if this name was applied strictly to the type as described herein.

BETATAKIN BLACK ON WHITE: new type

SYNONYMS: (a) Black-on-white Ware, Kidder & Guernsey, 1919, p. 130; (b) Kayenta Black-on-white, Kidder, 1924, p. 71; (c) 3rd Tusayan, Gladwin, W. & H. S., 1930 a, pp. 180–191.

ILLUSTRATIONS: AT 107 (Fig. 52).

TYPE SPECIMENS: Sherds Nos. AT 104–110 in the Type Collection of the Museum of Northern Arizona.

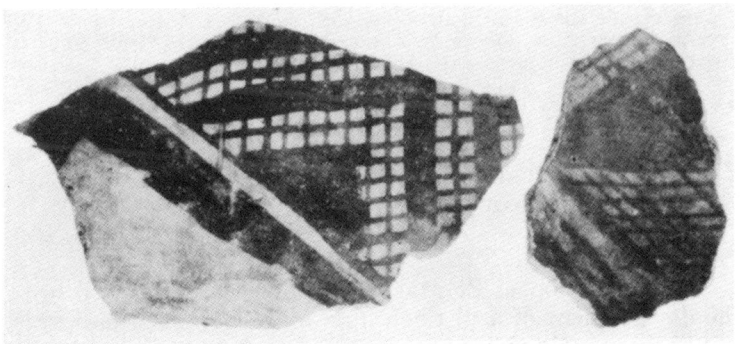

Fig. 52. Betatakin B/W ($\frac{2}{3}\times$).

TYPE SITE: Betatakin Pueblo (NA 2515), Tsegi drainage, Navajo National Monument, Navajo County, Arizona.
STAGE: Pueblo III.
TIME: ca 1275–1300 A.D.

DESCRIPTION:
Constructed: by coiling. *Fired:* in reducing atmosphere. *Core:* dark gray to light gray. *Temper:* not very abundant fine grains

quartz sand, often almost invisible. *Vessel walls:* strong. *Texture core:* fine. *Fracture:* shattering to very slightly crumbling. *Surface finish:* bowl interiors, jar exteriors, impacted; not highly polished. *Surface color:* pearl gray to light bluish gray. *Forms:* bowls, jars. *Recorded range thickness bowl walls:* 2.9 to 4.1 mm; greatest individual range recorded, 1.9 mm; average thickness, ca 4 mm. *Rims:* jars, IC3. *Decoration:* painted. *Paint:* black, usually dense but dull; occasionally gritty though usually fairly smooth, apparently due to polishing after application of paint. *Designs:* confined to bowl interiors and jar exteriors; stripes and rectangular or triangular panels of square or diamond cross-hatching; width individual hatchures somewhat less than that of interspaces; occasional large solid triangles; general effect, "open-work," rather than negative.

COMPARISONS: Kayenta Black-on-white, more highly polished, dead white in surface color; painted decoration covers more of surface, producing negative rather than open-work effect; execution design and manufacture very much better.

Wupatki Black-on-white, temper particles about same size but much more abundant; texture core, fine; execution design less precise, cross-hatching less frequent, plain hatching fairly frequent; unpainted surfaces less well-smoothed, never polished; scraping marks usually conspicuous; vessel walls medium strong.

Hoyapi Black-on-white, general character of design usually negative rather than open-work; texture core, usually somewhat more fine; vessel walls usually somewhat more strong with more decided ring; small individual sherds often difficult to distinguish; paint usually gritty and frequently purplish in spots.

RANGE:

Sherds have been obtained from Betatakin, Kiet Siel, and Turkey Cave pueblos and NA 2709, all in the Tsegi drainage, Navajo County, Arizona.

REMARKS:

The recognition of Betatakin Black-on-white is based upon the development of a distinct style of design sometime in the last quarter of Pueblo III. Objectively, this type seems to be a development from Sosi Black-on-white by the addition of crosshatching to the unpainted areas of the Sosi Style. With a refinement of the paste the peak of perfection of pottery vessels in the Tsegi was subsequently reached with the production of Kayenta Black-on-white, a type apparently essentially a development from and refinement of Betatakin Black-on-white. Moreover, the distinctions between Sosi Black-on-white and Betatakin Black-on-white imply a fairly long time interval during which it seems plausible to postulate an intermediate type between the last named types. As yet however, sufficient material has not been available for the identification and description of such a type.

KAYENTA BLACK-ON-WHITE

SYNONYMS: (a) Black-on-white Ware, Kidder & Guernsey, 1919, pp. 130–134; (b) Kayenta Black-on-white Ware, Kidder, 1924, Pl. 30, 31; (c) Tokonabi (Kayenta) Ware, Fewkes, 1926, p. 9; (d) Sagi Black-on-white, Gladwin, W. & H. S., 1934, Fig. 7.
DESCRIBED BY: Kidder & Guernsey, loc. cit.
NAMED BY: Kidder, 1924, p. 71.

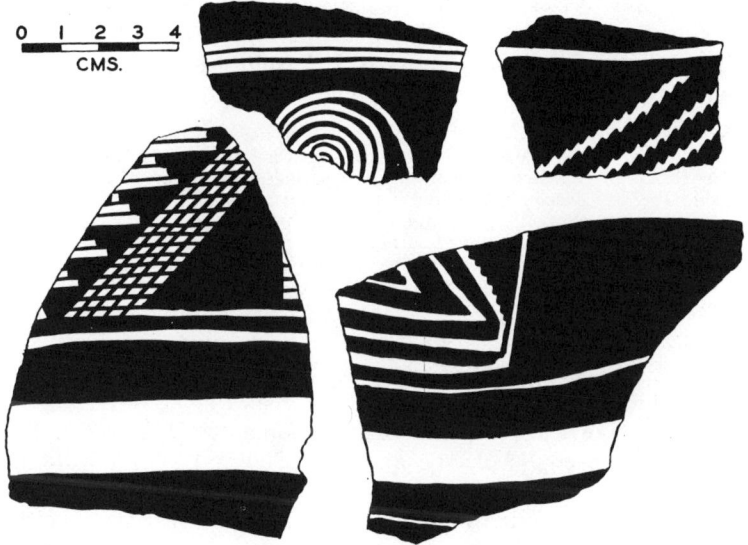

Fig. 53. Kayenta B/W ($\frac{1}{2}\times$).

ILLUSTRATIONS: Kidder & Guernsey, loc. cit.; Kidder, loc. cit; (Drawing) Fig. 53.
TYPE SPECIMENS: Cotype sherds Nos. AT 128, 1043, 3076–3093 in the Type Collection of the Museum of Northern Arizona.
TYPE SITE: Long House Pueblo (NA 897), equals Ruin A (Kidder & Guernsey, 1919), Marsh Pass, Navajo County, Arizona.
STAGE: Late Pueblo III.
TIME: ca 1275–1300 A.D.

DESCRIPTION (revised):

Constructed: by coiling. *Fired:* in reducing atmosphere. *Core:* usually light gray. *Carbon streak:* rare. *Temper:* small amounts very fine quartz sand, usually almost invisible; occasional small opaque angular fragment, red or black. *Vessel walls:* very strong. *Texture core:* very fine. *Fracture:* shattering. *Surface finish:* bowl interiors, jar exteriors, impacted; well-polished. *Surface color:* dead white to light pearl gray. *Forms:* jars (predominate), bowls, colanders. *Recorded range thickness jar walls:* 2.2 to 8.6 mm; average thickness (98 sherds), 4.3 mm. *Decoration:* painted. *Paint:* black, occasionally brownish, almost always rich and dense; never gritty. *Pigment:* carbon (test by Colton). *Design:* execution, excellent; characterized by negative or "mosquito-bar" effect (see Kidder & Guernsey, loc. cit., pp. 130–134; Kidder, loc. cit.; Hargrave, 1932, p. 23); wide stripes frame rectangular or triangular panels in which occur narrow-line cross-hatching, usually diagonal, with solid elements as triangles, bars, stepped elements; occasionally opposed stepped elements in panels without hatchure; rarely interlocking scrolls; rarely finely barbed wide lines or stripes.

COMPARISONS: Hoyapi Black-on-white, surface color never dead white, often fairly dark pearl gray; decorated surfaces less well-polished, scraping marks often conspicuous on unpainted surfaces; execution of design considerably less excellent; hatchure lines not always exactly parallel or evenly spaced; paint generally gritty and frequently purplish in spots.

Betatakin Black-on-white, surface color never dead white, often dark pearl gray; painted surfaces only moderately polished, scraping marks often conspicuous on unpainted surfaces; execution of design considerably less excellent; open-work rather than negative design.

RANGE:

Sherds have been obtained from Swallows Nest (NA 2507), Betatakin Pueblo (NA 2515), Kiet Siel Pueblo (NA 2519), Turkey Cave Pueblo (NA 2520), Loloma Ki (NA 2530), Bat Woman House (NA 2531), and NA 2709 and 2727, all in the Tsegi drainage; also from late Pueblo III sites in the upper Klethla Valley and Marsh Pass; occasionally intrusive in the Hopi Country, Navajo County, Arizona.

REMARKS:

Kayenta Black-on-white falls somewhat in the same category as Tusayan Black-on-white in that its distribution and abundance is not as generally believed. The Kayenta Style of Decoration is more widespread than the type and has thus given rise to erroneous impressions of the distribution of the type, Kayenta Black-on-white.

POLACCA SERIES

This series of types occurring consistently in the Hopi Country is closely related to Kayenta Series but is conspicuous for certain minor differences. Reasons for these differences have not been determined.

KIA-KO BLACK-ON-WHITE: new type

SYNONYMS: (a) Proto-Kayenta Black-on-white, Kidder, 1924, p. 94; (b) Tusayan Black-on-white, Gladwin, W. & H. S., 1934, tenth figure.

ILLUSTRATIONS: Gladwin, W. & H. S., loc. cit.

TYPE SPECIMENS: Sherds Nos. AT 111–127 in the Type Collection of the Museum of Northern Arizona.

TYPE SITE: NA 1712, about one mile north of the Indian School at Kiakochomovi (Lower Oraibi) Pueblo, in Oraibi Wash, Hopi Indian Reservation, Navajo County, Arizona.

STAGE: Pueblo II–III (?).

TIME: ca 1100–ca 1150 A.D.

DESCRIPTION:

Constructed: by coiling. *Fired:* in reducing atmosphere. *Core:* dark gray to light gray. *Carbon streak:* frequent. *Temper:* medium fine quartz sand; rarely few small angular fragments, black, gray, or tan. *Vessel walls:* medium strong. *Texture core:* medium to fine. *Fracture:* shattering. *Surface finish:* bowl interiors and exteriors, and jar exteriors, impacted, or coated with thin (white) slip; bowl interiors and jar exteriors, moderately polished; scraping marks noticeable on unslipped, and sometimes on slipped surfaces. *Surface color:* dead white or pearl gray. *Forms:* bowls, jars (predominate). *Recorded range thickness bowl walls:* 3.4 to 5.4 mm; greatest individual range recorded, 1.2 mm; average thickness (28 sherds), 4.5 mm. *Recorded range thickness jar walls:* 3.6 to 5.7 mm; greatest individual range recorded, 1 mm; average thickness (35 sherds) 4.6 mm. *Rims:* bowls, IA3, IA4, IIIA1. *Decoration:* painted. *Paint:* black, occasionally brownish; frequently flakes off. *Pigment:* carbon (test by Colton). *Designs:* usually confined to bowl interiors and jar exteriors; rarely also on bowl exteriors; elements—mostly straight stripes and wide lines with small solid triangles; barbed lines fairly frequent; width of lines and stripes on bowls ranges from two to eight mm; average (39 lines and stripes), 4.9 mm; on jars from 1 to 7 mm, average (47 lines and stripes), 4.8 mm.

COMPARISONS: Sosi Black-on-white, considerably bolder in treatment; stripes and lines wider and solid elements larger; small sherds of Kia-ko Black-on-white and Sosi Black-on-white may be indistinguishable.

Flagstaff Black-on-white, somewhat richer and dense paint; elements usually more closely massed covering the surface more generally; coarse crosshatching and pinnate lines in series sometimes present.

Deadmans Black-on-white, paint somewhat more dense and rich, stripes and lines generally wider, solid triangles and pendent dots frequent; small sherds sometimes indistinguishable.

RANGE:

Abundant at the type site and at NA 2584 on upper Weepo Wash near Pinyon Trading Post on Black Mesa, Navajo County, Arizona.

REMARKS:

Named for Kia-ko-cho-movi Pueblo. Apparently Kia-ko Black-on-white is a common and sometimes an abundant type in the Hopi Country proper in sites of early Pueblo III and possibly also in late Pueblo II. The type site is a D-shaped pithouse.

POLACCA BLACK-ON-WHITE: new type

SYNONYM: Proto-Kayenta Black-on-white, Kidder, 1924, p. 94.
ILLUSTRATION: AT 86 (Fig. 54); Fig. 55.
TYPE SPECIMENS: Sherds Nos. AT 79–96 in the Type Collection of the Museum of Northern Arizona.
TYPE SITE: Hoyapi Pueblo (NA 837), in lower Polacca Wash, about six miles south of Shungopovi, Hopi Indian Reservation, Navajo County, Arizona.
STAGE: Pueblo III.
TIME: ca 1150–ca 1250 A.D.

Fig. 54. ($\frac{1}{2}\times$).

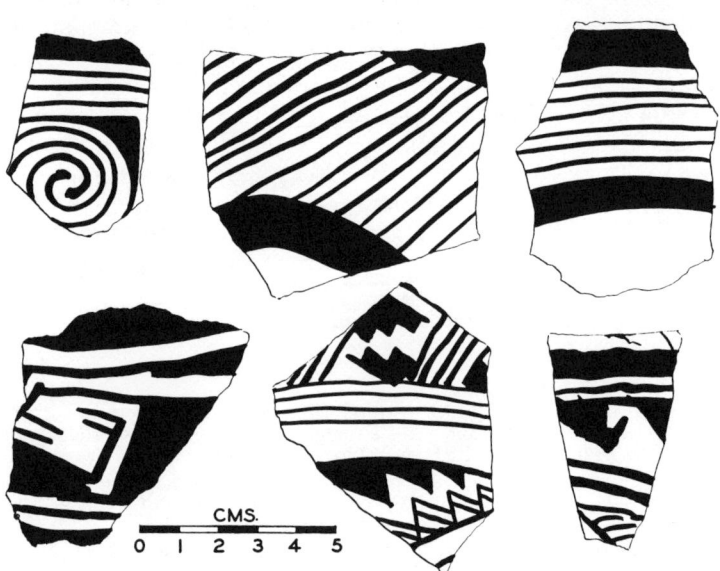

Fig. 55. Polacca Black-on-white ($\frac{1}{2}\times$).

DESCRIPTION:

Constructed: by coiling. *Fired:* in reducing atmosphere. *Core:* light gray to dark gray. *Carbon streak:* occasional. *Temper:* fairly fine quartz sand, usually inconspicuous; sometimes large grains noticeable on surface. *Vessel walls:* strong; occasionally warped. *Texture core:* medium to fine. *Fracture:* shattering. *Surface finish:* interior bowl surfaces, exterior jar surfaces, impacted, or coated with thin (white) slip; usually moderately polished; exterior bowl surfaces, scraped, scraping marks noticeable on both surfaces, especially on unslipped surfaces; slip somewhat fugitive, often flakes off from weathering. *Surface color:* dead white or pearl gray. *Forms:* bowls, jars (predominate), seed jars (rare), jugs. *Recorded range thickness bowl walls:* 2.3 to 6.9 mm; greatest individual range recorded 3.3 mm; average thickness (66 sherds), 4.8 mm. *Recorded range thickness jar walls:* 1.8 to 6.8 mm; greatest individual range recorded, 2.5 mm; average thickness (100 sherds), 4.5 mm. *Rims:* bowls, IA3 (predominate), IA4, IA6, IIA3, IIIA2, IIIA3, IIIA4, IIIA5, IIIB3, IC2; jars, IA3, IIA3, IIIA3. *Decoration:* painted. *Paint:* black, sometimes purplish. *Pigment:* carbon or iron-carbon (tests by Colton and F. G. Hawley); frequently metallic, sometimes vitreous, sometimes dull and lifeless, often gritty, usually dense, sometimes watery; often flakes off. *Designs:* confined to bowl interiors and jar exteriors; rim dotted (rarely) on forms IA3, IA4, IIIB3; elements—mostly straight narrow lines, occasional wide line and stripe; designs—bowls, horizontal band just below rim framed by stripes above and below, usually four to eight horizontal narrow lines between; sometimes diagonal lines and solid triangle within band; jars, horizontal band just below rim framed by stripes above and below and filled with diagonal hatchuring of narrow lines; sometimes divided into diagonal panels containing vertical hatchures; occasionally interlocking scrolls, interlooking hooked triangles and opposed solid stepped elements; width of stripes framing bands and panels, two to ten times greater than width of hatchures; brush work bold and sloppy.

COMPARISONS: Dogoszhi Black-on-white, hatchure less bold, more regular in execution, panels of smaller area, usually rectangular, much greater in one dimension than in other—almost like bands; spaces between hatchures about equal to width of hatchures themselves; solid elements absent; framing lines about same width as hatchures.

Padre Black-on-white, heavily slipped, core dark gray, hatchures slightly wider, uniformly spaced; temper mostly fine opaque angular fragments.

RANGE:

Abundant at type site. Sherds also have been examined from

Ma-chon-pi (NA 835) at Hotevilla on upper Dinnebito Wash, Hopi Indian Reservation, Arizona.

REMARKS:

For several years Hargrave has recognized the general occurence of an undescribed black-on-white type in the Hopi Country that seemed to precede and to partly parallel the Kayenta Style of Decoration in point of time. The general acceptance of Tusayan Black-on-white as a stage criterion for this time range made unnecessary the description of this new type. But with the recent discovery that Tusayan Black-on-white occurs too infrequently to be used exclusively as a stage criterion, other types from the Hopi Country must be described.

Polacca Black-on-white, in the field, gives the impression of a mixture of lines. Often a negative effect in design is approached. With a greater knowledge of the pottery of the Hopi Country, it is probable that a separation will be made from this type. The basic description of Polacca Black-on-white shows a mixture of characters in paste and technique of manufacture that is not in keeping with specific knowledge of Pueblo Ceramics in general. This mixture is indicative of intergrades from an early type but still it does not connect with Deadmans Black-on-white which is known to be earlier than Polacca Black-on-white.

HOYAPI BLACK-ON-WHITE: new type

SYNONYM: Kayenta Black-on-white, Kidder, 1924, p. 94.
ILLUSTRATION: Fig. 56.
TYPE SPECIMENS: Sherds Nos. AT 97–103 in the Type Collection of the Museum of Northern Arizona.
TYPE SITE: Hoyapi Pueblo (NA 837) in lower Polacca Wash about six miles south of Shungopovi, Hopi Indian Reservation, Navajo County, Arizona.
STAGE: Pueblo III.
TIME: ca 1275–ca 1300 A.D.

DESCRIPTION:

Constructed: by coiling. *Fired:* in reducing atmosphere. *Core:* dark gray to light gray. *Temper:* small quantities fine quartz sand, often almost invisible; rarely few opaque angular fragments, gray or black. *Vessel walls:* usually very decided ring; often warped. *Texture core:* fine to very fine. *Fracture:* shattering. *Surface finish:* both surfaces bowls and exterior surfaces jars, smoothed, impacted, or coated with thin (white) slip; sometimes moderately polished; smoothing marks sometimes noticeable but not conspicuous. *Surface color:* bluish white or

Fig. 56. Hoyapi Black-on-white ($\frac{1}{2}\times$).

deep pearl gray. *Forms:* bowls, jars (predominate), dippers. *Recorded range thickness bowl walls*: 2.6 to 6.9 mm; individual range often great, sometimes 3.3 mm; average thickness, ca 4.5 mm. *Recorded range thickness jar walls:* 2.9 to 6.7 mm; greatest individual range recorded, 2.6 mm; average thickness (63 sherds), 4.7 mm. *Rims:* bowls, IA3, IA4, IA6, IIA4, IIIA3; jars, IA3, IIC2. *Decoration:* painted. *Paint:* black, sometimes brownish; usually dense and dull, frequently gritty and vitreous. *Pigment:* carbon (test by Colton). *Design:* confined to bowl interiors and jar exteriors; normally, single encircling stripe (6 to 11 mm wide) just beneath rim; decorative band, framed by wide stripes above and below with triangular or rectangular panels usually containing checkered patterns or crosshatchure in negative style; occasionally very large solid areas; sometimes narrow bands of hatchure with framing lines of about same width as individual hatchures; bottom sherd of one bowl shows painted "bird track"; brush work sloppy, frequently an over-carrying of hatchure lines, usually not quite evenly spaced or exactly parallel; rims occasionally painted with dots.

COMPARISONS: Wupatki Black-on-white, temper about same size, much more abundant; texture core medium to fine; execution design generally less precise, cross hatchure usually rather coarse and less frequent; plain hatchure fairly frequent; general character design "open-work" rather than "negative"; unpainted surfaces less well smoothed; not polished; scraping marks usually conspicuous; vessel walls, medium strong.

Betatakin Black-on-white, general character design usually open-work rather than negative; texture core usually somewhat less fine; vessel walls somewhat less strong, less decided ring; small individual sherds often difficult to distinguish.

Kayenta Black-on-white, surface color dead white or very light pearl gray, painted surfaces very well-polished, undecorated surfaces very well-smoothed; execution design excellent, more decidedly negative than any other type, often with mosquito bar effect; hatchure lines very evenly spaced, usually exactly parallel.

RANGE:

Abundant at the type site. Sherds also have been examined from Ma-chon-pi (NA 835) at Hotevilla on upper Dinnebito Wash, Hopi Indian Reservation.

REMARKS:

Hoyapi Black-on-white expresses the same general cultural traits as shown by Kayenta Black-on-white but it is decidedly inferior in quality, in composition of paste, and in the execution of design. Its development probably parallels closely the development of the Kayenta type in the use and combination of design motifs, except possibly with a stronger expression of White Mountain influence as seen in the more general use of stepped elements. The great difference in quality of the two types hardly can be accounted for solely on the basis of materials used since later pottery types in the Hopi Country are superior in workmanship to Hoyapi Black-on-white. Since the time range of Hoyapi Black-on-white and Kayenta Black-on-white appears to coincide closely, and also, since these types were made during the last half of the 13th century when the Pueblo III stage began to decline, the relative security provided by the rough country of Black Mesa, Marsh Pass and the Tsegi Canyons, as compared to the more open Hopi Country, may have given leisure time to the makers of Kayenta Black-on-white for the development of arts and crafts. Apparently the Hopi Country was a mecca for many peoples at about this time, a condition that would cause much unrest (Hargrave, 1930, 1931b, 1932a).

A more practical explanation for the poor quality of Hoyapi Black-on-white may be in the use of coal for firing pottery. A high per centage of the sherds of this type are extremely overfired—often to the point of fusing pigment and paste. Inexperience in handling this new fuel could explain the poor quality of the vessel but the poorly executed design must be explained by a less material cause.

Intergrades may be expected between the general range of

Hoyapi Black-on-white and Kayenta Black-on-white because sherds from Ma-chon-pi at Hotevilla on the western edge of the Hopi Mesas are so intermediate in character that they could be assigned to either type.

WUPATKI SERIES

At the south edge of the normal area of Tusayan White Ware is found the Wupatki Series which centers about the San Francisco Mountains.

FLAGSTAFF BLACK-ON-WHITE

SYNONYMS: (a) Tusayan Pottery, Mason, 1898, Figs. 44–45; (b) Black-on-white Ware, Kidder and Guernsey, 1919, pp. 130–134; (c) "Proto-Kayenta" Black-on-white, Kidder, 1924, p. 72; (d) Tusayan Black-on-white, Hargrave, 1929, p. 2; (e) 3rd Tusayan, Gladwin, W. & H. S., 1930 a, pp. 180–191.
DESCRIBED BY: Hargrave, 1932, p. 16.
NAMED BY: Hargrave, loc. cit.
ILLUSTRATIONS: Colton, 1932, Pl. 1, 4; Hargrave, loc. cit., Pl. VII, 4; Fig. 57.

Fig. 57. Flagstaff Black-on-white ($\frac{1}{2}\times$).

TYPE SPECIMENS: Bowl No. NA 1814B.14 and type sherds Nos. AT 11–13; cotype sherds Nos. 14–33 and 4274 in the Type Collection of the Museum of Northern Arizona.
TYPE SITE: Two Kivas Pueblo (NA 700), San Francisco Mountains, Coconino County, Arizona.
STAGE: Pueblo III.
TIME: ca 1125–1200 A.D.

DESCRIPTION (revised):

Constructed: by coiling. *Fired:* in reducing atmosphere. *Core:* dark gray to light gray. *Carbon streak:* frequent. *Temper:* abundant fine quartz sand, frequently almost invisible even with power glass, often conspicuous on unslipped surfaces. *Vessel walls:* strong. *Texture core:* fine. *Fracture:* slightly crumbling. *Surface finish:* exterior bowl surfaces and interior jar surfaces scraped; not polished; scraping marks generally conspicuous on exterior bowl surfaces; sometimes very thinly slipped with (white) slip; moderately well-polished; both slipped and unslipped surfaces frequently pitted; exterior surface jars similar to interior surface bowls. *Surface color:* exterior bowl and interior jar surfaces, light gray with bluish tint; interior bowl surfaces and exteriors jar surfaces, dead white, sometimes with slight bluish tint. *Forms:* bowls, jars. *Recorded range thickness bowl walls*: 2 to 6.4 mm; greatest individual range recorded 3.2 mm; average thickness (58 sherds), 4 mm. *Recorded range thickness jar walls:* 1.8 to 5.4 mm; greatest individual range recorded, 1.3 mm; average thickness (31 sherds), 4 mm. *Rims:* bowls, IA3 (predominate), IA4, IA6, IIIA3, IIIA4, IB3, IIIB3, IC3, IIC3 *Decoration:* painted. *Paint:* black. *Pigment:* carbon (test by Colton). *Designs:* confined to bowl interiors, jar exteriors; bowl rims, undecorated, except widely flaring forms; usually all-over patterns of stripes and straight wide lines; barbed lines usually in opposed pairs; pinnate lines, diagonal or rectangular cross-hatching; sometimes with dots in open squares; small solid triangles, sometimes with interlocking hooks; barbed and pinnate lines very frequent (diagnostic).

COMPARISONS: Kia-ko Black-on-white, paint somewhat less rich and dense; elements not closely massed, leaving relatively large part of area unpainted; cross-hatching and pinnate lines absent.

Sosi Black-on-white, usually considerably bolder in treatment of design, stripes and lines wider; solid elements larger; barbs much less frequent; pinnate lines and cross-hatching absent; frequently somewhat more highly polished.

Tusayan Black-on-white, temper infrequent fine grains quartz sand, sometimes almost invisible; texture core, fine; fracture, shattering; design covers most of surface, producing nearly open-work effect; large solid masses, frequent; pinnate lines frequent, relatively less bold; decorated surfaces better smoothed, not gritty; undecorated surfaces well-smoothed, rarely pitted.

RANGE:

Northeast of San Francisco Mountains to and including the Hopi Indian Reservation from Jeddito Trading Post, Navajo County, west beyond Tuba City to Willow Springs, Coconino County, Arizona. Also on Rainbow and Kaibito plateaus.

REMARKS:

Recent discovery of Flagstaff Black-on-white in quantity at a pithouse site (NA 1712) in upper Oraibi Wash, Hopi Indian Reservation, Navajo County, discredits the idea of an imitation of Tusayan Black-on-white (Hargrave, 1392, p. 16) and suggests that Flagstaff Black-on-white may be more fundamental than previously thought. Flagstaff Black-on-white appears in an obviously earlier horizon than does Tusayan Black-on-white.

WUPATKI BLACK-ON-WHITE

DESCRIBED BY: Colton, H. S., 1932, p. 11.
NAMED BY: Colton, loc. cit.
ILLUSTRATIONS: Colton, 1932, Pl. 1, No. 6; Hargrave, 1932, Pl. VII, No. 6; Fig. 58.

Fig. 58. Wupatki Black-on-white ($\frac{1}{2}\times$).

TYPE SPECIMENS: Type sherds not separated by describer. Cotype sherds Nos. AT 129–150 in the Type Collection of the Museum of Northern Arizona.
TYPE SITE: Wupatki Pueblo (NA 405), Wupatki National Monument, Coconino County, Arizona.
STAGE: Pueblo III.
TIME: ca 1150–ca 1200 A.D.

DESCRIPTION (revised):

Constructed: by coiling. *Fired:* in reducing atmosphere. *Core:* light gray to dark gray; rarely almost black or slightly brownish. *Carbon streak:* occasional. *Temper:* fairly abundant fine quartz sand, sometimes almost invisible, occasionally small black angular fragments. *Vessel walls:* medium strong. *Texture core:* fine to medium. *Fracture:* shattering to slightly crumbling. *Surface finish:* exterior bowl surfaces, interior jar surfaces, usually scraped, unpolished, scraping marks conspicuous; bowl exteriors, rarely thinly slipped (white); bowl interiors, jar exteriors, polished; scraping marks visible unless slipped; often impacted. *Surface color:* dead white or (more frequently) light bluish gray. *Fire clouds:* common. *Forms:* bowls (predominate), jars. *Recorded range thickness bowl walls:* 2.5 to 6.2 mm: greatest individual range recorded, 1.9 mm; average thickness (16 sherds), 4.4 mm. *Recorded range thickness jar walls:* 2.2 to 5.8 mm; greatest individual range recorded, 2.6 mm; average thickness, ca 4 mm. *Rims:* bowls, IA3, IA4; jars, IA2. *Decoration:* painted. *Paint:* black, rarely purplish; usually dense and dull; sometimes polished and reflects light; occasionally slightly gritty. *Pigment:* carbon (test by Colton). *Designs:* confined to bowl interiors, jar exteriors; all-over designs; paint covers greater part of decorated area, producing open-work effect; design usually band around vessel framed with one of three lines, outer line widest; excellence of painted decoration superior to technique of manufacture; elements—stripes and wide lines (3 to 7 mm wide), large solid triangles, rectangles and stepped elements; motifs—diagonal and rectangular cross-hatching; coarse to fine diagonal hatching in triangular panels; rims undecorated or ticked with small lateral dashes.

COMPARISONS: Hoyapi Black-on-white, temper particles about same size, present in considerably smaller quantities; texture core, usually fine to very fine; execution design generally more precise, cross-hatching more frequent, plain hatching rare, negative character of design more evident; unpainted surfaces well-smoothed, polished; vessel walls, very strong with decided ring.

Betatakin Black-on-white, temper particles about same size, present in smaller quantities; texture core usually fine; execution of design more precise, cross-hatching more frequent, plain hatching rare, negative character of design more evident; unpainted surfaces well-smoothed, sometimes polished; vessel walls, strong.

RANGE:

Recorded only from San Francisco Mountain region, Coconino County, Arizona. Sherds have been found at Wupatki Pueblo (NA 405), Turkey Hill Pueblo (NA 660), and at sites near Leupp, Arizona.

REMARKS:

Wupatki Black-on-white apparently supersedes Flagstaff Black-on-white in the San Francisco Mountain region and for the present may be considered as representative of the Kayenta Style of Design in that region. This style is expressed in the open-work effect, few other characters of Kayenta Black-on-white being recognized. The time range of Wupatki Black-on-white does not necessarily coincide with the time range of Kayenta Black-on-white.

Hargrave has stated that the temper of Wupatki Black-on-white is "sherd" (1932, p. 20). This was an error.

MESA VERDE WHITE WARE

Probably less is known about the pottery of Mesa Verde National Monument and the surrounding country than in any other major culture division. Although spectacular houses of the "Ancient Pueblo Peoples" are annually seen by many thousands of visitors, still so little is specifically known about the pottery made by these people that only two types can be included in Mesa Verde White Ware. Moreover, the incompleteness of descriptions of these types means a poorly described ware. Mesa Verde White Ware is here recognized as a distinct ware although the distinctions are poorly defined. Undescribed types are known to occur in the area where recognized types of Mesa Verde White Ware are dominant. It is logical, therefore, to believe that some of these types belong to this ware.

KEY 17: MESA VERDE WHITE WARE

Temper predominantly quartz sand........Mancos Black-on-white (p. 230)
Temper predominantly light-colored angular fragments...............
　　　　　　　　　　　　　　　　　Mesa Verde Black-on-white (p. 231)

MESA VERDE WHITE WARE: new ware

SYNONYM: *Mesa Verde Ware*, Kidder, 1924, p. 62.
STAGES: Pueblo II (?)–III.
TIME: Probably between 1050–1300 A.D.

DESCRIPTION:

Constructed: by coiling. *Fired:* in reducing atmosphere. *Core:* gray to blue gray. *Carbon streak:* sometimes present. *Temper:* quartz sand with predominance of light-colored angular fragments and lesser amount black angular fragments. *Vessel walls:*

medium strong to strong. *Texture core:* fine to medium (?). *Fracture:* shattering to crumbling (?). *Surface finish:* "rough" or smoothed, slipped; crazed; sometimes coils unobliterated. *Surface color:* gray, slaty gray, chalky white. *Forms:* bowls, jars, jugs, mugs, dippers. *Recorded range thickness bowl walls:* 4 to 5 mm. *Recorded range thickness jar walls:* 5 to 7 mm; vessel walls rather uniform thickness. *Rims:* bowls, IA2, IA3, IA4, IA5, IIA4, IIIA1, IIIA2, IIIA3, IIIA4, IB3, IC3; jars; IA3, IIIA3. *Decoration:* painted. *Paint:* rich, dense, or flat black; frequently brownish or reddish brown; sometimes greenish tint; weak, sometimes watery. *Designs:* painted; geometric, occasionally zoomorphic. *Elements:* large. *Motifs:* large solid lines and triangles; some diagonal hatchure (panels and triangles); hatchure, coarse; rims, generally squarish, frequently decorated with dots or ticks.

RANGE:

Upper San Juan River drainage including Chinle Creek in Arizona.

REMARKS:

The name is derived from Kidder's "Mesa Verde ware" since the term was used to collectively include the black-on-white types from the region. This ware description, based upon two types only, necessarily is incomplete and inadequate.

MANCOS BLACK-ON-WHITE

SYNONYM: Proto-Mesa Verde Black-on-white, see Martin, 1936, p. 112.
ILLUSTRATIONS: Martin, loc. cit., Figs. 28–39 incl.
DESCRIBED BY: Martin, loc. cit., pp. 80–94.
NAMED BY: Gladwin, W. & H. S., 1934, p. 28, Fig. 8 (see Martin, loc. cit.).
TYPE SPECIMENS: Field Museum of Natural History, Chicago.
TYPE SITE: Lowry Ruin, nine miles west of Ackmen, Montezuma County, Colorado (Martin, loc. cit., p. 15).
STAGE: Probably Pueblo II–early III (?).
TIME: Not specifically stated (see Martin, loc. cit., pp. 110–114, also pp. 194–201).

DESCRIPTION (revised):

Constructed: by coiling. *Fired:* in reducing atmosphere. *Core:* gray to blue gray. *Carbon streak:* present. *Temper:* ground sherds. *Vessel walls:* hardness 6 (66%), 5 (28%), 4 (6%). *Texture core:* "smooth and even." *Surface finish:* bowl exteriors, generally rough, infrequently smooth; bowl interiors smoother than exteriors; surface occasionally imperfectly polished; dipper and jar exteriors similar to bowls; sometimes coils unobliterated;

interior surfaces bowl forms, generally slipped; slip thin, chalky, unpolished; gray base-color often visible through slip; brush marks, occasional; jar exteriors, generally slipped. *Surface color:* unslipped surfaces, gray; slipped surfaces chalky white to slaty gray. *Fire clouds:* uncommon. *Forms:* bowls, dippers, jars, pitchers, mugs. *Recorded range thickness bowl walls* (includes dippers): 4 to 5 mm. *Record range thickness jar walls*: 5 to 7 mm. *Rims:* bowls, IA2, IA3, IA4, IA5, IIA1, IIA2, IIIA3, IIIA4, IC3. *Decoration:* painted. *Paint:* transparent brown, greenish brown, reddish brown, dense or flat black. *Pigment:* iron (tests by Anna O. Shepard). *Designs:* geometric; crudely and unevenly applied; bowls and dippers—generally exterior surfaces (two known exceptions), interiors continuous band or divided band, quartered, all-over, and pendent from rim. *Motifs:* bowls—checkerboard in rectangular or triangular units, alternate hatchured squares and open squares with single dots, opposed triangles in panels, vertical lines and large triangles in panels, vertical sets parallel lines set-off from one another by solid and open triangles; "interior divided into quarters by two lines intersecting at right angles, half of each line bearing pendent triangles and the other half of each, upthrust triangles, or by two rows of polka dots, each row intersecting at right angles; sets of oblique parallel lines set at nearly right angles to other sets"; vertical lines pendent from rims, free-standing terraces attached to rim and others isolated; jars—decoration upper portion from rim to about base of shoulder; designs, in general, similar to designs on bowls; rims—infrequently ticked.

RANGE:

Southeastern Utah, southwestern Colorado, north of the San Juan River. Probably will be found in all sites of the Mesa Verde subculture occupied during the life of Mancos Black-on-white.

MESA VERDE BLACK-ON-WHITE

SYNONYM: Decorated Smooth Ware, Morris, 1919, p. 174.
DESCRIBED BY: Nordenskiöld, 1893, p. 82.
NAMED BY: Kidder, 1924, pp. 63–66.
ILLUSTRATIONS: Norkenskiöld, loc. cit., Figs. 50–57, plates XV–XXXII; Kidder, figs. 9–10, plates 25–26.
STAGE: Pueblo III.
TIME: Probably between 1200–1300 A.D.

DESCRIPTION (revised):

Constructed: by coiling. *Fired:* in reducing atmosphere. *Core:* gray. *Temper:* predominantly light-colored angular fragments, occasionally some black angular fragments, and some quartz sand; temper fine and abundant; conspicuous. *Surface finish:* smooth; slipped; slip chalky; finely crazed. *Surface color:* gray, bluish gray, chalky white. *Forms:* jars, jugs, mugs, bowls, dippers. *Decoration:* painted. *Paint:* black. *Pigment:* carbon (Hawley, 1929). *Designs:* geometric; occasionally zoomorphic; decoration bowls, interior, sometimes exterior; elements, large; balanced framing lines above and below band decoration; repeated units generally; hatchures, coarse; bounding lines equal in width to width of hatchure lines; rims, square, flat often decorated with black dots or ticks.

RANGE:

San Juan drainage above mount of Chinle Creek, San Juan County, Utah, and late Pueblo III sites in southwestern Colorado and northwestern New Mexico. Traded to Tsegi Canyons, Navajo County, Arizona.

LITTLE COLORADO GRAY WARE

Little has been published about utility types from sites along the tributaries of the Little Colorado River. Investigations have shown, however, that in a part of this area, at least, utility vessels fired in a reducing atmosphere have conspicuous fragments as temper. The material from which this temper was prepared has not been determined. Styles of decorating vessels in Little Colorado White Ware are the same as those found in Tusayan Gray Ware. The principal objective difference between these wares is in the temper. Little Colorado Gray Ware probably is a companion ware to Little Colorado White Ware.

LITTLE COLORADO GRAY WARE: new ware
STAGES: Probably Pueblo I–III.
TIME: Probably between 700–1200 A.D.

DESCRIPTION:

At present same as Little Colorado Corrugated.

LITTLE COLORADO CORRUGATED: new type
TYPE SPECIMENS: Sherds Nos. AT 1595–1617, 1651–1655 in the Type Collection of the Museum of Northern Arizona.
TYPE SITE: Klageto Pueblo (NA 1016), upper Leroux Wash, Apache County, Arizona.
STAGES: Pueblo II (?)–III.
TIME: Probably between 900–1200 A.D.

DESCRIPTION:

Constructed: by coiling. *Fired:* in reducing atmosphere. *Core:* dark gray to light gray. *Temper:* abundant opaque angular fragments, generally gray; occasionally some quartz sand; temper generally conspicuous on surfaces; color core and surface usually almost same color. *Vessel walls:* medium strong. *Texture core:* fine to coarse. *Fracture:* slightly crumbling. *Surface finish:* interior surfaces fairly well-smoothed, somewhat gritty; coils on exterior surfaces unobliterated, except that neck is scraped for distance of 1 to 4 cm below rim; coils treated in great variety of ways, sometimes flattened, sometimes deeply finger-dented; sometimes rounded; various combinations on same vessel. *Surface color:* light gray to almost black. *Forms:* jars. *Recorded range thickness jar walls:* 4.5 to 9.7 mm; greatest individual range recorded, 2.5 mm; average thickness ca 6 mm. *Rims:* jars, IA3, IIIA3, IIIB3. *No painted decoration.*

RANGE:

Little Colorado River Valley and northern tributaries between the New Mexico-Arizona line and the San Francisco Mountain region (trade), except in the Jeddito and more westerly washes.

LITTLE COLORADO WHITE WARE

In the area occupied by this ware are many types conspicuous for the temper used. These types belong to Little Colorado White Ware. It is not because of the material used for temper that is the basis for recognizing this ware, however, but it is because the material was especially prepared for the purpose. Certain objective characters other than temper are also identifying factors in the recognition of types in this ware. Still other characters than those given are characteristic of the ware, or, rather of some types in the ware, but they are difficult to describe accurately.

In general, Little Colorado White Ware lies between Tusayan White Ware and the area occupied by the early types in Mogollon Brown Ware, the oldest known ware in which vessels were constructed by coiling.

KEY 18: LITTLE COLORADO WHITE WARE

Kana-a Style of Design................Dead River Black-on-white (p. 235)
Deadmans Style of Design...............Holbrook Black-on-white (p. 235)
Walnut and Flagstaff Styles of Design (Fig. 5)........................
                                                  Walnut Black-on-white (p. 237)
Dogoszhi Style of Design..................Padre Black-on-white (p. 235)
Tularosa Style of Design................Tularosa Black-on-white (p. 240)
                                                  Klageto Black-on-white (p. 242)
                                                 Pinedale Black-on-white (p. 241)

LITTLE COLORADO WHITE WARE: new ware

SYNONYMS: Gray Ware, Hough, 1903.
STAGES: Pueblo I–IV.
TIME: ca 750–1375 A.D.

DESCRIPTION:

Constructed: by coiling. *Fired:* in reducing atmosphere. *Core:* dark gray to light gray. *Temper:* abundant opaque angular fragments varying size, mostly fine, usually gray or tan; quartz grains rare. *Texture core:* fine to medium. *Vessel walls:* medium strong to strong. *Fracture:* slightly crumbling. *Surface finish:* bowl interiors and jar exteriors always coated with thin dead white or light oyster gray slip; usually fairly well-polished; often crazed; exterior bowls scraped, not well-smoothed; often somewhat bumpy, usually pitted; usually coated with thin white slip or wash; not polished; often chalky; jar interiors usually fairly well-smoothed. *Surface color:* gray or white. *Forms:* jars (predominate in most types), bowls (only form reported in Holbrook Black-on-white), jugs, dippers, occasionally eccentric forms. *Recorded range thickness bowl walls:* 2.9 to 8.1 mm; greatest individual range recorded, 3.5 mm; average thickness, ca 5.5 mm. *Recorded range thickness jar walls:* 3.4 to 8.6 mm; greatest individual range recorded, 2.5 mm; average thickness, ca 5.5 mm. *Rims:* bowls, IA3, IA4, IIIA2, IIIA3, IIIA4, IIIA7, IB3, IIB3, IIIB3, IC2, IC3; jars, IA3, IA7, IIIA2. *Decoration:* painted, black, usually dense, dull, occasionally thin and watery with brownish tint in most types; sometimes near-glaze. *Pigments:* carbon, iron-carbon, manganese-iron-carbon. *Designs:* bowl interiors and jar exteriors in all types; rarely also on bowl exteriors.

RANGE:

Little Colorado Valley from Petrified Forest National Monument to San Francisco Mountain region, Coconino County; also Tonto Basin, Verde Valley, and upper Gila River drainage.

REDUCING ATMOSPHERE

WALNUT SERIES

Just east of the San Francisco Peaks, Arizona, is a thickly populated area where some types in this series are abundant.

DEAD RIVER BLACK-ON-WHITE

DESCRIBED BY: Mera, 1934, p. 8.
NAMED BY: Mera, loc. cit.
TYPE SPECIMENS: Cotype sherd No. AT 887 in the Type Collection of the Museum of Northern Arizona.
TYPE SITE: LA 1485 (location not designated).
STAGE: Pueblo I.
TIME: Probably between 750-800 A.D.

DESCRIPTION (revised):

Constructed: by coiling. *Fired:* in reducing atmosphere. *Core:* gray. *Temper:* abundant fine opaque angular fragments, gray or tan; rarely occasional grain quartz sand. *Texture core:* fine. *Vessel walls:* medium strong. *Fracture:* crumbling. *Surface finish:* carefully scraped, scraping marks not always noticeable; exterior surface, coated with (dead white) slip; fairly well-polished. *Surface color:* gray or white. *Form:* jars. *Wall thickness:* cotype sherd, 5.2 to 6 mm. *Decoration:* painted, black. *Decorative style:* Kana-a.

RANGE:

Petrified Forest and surrounding territory, Arizona.

HOLBROOK BLACK-ON-WHITE

DESCRIBED BY: Mera, 1934, pp. 8–9.
NAMED BY: Mera, loc. cit.
TYPE SPECIMENS: Cotype sherds Nos. AT 1498, 1579–1581, 1658 in the Type Collection of the Museum of Northern Arizona.
TYPE SITE: LA 1486 (location not designated).
STAGE: Pueblo II.
TIME: ca 900–1100 A.D.

DESCRIPTION (revised):

Constructed: by coiling. *Fired:* in reducing atmosphere. *Core:* gray. *Temper:* abundant opaque angular fragments, gray or tan, varying size, mostly fine; occasionally grains quartz sand. *Texture core:* fine to medium. *Vessel walls:* medium strong. *Fracture:* slightly crumbling. *Surface finish:* interior and exterior bowl surfaces coated with moderately heavy (dead white) slip; sometimes chalky and fugitive on exterior surface; interior surfaces fairly well-polished, sometimes coarsely crazed; scraping marks generally noticeable through slip on undecorated portions; exterior surfaces not smoothed, not polished, sometimes bumpy, often pitted. *Surface color:* gray or white. *Form:* bowls. *Recorded range thickness bowl walls:* 3.7 to 5.9 mm; greatest individual range recorded, 1.6 mm; average thickness, ca 5 mm. *Rims:* bowls, IIIA2. *Decoration:* painted, black, usually dense; often badly weathered. *Designs:* usually on interiors. *Decorative style:* Deadmans.

COMPARISONS: Deadmans Black-on-white has abundant quartz sand temper and no conspicious slip.

RANGE:

Petrified Forest National Monument, Arizona, and surrounding territory to San Francisco Mountain region, Coconino County, Arizona.

PADRE BLACK-ON-WHITE: new type

TYPE SPECIMENS: Sherds Nos. AT 1471, 1476, 1584–1590 in the Type Collection of the Museum of Northern Arizona.

TYPE SITE: Two Kivas Pueblo (NA 700), Walnut Creek, San Francisco Mountain region, Coconino County, Arizona.

STAGE: Pueblo III.

TIME: ca 1100–1200 A.D.

DESCRIPTION:

Constructed: by coiling. *Fired:* in reducing atmosphere. *Core:* gray. *Temper:* abundant opaque rarely occasional grain quartz sand. *Texture core:* fine to medium. *Vessel walls:* medium strong. *Fracture:* slightly crumbling. *Surface finish:* bowl interiors and jar exteriors coated with fairly heavy (dead white or oyster gray) slip; well-polished; sometimes crazed; bowl exteriors usually scraped; not smoothed, often bumpy, pitted; coated with chalky slip or wash; rarely finished and slipped on interiors; interior jar surfaces fairly carefully smoothed, scraping marks noticeable, fine and uniform; sometimes chalky (white) wash inside neck; slip frequently flakes off; scraping marks often visible through slip. *Surface color:* white, gray. *Forms:* jars, bowls. *Recorded range thickness bowl walls:* 4.2 to 5.5 mm; average thickness, ca 5 mm. *Recorded range thickness jar walls:* 4.9 to 6.4 mm; greatest individual range recorded, 1.4 mm; average thickness, 5.7 mm. *Rims:* bowls, IIB3. *Decoration:* painted; black, usually dense, sometimes slightly thin and watery. *Designs:* bowls, usually interior surfaces; jars, exterior surfaces only. *Decorative style:* Dogoszhi. *Motifs:* frequently rectangular and triangular panels usually containing narrow-line hatchure; sometimes fairly coarse rectangular cross-hatchure, framing lines about same width as hatchures or slightly wider; occasionally solid triangles and stepped elements combined with hatchure.

COMPARISON: Dogoszhi Black-on-white, usually not noticeably slipped, never thickly slipped; surface gritty, paint somewhat more watery, hatchures slightly narrower with spaces between often slightly wider than hatchures, panels usually smaller; temper fine quartz sand.
   Polacca Black-on-white, not slipped, temper fine quartz sand; hatchures slightly narrower, carelessly spaced; panels often curved; paint sometimes light purplish.

RANGE:

San Francisco Mountain region, particularly throughout lower parts of Walnut and Padre canyons, Coconino County, Arizona; also across Little Colorado River Valley to Machonpi (NA 835) near Hotevilla.

WALNUT BLACK-ON-WHITE

DESCRIBED BY: Hargrave, 1932, p. 20.
NAMED BY: Hargrave, loc. cit.
ILLUSTRATIONS: Hargrave, loc. cit., Pl. III, H; Pl. VI, G; Figs. 59, 60.
TYPE SPECIMENS: Bowl No. NA 1814B10, effigy No. NA 1814B12 and sherds Nos. AT 1375, 1377, 1470, 1472–1475, 1477–1479, 1481–1497, 1499–1509, 1511, 4275–4278 in the Type Collection of the Museum of Northern Arizona.
TYPE SITE: Two Kivas Pueblo (NA 700), Walnut Creek, Coconino County Arizona.
STAGE: Pueblo III.
TIME: ca 1100–1250 A.D.

DESCRIPTION (revised):

Constructed: by coiling. *Fired:* in reducing atmosphere. *Core:* gray. *Temper:* abundant opaque angular fragments, gray or tan, varying size, mostly fine; rarely occasional grain quartz sand. *Texture core:* medium. *Fracture:* slightly crumbling. *Surface finish:* bowl interiors and jar exteriors carefully smoothed and evenly coated with thick paper-white slip; frequently somewhat bumpy; scraping marks usually very conspicuous; sometimes coated with thin dead white wash, unevenly applied, polished only in rare instances of exterior decoration; jar interiors moderately smoothed; exterior bowl surfaces occasionally corrugated, corrugations clapboard style or indented. *Surface color:* gray or white. *Forms:* bowls, jars, pitchers, dippers, effigies. *Recorded range thickness bowl walls:* 2.9 to 8.1 mm; greatest individual range recorded, 3.5 mm; average thickness, ca 4.5

Fig. 59. Walnut Black-on-white ($\frac{1}{2}\times$).

mm. *Recorded range thickness jar walls:* 4 to 6.4 mm; greatest individual range recorded, 1.1 mm; average thickness, ca 5 mm. *Rims:* bowls, IA3, IA4, IIIA2, IIIA3, IIIA4, IIIA7, IB3, IIIB3, IC2, IC3; pitchers, IB2. *Decoration:* painted; black, usually thin and watery, occasionally dense, almost always lacking in sharpness of outline. *Pigment:* carbon (test by Colton). *Designs:* usually bowl interiors, jar exteriors, rarely also on bowl exteriors. *Patterns:* bowl interiors either all-over lay-out or wide band with open circle in bottom; band lay-out always framed above and below with wide encircling line; all-over lay-out sometimes framed just below rim, sometimes carries to rim; usually balanced, sometimes almost negative of solid elements and straight lines; usually wide lines and

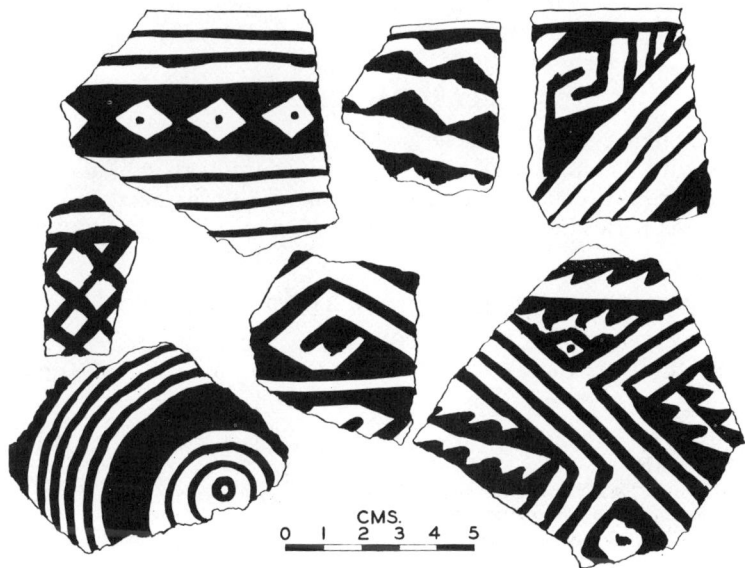

Fig. 60. Walnut Black-on-white ($\frac{1}{2}\times$).

stripes, opposed steps, solid triangles, triangular scrolls, zig-zag lines, barbed lines in opposed pairs producing negative lightning effect; curved lines rare, hatching absent; open squares and diamonds with occasional dots; bowl exteriors rare wide band with elements similar to elements on interiors; jar exteriors decorated in two bands, one around neck and one around body, both sometimes continuous, usually divided into rectangular panels by from two to four vertical lines; panels filled with solid elements in general similar to those on bowl interiors.

RANGE:

Tributaries of Little Colorado River, east of San Francisco Mountains, Coconino County, Arizona, to and including Petrified Forest National Monument. Also found in Verde Valley and Tonto Basin, Arizona.

REMARKS:

There is some similarity to Roosevelt Black-on-white* which has not been described in sufficient detail to compare the two types point by point. However, Roosevelt Black-on-white is predominantly water-worn quartz sand with less abundant angular fragments. The paint also is dense and richer with sharp clear-cut outlines; there is sometimes a suggestion of glaze. Jar necks of Roosevelt Black-on-white almost always are decorated with independent panels or isolated solid elements.

TULAROSA SERIES

Although types in this series have many characters in common with Walnut Series, these same characters in Tularosa Series are not generally so conspicuous. The area occupied by Tularosa Series lies south and east of the normal area of Walnut Series.

TULAROSA BLACK-ON-WHITE

SYNONYM: Upper Gila Black-on-white, Haury, 1931.
DESCRIBED BY: Kidder, 1924, p. 98; also Gladwin, W. & H. S., 1931 pp. 32–35.
NAMED BY: Kidder, loc. cit.
ILLUSTRATIONS: Kidder, 1924, Pl. 44, a-1; Gladwin, 1931, Pl. XXXIII, B; XXXIV.
TYPE SPECIMENS: Cotype sherd No. AT 1592 in the Type Collection of the Museum of Northern Arizona.
TYPE SITE: Not designated.
STAGE: Pueblo III.
TIME: Probably between 1100–1200 A.D.

DESCRIPTION (revised):

Constructed: by coiling. *Fired:* in reducing atmosphere. *Temper:* abundant opaque angular fragments varying sizes, mostly fine, usually gray, occasionally tan or black; sand grains less abundant. *Texture core:* medium. *Fracture:* slightly crumbling. *Surface finish:* bowl interiors, jar exteriors well-smoothed and coated with thin oyster-gray or dead-white slip; well-polished; frequently crazed; bowl exteriors fairly carefully scraped, not smoothed, not slipped. *Surface color:* white. *Forms:* bowls, pitchers (predominate), dippers, eccentric; pitcher handles frequently animal figurine. *Decoration:* painted; black, paint frequently watery, often dense, sometimes brownish if thin, usually

* See Gladwin, 1931, p. 47.

fairly clear-cut along edges. *Pigment:* iron and carbon (test by Hawley). *Designs:* most frequent design balanced solid and hatchured elements, either angular or interlocking scrolls, one solid and one hatchured, either angular or curvilinear; sometimes simple narrow-line scrolls with as many as fifteen full circuits; small close-set key figures, arranged to cover large areas, fine-line herringbone design; hatchuring usually fine-line or narrow-line with interspaces equal to or less than width of individual hatchures; sometimes (usually on very small vessels) no hatchuring, the design composed wholly of small opposed solid steps or elongated rectangular panels containing narrow staggered lines in series; jar necks usually decorated with frets, solid elements, opposed steps, nests of chevrons, or balanced solid and hatchured elements; never with panels of vertical bars; bases of jars unpainted area of polygonal or star-shaped outline, rarely curvilinear; brush work and execution excellent; lines regular and arrangement accurate.

COMPARISONS: Roosevelt Black-on-white, figurine-shaped handles very rare; necks and shoulders of pitchers and jars painted with panels of short vertical bars or isolated solid elements; bases of pitchers and jars always unpainted circular area (never polygonal).

RANGE:

Upper tributaries of the Gila, San Francisco, Tularosa, Blue and Little Colorado rivers of southeastern Arizona and southwestern New Mexico.

PINEDALE BLACK-ON-WHITE

DESCRIBED BY: Haury, 1931, p. 62.
NAMED BY: Haury, loc. cit.
ILLUSTRATIONS: Haury, loc. cit., Pl. 19, Fig. 17.
TYPE SPECIMENS: Gila Pueblo, Globe, Arizona. Cotype sherds Nos. AT 1662–1691, 1703–1708 in the Type Collection of the Museum of Northern Arizona.
TYPE SITE: Pinedale Pueblo (NA 1069), Pinedale, Navajo County, Arizona.
STAGE: Pueblo III–IV (?).
TIME: ca 1290–1375 A.D.

DESCRIPTION (revised):

Constructed: by coiling. *Fired:* in reducing atmosphere. *Core:* light gray to dark gray. *Temper:* abundant medium sized opaque angular fragments, usually gray, sometimes black or tan; occasional grain quartz sand. *Texture core:* medium to fine. *Vessel walls:* strong. *Fracture:* crumbling. *Surface finish:* exteriors jars and bowl interiors well-smoothed, coated with thin tenacious slip; usually well-polished, sometimes crazed; slip extends well down interior jar necks; interior surfaces jars evenly scraped; sometimes smoothed, scraping marks sometimes conspicuous, sometimes almost invisible. *Surface color:* dead white or oyster gray. *Forms:* jars (abundant), bowls (rare). *Recorded range thickness jar walls:* 3.4 to 8.6 mm; greatest individual range recorded, 2/5 mm; average thickness, ca 5 mm. *Rims:* bowls, "gently incurved"; jars, IA3, IA7, IIIA2. *Decoration:* painted; black, usually rich and dense, sometimes near glaze but occasionally watery; rarely brownish. *Design:* jar necks usually stripe along rim or immediately below on exterior; solid stepped elements, triangles, vertical bars or short lines pendent from rim stripe; lines wide to fine, sometimes staggered; jar bodies single broad field from near base of neck well down toward vessel base, bordered above and below with wide stripes; band occupied by panels stepped, triangular or curved with narrow-line hatchuring with interspaces usually slightly narrower than hatchures, averaging 25 to inch; elongated solid triangles, rectangular cross-hatching occasional; ticked, serrated and zigzag lines rare; decoration bowls all-over patterns on interiors, similar to jar exteriors, isolated geometric or zoomorphic figures on bowl exteriors occasional; continuous exterior decoration rare; framing line frequent just below rim; painted rims rare.

RANGE:
Silver Creek drainage, Navajo County, Arizona.

REMARKS:
Cotype material used in description was separated by Haury and donated to the Museum of Northern Arizona by the National Geographic Society from material collected by the Society's Beam Expedition, 1929 (see Douglass, 1929; Haury, loc. cit.).

KLAGETO BLACK-ON-WHITE: new type

ILLUSTRATIONS: (Drawings) Fig. 61.
TYPE SPECIMENS: Jar no. 243–941 and sherds Nos. AT 1299–1311, 1335–1345, 1399–1409, 1418–1434 in the Type Collection of the Museum of Northern Arizona.
TYPE SITE: Kintiel Pueblo (NA 1015), Le Roux Wash, north of Chambers, Apache County, Arizona.
STAGE: Pueblo III.
TIME: ca 1250–1300 A.D.

DESCRIPTION (revised):
Constructed: by coiling. *Fired:* in reducing atmosphere. *Core:* light gray to dark gray, occasionally tan or cream near surfaces.

Temper: abundant opaque angular fragments varying sizes, mostly fine, usually gray, occasionally tan; occasional grain quartz sand that rarely penetrates slip. *Texture core:* fine to medium. *Vessel walls:* strong. *Fracture:* crumbling. *Surface finish:* jar exteriors and both bowl and dipper surfaces coated with fairly heavy bluish-gray to dead white slip; well-polished; coarsely crazed; jar interiors well-scraped, sometimes smoothed,

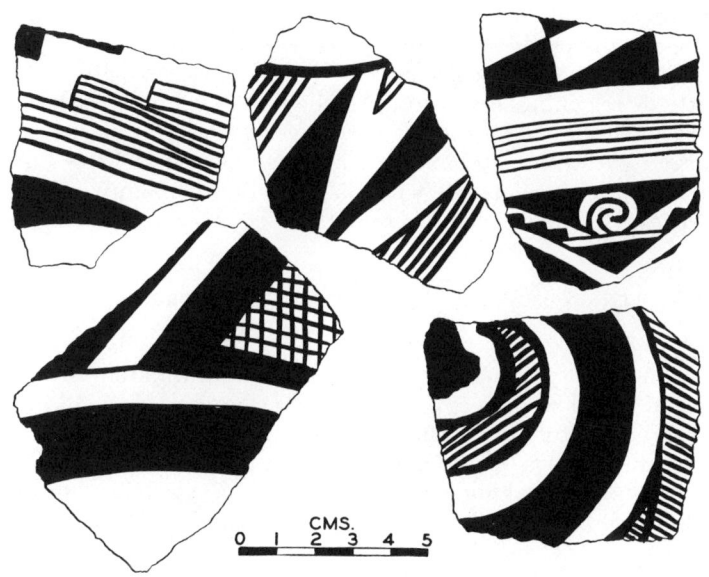

Fig. 61. Klageto Black-on-white ($\frac{1}{2}\times$).

gritty. *Surface color:* bluish-gray to dead white. *Forms:* jars (predominate), bowls, dippers. *Recorded range thickness jar walls:* 3.5 to 8.5 mm; greatest individual range recorded, 2 mm; average thickness, ca 5.5 mm. *Recorded range thickness bowl walls:* 5.3 to 8.1 mm; greatest individual range recorded, 1.2 mm; average thickness, ca 6.5 mm. *Recorded range thickness dipper walls:* 3.6 to 6.6 mm; greatest individual range recorded, 2.2 mm; average thickness, ca 5 mm. *Rims:* bowls, IIIA7; dippers IA3, IIA2, IIA3, IIA7, IIIA3, IIIA7; dippers have round hollow handles. *Decoration:* painted; black, usually very thick and dense, often rich red-brown; often slightly gritty. *Pigment:* iron-carbon (test by Colton); manganese-iron-carbon (test by Hawley). *Designs:* bowls, usually all-over designs; dippers, almost always on interiors, usually all-over designs, upper surface of handles, rarely zoomorphic figures on exteriors; jars, in two bands, one around neck, one from base of neck to below largest diameter of body; in general painted areas about balance unpainted areas, often producing open-work and sometimes negative effect. *Elements:* single stripes, narrow or wide lines in series from 2 to 4; rectangular or triangular panels containing rectangular and occasionally diagonal cross-hatching of varying degrees of fineness, wide staggered lines in series, narrow or wide-line hatching; solid stepped elements, sometimes in opposed pairs, sometimes singly in triangular panels framed by parallel lines in series; solid triangles, usually in pairs with interlocking hooks or attached solid stepped elements; occasionally open rectangles with several rows of isolated dots; curved lines very rare; execution in general bold and free but of high degree of exactitude with sharp outlines, in many instances brushwork careless; lines frequently over-carry at intersections.

RANGE:

Upper Leroux Wash, Apache County, Arizona.

REMARKS:

From the type material examined several different styles of design might well be isolated and described but since all of the material is from the same relatively small area of about the same date, it has been thought no good purpose could be served at present by making such a separation. Eventually, however, subdivision into several types may be found feasible.

BIDAHOCHI WHITE WARE

It is not often that a ware would be recognized on the basis of one type. Later will be considered miscellaneous types, i.e., types that do not fit a ware description. Conceivably there may be two or more types that obviously belong to the same ware yet there might not be sufficient data to warrant a ware description; inversely there could be one type that also could be a ware, the type description and ware description being the same. Bidahochi White Ware has only one type.

Bidahochi White Ware, as a ware, is recognized because it is identical in ware characters to Jeddito Yellow Ware, with the exception that vessels of this white ware were fired in a reducing atmosphere, thus the only difference between the two wares is the surface color.

BIDAHOCHI WHITE WARE: new ware

STAGE: Pueblo IV.
TIME: Probably between 1325–1400 A.D.
DESCRIPTION:

At present identical to Bidahochi Black-on-white, as revised, the only known type of this ware.

BIDAHOCHI BLACK-ON-WHITE

DESCRIBED BY: Caywood & Spicer, 1935, pp. 52–53, 57–59.
NAMED BY: Caywood & Spicer, loc. cit., P. 52.
ILLUSTRATIONS: Caywood & Spicer, loc. cit., Pl. XI, B; Pl. XII, A.
TYPE SPECIMENS: Cotype sherds Nos. AT 1033–1040, 1076–1081 in the Type Collection of the Museum of Northern Arizona.
TYPE SITE: Bidahochi Pueblo (Na 1054), upper Cottonwood Wash, above Indian Wells, Navajo County, Arizona.
STAGE: Pueblo IV.
TIME: Probably between 1325–1400 A.D.
DESCRIPTION (revised):

Constructed: by coiling. *Fired:* in reducing atmosphere. *Core:* light gray to nearly pure white. *Temper:* very fine grains quartz sand, almost invisible to naked eye; inconspicuous even under power glass. *Vessel walls:* medium strong to strong. *Texture core:* fine to very fine. *Fracture:* shattering. *Surface finish:* bowl interiors and jar exteriors, impacted; well-polished; bowl exteriors, smoothed, polished, scraping marks often noticeable; jar interiors, scraped, sometimes lightly smoothed, usually somewhat bumpy; impacted surfaces sometimes flake, leaving deeply pitted appearance. *Surface color:* dead white to very light pearl gray. *Forms:* bowls (predominate), jars, dippers. *Recorded range thickness bowl walls:* 5 to 6.2 mm; greatest individual range recorded, 1.1 mm; average thickness jar walls: ca 5 mm. *Rims:* bowls, IA3, IA4, IA6, IIIA6. *Decoration:* painted. *Paint:* black, usually very rich and dense, occasionally vitreous, sometimes blistered; occasionally watery with brownish purplish, or greenish tint. *Pigment:* carbon (tests by Colton and F. G. Hawley) or iron-manganese (Caywood & Spicer, loc. cit.). *Designs:* confined to interior bowl surfaces, exterior jar surfaces; no rim decoration; general character bold; brushwork free, not very precise, lines often over-carry and sometimes do not meet. *Elements:* horizontal and diagonal stripes, narrow and wide lines, sometimes in series; diagonal stripes, narrow wide lines, sometimes in series; solid stepped elements, often interlocking; staggered wide lines, solid triangles; rectangular or triangular panels containing fine to coarse diagonal cross-hatching; "pseudo-checker-board," occasional. *Decorative style:* almost identical to style on Jeddito Black-on-yellow.

RANGE:

Reported from type site, from Hoyapi Pueblo (NA 837) on Polacca Wash, from NA 1024 on upper Cottonwood Wash; from NA 2597 on Corn Creek, Navajo County, and six miles southeast of Leupp, Coconino County; also as trade from Tuzigoot Pueblo (NA 1261), upper Verde River Valley, Yavapai County, Arizona (Caywood & Spicer, loc. cit.).

REMARKS:

This type is identical to Jeddito Black-on-yellow except that it is fired in a reducing atmosphere; *when refired in an oxidizing atmosphere sherds of Bidahochi Black-on-white are indistinguishable from Jeddito Black-on-yellow, except that the paint changes in appearance when refired.* No sherds of this type have been reported from sites in the Jeddito Valley or on the Hopi Mesas, with the exception of Hoyapi Pueblo.

MISCELLANEOUS TYPES

In reviewing pottery types fired in a reducing atmosphere it was seen that some well known black-on-white types of the region objectively did not belong to the white wares presented herein. Upon investigation it was realized that the published descriptions for the most part were inadequate for type identification or for ware designation. Further, sherds of these types and of undescribed yet recognized types were consistent in basic objective characters and were identified as belonging with a group of types dominant east of the Hopi Country. To those students familiar with the appearance of Basket Maker–Pueblo pottery, these types would be called "Chaco." Some familiar type names will, therefore, be found missing from this work. Unfortunately there was not enough material available to revise these old type descriptions or to determine ware characters.

There are also types that have been adequately described for type and ware identification but that do not belong to any known ware. Since a ware description is based upon type descriptions, types must be described first. So until all wares have been identified, described, and named, there will be described types that cannot be assigned to a ware. In this category is Jeddito Black-on-white. A revised description is as follows:

JEDDITO BLACK-ON-WHITE

DESCRIBED BY: Hargrave, 1932, p. 16.
NAMED BY: Hargrave, loc. cit.
TYPE SPECIMENS: Sherds Nos. AT 919–921 and 1074 in the Type Collection of the Museum of Northern Arizona.
TYPE SITE: Bidahochi Pueblo (NA 1054), upper Cottonwood Wash, near Indian Wells, Navajo County, Arizona.
STAGE: Pueblo III–IV (?).
TIME: About 1275–1350 A.D.

DESCRIPTION (revised):

Constructed: by coiling. *Fired:* in reducing atmosphere. *Core:* gray. *Temper:* fairly abundant fine quartz sand, evenly distributed. *Vessel walls:* medium strong to weak. *Texture core:* medium to fine; somewhat porous. *Fracture:* slightly crumbling. *Surface finish:* both bowl surfaces and exterior jar surfaces coated with moderately heavy slip, usually fairly well-polished; scraping marks often noticeable on less well-polished surfaces; decorated surfaces more highly polished than undecorated; slip often flakes off from weathering. *Surface color:* bluish white or pearl gray. *Forms:* bowls, jars; bowls occasionally have single horizontal handle. *Recorded range thickness bowl walls:* 6.6 to 7.9 mm; greatest individual range recorded, 1.3 mm; average thickness, ca 7 mm. *Recorded range thickness jar walls:* 5.8 to 8.7 mm; greatest individual range recorded, 1.9 mm; average thickness, ca 7.5 mm. *Decoration:* painted. *Paint:* black; often watery, rarely brownish or purplish in thin spots; sometimes flakes off. *Design:* wide horizontal band around vessel, framed above and below with one to three stripes or wide lines, outer stripe or line usually widest, often touches edge of rim; negative effect sometimes attained with diagonal or rectangular crosshatching with solid figures superimposed. *Elements:* solid areas, keys, and stepped elements; scrolls. *Rim decoration:* uncommon; series of dots, solid stripe, or wide line.

RANGE:

Recorded sparsely from near Indian Wells and in the Jeddito Valley, Navajo County, Arizona.

KOKOP BLACK-ON-WHITE: new type

TYPE SPECIMENS: Sherds Nos. AT 925–944 in the Type Collection of the Museum of Northern Arizona.

TYPE SITE: Kokopnyama Pueblo (NA 1019), Jeddito Valley, Navajo County, Arizona.

STAGE: Late Pueblo III–early Pueblo IV.

TIME: About 1300 A.D.

DESCRIPTION:

Constructed: by coiling. *Fired:* in reducing atmosphere. *Core:* gray. *Carbon streak:* common. *Temper:* fine quartz sand with small quantities angular fragments, black or tan. *Vessel walls:* medium strong. *Texture core:* medium to fine. *Fracture:* slightly crumbling. *Surface finish:* bowl interiors and jar exteriors usually impacted and highly polished, occasionally crazed; never slipped; scraping marks noticeable on less well-polished specimens; bowl exteriors usually fairly well-smoothed but with scraping marks noticeable; sometimes highly polished and crazed; sometimes slightly bumpy. *Surface color:* dead white or light pearl gray. *Fire clouds:* occasional. *Forms:* bowls (predominate), jars, ladles. *Recorded range thickness bowl walls:* 3 to 7.7 mm; greatest individual range recorded, 2.6 mm; average thickness, 5.2 mm. *Recorded range thickness jar walls:* 3.6 to 5.8 mm; greatest individual range recorded, 1 mm; average thickness, ca 4.8 mm. *Rims:* bowls, IA3, IIIA3, IB3; jars, IA3, IIB3, IIB4. *Decoration:* painted. *Paint:* black, usually dense but dull, sometimes reflects light; sometimes watery with brownish or greenish tinge. *Design:* confined to bowl interiors and jar exteriors; bottoms of bowls, unpainted; elements and motifs—chiefly wide lines, solid triangles, open squares with dots, diagonal cross-hatching, wide-and-narrow-line hatching, wide *staggered* lines in series, fine lines in series of up to 10 lines; design usually band of varying width around sides of vessel, one or two wide framing lines at top and bottom of band, upper framing usually just below rim; negative designs of Kayenta Style.

RANGE:

Undetermined. Abundant at type site.

REMARKS:

The type material was collected by the National Geographic Society Beam Expedition, 1929 (Hargrave, 1931), and donated to the Museum of Northern Arizona. Among the type material are sherds of widely varying styles of design. Separation on the basis of design was not considered feasible because of insufficient material for study.

This type was placed in a hypothetical ware for convenience in study. Unfortunately, this ware name, Puerco White Ware, inadvertently appeared in print (Hargrave, 1935 a). Reasons for not retaining this ware name and for not presenting a ware description has already been given.

WIDE RUIN BLACK-ON-WHITE: new type

TYPE SPECIMENS: Sherds Nos. AT 1319–1334, 1378–1392, 1442–1457 in the Type Collection of the Museum of Northern Arizona.

TYPE SITE: Kintiel (=Wide Ruin) Pueblo (NA 1015), Le Roux Wash, north of Chambers, Apache County, Arizona.

STAGE: Pueblo III.

TIME: About 1275 A.D.

DESCRIPTION:

Constructed: by coiling. *Fired:* in reducing atmosphere. *Core:* gray. *Temper:* moderately fine quartz sand, sometimes some basalt (?) sand, and lesser amounts opaque angular fragments, gray, black, or tan. *Vessel walls:* medium strong. *Texture core:* medium to fine. *Fracture:* slightly crumbling. *Surface finish:* interior surfaces bowls and exterior surfaces jars coated with moderately heavy pearl gray or dead white slip; usually well-polished but sometimes chalky, often coarsely crazed; exterior surfaces bowls sometimes finished like interiors, more often moderately polished but not slipped and slightly bumpy; jar interiors fairly well-smoothed but gritty. *Surface color:* pearl gray or dead white; unslipped surfaces usually light gray. *Forms:* bowls, jars. *Recorded range thickness bowl walls:* 3.3 to 6.7 mm; greatest individual range recorded, 2.2 mm; average thickness, ca 5.2 mm. *Recorded range thickness jar walls:* 2.9 to 7.3 mm; greatest individual range recorded, 3.7 mm; average thickness, ca 5.2 mm. *Rims:* bowls, IA3, IA7. *Decoration:* painted. *Paint:* black, usually dense and dull, sometimes vitreous; often brownish; brush marks often noticeable. *Pigment:* iron-carbon (test by Colton). *Design:* confined to bowl interiors and jar exteriors; painted areas about evenly balanced with background; at least four styles of design can be distinguished: (1) sherds Nos. 13–19–1330, 1449–1452, elements and motifs principally diagonal or rectangular cross-hatching of fine to narrow lines, producing open-work effect; wide and narrow straight lines, singly or in series, with interspaces about equal to width of lines or up to three times width of lines; single wide stripes; solid stepped elements, usually in opposed or balanced pairs; rims undecorated or painted with transverse dashes, 2 to 3 mm wide and 3 to 5 mm apart; (2) sherds Nos. 1331–1334, 1453, elements and motifs chiefly narrow straight lines in series of from 3 to 6, with interspaces about equal to width of lines; narrow-line open-work cross-hatching; rectangular panels containing wide staggered lines in series; wide lines with small pendent isosceles triangles on one or both sides; (3) sherds Nos. 1442–1448, elements and motifs chiefly narrow straight lines in series, narrow-line open-work cross-hatching; wide stripes; solid elements, either triangular or of irregular shape, but almost always having attached interlocking hooks, occasionally if hooks are large, they are open and cross-hatched or are modified into pendent stepped elements; (4) sherds Nos. 1378–1392, 1454–1457, elements and motifs chiefly curved stripes and curved bands, the latter usually containing transverse narrow-line hatching with interspaces about equal to width of hatchures; bands sometimes divided into panels, with longitudinal hatching; triangular panels with hatching and solid triangles.

RANGE:

Upper Le Roux Wash and Rio Pueblo Colorado, Apache County, Arizona.

REMARKS:

Although it is likely that a thorough study of this type would warrant its subdivision into several types on the basis of design, it has not been deemed advisable to make such separation herein, partly because sufficient type material has not been available and partly because all type material comes from a limited area and is about the same horizon.

B: CONSTRUCTED BY PADDLING

There has been recognized only one ware in which vessels were constructed by paddling but which were fired in a reducing atmosphere.

SAN FRANCISCO MOUNTAIN GRAY WARE

Large storage jars of this ware have been found side by side with large storage jars (of Rio de Flag Brown) that were fired in an oxidizing atmosphere. Yet there is no reason to believe that both were not indigenous. It is not known why both atmospheres probably were in use at the same time at so early a date, but there is information that tends to show that San Francisco Mountain Gray Ware is developed from Rio de Flag Brown (of Alameda Brown Ware) by a change of firing atmosphere. This development is also indicated by a change in temper (Hargrave, 1932, p. 13).

KEY 19: SAN FRANCISCO MOUNTAIN GRAY WARE

Undecorated............................Deadmans Gray (p. 252)
Red slipped surface....................Deadmans Fugitive Red (p. 252)
Black painted design...................Deadmans Black-on-gray (p. 253)

SAN FRANCISCO MOUNTAIN GRAY WARE:
new ware

STAGES: Pueblo I–II.
TIME: Pre-700–ca 1050 A.D.

DESCRIPTION:

Constructed: by paddling. *Fired:* in reducing atmosphere. *Core:* gray. *Temper:* abundant fine quartz sand, occasional grain black angular fragments, and numerous fine mica-like particles. *Vessel walls:* medium strong. *Texture core:* fine. *Fracture:* slightly crumbling. *Surface finish:* bowl interiors, jar exteriors, polished, impacted; not slipped; interior jar surfaces, fairly well-smoothed, anvil marks, definite but not generally conspicuous; mica-like particles visible on surface. *Surface color:* light bluish-gray; pinkish or red in part when painted with fugitive paint. *Forms:* bowls, jars. *Decoration:* unpainted or painted with mat red or black design. *Elements:* mostly fine and narrow lines, small solid triangles, pendent dots.

RANGE:

San Francisco Mountains, Coconino County, southeast to Walnut Creek, and south to the Verde Valley, Yavapai County, Arizona.

DEADMANS GRAY

DESCRIBED BY: Hargrave, 1932, p. 12.
NAMED BY: Colton, 1931, p. 9.
TYPE SPECIMENS: Pitcher No. 721-A. 306, type sherd No. AT 2391, co-type sherds 4517–4531 in the Type Collection of the Museum of Northern Arizona.
TYPE SITE: NA 1238, Medicine Valley, San Francisco Mountains, Coconino County, Arizona.
STAGES: Pueblo I–II.
TIME: Pre-700–ca 1050 A.D.

DESCRIPTION (revised):

Constructed: by paddling. *Fired:* in reducing atmosphere. *Core:* gray. *Temper:* abundant fine quartz sand; occasional grain dark angular fragment; abundant fine mica-like particles. *Vessel walls:* medium strong. *Texture core:* fine. *Fracture:* slightly crumbling. *Surface finish:* exterior jar surfaces and interior bowl surfaces, polished and impacted; not slipped; interior jar surfaces, fairly well-smoothed; not polished; anvil marks definite but not conspicuous; mica-like particles glitter on surfaces. *Surface color:* light bluish-gray. *Forms:* bowls, jars. No painted decoration.

RANGE:

San Francisco Mountain region, Coconino County, to Chino Valley and Skull Valley, Yavapai County, Arizona.

REMARKS:

The name is derived from the type locality Deadmans Flat. This type may have developed from Rio de Flag Brown.

DEADMANS FUGITIVE RED

DESCRIBED BY: Hargrave, 1932, p. 14.
NAMED BY: Colton, 1931, p. 9.
TYPE SPECIMENS: Jar No. 41–29, and sherds Nos. AT 2408–2412 in the Type Collection of the Museum of Northern Arizona.
TYPE SITE: Medicine Fort (NA 862), Medicine Valley, San Francisco Mountains, Coconino County, Arizona.
STAGES: Pueblo I–II.
TIME: Pre-700–ca 1050 A.D.

DESCRIPTION (revised):

Constructed: by paddling. *Fired:* in reducing atmosphere. *Core:* gray. *Temper:* abundant fine quartz sand; occasional grain dark angular fragment; abundant fine mica-like particles. *Vessel walls:* medium strong. *Texture core:* fine. *Fracture:* slightly crumbling. *Surface finish:* exterior surfaces jars and interior surfaces bowls polished and impacted; not slipped;

interior surfaces jars fairly well-smoothed but not polished; anvil marks definite but not conspicuous; mica-like particles glitter on surfaces. *Surface color:* light bluish-gray, in part; in part pink or red. *Forms:* bowls, jars. *Decoration:* red fugitive paint on greater part of vessel; rims generally have red lip; no drawn design.

RANGE:

San Francisco Mountain region.

REMARKS:

The earliest reported find of this type is from a late Pueblo I pithouse (NA 1563). Sherds of this type vary considerably in the shade of red because of the effect of weathering. Specimens recovered from caves have a thick, deep red coat but on specimens dug from the ground in the open, the wash is powdery and generally pale. Sherds from the surface of the ground rarely have more than a pinkish tint. Vessel forms vary in size from small bowls to large storage jars. Since a red decoration could not be produced by firing a vessel in a reducing atmosphere, it would be necessary to paint the vessel after it was fired. The fugitive character of the paint could thus be accounted for.

DEADMANS BLACK-ON-GRAY

DESCRIBED BY: Hargrave, 1932, p. 14.
NAMED BY: Colton, 1931, p. 10.
ILLUSTRATION: Bowl 627/A 142 (Fig. 62).
TYPE SPECIMENS: Bowl No. 627/A142, type sherd No. AT 1026, and cotype sherds 1027–1028 in the Type Collection of the Museum of Northern Arizona.
TYPE SITE: NA 2050, Deadmans Wash, San Francisco Mountains, Coconino County, Arizona.
STAGES: Pueblo I–II.
TIME: Pre-700–ca 1050 A.D.

DESCRIPTION (revised):

Fig. 62. Deadmans Black on gray ($\frac{1}{6} \times$).

Constructed: by paddling. *Fired:* in reducing atmosphere. *Core:* gray. *Temper:* abundant fine quartz sand; occasional grain black angular fragment; abundant fine mica-like particles. *Vessel walls:* medium strong. *Texture core:* fine. *Fracture:* slightly crumbling. *Surface finish:* exterior jar surfaces and interior bowl surfaces, polished and impacted; not slipped; interior jar surfaces fairly well-smoothed, not polished; anvil marks definite but not conspicuous on interior jar surfaces;

mica-like particles glitter on surfaces. *Surface color:* light bluish-gray. *Forms:* bowls, jars. *Decoration:* painted, black. *Paint:* dull, usually thin. *Design:* confined to bowl interiors and jar exteriors; fine and narrow lines, often in series with interspaces about 4 times as wide as lines; small solid triangles, often with pendent dots or short fringe-like lines.

RANGE:

Headwaters of Verde River, Cataract Creek, and Cedar, Deadmans, Kana-a and Walnut drainages, in Yavapai and Coconino counties, Arizona.

GLOSSARY

ANGULAR INCLUSIONS—Fragments of crushed material added to clay.
ANTHROPOMORPHIC—Man-shaped.
APPLIQUE—Ornaments cut from one fabric or material and fastened on another.
BARBED LINE—A line with triangular barbs on one or both sides; saw-tooth.
BAR—A strip of solid color and of uniform width of more than 4 mm., which is not continuous and the ends of which terminate without junction with other elements in the design.
BODY—(1) The central or principal part of a vessel, as distinguished from the rim, neck or handles. (2) The mixture of clay and powdered rock of which pottery is composed.
BOTTLE—A vessel with comparatively narrow neck or mouth, and without handles.
BOWL—A concave vessel, usually hemispherical or nearly so, without a neck.
BRITTLE—Easily broken or snapped.
BURNISH—To make smooth or glossy by friction, giving a metallic lustre.
CANTEEN—A vessel with a small mouth usually flattened on one side, provided with means of suspension used for carrying water or other liquid.
CARBON STREAK—The black or gray color of the central portion of a vessel wall, caused by the presence of unburned carbon particles, in contrast to the lighter colored portions near the surface, in which the carbon particles have been burned.
CAULDRON (CALDRON)—A large kettle or boiler. Holmes uses this term to describe "large pot-like vessels," similar to vase but with relatively larger orifice.
CERAMICS—The art of making articles from earth by the agency of fire, as glass, enamel, pottery, cement.
CHEVRON—An isolated geometric figure formed by the terminal intersection of two relatively short straight lines or hatchures.
CLAY—A finely divided hydrous aluminum silicate derived usually from the weathering of feldspars.
CLEAVAGE—The structure possessed by some wares, causing them to break more readily in one direction than in others.
COAT—This word, as a noun, is synonymous with *slip, wash,* or *paint;* and should not be so used. It is appropriate as a verb, to indicate the process of applying a slip, wash or paint to all or substantially all of a vessel surface.
COIL (or COILED) POTTERY—Pottery vessels, in the construction of which fillets of clay (approximately cylindrical) are coiled one upon another, either as a series of concentric rings or as a continuous spiral. In the finished vessel the fillets may display their original form, may be wholly or partly obliterated by flattening, or smoothing with a scraper or by the paddle-and-anvil method, or may be distorted in various ways such as by indentations made with the finger-tips, incisions made with a hard instrument, etc.
COLANDER—A vessel having the bottom or lower part perforated for use as a sieve.
COMPOSITION—The art or practice of so combining the parts of a work of art as to produce a harmonious whole.
CONCHOIDAL (as applied to *Fracture*)—A break which shows curved surfaces like a shell.
CORE (Ceramics)—The inner portion distinct from the surfaces of a piece of pottery.
CORRUGATE—To form or shape into wrinkles or folds, or alternate ridges and grooves. N.B. Holmes uses *ribbed* to refer to unindented coils, and *corrugated* to refer apparently to cases in which coils are not obliterated.

Co-Type—An additional vessel or sherd on which the original description has been amplified.
Crackled—Having the appearance of being marked with minute cracks. (Syn.—*crazed*)
Crazed—Marked with minute cracks. (Syn.—*crackled*)
Crenelation—Furnished with battlements. Applied to a molding of embattled or indented pattern.
Crenate—To cut the margin into notches or scallops.
Cross-Hatched—Marked with two or more intersecting series of parallel lines.
Crumbly—Reduced to fragments by little pressure.
Design—An arrangement of elements, motives, or patterns, making a complete composition.
Depth—Degree of saturation and brilliance, increasing as saturation of color increases, and brilliance decreases.
Diaper Pattern—A pattern consisting of the constant repetition of one or more units of design. The figures connected with one another, or grow out of one another with continuously flowing or straight lines; or the surface may be wholly occupied by the successive units, the outline of one forming part of the outlines of others adjoining.
Disk—A flat, thin, rounded artifact.
Dish—A large piece of pottery, usually eliptical in form; a platter.
Dull—Lacking luster or brilliance, as of a color. Of low saturation of color. Without gloss. (Syn.—*thin*)
Effigy—An image or representation of an animate or inanimant object.
Element—The units out of which a motive is built.
Enamel—An opaque vitreous substance applied by fusion to the surface of glass, pottery, metal, etc. When transparent it is usually called a glaze.
Fillet—A part of an ornament resembling a ribbon. A border or outline of broad or narrow lines, used in giving relief to ornamentation. A little band; a thin, narrow strip or ribbon of clay.
Figurine—A small carved or molded figures; especially a statuette in pottery or the like.
Fire—To subject material to intense heat; to bake, to burn in a kiln.
Fire Cloud—A black or gray area on the surface of a vessel, caused either by exclusion of oxygen from that portion during firing, or by incomplete oxidation of carbon particles deposited from smoke.
Flask—A small bottle-shaped vessel; especially, one with a broad, flat body. (See *Canteen*)
Flat (paint)—Uniform in hue or shade. Having little appearance of relief. Contrast with gloss.
Float—To smooth with a trowel or smooth stone, bringing the water in the damp clay to the surface. To impact is a better word.
Fluted—Marked with grooves or channels of *curved section*, usually in parallel series.
Friable—Easily crumbled, pulverized, or reduced to powder.
Fugitive (in pottery)—A paint which will wash off with water is said to be fugitive.
Fuse—To liquefy by heat; to render fluid; to dissolve or melt.
Glaze—To encrust or overlay with a thin transparent surface of a material resembling glass.
Granular—Having a surface texture or structure appearing to consist of grains.
Ground—A surface prepared for decoration. The surface upon which a picture is painted, as a preliminary tone laid on a canvas. A flat surface, for figures in relief.
Grog—The refractory materials, such as crushed pottery, sand, etc., which are added to clay in the manufacture of pottery. Syn. *Temper.*
Hardness—The cohesion of the particles on the surface of a body, as determined by its capacity to scratch or be scratched by another.

GLOSSARY

Hatching—The process or result of drawing fine lines in close proximity to each other, to give the effect of shading.

Hatchure—A short parallel line used in drawing especially in shading.

Herringbone—An arrangement of materials or decorative patterns, in rows of parallel lines, which in any two successive rows the lines slope at angles. (A series of chevrons)

Incise—To cut into a hard object with a sharp instrument removing part of the material.

Indent—To press into a material a hard instrument, making a design without removing any of the material.

Jar—A deep vessel with a constricted neck. Syn. *olla*.

Jug—A large, deep vessel with a narrow mouth and a handle.

Kiln—A heated chamber for the purpose of burning or hardening anything.

Leach—To subject a material to the action of percolating water, which removes the soluble parts.

Lines—(1) FINE LINE—A line up to 1 mm. in width. (2) NARROW LINE—A line from 1 to 2 mm. in width. (3) WIDE or BROAD LINE—A line from 2 to 4 mm. in width. See also stripe.

Lug—That which projects like an ear, and by which anything is supported, carried, or grasped, or to which a support is fastened. N.B. Distinguished from handle.

Maze—Any intricate or involved enclosure; also, a representation of such, as in a print. Labyrinth.

Meander—A winding path or course; usually angular.

Model—To shape a pottery vessel by use of the hands only, without aid of potter's wheel, paddle, anvil or other tool; and from lumps rather than fillets of clay.

Motive (Motif)—A combination of *elements*.

Mug—A small cylindrical vessel with a handle.

Overcarried—Said of a line which intersects another line, and extends slightly beyond it, usually due to careless execution on the part of the painter.

Over-Fired—Having been fired for a longer time or at a higher temperature than is usual or than was intended.

Oxidizing Atmosphere—An oxidizing atmosphere contains free oxygen, which with sufficient heat will unite with materials placed in it.

Paddle-and-Anvil Method—A method of constructing pottery vessels by pressure in which a smooth stone or mushroom-shaped pottery tool (called the anvil) is held inside the vessel as the walls are built up, and the exterior is shaped by pounding or patting with a paddle (usually of wood), the anvil being used to sustain the blow. The vessel walls may be built up either by the use of coils or lumps of clay.

Paint—To apply coloring matter.

Pale (of color)—Wanting in vividness of hue or luster.

Paste—The moistened clay, etc., used in making pottery or porcelain.

Pattern—An artistic or mechanical design, built out of a definite arrangement of elements and motives.

Pigment—A colored powder or easily powdered substance which when mixed with a suitable vehicle, in which it is relatively insoluble, forms paints.

Pinnate Line—Featherlike; a line to which small high triangles (either solid or open) are pendant at regular intervals on both sides.

Plaque—A flat, thin piece of metal, clay or the like, used for ornament.

Plate—A shallow, usually circular vessel.

Platter—A large plate or dish.

Polish—To make smooth or glossy by friction.

Polychrome—A decorative scheme, in which more than two colors are used. Applied to a vessel or sherd or to a class of vessels or sherds on which such a decorative scheme appears.

Pot—Any ceramic container.

Pottery—Ware made from earthy material, usually clay, shaped while moist and hardened by heat.

PUKI—A shallow pottery dish in which a pottery vessel rests during the process of manufacture. (Gifford, 1928, p. 354.)
RAY—A thin line, being one of a number of lines diverging from a common center.
REDUCING ATMOSPHERE—A reducing atmosphere contains no free oxygen; materials placed in it with sufficient heat will have some of the oxygen removed.
REFIRED—Having been fired more than once.
REFRACTORY—Capable of enduring a high temperature without softening.
ROPE—Used as synonym for *fillet* in reference to coiling. N.B. *Fillet* is preferable, because *rope* connotes a twining or plaiting process.
SAUCER—A small plate.
SCALLOP—One of continuous series of circle segments forming a border. This is also called a *common cycloid*.
SCORED—Marked with coarse lines or grooves.
SCRAPE—To rub over the surface of with a blunt instrument that removes portions of the surface.
SCROLL—An ornament resembling a roll of paper, loosely rolled. Any of various spiral or convoluted forms based on the curves taken by a roll of paper.
SERIES—A group of pottery types within a ware which have a genetic relation to each other.
SERRATE LINE—Notched or toothed on the edge like a saw.
SHATTER (as applied to *Fracture*)—To break violently into pieces; to splinter.
SHERD (Archaeology)—A fragment of a pottery vessel. Syn. *Shard*.
SHOULDER—An angle and the parts adjacent thereto in a vessel, made by an abrupt *inward* curvature of the body.
SLIP—Potters clay in a liquid state, used for the decoration of ceramic ware.
SMUDGE—A black surface on pottery produced intentionally by smoke. It is the same as a fire cloud which is produced unintentionally.
SPIRAL—The path of a point that revolves around an axis while continuously receding from it. Syn. *Scroll*.
SQUIGGLY—Wriggling, wavy, twisting.
STAGGERED—Placed alternately at equal distances on either side of a median line.
STYLE—A distinctive or characteristic manner or method. The quality which gives distinction to artistic expression; distinctive mode of presentation or expression in any art or product.
STRENGTH—Power to resist force.
STRIATED—Marked with fine parallel grooves.
STRIPE—A strip of solid color and uniform width of more than 4 mm., either continuous and in the form of a closed circle around the vessel, or bounded at the ends by junction with other elements; may be either straight or curved.
TABLE TYPE—Small vessels often decorated, presumably used for serving food.
TECHNIQUE—Expert method in execution of the details of accomplishing something; the formal elements, collectively, of an art.
TEMPER (see GROG)—Refractory materials such as crushed pottery, sand, etc., which are added to clay in the manufacture of pottery.
TEXTURE—Disposition or manner of union of the particles or smaller constituent parts of a body or substance.
THIN (of paint)—Lacking in density of paint material in the vehicle.
TICKED LINE—A line to which very short lines set at an angle and at regular intervals are pendent on one or both sides
TOOL—To ornament a clay surface with an instrument.
TOPOTYPE—A sherd similar to a type sherd from the site on which the sherds were gathered which formed the basis of the original description.
TRAY—An open receptacle, with flat bottom and low rim.
TWILL—An appearance of diagonal lines or ribs produced in textile fabrics by passing the weft threads over *one* and under *two or more* warp threads.

GLOSSARY

TYPE (Pottery)—A group of pottery vessels which are alike in every characteristic except form.
TYPE SITE—A site on which part of the sherds were gathered which form the basis of the original description of a pottery type.
TYPE SHERDS—Sherds on which the original description of a pottery type was based.
UTILITY TYPE—Large vessels, seldom decorated, used for cooking or storage.
VASE—A jar with a tall narrow neck.
VEHICLE—The liquid element contained in paint, which serves to carry the pigment.
VITREOUS—Resembling glass, as in color, composition, lustre, brittleness, hardness, etc.
VOLUTE—A spiral or scroll-like ornamentation.
WARE—A group of pottery types having certain characteristics in common based on certain basic techniques of manufacture.
WASH—To cover with a thin or watery coat of color; to tint lightly and thinly.
WHORL—The small flywheel of a spindle.
WIPE—To rub or remove by rubbing with skin or a textile.
ZIGZAG—One of a series of short, sharp turns or angles in a course. As the letter Z. ZIGZAG LINE—a continuing series of zigzags.
ZOOMORPHIC—Animal shaped.

BIBLIOGRAPHY

BARTLETT, KATHARINE
1934 The Material Culture of Pueblo II in the San Francisco Mountains, Arizona. Museum of Northern Arizona, Bulletin 7, August, 1934.

BATESON, WILLIAM
1913 Problems of Genetics. Yale University Press. 1913.

BUNZEL, R. L.
1929 The Pueblo Potter: A Study of Creative Imagination in Primitive Art. Columbia University Press. New York. 1920.

BYERS, DOUGLAS S.
1935 An Ancient Cave Town in Arizona. Harvard Alumni Bulletin, pp. 1070–1075. Cambridge, Mass. 1935.

CAYWOOD, LOUIS R.
1936. Two Pueblo Ruins in West Central Arizona: Part II, Fitzmaurice Ruin. University of Arizona Bulletin, Vol. VII, No. 1, Social Science Bulletin No. 10, pp. 87–115. Tucson, January 1, 1936.

CAYWOOD, LOUIS R. AND SPICER, EDWARD H.
1935 Tuzigoot: The Excavation and Repair of a Ruin on the Verde River near Clarkdale, Arizona. Field Division of Education, National Park Service. Berkeley, California. 1935.

CLARKE, ELEANOR P.
1935 Designs on the Prehistoric Pottery of Arizona. University of Arizona Bulletin, Vol. VI, No. 4, Social Science Bulletin No. 9, pp. 1–76. Tucson. May 15, 1935.

COLTON, HAROLD S.
1931 The Archaeological Survey of the Museum of Northern Arizona. Museum of Northern Arizona, Museum Notes, Vol. 4, No. 1. July, 1931.
1932 A Survey of Prehistoric Sites in the Region of Flagstaff, Arizona. Bureau of American Ethnology, Bulletin 104. Washington, 1932.
1932a Sunset Crater: The Effects of a Volcanic Eruption on an Ancient Pueblo People. American Geographic Society, The Geographic Review, Vol. 32, No. 4, pp. 582–590. 1932.
1933 Pueblo II in the San Francisco Mountains. Museum of Northern Arizona, Bulletin 4. May, 1933.
1935 Stages in Northern Arizona Prehistory. Museum of Northern Arizona, Museum Notes, Vol. 8, No. 1, pp. 1–7. July, 1935.

COLTON HAROLD S. AND HARGRAVE, LYNDON L.
1935 Naming Pottery Types and Rules of Priority. Science, Vol. 82, No. 2133, pp. 462–463. November 15, 1935.

COLTON, M. R. F.
1931 Technique of the Major Hopi Crafts. Museum of Northern Arizona, Museum Notes, Vol. 3, No. 12. June, 1931.

CUMMINGS, BYRON
1935 Prehistoric Pottery of the Southwest. Arizona State Museum. The Kiva, Vol. 1, No. 2. Tucson. 1935.

CUSHING, F. H.
1886 A Study of Pueblo Pottery as Illustrative of Zuni Culture Growth. Fourth Annual Report, Bureau of Ethnology, pp. 373–510. Washington. 1886.

DOUGLASS, A. E.
1929 The Secret of the Southwest Solved by Talkative Tree Rings. National Geographic Magazine. December, 1929.
1935 Dating Public Bonito and Other Ruins of the Southwest. National Geographic Society, Contributed Technical Papers: Pueblo Bonito Series, No. 1. Washington. 1935.

BIBLIOGRAPHY

FEWKES, F. W.
- 1898 Archaeological Expedition to Arizona in 1895. Bureau of American Ethnology, 17th Annual Report, Part 2, pp. 519–744. Washington. 1898.
- 1904 Two Summers' Work in Pueblo Ruins. Bureau of American Ethnology, 22nd Annual Report, Part 1, pp. 3–195. Washington. 1904.
- 1909 Antiquities of Mesa Verde National Park, Spruce Tree House. Bureau of American Ethnology, Bulletin 41. Washington. 1909.
- 1911 Preliminary Report on a Visit to the Navajo National Monument, Arizona. Bureau of American Ethnology, Bulletin 50. Washington. 1911.
- 1926 An Archaeological Collection from Young's Canyon, near Flagstaff, Arizona. Smithsonian Miscellaneous Collections, Vol. 77, No. 10 (Publication 2833). Washington. January 12, 1926.
- 1927 Archaeological Field-Work in Arizona: Field Season of 1926. From "Explorations and Field-work of the Smithsonian Institution in 1926." Smithsonian Miscellaneous Collections, Vol. 78, pp. 207–232. Washington. 1927.

GLADWIN, WINIFRED AND HAROLD, S.
- 1929 The Red-on-Buff Culture of the Gila Basin. Gila Pueblo. Medallion Papers, No. III. Globe, Arizona. 1929.
- 1930 A Method for the Designation of Southwestern Pottery Types. Gila Pueblo. Medallion Papers, No. VII. The Medallion, Globe, Arizona. 1930.
- 1930a An Archaeological Survey of Verde Valley. Gila Pueblo. Medallion Papers, No. VI. The Medallion, Globe, Arizona.
- 1930b Some Southwestern Pottery Types: Series I. Gila Pueblo. Medallion Papers, No. VIII. The Medallion, Globe, Arizona. 1930.
- 1931 Some Southwestern Pottery Types: Series II. Gila Pueblo. Medallion Papers, No. X. The Medallion, Globe, Arizona. 1931.
- 1933 Some Southwestern Pottery Types: Series III. Gila Pueblo. Medallion Papers, No. XIII. The Medallion, Globe, Arizona. 1933.
- 1934 A Method for Designation of Cultures and Their Variations. Gila Pueblo. Medallion Papers, No. XV. The Medallion, Globe, Arizona. 1934.
- 1935 The Eastern Range of the Red-on-Buff Culture. Gila Pueblo. Medallion Papers, No. XVI. The Medallion, Globe, Arizona. 1935.

GIFFORD, E. W.
- 1928 Pottery-Making in the Southwest. University of California Publication in American Archaeology and Ethnology, Vol. 23, No. 8, pp. 353–373. Berkeley. 1928.

GUERNSEY, S. J.
- 1931 Explorations in Northeastern Arizona. Papers of the Peabody Museum of American Archaeology and Ethnology. Harvard University, Vol. XII, No. I. Cambridge, Mass. 1931.

GUTHE, C. E.
- 1925 Pueblo Pottery Making: A Study at the Village of San Illdefonso. Department of Archaeology, Phillips Academy, Andover, Mass. Yale University Press. New Haven, Conn. 1925.
- 1927 A Method of Ceramic Description. Papers of the Michigan Academy of Science, Arts and Letters, Vol. VIII, pp. 23–29. Ann Arbor, Michigan. 1927.

HARGRAVE, LYNDON L.
- 1929 Elden Pueblo. Museum of Northern Arizona. Museum Notes, Vol. 2, No. 5. 1929.
- 1930 Shungopovi. Museum of Northern Arizona. Museum Notes, Vol. 2, No. 10. 1930.
- 1931 Recently Dated Pueblo Ruins in Arizona: Excavations at Kin Tiel and Kokopnyama. Smithsonian Miscellaneous Collections, Vol. 82, No. 11 (Publication 3069), pp. 80–120. Washington, August 18, 1931.

1931a The Influence of Economic Geography Upon the Rise and Fall of the Pueblo Culture in Arizona. Museum of Northern Arizona, Museum Notes Vol. 4, No. 6, 1931.
1931b First Mesa. Museum of Northern Arizona. Museum Notes, Vol. 3, No. 8. 1931.
1932 Guide to Forty Pottery Types from the Hopi Country and the San Francisco Mountains, Arizona. Museum of Northern Arizona, Bulletin 1. 1932.
1932a Oraibi: A Brief History of the Oldest Inhabited Town in the United States. Museum of Northern Arizona. Museum Notes, Vol. 4, No. 7. 1932.
1933 Pueblo II Houses of the San Francisco Mountains, Arizona. Museum of Northern Arizona, Bulletin 4, pp. 15–73. 1933.
1933a A Review of Archaeological Activities in the San Francisco Mountain Region, Arizona. Museum of Northern Arizona. Museum Notes, Vol. 5, No. 7. January, 1933.
1935 Report on Archaeological Reconnaissance in the Rainbow Plateau Area of Northern Arizona and Southern Utah. University of California Press. Berkeley. 1935.
1935a The Jeddito Valley and the First Pueblo Towns in Arizona to be Visited by Europeans. Museum of Northern Arizona. Museum Notes, Vol. 8, No. 4. October, 1935.
1935b Concerning the Names of Southwestern Pottery Types. Southwestern Colorado Archaeological Society and the Museum of Western State College, Southwestern Lore, Vol. 1, No. 3, pp. 17–23. Gunnison, Colorado. December, 1935.
1936 Notes on a Red Ware from Bluff, Utah. Southwestern Colorado Archaeological Society and the Museum of Western State College, Southwestern Lore, Vol. 2, No. 2, pp. 29–34. Gunnison, Colorado, September, 1936.

HARGRAVE, LYNDON L. AND COLTON, HAROLD S.
1935 What Do Potsherds Tell Us? Museum of Northern Arizona. Museum Notes, Vol. 7, No. 12. June, 1935.

HARGRAVE, LYNDON L. AND SMITH, WATSON
1936 A Method for Determining the Texture of Pottery. American Antiquity, Vol. 2, No. 1. July, 1936.

HAURY, EMIL W.
1930 A Sequence of Decorated Redware from the Silver Creek Drainage. Museum of Northern Arizona. Museum Notes, Vol. 2, No. 11. May, 1930.
1931 Recently Dated Pueblo Ruins in Arizona: Showlow and Pinedale Ruins. Smithsonian Miscellaneous Collections, Vol. 82, No. 11 (Publication 3069). Washington. 1931.
1932 Roosevelt: 9:6—A Hohokam Site of the Colonial Period. Gila Pueblo. Medallion Papers, No. IX. Globe, Arizona. 1932.
1932a The Age of Lead Glaze Decorated Pottery in the Southwest. American Anthropologist (n.s.), Vol. 34, pp. 418–425. Menasha, Wis. 1932.
1934 The Canyon Creek Ruin and the Cliff Dwellings of the Sierra Ancha. Gila Pueblo. Medallion Papers, No. XIV. The Medallion, Globe, Arizona. January, 1934.
1936 Some Southwestern Pottery Types: Series IV. Gila Pueblo. Medallion Papers, No. XIX. The Medallion, Globe, Arizona. 1936.
1936a The Mogollon Culture of Southwestern New Mexico. Gila Pueblo. Medallion Papers, No. XX. The Medallion, Globe, Arizona. 1936.

HAWLEY, FLORENCE M.
1929 Prehistoric Pottery Pigments in the Southwest. American Anthropologist (n.s.), Vol. 31, pp. 731–754. Menasha, Wis. 1929.
1930 Prehistoric Pottery and Culture Relations in the Middle Gila. American Anthropologist (n.s.), Vol. 32, p. 522. Menasha, Wis. 1930.

BIBLIOGRAPHY

1930a   Chemical Examination of Prehistoric Smudged Wares. American Anthropologist (n.s.), Vol. 32, pp. 500–502. Menasha, Wis. 1930.
1934   The Significance of the Dated Prehistory of Chetro Ketl, Chaco Canyon, New Mexico. University of New Mexico Bulletin No. 246. July 1, 1934.
1936   Field Manual of Prehistoric Southwestern Pottery Types. University of New Mexico Bulletin, No. 291. April 22, 1936.

HODGE, F. W.
1923   Circular Kivas near Hawikuh, New Mexico. Museum of American Indian Heye Foundation, Vol. VII, No. 1. New York. 1923.

HOLMES, WILLIAM H.
1886   Pottery of the Ancient Pueblos. Bureau of Ethnology, Fourth Annual Report. Washington. 1886.

HOUGH, WALTER
1903   Archaeological Field Work in Northeastern Arizona: The Museum-Gates Expedition of 1901. United States National Museum, Annual Report for 1901, pp. 279–358. Washington. 1903.
1930   Explorations of Ruins in the White Mountain Apache Indian Reservation, Arizona. Proceedings of the United States National Museum, Vol. 78, Art. 13, pp. 1–21. Washington. 1930.
1932   Decorative Designs on Elden Pueblo Pottery, Flagstaff, Arizona. Proceedings United States National Museum, Vol. 81 (No. 2930), Art. 7, pp. 1–11. Washington. 1932.

KIDDER, A. V.
1924   An Introduction to the Study of Southwestern Archaeology. Department of Archaeology, Phillips Academy, Andover, Mass. Yale University Press, New Haven, Conn. 1924.
1927   Southwestern Archaeological Conference. Science, Vol. LXVI, No. 1716, pp. 489–491. November 18, 1927.

KIDDER, A. V. AND AMSDEN, C. A.
1931   Pottery of Pecos: Volume I. Department of Archaeology, Phillips Academy, Andover, Mass. Yale University Press. New Haven, Conn. 1931.

KIDDER, A. V. AND GUERNSEY, S. J.
1919   Archaeological Explorations in Northeastern Arizona. Bureau of American Ethnology, Bulletin 65. Washington. 1919.

KIDDER, A. V. AND SHEPARD, ANNA O.
1936   The Pottery of Pecos: Volume II. Department of Archaeology, Phillips Academy, Andover, Mass. Yale University Press, New Haven, Conn. 1936.

MAERZ, A. AND PAUL, M. REA
1930   A Dictionary of Color. McGraw Hill Book Co., New York. 1930.

MARTIN, PAUL S.
1936   Lowry Ruin in Southwestern Colorado. Field Museum of Natural History. Anthropological Series, Vol. XXIII, No. 1 (Publication 356). Chicago. 1936.

MASON, OTIS T.
1898   Woman's Share in Primitive Culture. D. Appleton and Co. New York. 1898.

MCGREGOR, JOHN C.
1932   Additional Prehistoric Dates from Arizona. Museum of Northern Arizona. Museum Notes, Vol. 5, No. 3. September, 1932.
1934   Dates from Tsegi. Tree Ring Bulletin, Vol. 1, No. 1. Flagstaff, Arizona. July, 1934.
1936   Dating the Eruption of Sunset Crater, Arizona. American Antiquity, Vol. II, No. 1, p. 15. July, 1936.
1936a   Culture of Sites Which Were Occupied Shortly Before the Eruption of Sunset Crater. Museum of Northern Arizona. Bulletin 9. October, 1936.
1937   Winona Village. Museum of Northern Arizona. Bulletin 12. October, 1937.

MERA, H. P.
1934 Observations on the Archaeology of the Petrified Forest National Monument. Laboratory of Anthropology. Technical Series, Bulletin No. 7. Santa Fe, New Mexico. 1934.

MORRIS, EARL H.
1917 The Place of Coiled Ware in Southwestern Pottery. American Anthropologist (n.s.), Vol. 19. Lancaster, Pa. 1917.
1921 Chronology of the San Juan Area. Proceedings of the National Academy of Science, Vol. 7, pp. 18–22. Philadelphia, 1921.

MORSS, NOEL
1931 Notes on the Archaeology of the Kaibito and Rainbow Plateaus in Arizona. Harvard University. Papers of the Peabody Museum of American Archaeology and Ethnology. Cambridge, Mass. 1931.

NORDENSKIÖLD, G.
1893 The Cliff-Dwellers of the Mesa Verde. (Translated by D. Lloyd Morgan). Stockholm. 1893.

ROBERTS, FRANK H. H. JR.
1929 Shabik'eschee Village. Bureau of American Ethnology, Bulletin 92. Washington. 1929.
1931 The Ruins at Kiatuthlanna Eastern Arizona. Bureau of American Ethnology. Bulletin 100. Washington. 1931.
1932 The Village of the Great Kivas on the Zuni Reservation, New Mexico. Bureau of American Ethnology. Bulletin 111. Washington. 1932.

ROGERS, MALCOLM J.
1936 Yuman Pottery Making. San Diego Museum Papers. No. 2, San Diego. Feb. 1936.

SCHMIDT, ERICK F.
1928 Time-Relations of Prehistoric Pottery Types in Southern Arizona. American Museum of Natural History, Anthropological Papers, Vol. XXX, Pt. V. New York, 1928.

SPENCER, J. E.
1934 Pueblo Sites of Southwestern Utah. American Anthropologist Vol. 36, No. 1. Menasha, Wis., March, 1934.

SPIER, LESLIE
1917 An Outline for a Chronology of Zuni Ruins. American Museum of Natural History. Anthropological Papers, Vol. XVIII, Pt. III, pp. 207–331. New York. 1917.
1918 Notes on Some Little Colorado Ruins. American Museum of Natural History. Anthropological Papers, Vol. XVIII, Pt. IV, pp. 333–362. New York. 1918.
1919 Ruins in the White Mountains, Arizona. American Museum of Natural History. Anthropological Papers, Vol. XVIII, Pt. V, pp. 363–387. New York. 1919.

STEVENSON, J.
1883 Illustrated Catalog of the Collections Obtained from the Indians of New Mexico and Arizona in 1879. Bureau of Ethnology. 2nd Annual Report. Washington. 1883.

INDEX

Adamana Brown 159
Adamana Fugitive Red 160
Adamana Polychrome 117
Adamana Series 159
Alameda Brown Ware 157
Alameda Red Ware 77
Alma Series 45
Arauca Plain 80
Arauca Polychrome 131
Awatobi Polychrome 155
Awatobi Yellow Ware 143

Betatakin Black-on-white 215
Bidahochi Black-on-white 245
Bidahochi Polychrome 151
Bidahochi White Ware 244
Black Ax Polychrome 81
Black Mesa Pueblo II 208
Bluff Black-on-red 69
Bluff Series 68

Chavez Pass Black-on-red 84
Chavez Pass Polychrome 84
Chavez Pass Series 83
Citadel Polychrome 75
Coconino Buff Ware 178, 179
Coconino Gray 201
Coconino Red-on-buff 182
Cultural stages xv

Dates 35
Dating pottery types 23
Deadmans Black-on-gray 253
Deadmans Black-on-red 71
Deadmans Black-on-white 208
Deadmans Corrugated 196
Deadmans Fugitive Red 252
Deadmans Gray 252
Deadmans Series 70
Deadmans Style 16
Dead River Black-on-white ... 235
Distribution by trade 27
Dogoszhi Black-on-white 209
Dogoszhi Polychrome 98
Dogoszhi Style 16

Elden Corrugated 63

Flagstaff Black-on-white 225
Flagstaff Red 163
Flagstaff Series 63
Flagstaff Style 16
Flagstaff Ware 163
Fourmile Polychrome 109

Geographical focus of
  manufacture 27
Gila Plain 174
Gila Polychrome 88
Gila Red 176
Gila Series 173
Gila White-on-red 177
Glossary 255

Hawikuh Glaze-on-white 130
Heshotauthla Polychrome 113
Holbrook Black-on-white 235
Homolovi Black-on-red 80
Homolovi Corrugated 134
Homolovi Orange Ware 132
Homolovi Plain 133
Homolovi Polychrome 82
Homolovi Series 78
Honani Tooled 202
Honani Series 202
Houck Polychrome 121
Houck Series 118
Hoyapi Black-on-white 222

Jeddito Black-on-orange 141
Jeddito Black-on-white 247
Jeddito Black-on-yellow 150
Jeddito Brown-on-yellow 150
Jeddito Corrugated 144
Jeddito Engraved 154
Jeddito Plain 144
Jeddito Polychrome 142
Jeddito Series 150
Jeddito Stippled 153
Jeddito Tooled 145
Jeddito Yellow 150
Jeddito Yellow Ware 146, 147

Kana-a Black-on-white 205
Kana-a Gray 195
Kana-a Style 16
Kawaioku Polychrome 156
Kayenta Black-on-white 217
Kayenta Polychrome 99
Kayenta Series 205
Kayenta Style 16
Key to Northern Arizona pottery
  types 36
Kia-ko Black-on-white 219
Kiet Siel Polychrome 100
Kiet Siel Gray 198
Kintiel Black-on-orange 125
Kintiel Polychrome 126
Kintiel Series 125

INDEX

Klageto Black-on-white..........242
Klageto Black-on-yellow.........123
Klageto Polychrome.............124
Klageto Series..................123
Kokop Black-on-orange..........149
Kokop Black-on-white...........248
Kokop Polychrome..............149
Kokop Series..................147
Kwaituki Polychrome...........148
Kwaituki Series...............140

Linden Corrugated..............60
Linden Series..................60
Lino Black-on-gray............194
Lino Fugitive Red.............193
Lino Gray.....................191
Lino Style....................15
Little Colorado Black-on-red....118
Little Colorado Corrugated.....232
Little Colorado Gray Ware......232
Little Colorado White Ware.233, 234

Mancos Black-on-white.........230
McDonald Corrugated............61
Medicine Black-on-red...........72
Medicine Gray.................199
Mesa Verde Black-on-white.....231
Mesa Verde White Ware.........229
Miscellaneous Types...........246
Moenkopi Corrugated...........197
Mogollon Brown Ware.......44, 45
Mogollon Red-on-brown..........47

Naming pottery types...........19

Oxidizing atmosphere............8
O'Leary Tooled................200

Padre Black-on-white..........236
Periods........................xv
Pinedale Black-on-red.........106
Pinedale Black-on-white.......241
Pinedale Polychrome...........107
Pinnawa Black-on-red..........113
Pinnawa Polychrome............115
Pinnawa Red-on-white..........129
Pinto Polychrome...............87
Polacca Black-on-white........220
Polacca Series................218
Pottery constructed by paddling.157
Pottery descriptions...........29
Prescott Gray Ware............183
Pre-Pueblo Black-on-white.....205
Prescott Red-on-brown.........186
Priority in Naming.............19
Proto-Kayenta Black-on-white..213
Proto-Mesa Verde Black-on-white
...............................230
Pueblo I Black-on-white.......205
Puerco Black-on-red...........120

Querino Polychrome............122

Reducing atmosphere........8, 188
Rims............................9
Rio de Flag Brown.............161
Rio de Flag Series............160
Rio de Flag Smudged...........162
Roosevelt Red Ware.........85, 86
Rules for naming...............19
Rules of priority..............21

Sagi Black-on-white...........217
Salado White-on-red............65
Salado Red.....................65
Salado Series..................64
San Francisco Mountain Gray
  Ware........................251
San Francisco Red..............48
San Juan Red Ware..............67
San Lorenzo Red-on-brown.......46
Santan Red....................175
Series..........................1
Series, definition..............3
Showlow Black-on-red...........78
Showlow Polychrome............111
Sikyatki Polychrome...........152
Silver Creek Corrugated........62
Slab-house Black-on-white.....205
Sosi Black-on-white...........211
St. Johns Polychrome..........104
Styles of design...............14
Sunset Red....................163

Techniques of pottery making....6
Tokonabi (Kayenta) Ware.......217
Tonto Polychrome...............90
Tonto Red.....................166
Tsegi Black-on-orange..........95
Tsegi Orange...................93
Tsegi Orange Ware..............92
Tsegi Polychrome...............96
Tsegi Red-on-orange............94
Tsegi Series..................191
Tularosa Black-on-white.......240
Tularosa Series...............240
Turkey Hill Red...............165
Tusayan Black-on-red...........74
Tusayan Black-on-white........213
Tusayan Corrugated............196
Tusayan Gray Ware.............189
Tusayan Polychrome.............96
Tusayan, Third................213
Tusayan White Ware............203
Tuwiuca Black-on-orange.......137
Tuwiuca Orange................136
Tuwiuca Polychrome............138
Tuzigoot Black-on-gray........172
Tuzigoot Black-on-red.........170
Tuzigoot Red..................169
Tuzigoot Red-on-black.........171
Tuzigoot White-on-red.........171

INDEX

Types....1
Type, definition....2

Upper Gila Black-on-white....240

Verde Black-on-gray....184
Verde Brown....167
Verde Polychrome....186
Verde Red-on-buff....168
Verde Series....167
Vessel Forms....33

Wallace Polychrome....114
Walnut Black-on-white....237
Walnut Corrugated....56
Walnut Series....235
Walnut Style....17
Walnut Wiped....180
Ware, definition....2
Wares....1
White Mountain Red Ware....101
Wide Ruin Black-on-white....249

Wingate Black-on-red....118
Wingate Corrugated....119
Winona Black-on-red....53
Winona Brown....162
Winona Corrugated....55
Winona Red....51
Winona Red-on-buff....181
Winona Red-on-tan....54
Winona Series....49
Winona Smudged....52
Winslow Orange Ware....134
Winslow Polychrome....139
Winslow Series....136
Woodruff Brown....58
Woodruff Incised....59
Woodruff Red....58
Woodruff Series....57
Woodruff Smudged....59
Wupatki Black-on-white....227
Wupatki Series....225

Zuni Glazed Ware....114
Zuni White Ware....127

Cumberland Trail Library System
Flora, Illinois 62839

Robinson Township Public
Library District
606 N. Jefferson Street
Robinson, IL 62454